Crusading and Pilgrimage
in the Norman World

Crusading and Pilgrimage
in the Norman World

Edited by
KATHRYN HURLOCK
AND
PAUL OLDFIELD

THE BOYDELL PRESS

© Contributors 2015

All Rights Reserved. Except as permitted under current legislation no part of this work may be photocopied, stored in a retrieval system, published, performed in public, adapted, broadcast, transmitted, recorded or reproduced in any form or by any means, without the prior permission of the copyright owner

First published 2015
Paperback edition 2018
The Boydell Press, Woodbridge

ISBN 978 1 78327 025 5 hardback
ISBN 978 1 78327 302 7 paperback

The Boydell Press is an imprint of Boydell & Brewer Ltd
PO Box 9, Woodbridge, Suffolk IP12 3DF, UK
and of Boydell & Brewer Inc.
668 Mount Hope Ave, Rochester, NY 14620–2731, USA
website: www.boydellandbrewer.com

A catalogue record for this book is available
from the British Library

The publisher has no responsibility for the continued existence or accuracy of URLs for external or third-party internet websites referred to in this book, and does not guarantee that any content on such websites is, or will remain, accurate or appropriate

Contents

List of Contributors	vii
Acknowledgements	viii
Abbreviations	ix
Timeline	xi

Introduction
Kathryn Hurlock and Paul Oldfield — 1

Part I

1 'Many others, whose names I do not know, fled with them': Norman Courage and Cowardice on the First Crusade
   William M. Aird — 13

2 The Enemy Within: Bohemond, Byzantium and the Subversion of the First Crusade
   Alan V. Murray — 31

Part II

3 Norman Italy and the Crusades: Thoughts on the 'Homefront'
   Joanna Drell — 51

4 The Norman Influence on Crusading from England and Wales
   Kathryn Hurlock — 65

5 The Secular Clergy of Normandy and the Crusades
   David S. Spear — 81

6 Norman and Anglo-Norman Intervention in the Iberian Wars of Reconquest before and after the First Crusade
   Lucas Villegas-Aristizábal — 103

CONTENTS

Part III

7 The Pilgrimage and Crusading Activities of the Anglo-Norman Earls of Chester
   Andrew Abram — 125

8 The Use and Abuse of Pilgrims in Norman Italy
   Paul Oldfield — 139

Part IV

9 Antioch and the Normans
   Emily Albu — 159

10 The Landscape of Pilgrimage and Miracles in Norman Narrative Sources
   Leonie V. Hicks — 177

11 Normans and Competing Masculinities on Crusade
   Natasha Hodgson — 195

Select Bibliography — 215

Index — 223

Contributors

Andrew Abram	Associate Lecturer in Medieval History, Manchester Metropolitan University
William M. Aird	Lecturer in Medieval History, University of Edinburgh
Emily Albu	Professor of Classics, University of California, Davis
Joanna Drell	Associate Professor of History, University of Richmond
Leonie V. Hicks	Senior Lecturer in Medieval History, Canterbury Christ Church University
Natasha Hodgson	Senior Lecturer in Medieval History, Nottingham Trent University
Kathryn Hurlock	Senior Lecturer in Medieval History, Manchester Metropolitan University
Alan V. Murray	Senior Lecturer in Medieval Studies, University of Leeds
Paul Oldfield	Lecturer in Medieval History, University of Manchester
David S. Spear	William E. Leverette, Jr. Professor of History, Furman University
Lucas Villegas-Aristizábal	Adjunct Assistant Professor, Richmond, the American International University, London

Acknowledgements

We would like to express our gratitude to all those who supported in various ways the work which has led to the production of this volume. We are grateful to Berthold Schoene and the Faculty of Humanities, Languages and Social Sciences at Manchester Metropolitan University for offering support and funding for the initial symposium out of which this publication was formed. We would also like to thank Nick Scarle for the production of the map and the support of the History department at the University of Manchester and its T. F. Tout fund which covered the costs of the cartographic services and the copyright fees for the book cover image. Finally, alongside our gratitude to all the individual contributors to this volume, we also would like to acknowledge the extremely valuable comments of the anonymous reviewer and the expertise of the editorial team (Caroline Palmer, Rohais Haughton and Rob Kinsey) at Boydell and Brewer which has guided us smoothly through the process.

Abbreviations

AA	Albert of Aachen, *Historia Ierosolimitana*, ed. and trans. Susan B. Edgington (Oxford, 2007)
Aird, *Robert Curthose*	William M. Aird, *Robert Curthose, duke of Normandy c. 1050–1134* (Woodbridge, 2008)
ANS	*Anglo-Norman Studies*
BB	*The Historia Ierosolimitana of Baldric of Bourgueil*, ed. Steven Biddlecombe (Woodbridge, 2013)
CCCM	*Corpus Christianorum Continuatio*
DEL	*The Conquest of Lisbon: De Expugnatione Lyxbonensi*, trans. Charles W. David, with Jonathan Phillips (New York, 2001)
EHR	*English Historical Review*
Gesta Regis Henrici Secundi	*Gesta regis Henrici Secundi Benedicti abbatis: The Chronicle of the Reigns of Henry II and Richard I. A.D. 1169–1192; known commonly under the name of Benedict of Peterborough*, ed. William Stubbs, 2 vols (London, 1867)
GN	Guibert of Nogent, *Dei Gesta per Francos et cinq autres textes*, ed. Robert B. C. Huygens, CCCM 127A (Turnhout, 1996)
GRW	William of Apulia, *Gesta Roberti Wiscardi*, ed. and trans. Marguerite Mathieu, *La geste de Robert Guiscard* (Palermo, 1961)
GT, Bachrach	*The* Gesta Tancredi *of Ralph of Caen: A History of the Normans on the First Crusade*, trans. Bernard S. Bachrach and David S. Bachrach (Aldershot, 2005)

ABBREVIATIONS

Hagenmeyer, GF	*Anonymi Gesta Francorum*, ed. Heinrich Hagenmeyer (Heidelberg, 1890)
Hill, GF	*Gesta Francorum: The Deeds of the Franks and the Other Pilgrims to Jerusalem*, ed. and trans. R. Hill (Oxford, 1962)
Hodgson, 'Reinventing Normans'	N. Hodgson, 'Reinventing Normans as Crusaders? Ralph of Caen's *Gesta Tancredi*', ANS 30 (2008), 117–32
Howden, *Chronica*	Roger of Howden, *Chronica*, ed. William Stubbs, 4 vols (London, 1868–71)
IC	Giraldus Cambrensis, *Opera VI: Itinerarium Cambriae*, ed. James F. Dimock (London, 1868)
Itin. Pereg.	*The Chronicle of the Third Crusade: The* Itinerarium Peregrinorum et Gesta Regis Ricardi, trans. Helen J. Nicholson (Aldershot, 1997)
JMH	*Journal of Medieval History*
MGH	Monumenta Germaniae Historica
OV	Orderic Vitalis, *The Ecclesiastical History of Orderic Vitalis*, ed. and trans. Marjorie Chibnall, 6 vols (Oxford, 1969–80)
RCaen	Ralph of Caen, *Gesta Tancredi in expeditione Hierosolymitana auctore Radulfo Cadomensi*, in *RHC*, iii, pp. 587–716.
RHC	*Recueil des historiens des croisades: historiens occidentaux*, 5 vols in 6 (Paris, 1844–95)
TCE	*Thirteenth Century England*
TRHS	*Transactions of the Royal Historical Society*

Timeline

911 × 918	The Treaty of Saint-Clair-sur-Epte: Rollo receives lands around the lower Seine from Charles the Simple
927	William Longsword succeeds Rollo as ruler of the nascent territory of Normandy
c. 940	Monastery of Jumièges refounded by William Longsword
942	Accession of Richard I, duke of Normandy
996	Accession of Richard II, duke of Normandy
c. 1000	Norman pilgrims at Salerno
c. 1010	Norman pilgrims at the shrine of St Michael at Monte Gargano
1026–27	Accession of Richard III, duke of Normandy
1027	Accession of Robert I, duke of Normandy
1035	Duke Robert I of Normandy's pilgrimage to Jerusalem; accession of William II, duke of Normandy
1053	Battle of Civitate
1059	Start of Norman conquest of Sicily, led by Count Roger I of Sicily; papal investiture of Robert Guiscard with new title of 'duke of Apulia and Calabria and in the future Sicily'
1064	Capture of Barbastro
1066	Battle of Hastings; William II, duke of Normandy, becomes William I, king of England
1081–82	First Norman invasion of Byzantine Empire
1084–85	Second Norman invasion of Byzantine Empire
1085	Conquest of Toledo; accession of Roger Borsa, duke of Apulia
1087	Translation of St Nicholas to Bari; accession of Robert II ('Curthose'), duke of Normandy; accession of William II ('Rufus'), king of England
1091	Fall of Noto: all of Sicily under Norman rule
1095	Pope Urban II's Clermont appeal
1096	Start of the First Crusade expedition
1097	Battle of Dorylaeum

TIMELINE

1098	Crusader capture of Antioch: Bohemond becomes the first prince of Antioch
1099	Crusader capture of Jerusalem; Battle of Ascalon
1100	Accession of Henry I, king of England
1105–6	Tour of western Europe by Bohemond, prince of Antioch
1106	Henry I, king of England, becomes duke of Normandy
1107–8	Bohemond's campaign against the Byzantines
1108	Treaty of Devol between Alexios Komnenos and Bohemond
1111	Accession of Bohemond II, prince of Antioch (under a regency until 1126); accession of William, duke of Apulia
1112	Roger II, count of Sicily, reaches his majority
1117	Annulment of Adelaide of Sicily's marriage to Baldwin I, king of Jerusalem
1126	Bohemond II, prince of Antioch, takes over direct rulership of the principality
1127	Roger II of Sicily, count of Sicily, becomes duke of Apulia
1130	Roger II establishes the kingdom of Sicily; death of Bohemond II, the last prince of Antioch directly descended from the male line of the Hauteville dynasty
1135	Accession of Stephen, king of England; Stephen also claims to be duke of Normandy in opposition to Empress Matilda, the daughter of Henry I of England
1144	Geoffrey Plantagenet, count of Anjou and husband of Empress Matilda becomes duke of Normandy
1147	Start of the Second Crusade expedition; conquest of Lisbon
1150	Accession of Henry II, duke of Normandy
1154	Henry II, duke of Normandy, crowned king of England; accession of William I, king of Sicily
1166	Accession of William II, king of Sicily
1169	Anglo-Norman conquest of Ireland
1177	Venice peace conference
1187	Battle of Hattin; Saladin's capture of Jerusalem
1188	Crusade preaching tour of England and Wales
1189	Accession of Richard I, king of England (and duke of Normandy); start of the Third Crusade expedition
1190	Accession of Tancred, king of Sicily
1190–91	Third Crusade forces winter in Sicily
1194	Staufen conquest of the kingdom of Sicily: Emperor Henry VI becomes king of Sicily
1195	Battle of Alarcos

TIMELINE

1198	Frederick II crowned king of Sicily
1199	Accession of John, king of England (and duke of Normandy)
1202	Start of the Fourth Crusade expedition
1204	Capetian capture of Normandy; capture of Constantinople
1212	Battle of Las Navas de Tolosa
1216	Accession of Henry III, king of England
1217	Start of the Fifth Crusade expedition
1220	Frederick II, king of Sicily, crowned Holy Roman Emperor
1225	Frederick II becomes king of Jerusalem through marriage
1259	Henry III of England renounces claim to duchy of Normandy

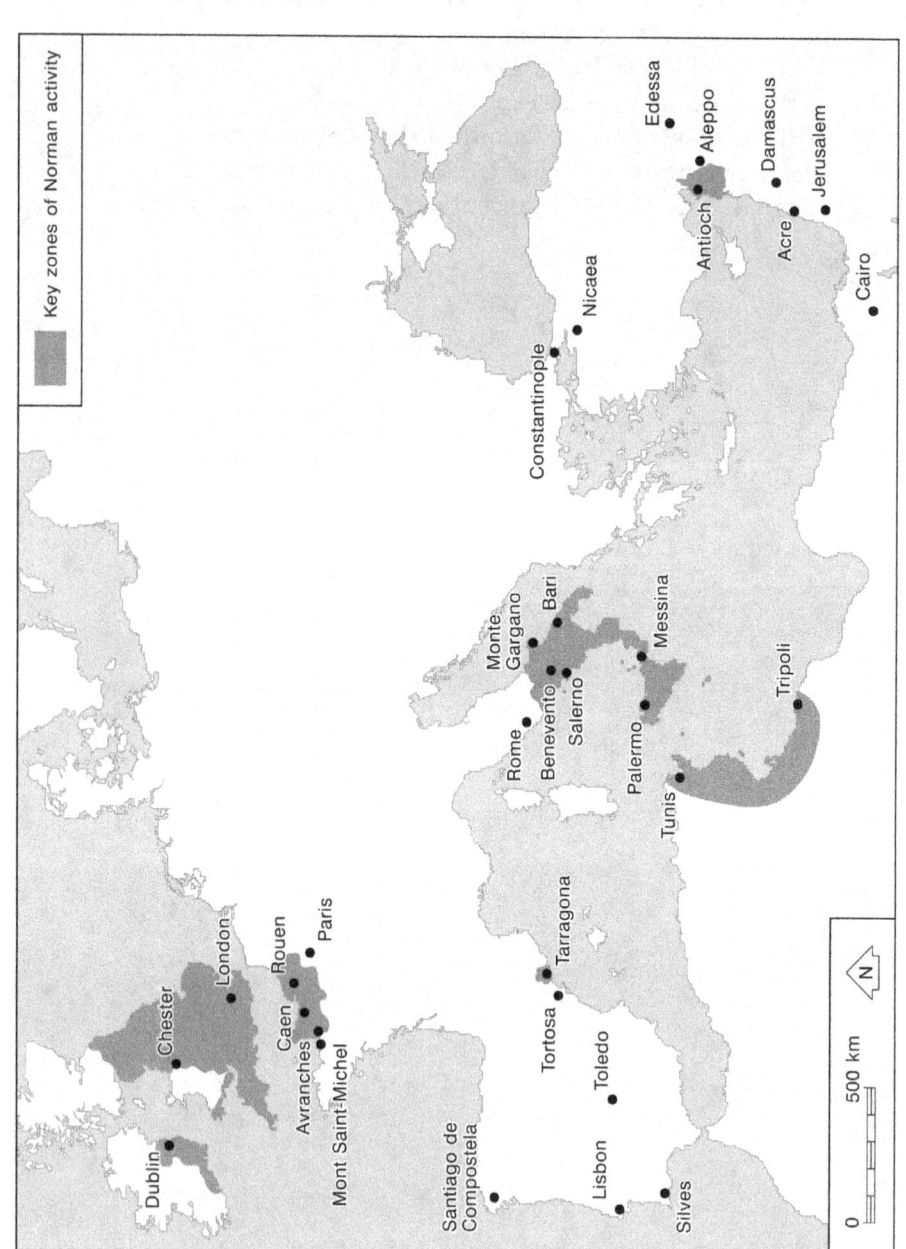

The Norman World. Produced by Nick Scarle

Introduction

KATHRYN HURLOCK AND PAUL OLDFIELD

The reputation of the Normans is rooted in an uneasy interplay between warfare and faith. The Normans were famed as warriors and at the same time noted for their religious devotion; their association as builders of both great castles and cathedrals is seemingly symbolic of the key juxtaposition inherent in Norman history. Yet, we might add a third defining feature of the Normans, one that underpinned the other two: mobility. The Norman proclivity to operate on and beyond established frontiers, and to move between different theatres of action across the medieval world, is a noteworthy one. In the Middle Ages few activities offered a better conduit to combine warfare, religiosity and movement than crusading and pilgrimage. It is no surprise then that both feature heavily in the phenomenal rise of the Normans from the tenth through to the early thirteenth century. And yet it is a surprise that the Norman relationship with crusading and pilgrimage has hitherto not received extensive scholarly treatment, at least not in the form of a single, focused volume.

Certainly, several journal articles and book chapters have been published on the subject of the Norman role in crusading and/or pilgrimage; for example, contributions by Emily Albu, John France, Aryeh Grabois, Natasha Hodgson, Graham Loud and Léan Ní Chléirigh.[1] Likewise, broader works on crusading, pilgrimage and sanctity address Norman input, sometimes directly, sometimes indirectly; for example in the works of Thomas Asbridge, Samantha Kahn Herrick, Kathryn Hurlock, Paul Oldfield, Jonathan

---

[1] E. Albu, 'Probing the Passions of a Norman on Crusade: The *Gesta Francorum et aliorum Hierosolimitanorum*', ANS 27 (2005), 1–15; John France, 'The Normans and Crusading', in *The Normans and Their Adversaries at War: Essays in Memory of C. Warren Hollister*, ed. Richard P. Abels and Bernard S. Bachrach (Woodbridge, 2001), pp. 87–102; A. Grabois, 'Anglo-Norman England and the Holy Land', ANS 7 (1985), 132–44; N. Hodgson, 'Reinventing Normans as Crusaders? Ralph of Caen's *Gesta Tancredi*', ANS 30 (2008), 117–32; G. A. Loud, 'Norman Italy and the Holy Land', in *The Horns of Hattin*, ed. B. Kedar (London, 1992), pp. 49–62; L. Ní Chléirigh, '*Gesta Normannorum*? Normans in the Latin Chronicles of the First Crusade', in *Norman Expansion: Connections, Continuities and Contrasts*, ed. K. J. Stringer and A. Jotischky (London, 2013), pp. 207–26.

Riley-Smith, Christopher Tyerman and Simon Yarrow.[2] But collectively – in addressing the inter-relationship between the Normans, crusading and pilgrimage – these existing works might only deal broadly with the subject, and do not aim to delve deeper; alternatively they might focus closely on one restricted area of it, or in many cases their main focus might lie elsewhere, and the Normans appear as a rather peripheral presence. Taken together, these works testify to the value and potential in studying crusading and pilgrimage in the Norman world, but demonstrate the clear need for more extensive examination collected within one volume. Inevitably, a single volume alone cannot fill completely such a lacuna in such a wide subject-field. But it is the aim of this present work to offer a first step towards doing so.

At the outset, in order to provide a framework for the present volume, it is necessary briefly to contextualise the subject, and to locate it within existing historiographical trends, some of which (crusader studies in particular) shift rapidly. First, it is crucial to acknowledge how contested and amorphous the very notion of a 'Norman world' is. Recent research continues to confirm that medieval identities were flexible constructs which could function in multiple forms. The Normans, as scholars such as Emily Albu, Marjorie Chibnall, Joanna Drell, John Gillingham, Graham Loud, Hugh Thomas and Nick Webber affirm, were expert at shifting their own identities, constructing them through historical writing, in opposition to 'others', and through the process of movement and conquest.[3] As the works of Webber and Léan Ní Chléirigh show, Normans looked different from different vantage points.[4] While internal Norman sources from the central Middle Ages might show us Normans who were labelled so due to certain characteristic features, some medieval commentators external to the

---

[2] T. Asbridge, *The Creation of the Principality of Antioch, 1098–1130* (Woodbridge, 2000); S. Kahn Herrick, *Imagining the Sacred Past: Hagiography and Power in Early Normandy* (Cambridge MA, 2007); K. Hurlock, *Britain, Ireland and the Crusades, c. 1000–c. 1300* (Basingstoke, 2013); P. Oldfield, *Sanctity and Pilgrimage in Medieval Southern Italy, 1000–1200* (Cambridge, 2014); J. Riley-Smith, *The First Crusade and the Idea of Crusading*, 2nd edn (London, 2009); C. Tyerman, *England and the Crusades 1095–1588* (Chicago, 1988); S. Yarrow, *Saints and Their Communities: Miracle Stories in Twelfth-Century England* (Oxford, 2006).

[3] E. Albu, *The Normans in Their Histories: Propaganda, Myth and Subversion* (Woodbridge, 2001); M. Chibnall, *The Normans* (Oxford, 2006); J. Drell, 'Cultural Syncretism and Ethnic Identity: The Norman Conquest of Southern Italy and Sicily', *JMH* 25 (1999), 187–202; J. Gillingham, 'Henry of Huntingdon and the Twelfth-Century Revival of the English Nation', in *The English in the Twelfth Century: Imperialism, National Identity, and Political Values* (Woodbridge, 2000), pp. 123–44; G. A. Loud, 'The Gens Normannorum. Myth or Reality?' *ANS* 4 (1982), 104–16; H. M. Thomas, *The English and the Normans: Ethnic Hostility, Assimilation and Identity, 1066–c.1220* (Oxford, 2005); N. Webber, *The Evolution of Norman Identity, 911–1154* (Woodbridge, 2005).

[4] Webber, *Evolution of Norman Identity*; Ní Chléirigh, 'Gesta Normannorum?' pp. 207–26.

Normans might as easily subsume them under wider 'national' groupings and the Normans disappear from sight. Furthermore, the Normans often opted for a strategy of assimilation with the native communities with which they interacted, and this could have obvious problematic consequences for Norman identity. In R. Allen Brown's apposite phrase, the Normans eventually 'adapted themselves out of existence'.[5]

This leaves the modern historian in something of a quandary when it comes to ascertaining who or what was Norman and when. In answer, all we can say for certain is that we might identify two poles of the spectrum: a maximum and a minimum view if you like. The former would view expansion (military or otherwise, but both denoting influence at the highest political echelons) and dynastic/regime change as key markers for mapping the Norman world. Thus, from their heartlands in Normandy – where the Normans could trace their roots back to the treaty of Saint-Clair-sur-Epte in 911 – the Normans expanded into England (from 1066), into Wales (1070s), into Scotland (early twelfth century), and into Ireland (late twelfth century). They also moved into southern Italy (from c. 1000), into the Iberian peninsula and into Byzantium (both from the mid-eleventh century), and into the Holy Land, particularly Antioch (from 1098). Moreover, from the 1140s, the kings of 'Norman' Sicily took control of a section of coastal North Africa (equating to parts of modern-day Tunisia and Libya). These Norman arenas would remain Norman, and the Normans within them would retain some form of Norman identity, as long as the political elites dominating them could trace their lineage back to Normandy, or as long as they individually retained certain affinities with it. Thus, England (and parts of Wales) might have remained Norman until the Angevin takeover of 1154, or indeed until the loss of Normandy in 1204.[6] Southern Italy could have been Norman until the Sicilian kings, of Norman Hauteville descent, were ousted by the German Staufen dynasty in 1194. Antioch could have been Norman until the descendants of the Norman Bohemond were replaced by Prince Raymond of Poitiers in 1136. Other zones in the Mediterranean – Iberia, Byzantium and North Africa – might too be incorporated into the Norman world, albeit more fleetingly, so long as individuals of Norman descent (however loosely defined) wielded significant territorial and political power in parts of these regions. Normandy of course, always remained Norman.

---

[5] R. Allen Brown, *The Normans and the Norman Conquest* (Woodbridge, 1985), p. 25.
[6] For a recent, important analysis of the relationship between Normandy and England see D. Bates, *The Normans and Empire* (Oxford, 2013).

In contrast, the minimum view would privilege direct links with the territory of Normandy in order to identify Normanness. Once these disappeared, so too did the Normans and their world. This approach focuses on the effects of movement and assimilation. Thus, in England, intermarriage, the declining influx of Normans arriving from Normandy, and the cultural reorientation of second-generation Normans who were not born in Normandy and who showed increased attachment to an English identity, could mean that we should not legitimately speak of 'Norman' England much past the first quarter of the twelfth century. This framework can be applied across all the zones of Norman activity; thus, for example, Norman southern Italy might have ended as early as *c.* 1100. In the present volume we do not intend to preference one model over the other, or indeed any of the variations that might fit between those two contrasting interpretations. Cautious of the highly subjective boundaries it can create, we have opted to implicitly acknowledge the maximum view, but only to allow room for manoeuvre for both our contributors and readers to make their own judgements.

Turning to crusading and pilgrimage, it is clear that the Normans made significant contributions to both movements. But to understand this fully we must again consider ongoing scholarly debates, particularly within crusader historiography. First, research over the last few decades has nuanced our understanding of certain features of crusading which were once widely accepted. Scholars like Paul Chevedden have, not without notable opposition it should be noted, pushed further than ever the notion that the call for a crusade by Pope Urban II in 1095 and the First Crusade (1096–99) that followed were not the beginning of the crusading movement proper.[7] In this interpretation, defining features of what would be identified as crusading post-1095 were already in place, certainly by the mid-eleventh century. Whatever one's view of the validity of such a thesis, it does carry significance for our subject, for at the very least it focuses attention on evidence for an earlier gestation of a 'crusading' ethos within three zones in the mid- to late eleventh century – Iberia, the south Italian mainland (and specifically the papal defeat by the Normans at the Battle of Civitate in 1053)

---

[7] Paul Chevedden, '"A Crusade from the First": The Norman Conquest of Islamic Sicily, 1060–1091', *Al-Masaq* 22 (2010), 191–225; and more broadly: P. E. Chevedden, 'The Islamic View and the Christian View of the Crusades: A New Synthesis', *History* 93 (2008), 181–200. For a brief critique of Chevedden's approach see Christopher Tyerman's review in *Crusades* 13 (2014) of Chevedden's contribution in the volume *Cultural Encounters during the Crusades*, ed. Kurt Villads Jensen, Kirsi Salonen and Helle Vogts (Odense, 2013).

and Sicily – in which the Normans were highly active.[8] Thus the Normans might be considered protagonists in some of the formative episodes which both pushed the Islamic frontier back and shaped subsequent crusading mentalities and papal ideologies. That the Normans had earlier experience of a redefined manifestation of holy warfare should encourage us to reconsider their subsequent actions in the First Crusade.[9] For it was in this latter venture that we arguably see Norman intervention at its most apparent, with separate Norman crusading forces led by Duke Robert Curthose and Bohemond of Taranto playing significant parts in the expedition and its immediate aftermath.

However, if we look beyond 1099 and the capture of Jerusalem, more traditional scholarship would claim a subsequent marked decline in Norman interest in crusading. How far we agree or disagree with this depends on our views on three important methodological approaches. First, returning to the earlier discussion, we must decide how to identify Normans. If we ascribe to the maximum view, we might indeed see their presence more frequently in the ensuing crusading movement. Second, we must consider how we define crusading. In the twentieth century, rather distinct 'schools' emerged which subscribed to vastly differing notions of what constituted a crusade. For some, it could only be a movement associated with the Holy Land. For others it was a movement defined by certain criteria, such as the way it was initiated, and the existence of distinct crusader vows and privileges, so that crusading could occur across a wide geographic expanse. Thus Iberia, the Baltic, and even movements against heretics and political enemies could be labelled crusades.[10]

This wider view of crusading inevitably then opens up the possibility of a wider Norman contribution. Furthermore, within crusader studies there has been an increased focus on a more holistic understanding of crusading activity. So, attention has diverted to crusading that falls outside those large expeditions which have traditionally been assigned numbers, the First, Second, Third Crusades, and so on. Smaller waves of expeditions and movement continuously moved back and forth between Europe and the various destinations of crusading, particularly the Holy Land, and these in many ways were as crucial to its functioning as the grander ventures. Here

---

[8] One might add here also Pope Alexander II's alleged bestowal of a papal banner to William the Conqueror in support of his claim to the English throne.

[9] See for example: J. Birk, 'Imagining the Enemy: Southern Italian Perception of Muslims in the Wake of the First Crusade', in *Just Wars, Holy Wars, and Jihads: Christian, Jewish, Muslim Encounters and Exchanges*, ed. S. H. Hashmi (Oxford, 2013), pp. 91–106.

[10] C. Tyerman, *The Debate on the Crusades* (Manchester, 2011), pp. 218–35.

again, we might find continued Norman activity. Equally, some studies have focused on the impact of crusading on the so-called 'home-front' in western Europe. People on a communal and individual level all across Europe were exposed to the culture of crusading through preaching, commerce and personal contact, and also contributed to it financially, emotionally and logistically without ever directly participating in a crusade.[11] Britain, Normandy, Iberia and southern Italy – all zones of Norman activity – were no exception.

Significantly too, this expansive interpretation of crusading also has relevance for an understanding of pilgrimage, which experienced a golden age of activity in the period from *c*. 1000 to *c*. 1300.[12] Particularly since Christopher Tyerman's seminal article, in which he demonstrated the amorphous and disorganised nature of crusading in the twelfth century, historians have increasingly acknowledged the overlap between crusading and pilgrimage.[13] Both movements often shared comparable terminology and spiritual frameworks, had certain performative acts in common, and also passed along similar routes heading for similar destinations.[14] The crusader could often metamorphose into a pilgrim and vice versa. When we see a Norman crusader it might well be worth considering whether he was a pilgrim too. Certainly, as many studies have made clear, and this current volume confirms, pilgrimage was very much at the heart of the Norman story.[15] There are many examples to choose from, but Norman devotion

[11] There is a vast literature on the interconnections between Europe and the Crusades: C. Tyerman, 'What the Crusades meant to Europe', in *The Medieval World*, eds. P. Linehan and J. L. Nelson (London, 2001), pp. 131–45; C. Morris, *The Sepulchre of Christ and the Medieval West* (Oxford, 2005); R. C. Smail, 'The International Status of the Latin Kingdom of Jerusalem', in *The Eastern Mediterranean Lands in the Period of the Crusades*, ed. P. M. Holt (Warminster, 1977), pp. 23–43; Oldfield, *Sanctity and Pilgrimage*, chapter 5; *Il mezzogiorno normanno-svevo e le cruciate, Atti delle XIV giornate normanno-sveve, Bari, 17-20 Ottobre 2000*, ed. G. Musca (Bari, 2002); M. Barber, 'Supplying the Crusader States: The Role of the Templars', in *The Horns of Hattin*, ed. Kedar, pp. 314–26; Loud, 'Norman Italy and the Holy Land', pp. 49–62; P. J. Cole, *The Preaching of the Crusades to the Holy Land, 1095-1270* (Cambridge, MA, 1991); C. T. Maier, *Preaching the Crusade: Mendicant Friars and the Cross in the Thirteenth Century* (Cambridge, 1998).

[12] Valuable overviews can be found in J. Sumption, *Pilgrimage: An Image of Mediaeval Religion* (London, 1975); D. J. Birch, *Pilgrimage to Rome in the Middle Ages: Continuity and Change* (Woodbridge, 1998); see also Oldfield, *Sanctity and Pilgrimage*, chapters 5 and 6.

[13] C. Tyerman, 'Were There any Crusades in the Twelfth Century?' *EHR* 110 (1995), 553–77. It should be noted that Tyerman's position remains contested; for a concise summary of alternative positions see N. Housley, *Contesting the Crusades* (Oxford, 2006), pp. 14–23.

[14] The development of saints associated with crusading highlights one way in which it merged with pilgrimage; see, for example: E. Lapina, 'Demetrius of Thessaloniki: Patron Saint of Crusaders', *Viator* 40 (2009), 93–112; M. Favreau-Lilie, 'The German Empire and Palestine: German Pilgrims to Jerusalem between the 12th and 16th Centuries', *JMH* 21 (1995), 321–41.

[15] See the valuable collection of essays in: *Culte et pèlerinages à Saint Michel en occident: les trois monts dédiés à l'archange*, ed. P. Bouet et al. (Rome, 2003); and also *Pellegrinaggi e itinerari dei santi nel mezzogiorno medievale*, ed. G. Vitolo (Naples, 1999); Saint George was also very popular among

INTRODUCTION

to Saint Michael at Mont-Saint-Michel and Monte Gargano in southern Italy, the famous pilgrimage to Jerusalem of Duke Robert of Normandy in 1035 and the pilgrim origin-stories of the Normans in southern Italy all testify to a long-standing connection between Normans and pilgrimage, and one that predated, and undoubtedly shaped, the Norman response to crusading.

The third and final methodological approach that we need to be aware of is linked to the ongoing debates over how to define the motivations of crusaders and pilgrims. Crusader historiography is littered with works addressing this theme, and they offer up a plethora of explanations: spiritual, psychological, eschatological, political, sociocultural and economic motivations seemingly influence some crusaders; notions of adventurism, family traditions or the need to assert status influenced others; while some may simply have been forced to go.[16] Since Jonathan Riley-Smith's important essay on crusading as an act of love, the idea of genuine religious motivations has enjoyed something of a resurgence.[17] However, taking the corpus of research as a whole it would seem that the current consensus, and the more compelling conclusion, is that multiple motivations co-existed in the same individual. Arguably it would be arbitrary and misleading to extract one, and, of course, profit and piety (the two traditional poles on the debate over motivations) could simultaneously motivate the same crusader. The Normans – deemed as warriors, parvenu Christians and opportunists (especially a figure like Bohemond) – feature heavily in these debates. But in this new light we might be able to arrive at more nuanced understandings of what prompted them to participate. Equally, the same motivating dynamics can be applied to acts of pilgrimage. Saints and their relics were considered to have supernatural qualities. A relationship with them could bring spiritual sustenance and help in the afterlife, and also cures and protection in the here and now. Saints and their shrines offered validation

---

the Normans: E. D'Angelo, 'San Giorgio e i normanni', in *San Giorgio e il Mediterraneo*, ed. G. de' Giovanni-Centelles (Vatican City, 2004), 195–217. See also C. Walsh, 'The Role of the Normans in the Development of the Cult of St Katherine', in *St Katherine of Alexandria: Texts and Contexts in Western Medieval Europe*, ed. J. Jenkins and K. J. Lewis (Turnhout, 2003), pp. 19–35.

[16] A brief, but useful overview of possible Crusader motivations is found in J. Flori, 'Ideology and Motivations in the First Crusade', in *The Crusades*, ed. Helen. J. Nicholson (Basingstoke, 2005), pp. 15–36; see also J. France, 'Patronage and the Appeal of the First Crusade', in *The First Crusade: Origins and Impact*, ed. J. Phillips (Manchester, 1997), pp. 5–20 and N. L. Paul, *To Follow in Their Footsteps: The Crusades and Family Memory in the High Middle Ages* (New York, 2012).

[17] J. S. Riley-Smith, 'Crusading as an Act of Love', *History* 65 (1980), 177–92. See also M. Bull, 'The Roots of Lay Enthusiasm for the First Crusade', *History* 78 (1993), 353–72, and his more extensive study: M. Bull, *Knightly Piety and the Lay Response to the First Crusade: The Limousin and Gascony, c. 970–c. 1130* (Oxford, 1993).

and support, not to mention the potential for great financial profit for the guardians of cults who would oversee pilgrim donations. Numerous communities and political elites aimed thus to establish links with particular saints, and so potent was this need that groups competed vigorously and resorted to violence and theft to gain possession of relics.[18] As we have already touched upon, and will see in the present volume, the Normans were not immune to these competing pressures and imperatives. Just as we have opted to avoid subscribing to one model for Norman identity, so too, and for the same reasons, have we decided to allow for as broad a perspective on definitions on crusading and pilgrimage, and on the debates over motivation and the extent of Norman participation in both. We feel that it is important to highlight the potential for conflicting approaches to the same subject, and even more important not to be prescriptive about its parameters. We hope that freedom enables the contributors to demonstrate the diverse ways of interpreting these contested points, and provides the reader with the tools to locate themselves within those same debates.

The collection of contributions gathered here has its roots in a symposium held at Manchester Metropolitan University in September 2012. Six of the essays in this volume were originally delivered at that event, with the remaining five contributors identified by the editors as being able to specifically address key themes which would complement and complete the overall project as envisaged by the editors. This collection of articles covers the entire geographic expanse of Norman activity – from the Celtic fringe via the Mediterranean to the Holy Land. It is hoped that together the contributions within the volume will enable the reader to form an understanding of two key underpinning themes: first, what was unique or different about the Normans and their relationship with crusading and pilgrimage; and second, how and why crusade and pilgrimage were important to the Normans. All the contributions, some explicitly, some implicitly, are informed by one or both of these questions. The contributions have been grouped into four thematic parts, the rationale for this hopefully being apparent from the preceding discussion in this introduction.

Part I examines the Normans and the First Crusade. William Aird's and Alan Murray's essays here address one of the pivotal episodes in the

---

[18] P. J. Geary, *Furta Sacra: Thefts of Relics in the Central Middle Ages* (Princeton, NJ, 1978); also useful are S. Barton, 'Patrons, Pilgrims and the Cult of Saints in the Medieval Kingdom of León', in *Pilgrimage Explored*, ed. J. Stopford (York, 1999), pp. 57–77 and J. Van Herwaarden, 'Pilgrimages and Social Prestige: Some Reflections on a Theme', in *Wallfahrt und Alltag in Mittelalter und früher Neuzeit*, ed. G. Jaritz and B. Schuh (Vienna, 1992), pp. 27–79.

Norman inter-relationship with crusading. In doing so they contribute to our understanding of what motivated the Normans to participate in the First Crusade, how it was recorded and why it played an integral role in Norman identity.[19] Part II explores ongoing crusading initiatives, revealing in what ways and why Normans continued to engage with the movement after the First Crusade. Joanna Drell examines the evidence for Norman southern Italy, Kathryn Hurlock for England and Wales, David Spear (through the specific prism of cathedrals) for Normandy, and Lucas Villegas-Aristizabal for Iberia. Part III comprises two essays which examine the significance of pilgrimage in diverse parts of the Norman world. Andrew Abram investigates the pilgrimage and crusading activities of the Anglo-Norman earls of Chester, while Paul Oldfield explores why pilgrims were deemed so important in southern Italy and the reasons why some of them were exploited, and consequently why pilgrimage could represent such a contentious topic.

Finally, the essays in Part IV focus on the ways in which crusading and pilgrimage were recorded in Norman narrative. As alluded to above, the Normans (following Marjorie Chibnall's well-known opinion) were in many senses constructed by the histories written about them, many of which they commissioned.[20] Thus, it is crucial to examine the messages and information derived from these sources. Emily Albu uses a range of Norman and non-Norman sources to explore the Normans' experience of Antioch and what this reveals about their wider attitude to crusading. Leonie Hicks' essay analyses a range of Norman historical works in order to elucidate how connections were made between landscape and sanctity. And, finally, Natasha Hodgson seeks to establish, through analysis of crusading narratives, how the Normans were perceived in the context of other crusading masculinities at a time when gendered identities were being radically redefined.

It should, hopefully, be clear that crusading and pilgrimage were European-wide phenomena. The Normans had no monopoly over either of them. The Normans were thus not unique in being involved in both, and this volume is driven as much by the aim to find comparison as it is to find difference. Ultimately, this volume aims in some respects to revise, in others to confirm, and to collectively offer a more holistic understanding

---

[19] Connor Kostick has looked at courage and cowardice in an article published after the symposium at which William Aird's paper was presented. Aird's paper takes a different approach to Costick's, looking at cowardice explicitly in relation to Norman identity. Conor Kostick, 'Courage and Cowardice on the First Crusade, 1096–99', *War in History* 20 (2013), 32–49.

[20] Chibnall, *The Normans*, p. 3.

of, the established paradigm of the Normans as crusaders *par excellence* and as opportunists who used religion to serve other agendas.

Part I

1

'Many others, whose names I do not know, fled with them'

Norman Courage and Cowardice on the First Crusade[1]

WILLIAM M. AIRD

Visitors to the great city of Antioch after its capture by the first crusaders in June 1098 might have noticed two memorials to certain less than heroic aspects of the siege. From the city walls dangled a number of ropes, and if our travellers had asked why these had been left there, they might have been told how several men, among them Normans from southern Italy, had deserted the crusade army when it was besieged by a great Turkish force led by Kerbogha, the emir of Mosul.[2] The anonymous author of the *Gesta Francorum*, arguably the most influential of the contemporary accounts of the First Crusade, had this to say about these deserters, the so-called 'secret rope-dancers' (*furtivi funambuli*) of Antioch:

> While this was going on, William of Grandmesnil, Aubré his brother, Guy Trousseau and Lambert the Poor, who were all thoroughly terrified [*timore perterriti*] by the battle of the previous day (8–9 June 1098), which had lasted until evening, let themselves down from the wall secretly during the night and fled on foot to the sea, and as a result both their hands and their feet were worn away to the bone. Many others, whose names I do not know, fled with them [*Multique alii fugerunt cum illis, quos nescio*]. When they reached the ships which were in St Simeon's port, they said to the sailors, 'You poor

---

[1] I am very grateful to Dr Kathryn Hurlock and Dr Paul Oldfield, the organisers of the symposium 'Pilgrimage and Crusading in the Norman World', for the invitation to present the paper upon which this chapter is based.

[2] For the siege of Antioch, see J. Birk, 'The Betrayal of Antioch: Narratives of Conversion and Conquest during the First Crusade', *Journal of Medieval and Early Modern Studies* 41:3 (2011), 463–85; Elizabeth Lapina, 'La représentation de la bataille d'Antioche (1098) sur les peintures murales de Poncé-sur-le-Loir', *Cahiers de civilisation médiévale* 52 (2009), 137–58 (I am grateful to Dr Lapina for sending me a copy of her article); J. France, 'The Fall of Antioch during the First Crusade', in *Dei gesta per Francos: Études sur les croisades dédiées à Jean Richard / Crusade Studies in Honour of Jean Richard*, ed. M. Balard, Benjamin Z. Kedar and Jonathan Riley-Smith (Aldershot, 2001), 13–20.

devils, why are you staying here? All our men are dead and we have barely escaped death ourselves, for the Turkish army is besieging the others in the city.' When the sailors heard this they were horrified and rushed in terror to their ships to put to sea. At that moment the Turks arrived and killed everyone whom they could catch. They burned those ships which were still in the mouth of the river and took their cargoes. And for us who stayed in Antioch, we could not defend ourselves against the attacks from the citadel, so we built a wall between us and it, and patrolled it day and night. Meanwhile we were so short of food that we were eating our horses and donkeys.[3]

William of Grandmesnil was not only a Norman who had settled in southern Italy, he was brother-in-law to the prominent crusade leader Bohemond of Taranto.[4] William had made a considerable reputation at the court of William the Conqueror and was offered the king's niece as a bride. However, this 'proud young knight [*superbus tiro*]' scorned honour and emigrated to Apulia, where he married Mabel Courte Louve, daughter of Robert Guiscard, duke of Apulia, acquiring control over fifteen castles. Following a failed rebellion, William took refuge at the court of the Byzantine emperor Alexios I.[5] William's brother Aubré also fled the siege of Antioch and there may have been yet another member of the Grandmesnil clan, Ivo, among the rope-dancers if Ralph of Caen's later account is accurate. Ralph also adds the name of Ralph of Fontenella from the Tourraine to the ignominious roll-call.[6] Abbot Suger of Saint-Denis confirms that one of the funambulists was Guy Trousseau, the son of Milo, lord of Montlhéry

---

[3] Hill, *GF*, pp. 56–57. For a recent study of this text, see C. Kostick, 'A Further Discussion of the Authorship of the *Gesta Francorum*', *Reading Medieval Studies* 35 (2009), 1–14.

[4] On the Grandmesnil family, see Marjorie Chibnall, *The World of Orderic Vitalis: Norman Monks and Norman Knights* (Woodbridge, 1996), pp. 21–2, 227; Joseph Decaëns, 'Le patrimoine des Grentemesnil en Normandie, en Italie et en Angleterre aux XIe et XIIe siècles', in *Les Normands en Méditerranée dans le sillage des Tancrède: Colloque de Cerisy-la-Salle (24–27 septembre 1992)*, ed. Pierre Bouet and François Neveux (Caen, 1994), pp. 123–40.

[5] *OV*, iv, 338–40 and n. 6. For William's career, see Geoffrey di Malaterra, *De rebus gestis Rogerii Calabriae et Siciliae comitis et Roberti Guiscardi ducis fratris eius*, ed. E. Pontieri (Bologna, 1927–8), p. 100; *The Deeds of Count Roger of Calabria and Sicily and of His Brother Duke Robert Guiscard, by Geoffrey Malaterra*, trans. K. B. Wolf (Ann Arbor, MI, 2005), p. 199; Evelyn M. Jamison, 'Some Notes on the *Anonymi Gesta Francorum*, with Special Reference to the Norman Contingent from South Italy and Sicily in the First Crusade', in *Studies in French Language and Medieval Literature presented to Mildred K. Pope* (Manchester, 1939), pp. 195–204 at 199–200; Mark Hagger, 'Kinship and Identity in Eleventh-Century Normandy: The Case of Hugh de Grandmesnil, c. 1040–1098', *JMH* 32 (2006), 212–30 at 214–15.

[6] *GT*, Bachrach, p. 101. This translation is of the edition in RCaen, pp. 603–716 at 662. My thanks to Daniel Roach for reference to a recent edition of Ralph of Caen's text: *Radulphus Cadomensis, Tancredus*, ed. E. D'Angelo, Corpus Christianorum Continuatio Mediaevalis 231 (Turnhout, 2011). All references here are to the *RHC* edition.

near Paris, 'that turbulent man and disturber of the kingdom'.[7] Lambert the Poor has been identified as the count of Clermont, near Liège.[8] William and his northern French companions were therefore men of some importance. Ralph of Caen noted that 'These were not obscure individuals, but rather important men among the paladins of the king of France.' It is also Ralph, a Norman cleric especially sensitive about this episode involving fellow countrymen, who noted that the ropes were left as memorials to cowardice. He tells us that, soon after the event, 'an edict was issued that no one was to dare to remove the ropes that stood as a monument of their shame to posterity'.[9] Eventually the ropes would have perished, but the memory of the dishonourable episode they represented may have endured and, if the injuries sustained by those who fled were as serious as reported, they may have borne scars on their hands and feet that advertised their shame. In addition, the term *furtivi funambuli*, reported by the English-born Norman monk Orderic Vitalis, may represent the characterisation of the deserters current in early twelfth-century northern France.[10] There was another 'monument of shame' erected to the dishonour of these deserters at Antioch.[11]

If visitors to Antioch had wished to relieve themselves during their stay in the city, they might have been directed to some tents that had been set aside as public latrines.[12] These tents had once belonged to the aforementioned Frankish nobleman, Guy the Red or Trousseau (*Trussellus*), and William the Carpenter, who was viscount of Melun and a relative of Hugh the Great, count of Vermandois, the brother of King Philip I of France. There is some conflation of this episode with the one discussed above, but, according to the *Gesta Francorum*, during the first months of the siege of Antioch, Guy, William and one of the key preachers of the Crusade, Peter the Hermit, had also absconded.[13] The anonymous author of the *Gesta Francorum* noted that:

---

[7] *Suger of Saint-Denis, Vita Ludovici Grossi Regis*, ed. and trans. H. Waquet (Paris, 1929), p. 36; *Suger, The Deeds of Louis the Fat*, trans. Richard C. Cusimano and John Moorhead (Washington DC, 1992), pp. 41 and 175–6.

[8] *GT*, Bachrach, p. 86 (RCaen, p. 650). For the identification of Lambert, see Hill, *GF*, p. 56, n. 6.

[9] *GT*, Bachrach, p. 102 (RCaen, p. 663).

[10] OV, v, pp. 98–9.

[11] On the memorialisation of the Crusades, see *Remembering the Crusades: Myth, Image, and Identity*, ed. Nicholas Paul and Suzanne Yeager (Baltimore, MD, 2012); Nicholas Paul, *To Follow in Their Footsteps: The Crusades and Family Memory in the High Middle Ages* (Ithaca, NY, 2012). Cf. Daniel Roach, 'The Material and the Visual: Objects and Memories in the *Historia Ecclesiastica* of Orderic Vitalis', *Haskins Society Journal* 24 (2012), 63–78.

[12] *GT*, Bachrach, p. 86 (RCaen, p. 650).

[13] AA, pp. 304–5. In Albert's text the desertions of William of Grandmesnil, William the Carpenter and Stephen of Blois are linked. Jonathan Riley-Smith, *The First Crusade and the Idea of Crusading*

> [b]ecause of this great wretchedness and misery – *a reference to the scarcity of supplies of food during the early months of the siege* – William the Carpenter and Peter the Hermit fled away secretly. Tancred went after them and caught them and brought them back in disgrace. They gave him a pledge and an oath that they were willing to return to the camp and give satisfaction to the leaders. William spent the whole of the night in my lord Bohemond's tent, lying on the ground like a piece of rubbish [*mala res*].[14]

Although these men were not themselves Normans, they were caught and punished by the southern Italian Normans, Bohemond and his nephew Tancred.[15] Ralph of Caen, who adds detail, joined Bohemond as his chaplain when the prince of Antioch was in France recruiting men for an expedition against the Byzantines in 1106. Later, probably soon after Bohemond's death in 1111, Ralph joined Tancred who had succeeded his uncle as ruler of Antioch.[16] It is likely, therefore, that Ralph's account of these memorials to cowardice has some basis. Very much associated with these deserters is another distinguished figure from northern France and a man intimately connected with the family of William the Conqueror. This was Stephen-Henry, count of Blois, Chartres and Meaux, who married the Conqueror's daughter Adela in late 1083.[17]

Stephen-Henry's conduct at Antioch was also criticised by contemporaries, although some were more sympathetic than others.[18] Just before the crusaders finally secured the city, Stephen-Henry decided to leave the expedition. According to the *Gesta* Anonymous:

> Now it happened that, before Antioch was captured, that coward[19] Stephen, count of Chartres, whom all our leaders had elected commander-in-chief,

---

(London, 1993), p. 161, dates the desertion to *c.* 20 January 1098. On Peter the Hermit, see J. Rubenstein, 'How, or How Much, to Re-evaluate Peter the Hermit', in *The Medieval Crusade*, ed. Susan Ridyard (Woodbridge, 2004), pp. 53–69; C. Morris, 'Peter the Hermit and the Chroniclers', in *The First Crusade, Origins and Impact*, ed. J. Phillips (Manchester, 1997), pp. 21–34 at 31.

[14] Hill, *GF*, 33.

[15] R. B. Yewdale, *Bohemond I, Prince of Antioch* (Princeton, NJ, 1924); R. L. Nicholson, *Tancred* (Chicago, 1940).

[16] Hodgson, 'Reinventing Normans', 117–32. My thanks to Dr Hodgson for sending me her article.

[17] Kimberly LoPrete, *Adela of Blois: Countess and Lord (c. 1067–1137)* (Dublin, 2007), p. 55. The count's given name was Henry and the 'Stephen' may have been added to advance a claim to the county of Meaux; see *ibid.*, p. 42, n. 84.

[18] *Fulcheri Carnotensis, Historia Hierosolymitana (1095–1127)*, ed. H. Hagenmeyer (Heidelberg, 1913), p. 228; cf. *Fulcher of Chartres: A History of the Expedition to Jerusalem 1095–1127*, trans. Frances Rita Ryan, ed. H. S. Fink (Knoxville, TN, 1969), p. 97.

[19] Hill, *GF*, p. 63: the word used is either *impudens* (shameless) or *imprudens* (of poor judgement or lacking foresight), which makes Hill's translation ('that coward') misleadingly unambiguous. The word *turpiter* can also have the connotation of defilement: see below n. 53. The translation 'coward', therefore, associates Stephen's departure with fear.

pretended to be very ill, and he went away shamefully [*turpiter*] to another castle which is called Alexandretta. When we were shut up in that city, lacking help to save us, we waited each day for him to bring us aid. But he, having heard that the Turks had surrounded and besieged us, went secretly [*latenter*] up a neighbouring mountain which stood near Antioch, and when he saw more tents than he could count he returned in terror [*uehementique captus timore*] and hastily retreated in flight with his army [*fugitque festinanter cum suo exercitu*].[20]

It is clear that the count of Blois withdrew from the crusade in two stages. At first he retreated to Alexandretta, a port to the north of Antioch, perhaps suffering with the illness reported. After the Franks took Antioch, Stephen-Henry returned as far as a mountain overlooking the city from where he saw that Kerbogha's army had now besieged the crusaders. It was the sight of 'more tents than he could count' (*innumerabilia tentoria*) that prompted Stephen-Henry to flee in terror.[21] The *Gesta* Anonymous added that Stephen-Henry met the Byzantine emperor at Philomelium, and told him that he was sure that, by now, the crusaders had all been killed. He then advised Alexios to withdraw.[22] The emperor called a secret council and summoned Bohemond's half-brother, Guy, who, like many Normans, was serving as a mercenary in the Byzantine army.[23] Alexios asked him for his advice about the story 'of this wretched count who has fled in such a shameful way'.[24] When Guy, who is described as a *miles honestissimus*, a contrast with Stephen-Henry the *infelix comes*, heard the news, he and his companions wailed with grief and threatened to abandon God if this was how the faith of the crusaders had been rewarded. Guy grieved painfully for Bohemond and when others tried to comfort him he said:

> 'Perhaps you believe this cowardly old fool of a knight [*semicano imprudenti militia*]? I tell you that I have never heard of any knightly deed [*de milites*] which he has done. He has retreated shamefully and indecently [*turpiter et inhoneste*], like a scoundrel and a wretch [*nequissimus et infelix*], and whatever the knave (*miser*) says, you may be sure that it is a lie.'[25]

---

[20] Riley-Smith, *The First Crusade*, p. 161: Stephen left Antioch on 2 June 1098 and the city fell the next day.
[21] James A. Brundage, 'An Errant Crusader: Stephen of Blois', *Traditio* 16 (1960), 380–95 at 388–9.
[22] Hill, *GF*, p. 63.
[23] *Ibid.*, pp. 63–5. On Guy in Byzantine service, see *The Alexiad of Anna Comnena*, trans. E. R. A. Sewter (Harmondsworth, 1969), pp. 188–91. W. B. McQueen, 'Relations between the Normans and Byzantium 1071–1112', *Byzantion* 56 (1986), 427–76 at 445–6.
[24] Hill, *GF*, p. 64.
[25] *Ibid.*, p. 65.

Despite Guy's assertion that Stephen-Henry was lying, Alexios decided to withdraw to Constantinople, thereby providing Bohemond with the justification for retaining control of Antioch. It is worth noting that Stephen-Henry's flight undermined his credibility as a witness. Notwithstanding his status as one of the leading nobles of northern France, he was no longer considered one of those trustworthy men (*probi homines*) medieval society usually called upon to render the truth. The desertion of Stephen-Henry, William the Carpenter, the Grandmesnils and their companions provides an opportunity to explore medieval representations of cowardice and courage. The desertions demonstrate that, despite their oaths, many of those who answered Pope Urban II's call failed to complete their armed pilgrimage, liberate Jerusalem and aid their co-religionists in the eastern Mediterranean. Their failure highlights the achievement of those who fulfilled their vows despite the arduous conditions of the march and the mortal dangers presented by siege and battle in an unfamiliar and often unforgiving environment.

Despite Philippe Contamine's attempt 'to mark out a trail' for a history of courage, relatively few historians have explored this theme as it relates to medieval warfare, and even fewer have explored the psychological effects of participating in the crusade.[26] This contrasts with the work of military historians dealing largely with later periods, such as John Keegan's influential *The Face of Battle* and Joanna Bourke's harrowing studies of modern warfare.[27] J. F. Verbruggen wrote about 'the psychology of knights on the battlefield', noting that earlier characterisations of medieval chivalric warriors displaying a contempt for death should be questioned because 'the knights were still human beings who feared for their lives in the presence of danger, and who behaved as men have always done in battle – in fear of death, mutilation, wounds and captivity'. Verbruggen suggested that the historian should 'look for courage in the manner in which they braved danger, for it is important to know how they overcame their fear and what made them fight bravely'.[28] In an early study of the First Crusade, Riley-Smith recognised the importance of those who deserted the

---

[26] Philippe Contamine, 'Towards a History of Courage', in *War in the Middle Ages*, trans. Michael Jones (Oxford, 1984), pp. 250–9 and cf. J. F. Verbruggen, *The Art of Warfare in Western Europe during the Middle Ages from the Eighth Century to 1340*, 2nd edn, revised and enlarged, trans. Colonel Sumner Willard and Mrs R. W. Southern (Woodbridge, 1997), p. 40.

[27] John Keegan, *The Face of Battle* (London, 1976); Joanna Bourke, *Dismembering the Male: Men's Bodies, Britain and the Great War* (London, 1996) and Bourke, *An Intimate History of Killing* (London, 1999).

[28] Verbruggen, *Art of Warfare*, pp. 37–44 at 38. On fear itself, see Joanna Bourke, *Fear: A Cultural History* (London, 2005).

pilgrimage and wrote about the fear and despair that the crusaders suffered on their march.[29] Recent studies of cowardice in medieval armies include those by Richard Abels, Steven Isaac and Stephen Morillo.[30] Influential on the work of these historians and on this paper is William Miller's study, *The Mystery of Courage*, which traces ideologies of courage and, necessarily, its antithesis, cowardice, drawing on a variety of texts from ancient Greece and Rome to memoirs from the American Civil War, the two world wars and Vietnam.[31] These studies assume that conceptualisations of courage and cowardice are culturally constructed and dependent upon specific situations for their effectiveness and meaning. As such, they must be nuanced according to context and are thus, as Contamine surmised, worthy of historical analysis. This is particularly interesting in the circumstances of the First Crusade. This armed pilgrimage was a new development in Christian warfare and the vows taken by those who committed themselves to the march to Jerusalem placed them under obligations that were significantly greater than if they had joined military expeditions to fight in the West for strictly secular purposes, however much those expeditions might have been influenced by pre-existing notions of 'holy war'.

The subject of courage and cowardice on the First Crusade also relates to the history of the emotions and representations of gendered identities. It can also elucidate the motives of those who decided whether to participate in the crusade or not. Beyond this, it is important to recognise that whether individuals, especially members of the medieval chivalric classes, were deemed courageous or cowardly affected not only their reputations and social standing, but also their ability to acquire and exercise effective political and social power.[32] The individuals named in this chapter were from the upper echelons of chivalric society; indeed Stephen-Henry of Blois may have led the crusade at one point. The behavioural expectations associated with medieval knights have a bearing on how far and in what circumstances displays of fearfulness were socially acceptable. At stake was not just social status, but perhaps also an individual's masculine identity. These men were scrutinised and measured not only by the expectations of

---

[29] Riley-Smith, *The First Crusade*, pp. 59, 61, 67, 71–2, 78, 85–6, 100, 116, 120–1 (desertion); [despair] 112 (despair); 71–3, 90, 112, 120–1, 154, 161 (fear).
[30] Richard Abels, '"Cowardice" and Duty in Anglo-Saxon England', *Journal of Medieval Military History* 4 (2006), 29–49; Steven Isaac, 'Cowardice and Fear Management: The 1173–74 Conflict as a Case Study', *Journal of Medieval Military History* 4 (2006), 50–64; Stephen Morillo, 'Expecting Cowardice: Medieval Battle Tactics Reconsidered', *JMH* 4 (2006), 65–73.
[31] William I. Miller, *The Mystery of Courage* (Cambridge, MA, 2000).
[32] On the term *miles/milites*, see C. Kostick, 'The Terms *milites*, *equites* and *equestris* in the Early Crusading Histories', *Nottingham Medieval Studies* 50 (2006), 1–21.

their families and comrades, but also by their own self-image. For a knight to manifest fear in battle, or take to his heels in flight, was to be associated with the behaviour of women.[33] A further consideration concerns the collective identity of the Normans who participated in the First Crusade.

By the end of the eleventh century, and largely through histories written for the Normans themselves, an image of the *gens Normannorum* as a people especially successful in warfare had been constructed.[34] However, the conduct of the Normans and their comrades on the First Crusade suggests that historians should not assume that these men were oblivious to the fear and hardships associated with medieval warfare.[35] Even the courage of those considered the most formidable warriors of the First Crusade might fail in the midst of battle. Generally acknowledged as the most effective general on the expedition, at least as far as Antioch, Bohemond seems to embody the martial qualities most associated with the *gens Normannorum*.[36] Descriptions of the Battle of Dorylaeum, 1 July 1097, provide contrasting representations of Bohemond's courage in battle. The *Gesta* Anonymous, at that stage in Bohemond's entourage and not yet as disillusioned by his lord's self-serving attitude as he was to be at Antioch, portrays the Norman coping well with the fight against the Turks.[37] After the capture of Nicaea, the crusaders advanced in two contingents, one of which was led by Bohemond and Robert Curthose, duke of Normandy. According to the *Gesta* Anonymous, when the Turks attacked, Bohemond ordered the knights to dismount and the army to pitch camp. The crusaders fought bravely with help from the women in the army, who brought water and encouragement for the soldiers. Bohemond sent word to the other contingent of the army asking them to bring aid and act 'manfully' (*viriliter*). When the other group arrived, the crusaders won a famous victory.

Later accounts offer interesting variations on this narrative. Robert the Monk associated the order for the knights to dismount with Bohemond

---

[33] M. Bennett, 'Military Masculinity in England and Northern France c. 1050–c. 1225', in *Masculinity in Medieval Europe*, ed. Dawn M. Hadley (Harlow, 1999), pp. 71–88. Patricia Skinner, '"Halt! Be men!": Sikelgaita of Salerno, Gender and the Norman Conquest of Southern Italy', *Gender and History* 12 (2000), 622–641. On constructions of masculinity and modern combat, see J. S. Goldstein, *War and Gender: How Gender Shapes the War System and Vice Versa* (Cambridge, 2001), pp. 251–331.

[34] R. H. C. Davis, *The Normans and Their Myth* (London, 1976); Loud, 'The *Gens Normannorum*: myth or reality?' *ANS* 4 (1981), 104–16; N. Webber, *Evolution of Norman Identity, 911–1154* (Woodbridge, 2005).

[35] J. R. Bliese, 'The Courage of the Normans: A Comparative Study of Battle Rhetoric', *Nottingham Medieval Studies* 35 (1991), 1–26.

[36] R. C. Smail, *Crusading Warfare 1097–1193* (Cambridge, 1956); John France, *Victory in the East: A Military History of the First Crusade* (Cambridge, 1994), 246–51.

[37] Hill, *GF*, pp. 18–21. Emily Albu, 'Probing the Passions of a Norman on Crusade: The *Gesta Francorum et aliorum Hierosolimitanorum*', *ANS* 27 (2005), 11.

and Robert of Normandy's recognition that the resolve of their troops was wavering.³⁸ Later in the battle the force of the Turkish assault threatened to rout the crusaders

> and if the Count of Normandy had not swung his horse round, brandishing his golden standard in his right hand, and bellowed the war-cry 'God wills it! God wills it!' this day would have been a disastrous one for our soldiers. However, once they had seen Bohemond and the Count of Normandy turn back, they regained their courage and decided to die rather than flee further.³⁹

Ralph of Caen described a rout of the crusader forces and it was only when Robert 'recalled to himself his lineage and the fact that he was a fighter' that the flight was halted. Ralph describes the duke of Normandy uncovering his head and shouting 'Normandy' to rally his fellow Norman Bohemond. In a short battle oration, Robert encouraged Bohemond and his men to stand fast and return to the offensive. Ralph's narrative specifically mentions the young men (*iuvenes*) of the Norman contingents responding to the duke's rhetoric, suggesting perhaps that these knights were particularly susceptible to a loss of nerve in battle.⁴⁰

In these accounts representations of courage and fearfulness in the various forms of medieval warfare are clear. However, fearfulness and cowardice should be distinguished when considering the conduct of the Normans and their Frankish comrades on the First Crusade. As Verbruggen and others have noted, fear of death or injury is an understandable and perfectly human reaction to the danger presented by combat.⁴¹ The decision to disengage from the fight and move away from the enemy cannot simply be characterised as 'cowardice', as the manoeuvre may be a tactical retreat or an orderly withdrawal rather than a rout. Martial courage in any era involves the mastery of both fear and the impulse to run away. As military historians have pointed out, training and codes of discipline can mitigate the levels of fear experienced by those called upon to fight. For Miller, displays of what appears to be courage can also be understood in a number of ways. Those who seem to give no thought to the possibility of injury or death may do so either through an inability to recognise the danger, or because their actions are instinctual, rather than rational. The narratives

---

³⁸ 'Roberti Monachi, Historia Iherosolimitana', *RHC*, iii, pp. 717–882 at 759–60; translated as *Robert the Monk's History of the First Crusade: Historia Iherosolimitana*, trans. Carol Sweetenham (Aldershot, 2005), pp. 107–8.
³⁹ *RHC*, iii, p. 761; trans. *Robert the Monk*, pp. 108–9.
⁴⁰ *GT*, Bachrach, p. 46 (RCaen, p. 622).
⁴¹ Verbruggen, *Art of Warfare*, p. 38.

presented here are concerned with three constructions of courage, namely what might be called 'heroic courage' or the ability to engage the enemy in battle, the courage to endure oppressive conditions and, finally, moral courage, or the ability to bear the disapproval and opprobrium of one's peers or society at large. Most societies tend to value the 'heroic' more highly than the less dramatic forms of courage.[42] Aggression rather than endurance tends to win more plaudits, especially among groups among whom the display of martial virtues is important to personal and social identity. In medieval accounts aggression is often gendered male. Endurance or suffering is gendered female and associated with women and other non-combatants.[43]

It seems incongruous for men later labelled cowards to answer the pope's call to arms, but both William the Carpenter and Stephen-Henry enjoyed reputations for martial prowess before they embarked on the crusade. Fulcher of Chartres lamented Stephen-Henry's departure as he was 'mighty in arms' (*validus armis*).[44] Guibert of Nogent explained that William gained his nickname, *Carpentarius*, 'not because he was a craftsman in wood, but because he prevailed in battle like a carpenter, by cutting men down'.[45] Although, like his brother-in-law Robert of Normandy, Stephen-Henry of Blois was approaching fifty years of age, he had performed heroic deeds in his youth and when he returned to his wife, she persuaded him to complete his vows calling to mind these former exploits.[46] In this honour-based society, the recklessness of youth might serve the adult well. Martial exploits performed during the knight's early career, as in Stephen-Henry's case, were often the basis of the reputation that could bring social status and dynastic wealth.[47] Stephen-Henry's loss of nerve, if that is what it was, at Antioch supports the idea that courage needed reinforcement through continual practice. It was a quality always subject to scrutiny and under threat. Youthful displays of courage raised expectations that Stephen-Henry would always act bravely. But he was a relatively old man on the First Crusade, perhaps living on his former reputation. Had people forgotten his

---

[42] Miller, *Mystery of Courage*, p. 107.
[43] *Ibid.*, pp. 232–53.
[44] *Fulcheri Carnotensis*, p. 228; *Fulcher of Chartres*, trans. Ryan, p. 97.
[45] GN, p. 179.
[46] LoPrete, *Adela of Blois*, p. 42, Stephen-Henry was born around 1048. See LoPrete, *Adela of Blois*, pp. 49–55, for his early career and marriage to Adela *c.* 1083.
[47] G. Duby, 'Youth in Aristocratic Society. North-Western France in the Twelfth Century', in *The Chivalrous Society: Essays by Georges Duby*, trans. Cynthia Postan (London, 1977), pp. 112–122; cf. J. R. Lyon, 'Fathers and Sons: Preparing Noble Youths to be Lords in Twelfth-Century Germany', *JMH* 34 (2008), 291–310.

earlier exploits? The *Gesta* Anonymous has Bohemond's half-brother, Guy call into question Stephen-Henry's former record: 'I tell you that I have never heard of any knightly deed which he has done.'[48] In a letter home to his wife from the siege of Antioch in 1098, the count of Blois claimed that the other leaders of the crusade had given him overall command of the army.[49] Unless he was fantasising, it seems incongruous that a known coward would have been given such a role. Until Antioch then, Stephen-Henry's courage was not an issue. Perhaps the illness, dismissed as a sham by the *Gesta* Anonymous, was genuine and contributed to his loss of nerve.[50] It is surely much harder to be brave when wracked with a debilitating malady. It should also be noted that Stephen did not desert before or during a battle and he seems to have played his part in earlier engagements.[51] What broke him, and what seems to have broken William the Carpenter, were the appalling conditions that the crusaders had to endure during the siege of Antioch. Just before reporting Stephen's desertion, the *Gesta* records that:

> So terrible was the famine that men boiled and ate the leaves of figs, vines, thistles and all kinds of trees. Others stewed the dried skins of horses, camels, asses, oxen or buffaloes, which they ate. These and many other troubles and anxieties, which I cannot describe, we suffered for the Name of Christ and to set free the road to the Holy Sepulchre; and we endured this misery, hunger and fear for six-and-twenty days.[52]

Ralph of Caen noted, when speaking of Count Stephen-Henry and William the Carpenter, that:

> These men, who shared a common generation and common manner of life, all hated labour and sought after pleasure. They were fighters. In between wars, however, they were accustomed to luxury.[53]

In Ralph's view, what Stephen-Henry and William lacked was the courage to endure the conditions of the siege. This was almost certainly the longest campaign and possibly the longest siege that these men had ever endured. In between the short battles were long marches through hostile terrain, often in debilitating climatic conditions, and always with the threat

---

[48] Hill, *GF*, 65.
[49] H. Hagenmeyer, *Die Kreuzzugsbriefe aus den Jahren 1088–1100. Eine Quellensammlung zur Geschichte des Ersten Kreuzzuges* (Innsbruck, 1901), no. X, pp. 149–52.
[50] Hill, *GF*, p. 63.
[51] *Ibid.*, p. 15: the siege of Nicaea. The *Gesta* Anonymous does not mention him at Dorylaeum.
[52] *Ibid.*, pp. 62–3.
[53] *GT*, Bachrach, p. 86 (RCaen, p. 651).

of surprise attacks by the enemy. Even for noblemen such as Stephen-Henry and William, who might not have shared all of the deprivations of the common soldiers, conditions tested their resolve and gradually their ability to endure was undermined. So, once courageous men, men who had even proved themselves in battle earlier on the crusade, reached their breaking-point and found that they could go no further. What were the consequences of being branded a coward?

According to the *Gesta*, once William the Carpenter had been captured and brought back by Tancred, Bohemond forced him to spend the night lying on the ground like a piece of rubbish (*mala res*).[54] In the morning, he was brought before Bohemond, and blushing with shame, he was berated:

> 'You wretched disgrace to the whole Frankish army – you dishonourable blot on all the people of Gaul! You most loathsome of all men whom the earth has to bear, why did you run off in such a shameful way? I suppose that you wanted to betray these knights and the Christian camp, just as you betrayed those others in Spain?' William kept quiet, and never a word proceeded out of his mouth. Nearly all the Franks assembled and humbly begged my lord Bohemond not to allow him to suffer a worse punishment. He granted their request without being angry and said, 'I will freely grant this for the love I bear you, provided the man will swear, with his whole heart and mind, that he will never turn aside from the path to Jerusalem, whether for good or ill, and Tancred shall swear that he will neither do, nor permit his men to do, any harm to him.'[55]

The striking detail is that William had previously deserted another campaign in Spain.[56] If the *Gesta* Anonymous was reporting fact, rather than prejudice, then William had form, so to speak. So, what was he doing on the crusade? Here we might pause before labelling William and others

---

[54] Hill, *GF*, p. 33. Cf. Guibert, *Dei Gesta*, pp. 216–17; R. Levine, *The Deeds of God through the Franks: A Translation of Guibert of Nogent's Gesta Dei per Francos* (Woodbridge, 1997), pp. 98–9. Guibert emphasises the fact that the deserters escaped by letting themselves down into the sewers, 'a worthy place for those who were giving such a bad example to the troops'. He adds the desertions of William of Normandy (Grandmesnil) and his brother Alberic, but, to protect them from shame, he declines to name the towns they were from because of his friendship with their families. He notes that there were others who deserted, who were denounced and held infamous everywhere when they returned home. He did not know all their names. Of those he knew well, he preferred not to name and humiliate them.

[55] Hill, *GF*, pp. 33–4.

[56] Guibert, *Dei Gesta*, 179; Riley-Smith, *The First Crusade*, 43: William the Carpenter joined a French army that marched into Spain in 1087 after the defeat of Alfonso VI of Leon-Castile at Sagrajas the year before. The French army diverted to besiege Tudela, but accomplished nothing and it was presumably here that William deserted. Marcus Bull, *Knightly Piety and the Lay Response to the First Crusade: The Limousin and Gascony, c. 970–c. 1130* (Oxford, 1993), pp. 83, 84–5. William's 'desertion' might be interpreted in a number of ways. For example, if nothing was to be gained, then raising the siege may have been the most rational of decisions.

cowards. Miller draws attention to the figure of the 'courageous coward', that is the man who tries sincerely to stand firm in the face of danger, but each time he puts himself in harm's way, his resolve collapses and he runs away.⁵⁷ Was William the Carpenter one of these 'courageous cowards'? The *Gesta* passage describes a ritual humiliation, but with redemption offered at the end. The charge against William was betrayal of the Christian army and there is the suggestion that because he had taken an oath to serve Christ his desertion may have been viewed as apostasy. William offered no excuses or explanations, although the *Gesta* Anonymous acknowledged that it was in the midst of 'great wretchedness and misery' that William fled. Ralph of Caen suggested that these noble deserters were lovers of luxury and, although accomplished warriors, they could not endure the privations of the siege.⁵⁸ It was the intercession of those he had betrayed that swayed Bohemond and allowed William to escape a more severe punishment. Out of the love he bore his companions, Bohemond agreed to let William go if he swore to continue to Jerusalem. Surely the *Gesta* Anonymous was aware of the irony here, given Bohemond's decision not to press on to Jerusalem after the capture of Antioch.⁵⁹ Despite this leniency, once again William the Carpenter 'sneaked off without delay, for he was greatly ashamed'.⁶⁰ Was William's subsequent desertion due to cowardice in the face of the enemy, or his inability to endure the opprobrium of his erstwhile comrades? His humiliation and restoration had put him in their debt and perhaps it was a situation that his own sense of status could not endure. His desertion here was a result of the lack of moral courage to bear this censure and there are parallels with the case of Stephen-Henry of Blois.⁶¹

Stephen-Henry's homecoming caused consternation which soon became condemnation. He had failed to complete his vow and to many it seemed that, whatever the reasons for his withdrawal from Antioch, he had abandoned his companions and deserted Christ's glorious army. It must be remembered that the count of Blois did not depart alone from Antioch. The *Gesta Francorum* noted that Stephen-Henry retreated 'with his army' (*cum suo exercitu*), and his decision placed his men in a difficult position for they were forced to choose between leaving their comrades at Antioch

---

⁵⁷ Miller, *Mystery of Courage*, 1–14.
⁵⁸ *GT*, Bachrach, p. 86 (RCaen, p. 651).
⁵⁹ On the *Gesta* Anonymous's response to the crusade, see Albu, 'Probing the Passions'.
⁶⁰ Hill, *GF*, p. 34.
⁶¹ William the Carpenter did return to the Holy Land and held a lordship in the principality of Antioch: *Regesta Regni Hierosolymitani (MCVII–MCCXCI)*, ed. R. Röhricht, 2 vols (Innsbruck, 1893–1904), i, p. 5, where William witnesses a grant by Tancred to the Genoese. Cf. Thomas Asbridge, *The Creation of the Principality of Antioch, 1098–1130* (Woodbridge, 2000), p. 184.

or renouncing their allegiance to their lord.[62] It is possible that this mirrored the decision to make the journey to Jerusalem they had taken at the beginning of the crusade. On that occasion, their loyalty to their lord may have prompted their participation as much as any religious vow, although in theory the decision to undertake the journey was a voluntary one.[63] The crusader's vow was a public affirmation that he would prove the truth of his words through his actions. In some respects the vow was akin to the boasts issued by the heroes of the medieval sagas and *chansons de geste*. In this way personal honour and social standing were intimately associated with the fulfilment of the crusader oath. In his condemnation of William the Carpenter's actions, Guibert of Nogent commented that '[h]is reputation in war was for boasting only, and not for deeds done'.[64]

Although writing after the events, Orderic Vitalis provided a characteristically lively account of Stephen-Henry's homecoming. He found life difficult, not least because, even before the crusaders captured Jerusalem in July 1099, a papal edict threatened anathema on anyone who deserted the expedition and failed to complete their vows. This was reissued by Pope Paschal II shortly after 1100 and it cannot have made Stephen-Henry's life easy.[65] Orderic recorded that:

> Stephen, count Palatine of Blois, was an object of contempt to almost everyone, and was continually reproached because he had fled disgracefully from the siege of Antioch, deserting his glorious comrades who were sharing the agonies of Christ. He was continually chided by many people, and was driven to embark on another crusade as much by fear as shame. His wife Adela also frequently urged him to it, and between conjugal caresses used to say, 'Far be it from you, my lord, to lower yourself by enduring the scorn of such men as these for long. Remember the courage for which you were famous in your youth, and take up the arms of the glorious crusade for the sake of saving thousands so that Christians may raise great thanksgiving all over the world, and the lot of the heathen may be terror and the public overthrow of their unholy law.' These speeches and many more like them were uttered by the wise and spirited woman to her husband; but he, knowing the perils and difficulties, shrank from undertaking such hardships a second time. At

---

[62] Hill, *GF*, p. 63.
[63] On this point see M. Bull, 'The Roots of Lay Enthusiasm for the First Crusade', *History* 78 (1993), 353–72 at 364; cf. Riley-Smith, *The First Crusade*, pp. 36–49. J. A. Brundage, *Medieval Canon Law and the Crusader* (Madison, WI, 1969), pp. 30–65; J. Muldoon, 'Crusading and Canon Law', in *The Crusades*, ed. Helen Nicholson (Basingstoke, 2005), pp. 37–57.
[64] Guibert, *Dei Gesta*, pp. 178–79 (trans. Levine, p. 79); cf. Miller, *Mystery of Courage*, pp. 134–6.
[65] Riley-Smith, *The First Crusade*, p. 125.

length he recovered his courage and strength, and took the road with many thousands of Frenchmen, persevering until he reached Christ's sepulchre in spite of the terrible difficulties encountered on the way.[66]

Orderic reiterates the *Gesta*'s association of Stephen-Henry's desertion with his betrayal of his comrades and Christ himself. Orderic also recognised that Stephen-Henry's motives for returning to the Holy Land were 'fear and shame' (*tam terrore quam confusione*), hardly honourable motives for such a pious enterprise. He lacked the moral courage to withstand the opprobrium heaped on him at home. His wife may have been especially sensitive to the issue, not only as the guardian of her family's honour, but also because she knew that her brother Robert had successfully fulfilled his vows. Her nagging even in between 'conjugal caresses' (how did Orderic know these intimate details?) made Stephen-Henry's home life uncomfortable. This episode also suggests that women might act as arbiters of chivalric behaviour. Countess Adela of Blois and perhaps many other aristocratic women in the early twelfth century were called upon to judge the conduct of their men. Adela was a formidable woman and jealous of her family's reputation. There was added pressure on Stephen-Henry for his father-in-law's triumphs must have been the standard by which his wife judged him. It was difficult for him to ignore the Conqueror's achievement as Adela's bed-chamber was decorated with a tapestry depicting her father's conquest of England. Stephen-Henry's conduct suffered by comparison with this constant reminder of Norman prowess.[67] Beyond these considerations, his tarnished reputation also seriously undermined Stephen-Henry's ability to rule his lands.[68]

In this society, accusations of cowardice brought with them assumptions about a lack of integrity and honesty. Guy had impugned Stephen-Henry's honesty in the presence of Emperor Alexios. Stephen-Henry thus returned to the Holy Land and completed his vows, but was killed in battle at Ramleh in May 1102.[69] A number of factors may have contributed to his decision to return to Jerusalem. His reputation had the potential to affect adversely the lives of his children, one of whom would become King Stephen of England.

---

[66] OV, v, pp. 324–5.
[67] On the tapestry, see Monika Otter, 'Baudri of Bourgueil, "To Countess Adela", *Journal of Medieval Latin* 11 (2001), 60–141. R. H. C. Davis, *King Stephen* (London, 1967), p. 1, n. 3.
[68] Lo Prete, *Adela of Blois*, pp. 111–15.
[69] There is doubt as to whether he died in battle or was captured and then executed: Brundage, 'An Errant Crusader', 391–4. On the crusade of 1101, see A. Mulinder, 'Albert of Aachen and the Crusade of 1101', in *From Clermont to Jerusalem: The Crusades and Crusader Societies, 1095–1500*, ed. A. V. Murray (Turnhout, 1998) pp. 69–77; Riley-Smith, *The First Crusade*, pp. 120–34.

In the opinion of this king's most recent biographer, Stephen-Henry made his decision in an attempt to ensure that his 'reputation would not be a burden to his children. That is why he had returned to the Holy Land and almost courted death.'[70] He suffered a martyr's death, but was this enough to restore his reputation? There is perhaps a hint that he had recovered his personal and family honour: Fulcher of Chartres recorded Stephen-Henry's death and described him as a *vir prudens et nobilis*.[71]

The count of Blois was not alone in suffering the consequences of his desertion from Antioch in 1098. Abbot Suger described Guy Trousseau as 'broken by the stress of a long trip and the irritation that comes from various afflictions, and by guilt for his unusual behaviour at Antioch when, in fear of Corboran (Kerbogha), he escaped over the wall and deserted God's host besieged within'. According to Suger he wasted away worrying that his daughter might be disinherited.[72] The count of Blois may have endured a more public disgrace, but Guy also seems to have incurred psychological damage as a result of his failure to fulfil his vow.

It is unknown how many deserted the crusade and as the sources tend to concentrate on the behaviour of the social elite, there may have been a steady stream of lower-status failed pilgrims returning to western Europe who were unnoticed in the sources. The crusade was unlike anything else that Latin Europe had seen. It was a pilgrimage and a military campaign that lasted years and covered thousands of miles. Conditions oscillated between periods of plentiful supplies enjoyed in comparative comfort and periods of deprivation, squalor and unimaginable terror. Even with the piety of the participants evident in the contemporary sources, many faltered and deserted. Fear in combat situations tends to be contagious and many of those who fled may have been responding to the actions of their comrades.[73] When those deserters were also among the leaders of the crusade it became a serious problem for the army. Even heroes like Bohemond wavered and the *Gesta Francorum* noted that the leaders had to demonstrate publicly their resolve by taking an oath 'that none of them, while he lived, would flee, either from fear of death or from hope of life'.[74] When these noblemen fled, the men in their retinues were faced with a hard choice. William the

---

[70] E. J. King, *King Stephen* (New Haven, CT, 2011), p. 7; cf. D. Crouch, *The Reign of King Stephen 1135–1154* (London, 2000), p. 11. If King Stephen was born in 1096, he may never have seen his father, nor retained any memory of him. Fulcher of Chartres (*Fulcheri Carnotensis*, p. 431; trans. Ryan, p. 165) makes it clear that Stephen-Henry returned to atone for his desertion.

[71] *Fulcheri Carnotensis*, p. 443; cf. *Fulcher*, trans. Ryan, p. 169.

[72] Suger, *Vita Ludovici*, p. 36.

[73] Miller, *Mystery of Courage*, p. 207.

[74] Hill, *GF*, p. 59.

Carpenter, Stephen-Henry of Blois, William of Grandmesnil and the others did not flee alone. In these circumstances there seems to have been no substantial difference between the behaviour of those identified as Normans and the other Frankish crusaders. The crusade itself served to subsume ethnic or regional identities by highlighting the common religious identity and pilgrim status of those who journeyed to Jerusalem, transforming even the bellicose Normans into 'a new type of Christian warrior'.[75] In terms of displays of courage and cowardice, the Normans were as prone to fear and as brave as their comrades. In fact, the evidence of Norman battle rhetoric suggests that they 'had to be warned much more frequently than others not to run away from a battle'.[76]

Desertion threatened the success of the First Crusade and the subject is worth exploring if only to highlight the courage and determination of those who reached Jerusalem. But courage and cowardice are complex concepts and historians should be circumspect in their use of the terms. Context is everything and often it is a question of numbers: one man flees, an army withdraws. Being a hero or a coward is a lonely business and it is paradoxical that both need a certain amount of courage. William the Carpenter and Stephen-Henry of Blois had both been courageous in battle, but, according to their judges, their companions on the crusade, they proved cowardly by deserting at Antioch. Whether Stephen-Henry was ill or not was in their eyes irrelevant. Former fearsome reputations like the Carpenter's counted for little. It took a great deal of courage to make the decision to withdraw and to accept the stigma of cowardice and the social exclusion that it threatened. Stephen-Henry's courage failed him again when he succumbed to the public opprobrium that attended his return to Blois. It was fear and shame, rather than, or perhaps as well as, courage, that drove him to a martyr's death. So, did Stephen-Henry display 'cowardly courage'? He died a heroic death, but was it for the wrong reasons? His obligations to family honour were met and his sense of self-worth may have been restored, but the memory of his desertion at Antioch remains.

---

[75] Hodgson, 'Reinventing Normans', 132.
[76] Bliese, 'The Courage of the Normans', 17.

2

The Enemy Within

Bohemond, Byzantium and the Subversion of the First Crusade*

ALAN V. MURRAY

All the preparations were thus made. The knights went by the plain and the foot-soldiers by the mountain, and they rode and marched all night until towards dawn, when they began to approach the towers of which Firuz, who had been watching all night, was warden. Then Bohemond dismounted at once and said to his men, 'Go on, strong in heart and lucky in your comrades, and scale the ladder into Antioch, for by God's will we shall have it in our power in a trice.' The men came to the ladder, which was already set up and lashed firmly to the battlements of the city, and nearly sixty of them went up to it and occupied the towers which Firuz was guarding. But when Firuz saw that so few of our men had come up, he began to be afraid, fearing lest he and they should fall into the hands of the Turks and he said (in Greek), 'Μικρούς φράγκους έχομεν' (which means, 'We have few Franks'). Where is the hero Bohemond? Where is that unconquered soldier?[1]

This famous passage from the anonymous *Gesta Francorum* narrates one of the most decisive incidents in the course of the First Crusade, describing how on the night of 2/3 June 1098, followers of Bohemond, son of Robert Guiscard, climbed up the walls of the city of Antioch on the Orontes to seize three towers commanded by one Firuz (or Pirrus), an officer in Turkish service, who had agreed to betray his section of the walls to the crusaders. The anonymous author dramatically conveys the uncertainty of

---

*Where dates are given in this chapter without further references or discussion, it is assumed that they derive from the chronology established by Heinrich Hagenmeyer, 'Chronologie de la Première Croisade', *Revue de l'Orient latin* 6 (1898), 214–93, 490–549; 7 (1899), 275–339, 430–503; 8 (1890–91), 318–82.

[1] Hill, *GF*, p. 46.

the situation, highlighting the danger that the traitor of Antioch was about to get cold feet because he did not immediately see the crusader leader. Eventually Bohemond arrived on the scene and, despite the breaking of one of the scaling ladders, his men effected an entry that delivered the city into the hands of the crusaders.[2]

As well as illuminating the difficulties of a clandestine military operation undertaken in darkness, the passage is interesting because of two stylistic features. The first relates to the purported direct speech. While the words of Bohemond and Firuz must be regarded as literary constructions rather than verbatim reproduction, they probably correspond to the import of what was actually said. The anguished exclamation of Firuz, 'Mikrous Frangkous ekhomen', is one of only a handful of instances in any of the crusade narratives where an utterance which must have been made in an Eastern language is represented in its original form (or an approximation of it) rather than in Latin, and this also tells us something about Bohemond's following. Antioch had been under Byzantine rule as recently as 1085 and still had a largely Greek-speaking population. It was thus likely that the Greek language was used by the traitor in Turkish service as the most practical way to communicate with Bohemond's forces, who included speakers of Greek from the island of Sicily and the Italian mainland.

The second noticeable feature is that Firuz is depicted as referring to Bohemond's men not as 'Normans', but as *Frangoi* (Franks). This is not in itself surprising, and indeed constitutes another indication of verisimilitude in the report. For centuries before the First Crusade, orthodox Christians and Muslims had tended to categorise all Western Europeans as *Frangoi* in Greek and *al-Ifranj* in Arabic. One of the remarkable things about the First Crusade is that its participants seem to have adopted the terminology which they heard repeatedly applied to them during their long campaign as a convenient group designation which emphasised their unity as Catholic Christians. This usage, in which the crusaders and their descendants in Outremer are called *Franci*, is reflected in many of the titles given to chronicles which were written to describe the momentous events.[3]

---

[2] On the context of this incident, see John France, *Victory in the East: A Military History of the First Crusade* (Cambridge, 1994), pp. 262–5.

[3] Michel Balard, '*Gesta Dei per Francos*: L'usage du mot *Francs* dans les chroniques de la Première Croisade', in *Clovis: Histoire et mémoire*, ed. Michel Rouche (Paris, 1997), pp. 473–84; Alan V. Murray, 'Ethnic Identity in the Crusader States: The Frankish Race and the Settlement of Outremer', in *Concepts of National Identity in the Middle Ages*, ed. Simon Forde, Lesley Johnson and Alan V. Murray (Leeds, 1995), pp. 59–73; Peter Thorau, 'Die fremden Franken – *al-farang al-gurubā*': Kreuzfahrer und Kreuzzüge aus arabischer Sicht', in *Saladin und die Kreuzfahrer*, ed. Alfried Wieczorek, Mamoun Fansa and Harald Meller (Mannheim, 2005), pp. 115–25; Antonius Hendrikus van Erp, *Gesta Francorum:*

Yet, unlike the *Gesta Francorum*, other authors writing in the Norman polities of Normandy, England, southern Italy and Antioch placed great stress on the Norman identity and contributions to the success of the crusade, building on an existing historiographical tradition of specifically Norman courage and military ability.[4]

These two points relate to key facets of the character of the Norman contribution to the First Crusade which will form the subject of this chapter. At the outset it is necessary to stress the distinction between the two Norman, or to be more accurate, predominantly Norman contingents in the crusade. Robert II Curthose, duke of Normandy, led a force of crusaders from Normandy, Brittany and England.[5] Bohemond and his nephew Tancred, son of Odo 'the Good Marquis', led a force originating from Apulia, Calabria, Campania and Sicily, who included not only men of Norman descent, but also Frenchmen and Romance-speaking Lombards.[6] Each contingent maintained its own autonomy within the command structure of the united crusader armies and pursued different policies during the three years that they spent in the East.[7] Indeed, despite the panegyric tendencies of Ralph of Caen, William of Malmesbury and Henry of Huntingdon, the achievements of the two Norman groups during the crusade were significantly different. At some points Robert Curthose acted assertively, as when he seized the port of Laodikeia during the winter of 1097–98, but in his strategic and tactical actions he showed much less initiative than Raymond

---

Gesta Dei? Motivering en rechtvaardiging van de eerste kruistochten door tijdgenoten en moslimse reactie (Amsterdam, 1982); Alan V. Murray, 'The Siege and Capture of Jerusalem in Western Narrative Sources of the First Crusade', in *Jerusalem the Golden: The Origins and Impact of the First Crusade*, ed. Susan B. Edgington and Luis García-Guijarro (Turnhout, 2014), pp. 191–215.

[4] G. A. Loud, 'The *Gens Normannorum*: Myth or Reality?' *ANS* 4 (1981), 104–16; Laetitia Boehm, 'Die *Gesta Tancredi* des Radulph von Caen: Ein Beitrag zur Geschichtsschreibung der Normannen um 1100', *Historisches Jahrbuch* 75 (1956), 47–72; J. R. Bliese, 'The Courage of the Normans: A Comparative Study of Battle Rhetoric', *Nottingham Medieval Studies* 35 (1991), 1–26.; Emily Albu, *The Normans in Their Histories: Propaganda, Myth and Subversion* (Woodbridge, 2001), pp. 152–5; John France, 'The Normans and Crusading', in *The Normans and Their Adversaries at War: Essays in Memory of C. Warren Hollister*, ed. Richard P. Abels and Bernard S. Bachrach (Woodbridge, 2001), pp. 87–102; Hodgson, 'Reinventing Normans', 117–32.

[5] Charles Wendell David, *Robert Curthose, Duke of Normandy* (Cambridge, MA, 1920), pp. 221–9. Unfortunately the biography by William Aird, *Robert Curthose Duke of Normandy, c. 1050–1134* (Woodbrige, 2008), does not deal with Robert's participation in the crusade.

[6] Evelyn M. Jamison, 'Some Notes on the *Anonymi Gesta Francorum*, with Special Reference to the Norman Contingent from South Italy and Sicily in the First Crusade', in *Studies in French Language and Medieval Literature presented to Professor Mildred K. Pope* (Manchester, 1939), pp. 183–208, reprinted in Jamison, *Studies on the History of Medieval Sicily and South Italy*, ed. Dione Clementi and Theo Kölzer (Aalen, 1992), pp. 275–300. The term 'southern Italy' could be regarded as insufficiently specific if not anachronistic, but it will be used in this chapter as a convenient designation for the totality of the Norman-ruled domains of Apulia, Calabria, Campania and Sicily.

[7] France, 'The Normans and Crusading', p. 91.

of Saint-Gilles, Godfrey of Bouillon, Baldwin of Boulogne or Bohemond himself.[8] He also distinguished himself for his bravery at the Battle of Ascalon on 12 August 1099.[9] William of Malmesbury, Henry of Huntingdon and the *Historia Belli Sacri* written at Montecassino all claim that after the capture of the Holy City in July 1099 the rulership of Jerusalem was offered to Robert Curthose.[10] However, if there is any substance in this report, it is probably a reflection of an electoral process in which candidates for the throne were canvassed about their willingness to serve, and Robert's evident reluctance to put himself forward is either an indication of his lack of ambitions in the East, or a recognition that he did not command sufficient support.[11] Robert's record thus contrasts with the ambition and assertiveness of the Normans of Italy, which was manifested in Bohemond's establishment of the principality of Antioch after his seizure of the city in 1098, and Tancred's shorter-lived attempt to create an independent lordship in Galilee after the capture of Jerusalem in 1099.

The aim of this chapter is not to add to the extensive literature on the concept of *Normannitas* in medieval historiography, but to analyse the activity of the army of Bohemond in the crusade as the more dynamic of the two Norman forces, examining not only actual events but also various potential outcomes which, although not realised, tell us something about the aims and attitudes of different protagonists. It will argue that, in the course of the expedition, the southern Italian leadership pursued policies which were fundamentally different from those of the crusader contingents which originated from north of the Alps, and were at variance with the aim of the liberation of the Holy Land.

The first significant point is the timing of the decision of Bohemond and his followers to join the crusade. During the struggles of the Investiture Contest, the Norman rulers of southern Italy had been strong supporters of the Reform papacy, and in return the popes offered them ideological support and validation of their conquests.[12] It has even recently been argued that Urban II conceived of his crusade to liberate the Holy Land as

---

[8] France, *Victory in the East*, pp. 214–19.

[9] Hill, *GF*, pp. 95–6.

[10] William of Malmesbury, *Gesta Regum Anglorum: The History of the English Kings*, ed. and trans. R. A. B. Mynors, Rodney M. Thomson and Michael Winterbottom (Oxford, 1998), p. 702; Henry of Huntingdon, *Historia Anglorum* (London, 1879), p. 236; 'Historia Belli Sacri' ('Historia de via Hierusolymis'), *RHC*, iii, p. 225.

[11] Alan V. Murray, *The Crusader Kingdom of Jerusalem: A Dynastic History, 1099–1125* (Oxford, 2000), pp. 63–69. David, *Robert Curthose*, p. 114, dismisses the offer of the throne to Robert as pure invention.

[12] G. A. Loud, *The Age of Robert Guiscard: Southern Italy and the Norman Conquest* (Harlow, 2000), pp. 186–233.

a continuation of a movement which had begun with the conquest of Islamic Sicily.[13] This is not the place to examine the detailed arguments of Paul E. Chevedden on this question; suffice to say that, irrespective of its significance concerning the genesis of the crusade movement, much of the evidence adduced by him is testimony to a close co-operation between the Reform papacy and the rulers of southern Italy. In view of this commonality of interest and tried alliance, it might well be expected that Urban II would count on the military assistance of the Normans in his campaign to free the Holy Land. What is striking is how relatively late Bohemond and his followers signed up to the papal enterprise.

Most of the northern princes who took the Cross did so during the winter of 1095–96 after Pope Urban II's appeal at the council of Clermont in November 1095. The departure date proclaimed by the pope was 15 August 1096, but many groups of crusaders left before this time. According to the *Gesta Francorum*, Bohemond was besieging the rebellious city of Amalfi along with his uncle Count Roger I of Sicily and his half-brother Roger Borsa when he became aware of French crusaders who were travelling down the peninsula, making for the Apulian ports where they intended to take ship across the Adriatic to Byzantine territory. It was only at this point that Bohemond decided to take the Cross, and it is an indication of the hurried nature of preparation that he recruited most of his following from the retinues of his two kinsmen.[14] The most likely date for this event, according to Jamison, is June or July 1096, but other authorities such as Pryor have placed it in September.[15] The Norman forces landed on the eastern Adriatic coast in late October and reached Constantinople on 26 April 1097, although Bohemond himself hurried ahead of them, arriving in the Byzantine capital around 10 April. Pryor argues that a decision to join the crusade in September was far too late to allow adequate time for Bohemond to mobilise his forces in time for the known date of the sea crossing, concluding that this 'gives the lie to the story of the *Gesta Francorum* that he did not know about Clermont and the launching of the crusade'.[16] Whether Bohemond was aware of the messages of the church council of November 1095 is a separate matter, but two objections can be raised to the argument

---

[13] Paul Chevedden, 'The Islamic View and the Christian View of the Crusades: A New Synthesis', *History* 93 (2008), 181–200; Paul Chevedden, '"A Crusade from the First": The Norman Conquest of Islamic Sicily, 1060–1091', *Al-Masaq* 22 (2010), 191–225.

[14] Hill, *GF*, pp. 7–8.

[15] Jamison, 'Some Notes on the *Anonymi Gesta Francorum*', pp. 188–93; John Pryor, 'Modelling Bohemond's March to Thessalonike', in *Logistics of Warfare in the Age of the Crusades*, ed. John H. Pryor (Aldershot, 2006), pp. 1–24.

[16] France, *Victory in the East*, pp. 103–4; Pryor, 'Modelling Bohemond's March', p. 1.

that he took the Cross in direct response to the pope's appeal. First, if this were the case, then it seems strange that such an experienced campaigner as Bohemond would have waited so late to make his preparations for the crusade. Second, in such a case the author of the *Gesta Francorum* would have had every incentive to show Bohemond acting in accordance with the aims of Urban II rather than being surprised by the arrival of transient crusaders from France. We can better accommodate the chronology of the Adriatic crossing with the evidence of the *Gesta Francorum* if we accept Jamison's argument that Bohemond's decision should be dated to June or July.

Before making his appeal at Clermont, Urban II had certainly been in contact with Raymond of Saint-Gilles, count of Toulouse, and Adhemar, bishop of Le Puy; there is no reason why he could not have negotiated with the Norman leaders of southern Italy if he had wished to secure their support for the forthcoming crusade. For whatever reason, however, it seems that the pope decided not to count on his traditional allies. The manner and timing of Bohemond's decision suggest that his motivation was essentially opportunistic, in contrast to the transalpine princes who had spent the best part of a year contemplating their decisions to join the expedition, raising finance and making logistical preparations.

Unlike the contingents of the other leaders, Bohemond, Tancred and their followers already possessed considerable knowledge of the Christian and Muslim East. There were two dimensions to this issue. First, the conquest of southern Italy had brought the Normans into close contact with Greek and Arabic cultures. While the majority population of the mainland consisted of Lombards who spoke a form of what later became Italian, the Norman domains also contained substantial numbers of Greek-speakers, especially in Calabria, the Terra d'Otranto and the north-east of Sicily. There were many Greeks among the secular and monastic clergy. The remainder of Sicily was predominantly inhabited by Arabic-speakers, mostly Muslims but with a Christian minority, and the 'Saracens', as they were known, often provided soldiers for the rulers of the island.[17] Bohemond's contingent included speakers of Greek and Arabic. Communications with the traitor Firuz during the siege of Antioch were carried out in Greek by a 'certain interpreter of languages, a Lombard by race and a member of Bohemond's household', while we also know that an Arabic interpreter was sent to negotiate with the population of the Muslim-held city of

---

[17] Loud, *The Age of Robert Guiscard*, pp. 12–13, 54–9.

Ma'arrat al-Numan in December 1098.[18] Tancred and his kinsman Richard of the Principate are recorded as communicating in Arabic, while it has been argued convincingly by Jonathan Shepard that Bohemond himself had acquired a working knowledge of Greek before the crusade.[19] Second, having conquered the last Byzantine enclaves in Apulia, the Normans had a clear appreciation of the military weakness of the empire, and, like their Angevin successors in the late thirteenth century, they came to identify the territories of Epiros and Albania as ripe targets for expansion.[20] In 1081–82 and 1084–85 Robert Guiscard led large invasions of this area, directed primarily at Dyrrachion (modern Durrës, Albania), the naval base at the western end of the Via Egnatia, the great military road that linked the coast with Constantinople.[21]

Most of Guiscard's possessions were earmarked to be inherited by Roger Borsa, his eldest son by the Lombard princess Sichelgaita, and it is probable that his projected conquests in the Balkans were intended to make provision for his other sons, who of course included Bohemond, whose mother was Guiscard's repudiated first wife Alberada. Bohemond's interest in these enterprises can be seen from the fact that he played a major role during both expeditions, which must have given him valuable first-hand acquaintance of Byzantine military and political practice.[22] Thus the cultural knowledge deriving from the nature of the southern Italian territories as well their experience of Byzantium gave Bohemond and his followers an edge in any dealings with the rulers and populations of the territories through which the crusade would pass.

The point has been well made that, despite his late decision to join the crusade, Bohemond arrived at Constantinople before Raymond of Saint-Gilles and some other northern crusaders. Bohemond evidently regarded the expedition as a great opportunity which had to be seized, even if his hasty preparations and relatively modest forces put him at a certain

---

[18] AA, pp. 274–5: *interpretem linguarum genere Longobardorum de domesticiis Boemundi*; Hill, GF, p. 79: *Boamundus igitur fecit per interpretem loqui Saracenis*.
[19] Jonathan Shepard, 'When Greek Meets Greek: Alexius Comnenus and Bohemond in 1097-98', *Byzantine and Modern Greek Studies* 12 (1988), 185–277 (here 251–8).
[20] Graham Loud, *The Age of Robert Guiscard: Southern Italy and the Norman Conquest* (Harlow, 2000), pp. 210–23.
[21] Klaus Belke, 'Roads and Travel in Macedonia and Thrace in the Middle and Late Byzantine Period', in *Travel in the Byzantine World*, ed. Ruth Macrides (Aldershot, 2002), pp. 73–90 (here 74–9); Elena Koycheva, 'Civitates et Castra on Via Militaris and Via Egnatia: Early Crusaders View' [sic], *Revue des études sud-est européennes* 44 (2006), 139–44; Koytcheva [sic], 'Travelling of the First Crusaders across the Byzantine Balkans', Ηπειρωτικα Χρονικα 36 (2002), 17–24.
[22] William B. McQueen, 'Relations between the Normans and Byzantium 1071–1112', *Byzantion* 56 (1986), 427–74; R. Upsher Smith, Jr, '*Nobilissimus* and Warleader: The Opportunity and the Necessity behind Robert Guiscard's Balkan Expeditions', *Byzantion* 70 (2000), 507–26.

disadvantage compared to the transalpine leaders.²³ A knowledge of the Greek language explains how Bohemond was able to act as a trusted intermediary in negotiations between the crusade leaders and the Byzantine emperor, Alexios I Komnenos which resulted in the leaders taking oaths to Alexios; the precise import of these is still a matter of debate, but they undoubtedly foresaw the restitution of any territory held by the Byzantine empire prior to the Turkish invasions of the late eleventh century.²⁴ However, Bohemond differed from the other leaders in the nature of the relationship that he aspired to establish with the emperor. According to Anna Komnene, Bohemond demanded that the emperor appoint him to the grand domesticate of the East (*domestikaton aitoumenos tēs anatolēs*).²⁵ It is not immediately apparent what this position implied. In previous negotiations with the Normans of southern Italy, Byzantine emperors had sometimes offered to grant them high-sounding but essentially insubstantial titles, yet given his military ability and the experienced troops under his command, Bohemond was unlikely to be satisfied with a mere honorific dignity. The title of *domestikos* normally denoted one of the highest-ranking commanders of the Byzantine armed forces, and although the precise commands of *domestikoi* changed somewhat in the Komnenian period, the specific title described by Anne implied a considerable responsibility at a time when the crusade armies were preparing to cross over to the Asian shore.²⁶ The huge Turkish incursions in the aftermath of the Battle of Mantzikert in 1071 had left only a few pockets of Anatolian territory under Byzantine control, mostly along the Black Sea coast, although by the 1090s Alexios Komnenos had been able to push into Bithynia and establish some military bases there.²⁷ Thus apart from a few garrisons in fortresses such as Helenopolis on the Gulf of Nikomedia, there were no substantial Byzantine forces stationed in Anatolia to warrant the appointment of a high-ranking commander before the arrival of the crusaders.

In asking for the domesticate of the East, therefore, Bohemond was not seeking to fill an existing vacancy, but was anticipating a new command. We know that when the crusaders advanced to Nicaea (modern Iznik, Turkey), they were accompanied by Byzantine soldiers equipped with siege

---

[23] Shepard, 'When Greek Meets Greek', pp. 242–4.
[24] *Ibid.*, pp. 237–40; France, *Victory in the East*, pp. 110–21.
[25] Anne Comnène, *Alexiade*, trans. Bernard Leib, 3 vols (Paris, 1937–76), ii, p. 234.
[26] John Haldon, *Warfare, State and Society in the Byzantine World, 565–1204* (London, 1999), pp. 118–19; John W. Birkenmeier, *The Development of the Komnenian Army, 1081–1180* (Leiden, 2002), p. 240.
[27] Jonathan Shepard, 'Cross-Purposes: Alexios Comnenus and the First Crusade', in *The First Crusade: Origins and Impact*, ed. Jonathan Phillips (Manchester, 1997), pp. 107–29 (here 117–18).

machines which were to play a decisive role in the capture of the city.[28] As Alexios and the crusade leaders planned their operations, it could be envisaged that, as the allies recovered further territory, more Byzantine troops would be sent into Anatolia to garrison the new conquests and help the crusaders to besiege new targets. As grand *domestikos*, Bohemond could see himself as commanding these forces, a position which would also give him a significant political advantage over the other crusader leaders. While they conceded a moral authority to Adhemar of Le Puy as papal legate, none of the princes was recognised as possessing military authority over all of the crusade armies, a situation that was never fully resolved, with tactical generalship being assigned on an ad hoc basis and strategic decisions taken in council.[29] Raymond of Aguilers reports that the princes had expected that Alexios himself would assume leadership of the crusade.[30] The emperor declined to take up this offer, but if Bohemond had indeed been given the position of grand *domestikos*, he would effectively have become Alexios's deputy in Asia, which would have made it difficult for the other princes to deny him overall command over the combined Byzantine-crusader forces.

Whether Bohemond intended to make a career in Byzantine service or to exploit his tenure of the domesticate to carve out a territory for himself cannot be surmised with certainty, since Alexios Komnenos refused his demands for such a command. The emperor did, however, make him an offer which is further testimony that, at least initially, he was prepared to buy into an alliance with the Normans. There is no reason to discount the report of the *Gesta Francorum* that in return for Bohemond's oath, the emperor was willing to grant him 'lands beyond Antioch, fifteen days' journey in length and eight in width' (*quindecim dies eundi terrae in extensione ab Antiochia retro daret, et octo in latitudine*).[31] This was territory which was still under Turkish or Arab control, but it still represented a considerable concession, since it potentially granted Bohemond an undisputed title to a vast principality. A conservative rate of march for military forces with substantial infantry components would be twenty kilometres per day, so if similar distances are implied by the terms of the grant, it could have amounted to a bloc of territory of some 45,000–50,000 square kilometres, that is approximately a quarter of the combined area of the modern states of

---

[28] Anne Comnène, *Alexiade*, iii, pp. 10–14.
[29] Conor Kostick, *The Social Structure of the First Crusade* (Leiden, 2008), pp. 244–69.
[30] Raymond of Aguilers, 'Raimundi de Aguilers canonici Podiensis historia Francorum qui ceperunt Iherusalem', *RHC*, iii, pp. 231–309 (here 237).
[31] Hill, *GF*, p. 12; Jamison, 'Some Notes on the *Anonymi Gesta Francorum*', pp. 193–5.

Syria and Lebanon.[32] It is important, however, that the grant excluded Antioch itself: the acquisition of the great city with its orthodox patriarchate and large Greek-speaking population was one of Alexios' main objectives and from what we know of Byzantine foreign policy throughout the twelfth century it is unlikely that he would be willing to trade such a prize for anything that Bohemond might provide.[33] Furthermore, as Jamison argues, if Bohemond had indeed been promised Antioch by the emperor then he would undoubtedly have made use of this title in his dealings with the other leaders over the possession of the city after its capture. In fact the concession of territory beyond Antioch by Alexios cost him nothing, but created the prospect of a new vassal state which could function as a buffer zone between restored imperial territory in northern Syria and the Saljūq kingdoms of Aleppo and Damascus.[34]

Alexios' negotiations with Bohemond offered the opportunity for closer co-operation with the Normans than with any of the other crusader contingents. It is well known how this relationship deteriorated, but it is also noticeable how Bohemond and Tancred frequently found themselves in opposition to other crusader leaders, and the two phenomena are related. As the crusaders approached the plains of Cilicia in the autumn of 1097, advance forces started to move ahead of the main armies with the aim of scouting the country ahead and encouraging the Christian Armenian population to rise up against the Turkish garrisons which controlled the coastal cities. This was a strategic decision taken by the crusade leaders in council, based on intelligence they were beginning to receive from these areas, but we can observe a significant degree of competition between them.[35] Tancred led a detachment to the city of Tarsos on the coast and began to treat with its Turkish garrison. In the meantime Baldwin of Boulogne arrived with a larger force of Lotharingian knights, and after impressing both garrison and population with the military strength of his brother, Duke Godfrey, he persuaded them to renege on their agreement with Tancred and admit the Lotharingian forces. Tancred moved on to Adana and took possession of it, but more reinforcements from Bohemond's contingent who arrived at Tarsos were denied shelter by Baldwin and massacred by

---

[32] John Haldon, 'Roads and Communications in the Byzantine Empire: Wagons, Horses, and Supplies', in *Logistics of Warfare in the Age of the Crusades*, ed. Pryor, pp. 131–58 (here 142–3).

[33] Jean-Claude Cheynet, 'The Duchy of Antioch during the Second Period of Byzantine Rule', in *East and West in the Medieval Eastern Mediterranean, I: Antioch from the Byzantine Reconquest until the End of the Crusader Principality*, ed. Krijnie Ciggaar and Michael Metcalf (Leuven, 2006), pp. 1–16.

[34] On the Saljūq kingdoms, see Taef Kamal El-Azhari, *The Saljūqs of Syria during the Crusades, 463–459 AH/1070–1154 AD* (Berlin, 1997).

[35] France, *Victory in the East*, pp. 167–8, 190–6.

the Turks, who then fled. Tancred then advanced to Mamistra, and after seizing the city, cast down its fortifications. Baldwin's troops had meanwhile followed along the same route and pitched camp outside the city. At this point open warfare broke out when Tancred, encouraged by Richard of the Principate, attacked Baldwin's forces but was repulsed with heavy casualties.[36] John France is undoubtedly correct in arguing that the expeditions of Baldwin and Tancred were not primarily intended as aggrandisement, but were undertaken with the approval of the crusade leaders and the imperial representative, Tatikios.[37] However, there was clearly an element of rivalry involved. The crusade armies had no central system of provisioning, and the possession of a fortified town and its agricultural hinterland would secure necessary food supplies for the contingent that controlled it. Even if Tancred and Bohemond merely wished to garrison the captured cities until they could be handed over to the Byzantines, their possession would give the Normans an important bargaining counter in negotiations with Alexios Komnenos.

In late 1097, therefore, it was possible that Bohemond and Tancred still intended to maintain and profit from their relationship with the emperor, but by the beginning of 1098 at the latest Bohemond had designs which excluded any restoration of Byzantine authority in any newly conquered lands. The fact and the manner of Bohemond's acquisition of Antioch were not only in blatant contravention of the crusaders' agreements with Alexios Komnenos; they also showed an underhand attitude towards the other crusader leaders. After entering northern Syria, the crusader contingents had attempted to acquire local expertise by employing native Christians or renegades; thus Godfrey and Baldwin had enlisted one Bagrat, brother of the Armenian lord Kogh Vasil.[38] Yet in establishing contacts and forging bonds with local people, their existing familiarity with the Greek and Arabic languages clearly gave the southern Italians an edge over the transalpine contingents. One was a Turk who agreed to convert to Christianity, taking the name Bohemond at baptism after his sponsor, and who accompanied the Norman troops on the fateful night of 2/3 June.[39] Firuz, the actual betrayer of Antioch, is described by the *Gesta Francorum* and Raymond of Aguilers in terms that suggest a Turkish origin.[40] By contrast, Ralph of

---

[36] AA, pp. 144–61.
[37] France, *Victory in the East*, pp. 193–6.
[38] AA, pp. 164–5.
[39] *Ibid.*, pp. 234–5, 270–4.
[40] Hill, *GF*, p. 44 (*de genere Turcorum*); Raymond of Aguilers, 'Raimundi de Aguilers canonici Podiensis historia Francorum', p. 251 (*quidam de turcatis, qui erat in civitate*).

Caen and William of Tyre call him an Armenian, which Rebecca Slitt has argued was simply a literary device to make Bohemond's friendship with him more palatable to a Christian readership.[41] Yet clearly these sources are all describing the same person. The most satisfactory explanation for the apparently contradictory identification as both an Armenian and a Turk is that Firuz was indeed of Armenian origin but had entered Turkish service, probably apostatising in the process. Certainly an Armenian from the region of Antioch is far more likely to have been conversant with Greek than an ethnic Turk would have been.

When the secret negotiations with Firuz had reached the point that the latter agreed to facilitate his entry into the city, Bohemond judged that he had an excellent chance of breaking the stalemate of the siege which had held up the crusade for most of the winter and spring of 1097–98. However, he was determined to engineer the situation to his own benefit. According to the best informed accounts, he persuaded the other leaders to agree in advance that any one of them who brought about the capture of Antioch was to have possession of it, using the threat of a Turkish relief to raise the stakes. In this game of poker Bohemond was playing his cards close to his chest, with an ace in the form of Firuz, while the other leaders' cards were on the table. It is not necessary to describe the capture of Antioch at length here, save to recognise that in order to justify his actions, Bohemond also had to persuade the other leaders – in some cases against their consciences – that the emperor had abandoned the crusade and that their agreements with him had thus been rendered invalid. Bohemond's arguments were buttressed by the fact that the imperial general Tatikios had left Antioch in February 1098.[42] For Bohemond, the possession of the city of Antioch was a far greater prize than the nebulous concessions of territory farther south; indeed, it offered – and in the event provided – the basis for expansion of his new lordship in all directions. Yet this great gain was bought at the cost of the effective functioning of the crusader-Byzantine alliance.

Bohemond was not the only, nor indeed the first, crusader leader to establish a lordship for himself. In February and March 1098, while the main armies were bogged down in the siege of Antioch, Baldwin of Boulogne

---

[41] RCaen, pp. 651–2, 654; Guillaume de Tyr, *Chronique*, ed. Robert B. C. Huygens, 2 vols (Turnhout, 1986), pp. 285–86; Rebecca L. Slitt, 'Justifying Cross-Cultural Friendship: Bohemond, Firuz, and the Fall of Antioch', *Viator: Medieval and Renaissance Studies* 38 (2007), 339–49 (here 339, 344).

[42] Hill, *GF*, pp. 44–6; AA, pp. 234–35, 270–75; John France, 'The Departure of Tatikios from the Army of the First Crusade', *Bulletin of the Institute of Historical Research* 44 (1971), 131–47; France, *Victory in the East*, pp. 262–8; John France, 'The Fall of Antioch during the First Crusade', in *Dei gesta per Francos: Études sur les croisades dédiées à Jean Richard / Crusade Studies in Honour of Jean Richard*, ed. M. Balard, Benjamin Z. Kedar and Jonathan Riley-Smith (Aldershot, 2001), pp. 13–20.

took off with a force borrowed from his brothers Godfrey of Bouillon and Eustace III of Boulogne and used it to liberate the cities of Edessa (modern Şanlıurfa, Turkey) and Turbessel (modern Tilbeşar) and adjacent parts of northern Syria and upper Mesopotamia. There were, however, significant differences between the establishment of the county of Edessa and that of Bohemond's new polity centred on Antioch in terms of the overall aims of the crusade. Baldwin's intervention was carried out in response to appeals from Armenian leaders and, because of the smallness of his Frankish retinue, Baldwin was obliged to co-operate with local indigenous lords, with whose families he and his leading supporters allied and intermarried; for all of its subsequent existence the county of Edessa was essentially a joint Frankish-Armenian polity.[43] The liberation of these Armenian lands also aided the progress of the crusade by securing supply lines for the forces besieging Antioch, and Baldwin's possession of his new territory was never disputed by the other crusade leaders.

The capture of Antioch and the immediate defeat of a Muslim relieving army under the emir Karbuqa of Mosul were followed by a period in which several of the crusader princes fanned out over northern Syria with the aim of securing strongpoints and supplies. Bohemond's claim to Antioch had been accepted by the other princes except Raymond of Saint-Gilles, who retained control of some sectors of the city.[44] Raymond and his large contingent from southern France then moved to the south-east, where he took control of the Jabal al-Summāq, a plateau to the east of the River Orontes, thus starting to establish a third crusader principality in Syria, around the town of Albara. However, when the combined contingents captured Ma'arrat al-Nu'mān to the south, Bohemond disputed its possession with Raymond. The count of Toulouse then evidently gave up his regional ambitions and continued south with the majority of the crusade contingents at the beginning of 1099, and the Jabal al-Summāq was subsequently incorporated into Bohemond's nascent principality.[45]

In these events we can observe Bohemond building alliances with the

---

[43] Alan V. Murray, *The Crusader Kingdom of Jerusalem: a Dynastic History, 1099–1215* (Oxford, 2000), pp. 61–2; Christopher MacEvitt, *The Crusades and the Christian World of the East: Rough Tolerance* (Philadelphia, 2008); James H. Forse, 'Armenians and the First Crusade', *JMH* 17 (1991), 13–22; Natasha Hodgson, 'Conflict and Cohabitation: Marriage and Diplomacy between Latins and Cilician Armenians, c. 1097–1253', in *The Crusades and the Near East: Cultural Histories*, ed. Conor Kostick (London, 2011), pp. 83–106.
[44] France, *Victory in the East*, pp. 297–8.
[45] Thomas Asbridge, 'The Principality of Antioch and the Jabal as-Summāq', in *The First Crusade: Origins and Impact*, ed. Phillips, pp. 142–52; John France, 'The Crisis of the First Crusade: From the Defeat of Kerbogha to the Departure from Arqa', *Byzantion* 40 (1970), 276–308.

other leaders to isolate Raymond politically. In part this succeeded because the count of Toulouse was increasingly seen as remaining perversely loyal to the emperor whose stock was now at rock bottom with the majority of crusaders. However, cultural and linguistic identities also played a major part. Chroniclers such as Fulcher of Chartres remarked on the linguistic diversity of the crusade armies, which included speakers of a wide variety of Romance, Germanic and Celtic dialects.[46] While the majority of crusaders spoke forms of northern French, the followers of Raymond of Saint-Gilles, who originated from Provence, Languedoc, Auvergne, Burgundy and Gascony, spoke various dialects of Occitan and Franco-Provençal. These southern varieties were not comprehensible to most French speakers, and vice versa.[47] This linguistic divide explains why the followers of Raymond were collectively known to the other, predominantly French-speaking crusaders, as *Provinciales*, that is 'Provençals', probably because the marquisate of Provence was one of the titles held by him.[48]

It is likely that most of the leaders could communicate with each other in French, if necessary drawing on the help of clerics who knew Latin, but the same did not apply at lower levels. There was a clear animosity between different groups, which is reflected in the partisan history of Ralph of Caen. It is telling that Ralph tends to contrast the southerners with the *Franci*, used here in the more restricted sense of (northern) French, which indicates how the Normans were perceived as belonging to the latter. In one chapter, entitled 'The Customs of the Provençals' (*Provincialium mores*), Ralph parades some prejudices which can only have derived from the experience of Normans during the crusade. He wrote that the Provençals differed as much from the French in their customs, their religious habits and their food as a hen differs from a duck, and highlights their lack of martial ability by citing a proverb, *Franci ad bella, Provinciales ad victualia* ('The French to battle, the Provençals to dinner').[49] This animosity sometimes spilled over into violence. On one occasion, during the long siege of Antioch, a dispute broke out between members of Bohemond's army and some of the southern French as they returned from foraging expeditions. The two parties began to fight, but eventually other crusaders were drawn

---

[46] Fulcher of Chartres, *Fulcheri Carnotensis, Historia Hierosolymitana (1095–1127)*, ed. H. Hagenmeyer (Heidelberg, 1913), pp. 202–3.

[47] Alan V. Murray, 'National Identity, Language and Conflict in the Crusades to the Holy Land, 1096–1192', in *The Crusades and the Near East: Cultural Histories*, ed. Kostick, pp. 107–30.

[48] Raymond of Aguilers, 'Raimundi de Aguilers canonici Podiensis historia Francorum', p. 244; RCaen, pp. 587–716, here 651, 660–1, 675–76; AA, pp. 300–1, 330–1, 334–6, 478–9, 600–1, 604–5, 608–9.

[49] RCaen, p. 651.

in, taking sides according to linguistic affiliations. Ralph of Caen states that 'those from Narbonne, Auvergne, Gascony and all of the Provençal people' took one side, while 'the Apulians were supported by the remainder of the French [literally 'of Gaul'], especially the Normans', while others, such as Bretons and Swabians, held to those who spoke their languages.[50] There were of course close connections between the Normans of southern Italy and the contingent led by Robert Curthose, and while the Norman dialect had some vocabulary and phonological features that made it distinctive from other French dialects, there was a far greater commonality of language between the various northern French groups than of any of them with the 'Provençals'. This divide probably helps to explain why Bohemond was able to count on the active or at least tacit support of most of the other crusaders in his disputes with Raymond of Saint-Gilles.

It was largely pressure from the large popular element in the crusade that forced the princes, Raymond of Saint-Gilles above all, to abandon their campaigning in Syria and continue the journey towards Jerusalem.[51] The most conspicuous absentees from the renewed expedition were Baldwin I, now count of Edessa, and Bohemond, who remained behind in Antioch. The latter had taken a crusading vow in quite flamboyant fashion, tearing up his rich cloak to make crosses for his knights to wear on their clothing, but at this time he showed no inclination to fulfil his promise by going on to Jerusalem. Some of his knights evidently took a different view, since they are found in the service of Godfrey of Bouillon or Baldwin I in Jerusalem in the years 1099–1100.[52] Tancred himself (presumably with his personal following), took service with Raymond, but the two men fell out at Arqa over payments that Tancred claimed he was owed, as a result of which he transferred his allegiance to Godfrey.[53]

Neither Bohemond nor Baldwin of Edessa fulfilled their crusading vows until Christmas 1099. Does this mean that both men were, equally, relatively unenthusiastic crusaders who were primarily concerned with territorial aggrandisement for themselves, their kinsmen and retinues? Bohemond's pilgrimage to Jerusalem and his activity during it were anything but disinterested. In September 1099 he was besieging the Byzantine-held city of

---

[50] *Ibid.*, pp. 675–6: *Qui alterutri linguae consonabat, modo cum ea verberat, interdum pro ea innocens verberatur. Narbonenses, Arverni, Wascones, et hoc genus omne Provincialibus: Apulis vero reliqua Gallia, praesertim Normanni conspirabant; Britones, Suevos, Hunos, Rutenos et hujus modi linguae suae barbaries audita tuebatur.*
[51] France, 'The Crisis of the First Crusade', 276–308.
[52] Alan V. Murray, 'Norman Settlement in the Latin Kingdom of Jerusalem, 1099–1131', *Archivio Normanno-Svevo* 1 for 2008 (2009), 61–85.
[53] AA, pp. 382–5.

Laodikeia (modern Lādhiqīyah, Syria), which was the main port in northern Syria and an obvious target for acquisition for the principality. He was able to exploit the arrival of a fleet under Daibert, archbishop of Pisa, the newly commissioned papal legate, by inducing him to join in the siege. It was only crusaders returning from Jerusalem who convinced the archbishop that he should not be attacking their Byzantine allies. Both Bohemond and Baldwin then accompanied the legate to Jerusalem, where they nominated him as patriarch of Jerusalem, and at Christmas Bohemond along with the newly elected ruler of Jerusalem, Godfrey of Bouillon, received a form of investiture at Daibert's hands.[54] The significance of this act, especially in the case of Godfrey, is problematic and has generated much debate. Yet it is at least apparent that while it was reasonable for the ruler of Palestine to seek validation from the patriarch of Jerusalem, the proper ecclesiastical authority for Antioch was the patriarch of that city. But as the occupant of that office was John of Oxeia, a Greek, Bohemond was clearly unwilling to undergo any ceremony that might imply subordination to the Byzantine emperor. His investiture by Daibert was simply a quick political fix to provide legitimation against possible claims from Byzantium in respect of the oaths rendered to the emperor in 1097.[55]

Baldwin of Edessa did not evidently feel a need to seek validation from either patriarch. This may be an indication that he did not anticipate any Byzantine claims on his territory. In fact, the establishment of his county could be regarded as a strategic action which fully conformed to the spirit of the liberation of Eastern Christendom as proclaimed by Pope Urban II. By contrast, Bohemond's acquisition of Antioch and subsequent expansion of his principality ran contrary to these aims, seriously damaging the relationship between the crusaders and their most important ally, the Byzantine emperor. To add to the injury of the loss of the Syrian metropolis, the subsequent Antiochene conquest of Cilicia deprived the empire of a predominantly Christian territory to which it had a reasonable expectation. Unlike Baldwin in Edessa, Bohemond and later Tancred made little attempt to make use of the native Christian population in administrative and military matters, since they feared possible co-operation with the Byzantines.[56] This distrust extended to the church: Bohemond secured the

---

[54] Michael Matzke, *Daibert von Pisa: Zwischen Pisa, Papst und erstem Kreuzzug* (Sigmaringen, 1998), pp. 150–62.

[55] On the relationship between Godfrey and Daibert, see Murray, *The Crusader Kingdom of Jerusalem*, pp. 81–93. Patriarch John is numbered variously as IV or V of that name in scholarship.

[56] The Franks maintained the important Byzantine office of *doux* of Antioch, but it was not held by Greeks until the 1130s: Reinhold Röhricht, *Regesta Regni Hierosolymitani*, 2 vols (Innsbruck, 1893–1904),

approval of Daibert to install Latin bishops in Tarsos, Artah and Mamistra, and by 1100 he had replaced John of Oxeia with the Frenchman Bernard of Valence.[57] Yet Bohemond still cherished grander ambitions against Byzantium. In 1105 he returned to the West and persuaded Pope Paschal II to support a new invasion of the empire's western provinces from Apulia. This was essentially another piece of aggrandisement, and it ended in failure.[58]

One can conclude that Bohemond's decision to join the crusade launched by Pope Urban II was opportunistic and intended to exploit whatever leverage he might be able to acquire against the Byzantine empire. By the time he reached Antioch he realised that he had a chance to exploit local conditions to seize the city and establish a principality for himself, even though his actions would and did cause a fundamental breach with Raymond of Saint-Gilles and ensure the enmity of Alexios Komnenos and his successors. Even after the conclusion of the crusade, his attempts to seize Laodikeia and Cilicia and his 'crusade' of 1107–8 show that his political aims were primarily directed, not against the Turkish powers of the East, but against the Byzantine empire. A wily son of a notoriously wily father, Bohemond was a skilful and adaptable politician whose ambitions were Byzantine in all modern senses of the word, but as a crusader he fell far short of the qualities of his transalpine comrades.

---

i, pp. 37, 38, 48–9, 57, 63–4, 72, 74 (nos. 149, 151a, 195, 196, 228, 253, 282, 292).

[57] Bernard Hamilton, 'The Growth of the Latin Church of Antioch and the Recruitment of Its Clergy', in *East and West in the Medieval Eastern Mediterranean*, ed. Ciggaar and Metcalf, i, pp. 171–84; Matzke, *Daibert von Pisa*, p. 161. It should also be noted that Baldwin sought approval for the installation of a bishop of Edessa. This, however, did not have the same significance as the imposition of a Latin hierarchy in Antioch, as the majority of the Armenian and Syrian population in Edessa were not members of the Orthodox church, which the Franks regarded as being part of the universal Catholic communion.

[58] Brett Whalen, 'God's Will or Not? Bohemond's Campaign against the Byzantine Empire (1105–1108)', in *Crusades – Medieval Worlds in Conflict*, ed. Thomas F. Madden, James L. Naus and Vincent Ryan (Farnham, 2010), pp. 111–25.

Part II

3

Norman Italy and the Crusades
Thoughts on the 'Homefront'

JOANNA DRELL

Never will I be comforted,
nor do I wish to be cheered.
The ships have arrived at port
and are about to set sail.
The noblest of men is leaving
for a land across the sea;
and I, alas, forlorn –
what am I to do?
…
Holy, holy, holy God,
who came to the Virgin
save and keep my love,
since you have taken him away from me.
…
The cross saves the people –
and it is my undoing.
The cross is the source of my pain.
and my prayers to God do me no good.
O pilgrims' cross,
why have you destroyed me?
Poor wretched me –
I am all in flames!

The Emperor rules
all the world in peace –
and on me he makes war,
for he has taken away my hope.
…

> When he took the Cross,
> he certainly did not think of me –
> that man who loved me so,
> and I loved him so.
> ...
> The ships have hoisted their sails;
> may they have a propitious journey,
> the ships, and my love,
> and the people who must travel there!
> O Father Creator,
> lead them to port,
> for they go to serve
> the holy Cross.[1]

Già mai non mi comforto, or 'never will I be comforted', by thirteenth-century Italian poet Rinaldo d'Aquino, details the emotional world, the sorrows and the frustrations of a woman who had just seen her lover off on crusade, most likely from the shores of Messina, Sicily. She expresses her feelings of abandonment, neglect; she asks what will happen to her, whether anyone had thought of her. She exclaims that while 'the Cross' may save others it 'destroyed' her and is her 'undoing'. She denounces those whom she holds accountable – in addition to her lover – including the emperor (Frederick II) who called the crusade, the Cross (i.e., the mission), and God.[2]

The poem belongs to a genre of thirteenth-century Sicilian lyric love poetry.[3] In this particular example, several broad themes converge: first, the crusades in the Mediterranean; next, Sicily and the kingdom of southern Italy, or the *Regno*; and finally the impact of the crusades on those left

---

[1] Karla Mallette, *The Kingdom of Sicily, 1100–1250: A Literary History* (Philadelphia, 2005), pp. 180–1.

[2] The poem exists in only one extant manuscript, likely due to its criticism of Frederick II: Mallette, *The Kingdom of Sicily*, pp. 80, 86–7. For further discussion see Vito Sivo, 'Il Mezzogiorno e le Crociate in alcuni testi letterari', in *Il mezzogiorno normanno-svevo e le crociate: Atti delle quattordicesime giornate normanno-sveve, Bari, 17–20 ottobre 2000*, ed. Giosuè Musca (Bari, 2002), p. 376.

[3] According to Mallette, 'the lament of the woman who watches her lover set sail on crusade was a set piece for medieval Romance poets': Mallette, *The Kingdom of Sicily*, p. 180. See also the discussion in Natasha R. Hodgson, *Women, Crusading and the Holy Land in Historical Narrative* (Woodbridge, 2007), especially pp. 113–15. Hodgson discusses representations of emotional departure scenes that appear in crusades narratives and poems prior to d'Aquino's Sicilian romance. One example, particularly reminiscent of emotions detailed in *Già mai non mi conforto*, appears in the twelfth-century chronicle of Fulcher of Chartres. Fulcher recounted the episode of a crusader who bid his wife farewell, thereby causing her to collapse in grief, 'fearing that she would never see him again, could not stand but swooned to the ground. Mourning her loved one whom she was losing in this life as if he were already dead': Fulcher of Chartres, *A History of the Expedition to Jerusalem 1095–1127*, trans. Frances Rita Ryan, ed. H. S. Fink (Knoxville, TN, 1969) Bk I, 6, p. 74; see also Hodgson, *Women, Crusading and the Holy Land*, p. 113.

behind. Two of these themes – the Crusades and Norman Italy – are among the most popular and widely researched fields of medieval history in recent decades. Scholarly conferences proliferate; articles and books have reached avalanche proportions. Moreover, Anglophone study of medieval southern Italy, excepting a few British scholars, barely existed twenty-five years ago but now thrives.

But despite the popularity of the two subjects – the crusades and Norman Italy – individually, when considered together, scholars usually focus on what the *Regno* did or did not contribute to the crusades. (Here, the crusading period refers to the crusades to the Holy Land, 1095–1291.) Previous examinations have emphasised the 'minimal' role of southerners in military campaigns, especially after the First Crusade. Based on evidence for military engagement in the Holy Lands, Helene Wieruszowski went so far as to argue that 'the crusade had no part in the Sicilian tradition', a claim reinforced by other scholars over the years, including Graham Loud, James Powell and John France.[4] In fact, Loud's article focused on the question, 'why did southern Italy and Sicily contribute so little to the Holy Land in the twelfth century?'[5] The notable exception to this 'minimalist' analysis is the study of Bohemond of Taranto, illegitimate son of Robert Guiscard, who took his army on the First Crusade, and to whom we will return later in this chapter.

While the southern Italians may not have made a great impression as armed combatants, the kingdom has itself been received as a geographical and ideological fulcrum for the crusades, an indispensable participant: a 'valuable bulwark' of the crusades;[6] a 'virtual turnstile' for Western sea

---

[4] Helene Wieruszowski, 'The Norman Kingdom of Sicily and the Crusades', in *A History of the Crusades*, vol. 2, *The Later Crusades 1189–1311*, ed. R. L. Wolff and H. W. Hazard (Madison, WI, 1969), p. 6, n. 8. Despite Orderic Vitalis' claims that Bohemond led a force of 30,000 men, scholars generally accept annalist Lupus Protospatharius' number of '500 knights' in Bohemond's company. See Evelyn Jamison, 'Some Notes on the *Anonymi Gesta Francorum*, with Special Reference to the Norman Contingent from South Italy and Sicily in the First Crusade', in *Studies in French Language and Medieval Literature presented to Professor Mildred K. Pope* (Manchester, 1939), pp. 183–208; G. A. Loud, 'Norman Italy and the Holy Land', in *The Horns of Hattin*, ed. B. Z. Kedar (London, 1992), pp. 49–50; For Lupus Protospatharius see excerpts in 'Composite Chronicles from Bari', trans. Tehmina Goskar and Patricia Skinner, in *Medieval Italy Texts in Translation*, ed. Kate Jansen, Joanna Drell and Frances Andrews (Philadelphia, 2009), p. 499. Though the southern Italian contingent during the Third Crusade may have been somewhat larger, overall the research concludes that there was not a significant southern Italian military presence during the crusades. France further remarked that there was no real Norman 'contingent' in the first crusade – they were Normans from Normandy. John France, 'The Normans and Crusading', in *The Normans and Their Adversaries at War: Essays in Memory of C. Warren Hollister*, ed. Richard P. Abels and Bernard S. Bachrach (Woodbridge, 2001), p. 91.
[5] Loud, 'Norman Italy and the Holy Land', p. 50.
[6] Wieruszowski, 'The Norman Kingdom of Sicily', p. 3.

powers to the East;[7] 'central to the history of the Crusades';[8] and more recently, in a provocative piece, 'a seedbed of crusades and crusading concepts'.[9] Such claims, many of them grounded in geography, strongly imply that the *Regno* was in no position not to be a player in the crusades.

I propose a different metric for evaluating the interplay of Norman Italy and the crusading movement. Rinaldo d'Aquino's distraught lover, while a literary construct, offers a glimpse into the personal cost of war, or to borrow from the late James Powell, 'the manner in which the crusading movement had entered into the fabric' of Norman Italian society and life.[10] Weaving together new research with rich evidence scholars have discussed in other contexts, I shall reconsider here how the crusades shaped the *Regno*. In effect, how were the crusades interwoven into the 'fabric' of Norman Italian life – not just socially, but also economically and politically? For example, what were those ships which arrived to carry away the woman's lover bringing with them? Whom did they bring? Could the goods, the ideas and the people that moved east to west rather than west to east have shaped the *Regno* in significant yet heretofore unconsidered respects either positive or negative, for good or ill? Approaching the topic from this perspective adds crusading's domestic impact to its acknowledged influence on the *Regno*'s transregional connections.

First, to what extent did the crusades affect the social fabric of southern Italian life? The evidence from southern Italy is sparse. Nevertheless, crusaders and pilgrims made preparations for their families before embarking on the arduous journey to Palestine. As a result, wills can be a helpful measure for contemporary awareness of the crusades, the dangers involved or planning required. However, given how few men from southern Italy went on crusade it is unsurprising that few wills record efforts to put affairs in order before departing to the Holy Land on crusade, or, more benignly, on pilgrimage. Occasionally someone like John from Avellino, son of John Dauferius, made preparations before he set off on pilgrimage in 1133. In the event of his death he assigned his wife Altruda to the guardianship of his

---

[7] Charles D. Stanton, *Norman Naval Operations in the Mediterranean* (Woodbridge, 2011), p. 180.

[8] Sarah C. Davis-Secord, 'Medieval Sicily and Southern Italy in Recent Historiographic Perspective', *Compass* 8/1 (2010), 69.

[9] Paul Chevedden, '"A Crusade from the First": The Norman Conquest of Islamic Sicily, 1060–1091', *Al-Masaq* 22 (2010), 206. See also Paul Oldfield, *Sanctity and Pilgrimage in Medieval Southern Italy, 1000–1200* (Cambridge, 2014), chapter 5, which stresses the region's pivotal role in pilgrimage and crusading traffic.

[10] James M. Powell, 'Crusading by Royal Command: Monarchy and Crusade in the Kingdom of Sicily (1187–1230)', in *Potere, società e popolo nell'età dei due Guglielmi: Atti delle quarte giornate normanno-sveve, Bari, 9–10 ottobre 1979* (Bari, 1981), p. 134.

father-in-law.[11] The year before, also in Avellino, Alferius, son of Ursus, prepared his will in the event of his death 'on the way to Jerusalem.'[12] If he was to die while away, and if his daughter, Maria, and unborn son or daughter were to die before they reached 'legitimate age' (presumably that age when they could receive their inheritances), all his possessions were to belong to the monastery of Saint Leonard, near the town of Avellino, excepting the *quarta* or marriage portion that belonged to his wife, Rolga. The language of the testament strongly suggests that Alferius leaves behind his pregnant wife to embark on crusade.[13] Our sad lady in Rinaldo d'Aquino's poem might have found comfort had her lover made any arrangements whatsoever for her. Moreover, the arrangements made for Altruda and Rolga reflect their husbands' active concerns for property ownership and inheritance strategies in the period before they set off to the Holy Land. It is well known that some women performed significant roles during the crusades in 'minding the homefront' in the absence of their husbands. Such women bring to mind David Herlihy's observations of over half a century ago: 'The great, external, dramatic events of the day, the wars and crusades, are the work of active men. But their accomplishments were matched and perhaps made possible by the work of women no less active.'[14]

A more detailed idea of both the logistics of crusading and the settling of personal matters is offered by none other than Bohemond of Taranto. According to chronicler Geoffrey Malaterra, while Bohemond was dutifully assisting his brother, Duke Roger Borsa, in the siege of Amalfi in 1096, he encountered a 'most fervent expedition' of Christians heading to the Holy

---

[11] For further discussion of wills and pilgrim activity, see Loud, 'Norman Italy and the Holy Land', pp. 55–61. Pasquale Cordasco discusses some of the extant wills men made before venturing to the Holy Land in his 'Echi delle Crociate nei documenti notarili meridionali', in *Il mezzogiorno normanno-svevo e le crociate*, ed. Musca, pp. 382–7.

[12] From the archive at the abbey of SS. Trinità of Cava de' Tirreni, Arca XXIII.25; see also Cava XVI-II.31. There are additional examples from the archive of Montevergine, *Codice diplomatico verginiano*, ed. P. M. Tropeano (Montevergine, 1977–2000), III.255 (1139), III. 206/206bis (1133).

[13] Cava Arca XXIII.25: *Ideo, sicut mihi congruum est, bona etenim mea voluntate et per hanc cartula iudico adque dispono ut si ego predictus alferio mortuus fuero in istam viam gerusolima que iturus sum et maria filia mea et ipsum filium meum vel filia mea si natum vel natam fuerit de rolga uxor mea morti fuerint antequam ad legitima etate perveniant, tunc integram ipsam rebus mea que est terra cum nucillitum quam abeo in loco ubi pontarola dicitur et propinquo ecclesia sancti laurentii, veniat in potestate de monasterio sancti leonardi quod constructum est propinquo civitate avellini et de eius rectori per ille finis et mensurie sicut monimine mee continent, except ipsa quarta parte quam ibidem abent supradicta rolga uxor mea*.

[14] David Herlihy, 'Land Family and Women in Continental Europe, 701–1200', *Traditio* 18 (1962), 113. For further discussion of the topic see Constance M. Rousseau, 'Home Front and Battlefield: The Gendering of Papal Crusading Policy (1095–1221)', in *Gendering the Crusades*, ed. Susan B. Edgington and Sarah Lambert (New York, 2002), pp. 31–44. See also Patricia Skinner, *Women in Medieval Italian Society, 500–1200* (Harlow, 2001), pp. 167, 171; Amy Livingstone, 'Aristocratic Women in the Chartrain', in *Aristocratic Women in Medieval France*, ed. Theodore Evergates (Philadelphia, 1999), p. 63.

Land.[15] Inspired to religious fervour, Bohemond lifted the siege, joined the expedition, named himself leader, and went home to make his 'crusader preparations'.[16] An Apulian charter describes Bohemond's financial preparations prior to departure, specifically the alienation of his lands ('immovables') to finance his voyage. In the text, Bohemond also commands his man to make the arrangements necessary to avoid future challenges from his heirs. Further, Bohemond tells his men to sell their holdings to raise money to go on crusade.[17]

Despite Bohemond's enthusiasm – his preparations were perhaps meant to serve as a public statement of his spiritual fervour – it is not clear whether society at large shared his passion. Such scholars as Loud and Powell have noted that contemporary awareness of crusading activities is not necessarily reflected in the evidence for church endowments. Southern Italians endowed few churches in the Holy Land, and there is little record of pious donations made in the name of crusaders in Norman Italy.[18] In general, any 'crusading echoes' found in notarial accounts in the crusading era are 'weak and distant'.[19] When measured by documentary evidence, the impact of the crusades on southern Italian society, like the degree of armed participation, seems to have been minimal.

A variety of explanations have been offered for the subdued social climate with regard to the crusades. At this time, concern among Norman Italian leaders for the safeguarding of the *Regno*'s political situation perhaps outstripped interest in crusading.[20] Count Roger's and Roger II's focus

---

[15] Geoffrey Malaterra, *The Deeds of Count Roger of Calabria and Sicily and of His Brother Duke Robert Guiscard, by Geoffrey Malaterra*, trans. Kenneth Wolf (Ann Arbor, MI, 2005), pp. 204–5.

[16] *Ibid.*, p. 204; Patricia Skinner, *Medieval Amalfi and Its Diaspora 800–1250* (Oxford, 2013), pp. 136, 136 n. 147. The pro-Norman chronicler, Ralph of Caen, also praises Bohemond's spiritual commitment, 'The same apostolic sermon that stirred the souls of other princes around the world to free Jerusalem from the yoke of the infidels also moved him': *GT*, Bachrach, p. 23.

[17] Luigi Rosso, 'I Normanni e il movimento crociato, una revisione', *Il papato e i normanni: Temporale e spirituale in età normanna* (Florence, 2011), pp. 167–8. Vito Sivo discusses literary evidence for Bohemond's role in the First Crusade, 'Il mezzogiorno e le crociate', pp. 356–9.

[18] Loud claims that 'enthusiasm very rapidly cooled', following a spurt of donation activity after the First Crusade. He concludes that southern Italians, overall, 'seem not to have been very active as pilgrims': Loud, 'Norman Italy and the Holy Land', p. 60, and more generally, pp. 52–62. See also Powell, 'Crusading by Royal Command', p. 137.

[19] According to Pasquale Cordasco, 'nei documenti notarili, in quasi duecento anni, gli echi delle Crociate son cosi fievoli e lontani': Pasquale Cordasco, 'Echi delle crociate', pp. 391–2.

[20] Powell cautions that a 'low level of participation in the crusading movement' should not be equated with a lack of interest or support; rather it may be seen as 'indirect confirmation of the manner in which the crusading movement in the Kingdom was subordinated to the interests of the monarchy': Powell, 'Crusading by Royal Command', p. 142. According to Powell, 'The subordination of crusader participation to royal control seems logically to have emerged in the Kingdom of Sicily from the military policies of the kings and to reflect the geographical position of the kingdom on the southeastern frontier of Latin Europe, exposed to threat from both the Byzantines and the Moslems': p. 146.

was on protecting their hold over newly conquered territories and creating stability. Count Roger did not want to jeopardise his previously established trade relations with Muslims, in particular in Africa; moreover, he wanted to revive Sicilian commerce following his conquest of the Island in 1091.[21] Arab historian Ibn-al-Athir (d. 1233) suggested that economic and commercial concerns underscored Roger's refusal to join the Franks against the Muslims. According to Al-Athir, Roger reasoned – emphatically! – that military costs and the disruption of trade would be too great. In response to the proposal to go to war

> Roger raised his leg and gave a loud fart. 'By the truth of my religion', he said, 'there is more use in [relations with the Muslims in Syria and North Africa] than in what you have to say! ... I shall be deprived of the money that comes in every year from agricultural revenues ... . Our mutual contacts and visits will be interrupted.[22]

Similarly, the Muslim chronicler/geographer, al-Idrisi, noted that both Count Roger and his son Roger II treated Muslims favorably by respecting their laws and religion.[23] Another, arguably 'superficial', explanation for the reluctance of Roger II to involve himself in the crusades was his bitterness over the repudiation of his mother Adelaide by King Baldwin of Jerusalem in 1117. William of Tyre remarked that as a result of her rejection, Adelaide's son (Roger II) and heirs 'conceived a mortal hatred against the [Latin] kingdom [of Jerusalem] and its people'.[24]

If southern Italians were not major military participants (in the sense of direct contribution to crusading expeditions), the crusades could be 'woven into the fabric' of southern Italian life by other means. This leads to a next category of analysis, the economic impact of the crusades, in

---

[21] Wieruszowski, 'The Norman Kingdom of Sicily', p. 6; Loud, 'Norman Italy and the Holy Land', p. 51; Chevedden, 'A Crusade from the First', p. 220. See also Hubert Houben, *Roger II of Sicily: A Ruler between East and West* (Cambridge, 1997), pp. 162-3.

[22] Ibn al-Athir, *The Chronicle of Ibn al-Athīr for the Crusading Period from al-Kamil fi'l-Ta'rikh*. Part I. trans. D. S. Richards (Aldershot, 2006) p. 13.

[23] Graham A. Loud, *Roger II and the Creation of the Kingdom of Sicily* (Manchester, 2012), p. 357. Historians have offered a spectrum of motivations for the Norman 'conquest' of southern Italy and Sicily. For a recent perspective see Chevedden, 'A Crusade from the First', pp. 206-20. Chevedden emphasises the religious aspect of the Norman conquest of Islamic Sicily, underscoring his position that Sicily was 'the seedbed of the crusades and crusading concepts' (p. 206). Drawing on the chronicles of Amatus of Montecassino, Geoffrey Malaterra, and others, Chevedden argues that the Normans were invoking the will of God, 'long before "god wills" became the battle cry of the Crusaders' (p. 208). His view contrasts with that of Hubert Houben, for example, who maintained that religion, while a factor in Norman actions, 'took a back seat to a desire of conquest': Houben, *Roger II of Sicily*, p. 20.

[24] William of Tyre, *A History of Deeds done beyond the Sea*, trans. E. A. Babcock and A. C. Krey (New York, 1941), i. p. 514; see also France, 'The Normans and Crusading' p. 96; Loud, 'Norman Italy and the Holy Land', pp. 57-9; Hodgson, *Women, Crusading and the Holy Land*, pp. 209-10.

particular on shipping and trade. Maritime centres including Palermo and Messina in Sicily, Bari, Brindisi, Barletta and Trani in Apulia were principal port cities for traffic to the Holy Land.[25] These cities served not only the foreign crusaders and pilgrims but also merchants who had been travelling to the Holy Land since well before 1095. The crusades increased traffic of all sorts to and from the south, but what do we know about the activities in these port cities?[26]

A multicultural and multiethnic array of voices – residents, visitors, travellers – extol the commercial and military strengths of the port cities on both sides of the peninsula and in Sicily. In these ports, commercial and agricultural markets thrived, ships were built and repaired, foreign soldiers and armies were housed and supplied. To give a sense of scale, by the 1220s, Frederick II was complaining about the financial burden of outfitting over 1,500 soldiers from all over Italy and 'north of the Alps', while also providing ships and the men to sail them.[27] Al-Idrisi, in his description of Palermo, *c.* 1150, remarked on both the military functions of the city and the busy markets that supported the town and its suburbs. He observed that 'it is from there [the port of Palermo] that fleets and armies departed on military expeditions and it is to there that they returned'; he further describes the 'arsenal for the construction of [these] ships' in the suburbs of Palermo.[28] In his 1185 portrait of Messina, the Spanish Muslim traveller, Ibn Jubayr, observed 'ships ranged along the quay like horses lined at their pickets or in their stables'; and the city was 'the focus of ships from the world over'.[29] He goes on to describe the shipyards of Messina and Palermo, 'containing fleets of uncountable numbers of ships'.[30] That many ships required a small army to care for them, as illustrated when English King Richard I's fleet docked in Messina in 1190 to await the king's arrival, 'many sorts of people [were] assigned to look after the fleet'.[31] In effect, the

---

[25] P. Oldfield, *City and Community in Norman Italy* (Cambridge, 2009), pp. 246–7; Donald Matthew, *The Norman Kingdom of Sicily* (Cambridge, 1992), p. 74.

[26] As the evidence from the Cairo Geniza has shown, Amalfitan merchants were already in Cairo in 996. Michel Balard, 'Notes on the Economic Consequences of the Crusades', in *Experience of Crusading*, ed. Marcus Bull, Norman Housley and Peter Edbury (Cambridge, 2003), pp. 233–5. Also Oldfield, *City and Community*, pp. 246–7.

[27] Matthew, *The Norman Kingdom of Sicily*, pp. 312–21.

[28] Loud, *Roger II and the Creation of the Kingdom of Sicily*, pp. 358, 359.

[29] *The Travels of Ibn Jubayr*, trans. Roland Broadhurst (London, 1952), pp. 338, 339.

[30] *Ibid.*, p. 343.

[31] *Itin. Pereg.*, p. 155.

Norman ports, but especially Messina, served as focal points for military and commercial operations in the crusading period.[32]

In addition to their military role, port cities served the many pilgrims who congregated from across the continent to make the journey to Jerusalem. In c. 1169, the Jewish traveller from Spain, Benjamin of Tudela, described his journey back from Jerusalem through Sicily, 'Most of the pilgrims who embark for Jerusalem assemble here [Messina], because the city affords the best opportunity for a good passage.'[33] In his account from 1102–3, the English pilgrim Saewulf illustrated the dangers of such voyages, as well as the critical supporting roles performed by the people on shore. In his description of the Apulian ports of Bari, Barletta, Trani, and Monopoli, Saewulf recounted how he set off with his group of pilgrims from Monopoli only to be shipwrecked three miles out, and forced to seek refuge in Brindisi where their ship was 'refitted'.[34] Some period later they were able to embark on their journey.

Turning to the western side of the southern Italian peninsula, close connections between the *Regno* and Genoa dated back to the early years of the twelfth century with the marriage of Count Roger – Roger II's father – to Adelaide of the prominent Ligurian Aleramici family.[35] Furthermore, Benjamin of Tudela, al-Idrisi and many others did not neglect to praise the busy markets, abundant resources and prosperity of the port centres along the western coast: Naples, Sorrento and Amalfi (in particular) – all cities that formed strong trading and commercial partnerships with northern Italian cities like Genoa and Pisa.[36] Their trade involved both the local agricultural markets and luxury merchandise from the Holy Land. To offer one example, though we know frustratingly little of his origins, the successful Genoese merchant Solomon of Salerno reflects the thriving commercial and personal bonds between the two cities in the twelfth century.[37] With commercial interests that spanned the Mediterranean, from Alexandria to Spain, Solomon of Salerno is credited with expanding Genoese trade in the

---

[32] For an overview of Norman naval capacity see Stanton's *Norman Naval Operations*, Appendix A, pp. 225–72.

[33] *The Itinerary of Benjamin of Tudela*, trans. M. N. Adler (London, 1907), p. 137; Matthew, *The Norman Kingdom of Sicily*, p. 75.

[34] *Peregrinationes Tres: Saewulf, John of Würzburg, Theodericus*, ed. R. B. C. Huygens with study by J. H. Pryor, Corpus Christianorum. Continuatio Mediaevalis 139 (Sydney, 1994), pp. 35–7, 59, lines 6–12.

[35] David Abulafia, *The Two Italies: Economic Relations between the Norman Kingdom of Sicily and the Northern Communes* (Cambridge, 1977), pp. 283–4; Stanton, *Norman Naval Operations*, p. 197.

[36] For the Privileges of 1156 between Messina and Genoa see Abulafia, *Two Italies*, p. 92; see also Matthew, *The Norman Kingdom of Sicily*, pp. 76–7.

[37] Abulafia, *Two Italies*, pp. 237–57; Steven A. Epstein, *Genoa and the Genoese 958–1528* (Chapel Hill, NC, 1996), p. 59.

twelfth century. His familiarity with *Regno* authorities at the highest level is suggested by a text from 1162 in which he is named 'King William's *fidelis*'.[38]

Overall, the crusading period witnessed the expansion and strengthening of southern Italian internal markets and connections with northern Italy; if anything, there was less international trade but more interregional trade. Contrary to old theories that these relationships initiated the long, slow decline of the southern Italian economy (the infamous *Problema del Mezzogiorno*), southern Italian markets were clearly not suppressed due to Norman authority, crusading or rapacious northern Italian towns like Genoa, Pisa and Venice.[39] To speculate, the extent to which the crusading movement can be directly credited with any of these developments in agricultural production and interregional trade would have depended on the readiness, flexibility and management of the ports in responding to the increase in traffic. Abulafia memorably remarked, 'Messina was a Norman phenomenon and a phenomenon of the Crusades'.[40] Crusaders, pilgrims and merchants benefited from the local commercial infrastructure on both coasts and Sicily. For example, Abulafia has discussed the 'sailors' rest and merchant hostel' that the Genoese were allowed to build in Messina after 1116.[41] Such facilities speak to a built environment created to support the bustling markets, military arsenals and transportation hubs.

Clearly related to the role of southern Italy's ports is the final category in this survey of the crusades' domestic/internal impact on southern Italy: specifically the emergence of the *Regno* as a player on the diplomatic stage as a consequence of the crusades. The focus here is the fostering of diplomatic ties in the twelfth century between the Norman kings of Italy and the rulers of England and France. When the southern Italian kings appear on the same diplomatic stage as Eleanor of Aquitaine, Richard the Lionheart and others, they are clearly engaging in the 'high politics' of the twelfth century.[42] Keeping in mind that there were pre-existing political

---

[38] Abulafia, *Two Italies*, p. 248.

[39] Davis-Secord, 'Medieval Sicily and Southern Italy', pp. 69–70; Abulafia, *Two Italies*, pp. 64–5. Matthew observes that the *Regno*'s economic prosperity was largely based on what was produced and cultivated in the kingdom, not on the great ports: Matthew, *The Norman Kingdom of Sicily*, pp. 74–7.

[40] Abulafia, *Two Italies*, p. 42.

[41] *Ibid.*, pp. 62–4. On travel infrastructure and pilgrimage in the region see Oldfield, *Sanctity and Pilgrimage*, chapter 5; and also P. Dalena, *Dagli itinera ai percorsi: viaggiare nel mezzogiorno medievale* (Bari, 2003).

[42] Loud, 'Norman Italy and the Holy Land', p. 50; see also G. A. Loud, 'The Kingdom of Sicily and the Kingdom of England, 1066–1266', *History* 88 (2003), 540–67; and the recent study of Sulamith Brodbeck, *Les Saints de la cathédrale de Monreale en Sicile* (Rome, 2010) which connects the hagiographical material displayed in the famous mosaic cycles at Monreale to Sicily's wider diplomatic relations. On the triangular relationship linking crusading/pilgrimage, royal ideology and diplomacy see also the chapter by Paul Oldfield in this volume.

and administrative connections between the *Regno* and Norman England, especially, the issue is to what degree adding the crusades to the mix altered these pre-existing connections?

For decades the kingdom of Sicily was a strategically significant and convenient 'stopover point' for crusading armies from the continent – for refuelling or for a layover during the winter or bad weather.[43] Though Roger II may have wanted to avoid upsetting his Muslim commercial allies, as mentioned earlier, he did not hesitate to indicate his support for Louis VII of France on his crusade to the Holy Land in 1146 – a venture known to posterity as the Second Crusade. Roger offered 'food supplies and transportation by water and every other need' to the French king, although Louis refused the offer, fearing objections from the pope or the Byzantines.[44] That said, Louis and his wife Eleanor needed Roger's assistance on their return from the Holy Land in 1149 when his forces rescued the queen after her ship was captured by Byzantine galleys. Eleanor and Louis were escorted back to Palermo 'rejoicing, with honour and triumph'.[45]

Sicily, the Norman kings and crusading became further embroiled in continental politics when King William II of Sicily, on his deathbed (1189), and incensed by the loss of Jerusalem after the Battle of Hattin (1187), donated a fleet to Henry II of England with two years' worth of supplies (money, provisions, equipment). Things became truly complicated in 1190–91, when William II's heir, King Tancred, hosted the crusading armies of both Philip II of France and Richard I of England, in Messina for a long stay of six months, apparently due to bad weather. Disagreements immediately arose over the return of Tancred's stepmother, Joanna, and her dowry to her brother, Richard I. (Tancred had imprisoned her upon the death of her husband, William II.) As a result Tancred refused to supply the king of England and his troops during their time in Messina and left them at the mercy of local Messinese authorities who were profiteering from them while, conversely, being generous to the French soldiers; thus

> [the locals] oppressed King Richard and his people as much as they could contrive. They prevented them from buying the food that such a large army needs, and decreed that nothing could be put out for sale, so that they would be forced to submit to the local authorities.[46]

---

[43] Davis-Secord, 'Medieval Sicily and Southern Italy', p. 69

[44] Odo of Deuil, *De profectione Ludovici VII in orientem*, ed. and trans. V. G. Berry (New York, 1948), pp. 10–11; France, 'The Normans and Crusading', p. 98.

[45] John of Salisbury, *Historia Pontificalis*, ed. and trans. M. Chibnall (Oxford, 1956), p. 60; Matthew, *The Norman Kingdom of Sicily*, p. 60.

[46] *Itin. Pereg.*, p. 166; France, 'The Normans and Crusading', pp. 100–1.

Peace was eventually made with the return of Joanna and her dowry to her brother. Included in this settlement were 'necessary foodstuffs for humans and horses ... laid out for sale at a reasonable price', as well as a well-dowered, royal wife (one of Tancred's daughters) for Richard's nephew, Arthur of Brittany.[47] This episode offers a further glimpse of crusader life – or the bias of its pro-Richard I author – as we learn that the English soldiers grew restless from inactivity and 'not achieving anything'.[48] Moreover, so great was their spiritual commitment that the English soldiers 'objected that their brothers in Christ were constantly struggling in the siege of Acre while they idled their time away in Messina'.[49] (Unsurprisingly, there is no mention of whether the French soldiers were restless.)

In essence, the crusading interests of Europe's continental powers, combined with southern Italy's geographic advantages, gave the Norman kings opportunities to establish and develop networks of communication. They built political alliances that would endure or test the kingdom in the century that followed.

This brief examination of domestic impacts of the crusades in southern Italy began with the despondent words of an inconsolable lady, as imagined by a male poet. Was it only through the voice of a woman that a statement critical of the war and political authority could be expressed? Could d'Aquino only critique the crusades and his emperor under his genre's veil of romance and drama? Other scholars have raised and will continue to debate this issue.[50] However the poem is a reminder that an enduring crusading legacy of southern Italy is the literary window of a poem like *Già mai non mi conforto*. Fictional works, including Occitan courtly romances, Arthurian stories and Boccaccio's tales, reflect the cultural diversity of individuals who passed through the *Regno*'s ports, each one with his own agenda: merchant, pilgrim, crusader. In addition to examples included in this study – from Spanish Jewish and Muslim travellers, to Arabic, English and French chroniclers, finally to a merchant with Salernitan ties who was fully integrated into Genoese society – crusading activity, by bringing people through the ports and markets of the south, enhanced the *Regno*'s multicultural character and reputation.

The crusades' impact on society and economy is a rich area for further study, especially as more evidence comes to light and older scholarship and

---

[47] *Itin. Pereg.*, pp. 168–9. See Hodgson, *Women, Crusading and the Holy Land*, pp. 206–9 for further discussion of these events by Richard of Devizes, and others.
[48] *Itin. Pereg.*, p. 172.
[49] *Itin. Pereg.*, p. 170
[50] See Mallette, *The Kingdom of Sicily*, pp. 86–7.

studies are revisited. Crusading activity had multiple consequences for the *Regno*. Focusing on the domestic impact of the crusades invites a reconsideration of the 'minimalist' argument for southern Italian engagement in the crusades. Though the Norman kingdom may have contributed few mounted knights and infantry, the *Regno* was a crucial player in facilitating the projection of military power by foreign troops through its transport and supplying of them, especially during the twelfth-century crusades. The fictional nobles who chose duty over love and left behind their lovers weeping on the Sicilian shores might have been seen as projections of that military power. The crusades were interwoven into the social, economic and political fabrics of Norman Italy. Whether as scenic backdrop, active participant, much-needed rest stop on a long journey or political actor, the *Regno* and its inhabitants became, irreversibly, a part of a broader Italian and European sociopolitical narrative.

4

The Norman Influence on Crusading from England and Wales

KATHRYN HURLOCK

The tradition that the Normans were at the forefront of the early crusading movement has a long history. From the 1130s, Norman and Anglo-Norman writers were keen to establish the idea that Norman crusaders were a united force, and they highlighted the piety and military qualities of the Norman people.[1] Several conflicts had already received papal backing by this time, and Norman mercenaries were fighting for the Byzantine emperor before the First Crusade, suggesting that they were already linked to the idea of Holy War and conflict in the East.[2] Interpretations based on early sources understandably emphasised the Norman involvement in crusading, with works complimentary to the Normans promoting their contribution at the expense of others.

However, the publication, in 1976, of D. C. Douglas' *The Norman Fate* saw one of the last works to highlight the Norman contribution to crusading as one of their most important triumphs, and their military role in the First Crusade as key to its success.[3] Studies have demonstrated that the Normans were not the unified group portrayed in the sources, and, therefore, that the contribution made to the First Crusade by Norman combatants such

---

[1] Barbara Packard, 'Remembering the First Crusade: Latin Narrative Histories 1099–*c*. 1300', unpublished PhD thesis (London, 2011), p. 105; Ralph of Caen alluded to the common origins of the Norman crusaders of Normandy and southern Italy at the time of the First Crusade when he praised Bohemond of Taranto, his nephew Tancred, and Robert Curthose, duke of Normandy, for propagating 'the unique glory of their fatherland' whilst on crusade: *GT*, Bachrach, pp. 44–5. In the case of the southern Italian Normans, the idea that the Normans were fulfilling expectations placed on them by their ancestors' reputation predated the crusades; here they were portrayed as champions of Christianity in the 1070s by Amatus of Monte Cassino. As Marjorie Chibnall put it, 'In Italy a new twist was being given to the myth of the Normans as a chosen people; even before the Crusade launched by Urban II in 1095 they were seen as the spearhead of counter-attacks against the Saracens': M. Chibnall, *The Normans* (Oxford, 2006), p. 119.

[2] J. Shephard, 'The Uses of the Franks in Eleventh-Century Byzantium', *ANS* 15 (1992), pp. 300–2; P. Magdalino, *The Byzantine Background to the First Crusade* (Toronto, 1996), pp. 11–13, 29–35.

[3] D. C. Douglas, *The Norman Fate, 1100–1154* (Berkeley, CA, 1976), pp. 156–93.

as Robert, duke of Normandy, and Bohemond of Taranto was not an indication of a wider interest among the Norman *gens*.[4] Indeed, what is clear is that the Normans across Europe did not form a cohesive group, and that not all Normans responded to the First Crusade with the same level of enthusiasm. What this chapter seeks to do is consider those of Norman descent who held lands in England and Wales from the time of the First Crusade (for want of a better term hereafter referred to as Anglo-Normans), looking at what role Anglo-Norman rule had on participation from England and Wales up to 1204 when King John lost Normandy, though Henry III did not renounce his claim to the duchy until 1259. It will also consider the legacy of Norman and Anglo-Norman crusading and its impact beyond this. Though participation from Normandy itself was almost non-existent after the First Crusade, it increased from England and Wales throughout the twelfth century under the leadership of the Anglo-Normans who settled in these areas after 1066, some of whom still held land in Normandy into the thirteenth century. It will also consider how interest in crusading traditions from the time of the First Crusade onwards may have prompted crusading activity, and how the domestic political situation at home influenced crusaders and crusading from England and Wales.

Positive influences on crusade participation are perhaps the easiest to determine. Whilst few crusaders have left records stating the motivations behind their decision to join the crusade, many more driving forces can be determined by looking at groups of crusaders and considering what broader factors positively influenced their choices. Active recruitment naturally spread the message of the Cross more systematically and to a broader audience, and this could increase the number of participants; so too could the establishment of family traditions, which arguably came to have more of an impact in England and Wales in the late twelfth and early thirteenth centuries. Perhaps most important, though, was the provision of strong leadership. In a society where military service took place in a retinue under the leadership of a lord, knightly and noble participation often spurred those used to serving to take the Cross themselves. Leadership also provided a focus for organisation and a figurehead to follow across Europe to the East.

At the time of the First Crusade, this leadership came in the form of

---

[4] For discussion of identity and the idea of unity, see France, 'The Normans and Crusading'; Alan V. Murray, 'How Norman Was the Principality of Antioch? Prolegomena to a Study of the Origins of the Nobility of a Crusader State', in *Family Trees and the Roots of Politics: The Prosopography of England and France from the Tenth to the Twelfth Century*, ed. K. S. B. Keats-Rohan (Woodbridge, 1997), pp. 349–59; N. Hodgson, 'Reinventing Normans as Crusaders? Ralph of Caen's *Gesta Tancredi*', ANS 30 (2008), 117–32.

Robert Curthose, duke of Normandy, one of the pre-eminent leaders of the Christian forces.[5] He was accompanied by men from Normandy and elsewhere in mainland northern Europe, as well as Anglo-Normans who no doubt joined his contingent, as he was the closest they had to a 'natural lord'.[6] Estimates vary, but Robert of Normandy's army may have included up to 1,000 knights and 8,000 infantrymen, some of whom could have been unnamed Anglo-Normans.[7] Among those who joined Curthose's retinue was Pagan Peverel, from the area around Huntington, 'an outstanding soldier ... and praiseworthy above all the nobles of the kingdom in matters of Warfare' (according to *the Book of Barnwell*), who acted as Curthose's standard-bearer, and went into the service of Henry I of England on his return to the West.[8] Pagan brought home 'most genuine relics in gold and precious topaz' from the crusade and he gave some to Barnwell Priory, where he refounded a college of canons.[9] William de Percy, who had been given land in the north by Hugh d'Avranches and founded Whitby Abbey, travelled from England, dying before the army reached Jerusalem.[10] Edith, sister of William de Warenne (who held land in southern England), joined him.[11]

Royal leadership was distinctly lacking for much of the twelfth century, as we shall see below, so noblemen from England and the Welsh March often filled the void. At the time of the Second Crusade, this meant Waleran de Beaumont, count of Meulan and earl of Worcester. He chose to travel under the leadership of the French king Louis VII in order to protect the interests of his Norman estates.[12] William of Warenne, earl of Surrey, and half-brother of Waleran, joined but served in the personal guard of

---

[5] *Robert the Monk's History of the First Crusade: Historia Iherosolimitana*, trans. Carol Sweetenham (Aldershot, 2005), pp. 89, 91.

[6] OV, v, p. 157.

[7] For differing views, see France, 'The Normans and Crusading', p. 91; Charles Wendell David, *Robert Curthose, Duke of Normandy* (Cambridge, MA, 1920), p. 228; John France, *Victory in the East: A Military History of the First Crusade* (Cambridge, 1994), pp. 129–30.

[8] Susan Edginton, 'Pagan Peverel: An Anglo-Norman Crusader', *Crusade and Settlement: Papers Read at the First Conference of the Society for the Study of the Crusades and the Latin East and presented to R. C. Smail*, ed. Peter Edbury (Cardiff, 1985), pp. 90–3; *Liber Memorandum Ecclesie de Barnewelle*, ed. J. W. Clark (Cambridge, 1907), pp. 41, 46, 54–5. Albert of Aix gives the names of two of Robert's standard bearers, but makes no mention of Pagan: Albert of Aix, 'Liber Christianae expeditionis', in *RHC*, iv, p. 362.

[9] N. L. Paul, *To Follow in Their Footsteps: The Crusades and Family Memory in the High Middle Ages* (New York, 2012), p. 121.

[10] William Farrer, ed., *Early Yorkshire Charters*, 6 vols (Edinburgh and Cambridge, 1915–16), ii, pp. 20, 197–8.

[11] Frank Barlow, *William Rufus* (New Haven, CT, 2000), p. 367.

[12] David Crouch, *The Beaumont Twins: The Roots and Branches of Power in the Twelfth Century* (Cambridge, 1986), pp. 65–6.

Louis VII. He died at the Battle of Cadmus (Anatolia) in January 1148.[13] The Anglo-Norman bishop Roger de Clinton, bishop of Chester, also joined the crusade.[14] After the failure of the Second Crusade, Henry II of England promised to undertake a crusade of his own, but he never fulfilled his vow and his promised army never materialised.[15] He raised significant sums of money for the assistance of the Holy Land in the 1170s and 1180s, but did not allow anyone to spend the money, rendering it effectively worthless.[16] His regular promises to go on crusade himself were hindered by rebellion at home and problems with the church, though even contemporaries doubted that he intended to fulfil his vow.[17]

The second contingent of crusaders to join the Second Crusade was drawn from the lower knightly and merchant class in England and Scotland, travelling independently from the Anglo-Norman nobility. This contingent comprised as many as 4,500 combatants, and was under the leadership of a small group of men, including some Anglo-Norman landowners.[18] These landowners comprised two constables of England, Saher de Archelle (an Anglo-Norman Lincolnshire landowner) and Hervey de Glanville (of East Anglia, who oversaw the 'ships from Norfolk and Suffolk'), in addition to Simon of Dover (overseeing shipping from Kent) and Andrew of London (possibly a descendant of an Italian family, who oversaw the ships from London).[19] William Vitalus led a further contingent from Southampton.[20] Intending to sail around the Iberian peninsula to the Holy Land (though it is likely the stop-off was premeditated), the crusaders were exhorted to make the final assault on Lisbon by an Anglo-Norman priest. Throughout the *De Expugnatione Lyxbonensi*, the Normans and English (*Normanni et Anglici*) are shown as working in concert under the leadership of these men.[21] Anglo-Norman crusaders took part in the conquests of Lisbon and

---

[13] Odo of Deuil, *De profectione Ludovici VII in Orientum*, ed. and trans. V. G. Berry (New York, 1948), pp. 55, 123. Jonathan Riley-Smith highlights the familial link between William and the comital house of Burgundy which produced a very high proportion of crusaders. Jonathan Riley-Smith, 'Family Traditions and Participation in the Second Crusade', in *The Second Crusade and the Cistercians*, ed. Michael Gervers (New York, 1992), pp. 102–3.

[14] E. J. King, *King Stephen* (New Haven, CT, 2011), p. 231.

[15] Tyerman, *England and the Crusades*, pp. 52–3; Hans Eberhard Mayer, 'Henry II of England and the Holy Land', *EHR* 97 (1982), 721–23.

[16] *Ibid.*, p. 722.

[17] *Ibid.*, p. 721.

[18] Jonathan Phillips, *The Second Crusade: Extending the Frontiers of Christendom* (New Haven, CT, 2010), p. 143; The *De expugnatione Lyxbonensi* says that the Anglo-Normans set up night watches of 500 men which worked on a nine-day rota, equalling 4,500 men. *DEL*, p. 129.

[19] *Ibid.*, pp. 55–7.

[20] *Ibid.*, pp. 101–5.

[21] *Ibid.*, pp. 105, 107, 109, 129, 135, 141, 143, 147, 171, 177.

Tortosa, before the majority of them continued their journeys to the Holy Land.[22]

At the time of the Third Crusade (1189–92), Richard I, king of England and duke of Normandy, provided leadership for the largest crusader army to leave England and Wales in the twelfth century. Richard had only recently become king, and spent little time in England itself, but his status made him the natural leader for the armies that came from his lands; as Beatrice Siedschlag put it, 'He was a prince who inspired devotion.'[23] His positive leadership provided finance for a crusade, equipped a fleet and encouraged hundreds of Anglo-Normans, Normans and others to join the crusade.[24] Importantly, his decision to organise and lead the army himself also meant that he poured vast sums of money into the enterprise, something that had hitherto been lacking as crusaders largely paid for themselves. He raised money via the Saladin Tithe instituted by his father, and by selling offices, extracting money from the Scots in return for concessions and calling in debts.[25] The money allowed Richard to equip a sizeable fleet and army, something which previous Anglo-Norman leaders had not done.

The numbers of men (and women) who participated in the crusades from England and Wales were understandably higher during those periods when a concerted effort was made to recruit combatants. The first time that this really occurred in England was in 1185. Henry II allowed the patriarch of Jerusalem, Heraclius, to preach at a council held at the priory of Saint John of Jerusalem in Clerkenwell on 18 March 1185. Heraclius' preaching was effective enough to bring his audience to tears.[26] More effective was the concerted effort made to recruit crusaders in 1188, led by Baldwin of Forde, the Anglo-Norman archbishop of Canterbury. In the spring of 1188, he embarked on a six-week Lenten tour of Wales and the Welsh border, preaching the Cross in what was a highly organised and stage-managed journey.[27] His motives for travelling primarily to Wales were numerous

---

[22] L. Villegas-Aristizábal, 'Norman and Anglo-Norman Participation in the Iberian *Reconquista c.* 1018–c. 1248', unpublished PhD thesis (Nottingham, 2007), pp. 176–84, 192–205.
[23] Beatrice N. Siedschlag, 'English Participation in the Crusades, 1150–1220', unpublished PhD thesis (Bryn Mawr, 1939), p. 71.
[24] For Richard I's impact on the crusade in this way, see *The Chronicle of Richard of Devizes*, trans. J. T. Appleby (London, 1963), pp. 5, 7, 9, 30; Ralph of Coggeshall, *Radulphi de Coggeshall Chronicon Anglicanum*, ed. Joseph Stevenson (London, 1875), p. 93; John Tate Appleby, *England without Richard, 1189-1199* (London, 1965), p. 19; Tyerman, *England and the Crusades*, pp. 80–1; Hurlock, *Britain, Ireland and the Crusades* pp. 46–7.
[25] *Ibid.*, pp. 46–7.
[26] *Gesta regis Henrici Secundi*, i, pp. 328, 336.
[27] *IC*; translated as *The Journey through Wales and the Description of Wales*, trans. Lewis Thorpe (Harmondsworth, 2004).

and have been discussed elsewhere, but as the tour also included towns in the border counties of Cheshire, Shropshire and Herefordshire, the tour understandably had an impact here, as well as on the Norman settlers who controlled land in Wales.[28] Baldwin ensured that he was accompanied by preachers who spoke Welsh, such as Siesyll, the abbot of Strata Florida, and both native Welsh and Anglo-Norman settlers were addressed by the preachers so ensure that the tour had maximum impact.

The tour spent its last few days travelling south from Chester to Hereford via Whitchurch, Oswestry, Shrewsbury, Ludlow and Leominster. At Chester, Gerald of Wales claims, 'many people' who heard the archbishop's sermons took the Cross.[29] When the tour reached Oswestry most of the Welshmen who arrived had already made their vows, but Baldwin was able to recruit the rest.[30] Shrewsbury appears to have been a particularly fertile recruiting ground. Here the archbishop's preaching and Gerald's own 'elegant sermons ... persuaded many folk to take the Cross'.[31] The preaching appears to have been met with enthusiasm, even allowing for Gerald's tendency to exaggerate his own successes. At Oswestry, their host was William FitzAlan, 'a hospitable young nobleman', who had invited the party to stay, suggesting that he was interested in what the archbishop had to say.[32] Participation from this area at the time of the Third Crusade was mixed. The lack of noble leadership from Cheshire may have dissuaded some from taking part, though important men from the area, like John de Lacy, constable of Chester, did reach the Holy Land.[33]

The preaching tour of 1188 is the best documented of all preaching efforts in England and Wales, thanks to the record of Gerald of Wales. There were few other recorded attempts at recruiting in this way during the twelfth century. In 1198, abbot Eustace of Fly came to England from Normandy in order to preach the crusade, but he appears to have been a lone voice.[34] Peter of Blois, archdeacon of Bath, wrote at least two sermons to promote the crusade.[35] He was widely travelled and served Henry II in

---

[28] Kathryn Hurlock, 'Power, Preaching and the Crusades in Pura Wallia c. 1180–1280', *TCE* 11 (2007), 95–6.
[29] *IC*, p. 142; trans. Thorpe, *Journey*, p. 200.
[30] *IC*, p. 142; trans. Thorpe, *Journey*, p. 200.
[31] *IC*, p. 144; trans. Thorpe, *Journey*, p. 202.
[32] *IC*, p. 142; trans. Thorpe, *Journey*, p. 201.
[33] Geoffrey Barraclough, *The Charters of the Anglo-Norman Earls of Cheshire, c. 1071–1237* (Record Society of Lancashire and Cheshire, 1988), p. 209; *Gesta Regis Henrici Secundi*, ii, p. 148; Howden, *Chronica*, iv, p. 88.
[34] Cole, *The Preaching of the Crusades to the Holy Land*, p. 88.
[35] Peter of Blois, *Petri Blesensis Bathoniensis in Anglia archidiaconi: opera omnia*, ed. J.-P. Migne, *Patrologia Latina* 207 (Paris, 1853), cols. 529–34, 957–76, 1057–70.

the Norman kingdom of Sicily at the court of Palermo, where his enthusiasm for the crusade could have been enhanced.[36] More informal methods of recruitment – such as the composition and performance of crusading lyrics – could have prompted an interest in crusading in the late twelfth century. Most lyrics were from Normandy and France, but one survives from England, written on the flyleaf of a genealogy of the dukes of Normandy, in which the performer calls on his audience to hear his song, 'for God calls us to His aid, and no *preudhome* ought to fail him'.[37]

Participation in the earliest crusades set a precedent for many families who subsequently saw other members join the armies setting out for the east. Family tradition and the common interests forged by familial links could prove a strong motivator.[38] This was something that promoters of the crusades were only too aware of, and emulating crusading ancestors and following in their footsteps are common themes in promotional material.[39] Pagan Peverel went on the First Crusade, and his son William on the Second; moreover, one of Pagan's daughters, Alice, appears to have transmitted a devotion to crusading to her descendants.[40] Gerard de Furnival, a Norman who went on the Third Crusade and subsequently settled in England, had a son – also Gerard – who went on the Fifth Crusade (1219–21). Bernard de Saint-Valery, a landholder of Hinton Waldrist in Berkshire, went on the Third Crusade; he was the grandson of Reginald de Saint-Valery, who went on crusade in the late 1150s with Thierry of Flanders.[41] By the time of the Fifth Crusade, the number of crusaders whose ancestors had taken the Cross in the twelfth century rose significantly. John de Lacy, constable of Chester, William Ferrers, earl of Derby, and William Longespée, earl of Salisbury, all had family members who had taken part in previous crusades.[42] Other Norman families who came to England in the

---

[36] Siedschlag, 'English Participation', p. 80; in Ireland, Henry of London, archbishop of Dublin and papal legate, and Thomas, abbot of Mellifont, were instructed to preach in 1217, the two men perhaps chosen to appeal to both the native and settler groups in Ireland; Hurlock, *Britain, Ireland and the Crusades* p. 34.

[37] Joseph Bedier and Pierre Aubry, eds., *Les Chansons de Croisade* (Paris, 1909), pp. 67–73; Siedschlag, 'English Participation', p. 81, n. 12; British Library, MS. Harley 1717, f. 251v.

[38] Riley-Smith, 'Family Traditions', pp. 101–9; Paul, *To Follow in Their Footsteps*; Kathleen Thompson, 'Family Tradition and the Crusading Impulse: The Rotrou Counts of the Perche', *Medieval Prosopography: History and Collective Biography* 19 (1998), 1–33.

[39] Riley-Smith, 'Family Traditions', p. 101.

[40] Paul, *To Follow in Their Footsteps* p. 121.

[41] *Epistolae Cantuarienses 1187–99*, in *Chronicles and Memorials of the Reign of Richard I* ed. W. Stubbs (London, 1865), p. 113; Siedschlag, 'English Participation', p. 113.

[42] Roger of Wendover, *Flores Historiarum*, ed. H. G. Hewlett, 3 vols (London, 1886–89), ii, pp. 135, 244; *The Cartulary of St. John of Pontefract*, ed. R. Holmes, 2 vols (Yorkshire Archaeological Society, Record Series, 1899–1902), ii, p. 37; Walter of Coventry, *Memoriale*, ed. W. Stubbs, 2 vols (London, 1872–73), ii, pp. 240–1; *Annales de Burton*, in *Annales Monastici*, ed. H. R. Luard, 5 vols (London,1864),

eleventh and twelfth centuries established traditions that carried on into the thirteenth century, such as the Bohuns, Cliffords, Verduns, Stutevilles and Beauchamps.[43] In 1224, Pope Honorius III played on family tradition when he wrote to Henry III, asking him to remember the contribution of his uncle, Richard I.[44]

Until the time of the Third Crusade, participation in crusading to the Holy Land and elsewhere was limited from England and Wales when compared to regions like France and Germany. One of the initial problems was a lack of strong leadership, in terms of leading a crusading army and recruiting for its membership. In particular, there was no effort on the part of the kings of England to lead a crusade until Richard I did so in 1189.[45] When Pope Urban II launched the First Crusade at the end of the Council of Clermont in November 1096, the subsequent tours that were sent across Europe to drum up support did not reach England.[46] There is no record of any of the bishops or clergy engaging in crusade preaching or promotion; this could have been because William Rufus forbade his clergy from going to the Council of Clermont. Even from Normandy, only three bishops and one abbot attended.[47] Efforts at recruitment appear non-existent. King William Rufus was not interested in supporting the crusade, though this is perhaps not surprising given his apparent lack of personal piety and abuse of the church. The king actually denied potential combatants permission to join the crusade, 'their obligation to provide military service to the king ... considered more important than that of fighting the Saracens'.[48] It was not that these men were required to, or chose to, stay in England because there was a need to defend the acquisitions of 1066, but that there were still opportunities in England under William Rufus and now, due to Robert Curthose's mortgaging of his duchy, in Normandy, which might be missed by those who went overseas.[49] The lack of leadership was largely filled by Robert Curthose, as we have seen, but crusaders from England also turned

---

i, p. 225; James M. Powell, *Anatomy of a Crusade, 1213-1221* (Philadelphia, 1990), p. 246. Tyerman, *England and the Crusades*, p. 180. For William Longespée's crusading career, see Simon D. Lloyd, 'William Longespee II: The Making of an English Crusading Hero', *Nottingham Medieval Studies* 35 (1991), 41–69 and 36 (1992), 79–125; *Nouveau recueil de contes, dits, fabliaux, et autres pieces inédits des XIIIe, XIVe et XVe siècles, pour faire suite aux collections Legarnd d'Aussy, Barbazan et Méon, mis au jour pour le premiere fois*, ed. A. Jubinal, 2 vols (Paris, 1839–42), ii, pp. 339–53.

[43] Hurlock, *Britain, Ireland and the Crusades* p. 87.
[44] *Foedera*, ed. T. Rymer, 16 vols. (London, 1816), i, pp. 172–3.
[45] *Ibid.*, p. 35.
[46] Riley-Smith, *The First Crusade*, p. 31.
[47] Frederic Duncalf, 'The Councils of Piacenza and Clermont', in *A History of the Crusades*, vol. 1: *The First One Hundred Years*, ed. Marshall M. Baldwin (London, 1969), p. 236.
[48] A. Graboïs, 'Anglo-Norman England and the Holy Land', *ANS* 7 (1985), 132.
[49] Tyerman, *England and the Crusades*, pp. 17–18.

to other noblemen. One, the lord of Thouars in Poitou, included Welsh, Irish and English crusaders in his army.[50]

No support came either from Archbishop Anselm of Canterbury, the man who might be expected to carry the pope's message and co-ordinate its dissemination. Although an Italian, Anselm's career had flourished in Normandy at Bec, and he had only recently (and reluctantly) been appointed archbishop in 1093. The archbishop fully embraced the reformist messages of the papacy and assisted in the reform of the church in England, but when it came to recruiting for the crusade his support was lacking.[51] His biographer, Eadmer, failed to show any interest in it too.[52] Anselm appears to have envisioned himself as papal legate in England, seeing it as more important for his position to defend his rights and dignities than to support the crusade.[53] His lack of support may have been an intentional echo of the dearth of interest shown by William Rufus for the crusade; when asked by the papal legate in 1095 if he could leave England, Anselm told the legate that the king had placed him (Anselm) in charge of the kingdom of England whilst the king was absent fighting in Scotland.[54] Encouraging others to leave England in the following year might have gone against this role. This appears to have been a motivating factor for his refusal to send soldiers to assist in the Spanish *Reconquista*.[55]

Matters in England did not improve for prospective crusaders until the second half of the twelfth century. Henry I, for example, discouraged Bishop Gerard of York from going on crusade in 1107.[56] At the time of the Second Crusade (1147–49), there was still little interest among the nobility;

---

[50] *The Canso d'Antioca: An Occitan Epic Chronicle of the First Crusade*, trans. Carol Sweetenham (Aldershot, 2003), p. 227. In 1177, a group of crusaders from England sought leadership outside the Anglo-Norman realm in the form of Philip of Flanders who set off on crusade to the Holy Land with English knights and 500 silver marks from Henry II of England. They included William Mandeville, Robert Pirou (preceptor of Temple Hirst), and Henry de Lacy, lord of Pontefract: Elijas Oksanen, *Flanders and the Anglo-Norman World* (Cambridge, 2012), p. 261; Tyerman, *England and the Crusades*, p. 48; *Early Yorkshire Charters*, iii, p. 289 (no. 1629); Beatrice A. Lees, *Records of the Templars in England in the Twelfth Century: The Inquest of 1185* (London, 1935) p. 276.

[51] Samu Niskanen, 'St Anselm's Views on Crusade', in *Medieval History Writing and Crusading Ideology*, ed. Tuomas M. S. Lehtonen and Kurts Villads Jensen (Helsinki, 2005), p. 65.

[52] Eadmer, *The Life of St Anselm, Archbishop of Canterbury*, ed. and trans. R. W. Southern (Oxford, 1972).

[53] Tomaž Mastnak, *Crusading Peace: Christendom, the Muslim World and Western Political Order* (Berkeley, 2002), p. 77.

[54] *The Letters of St Anselm of Canterbury*, trans. Walter Fröhlich (Kalamazoo, 1990–94), no. 191.

[55] Niskanen, 'St Anselm's Views on Crusade', p. 68.

[56] Riley-Smith, *The First Crusaders*, p. 88. Even those who managed to leave on crusade could be discouraged *en route* from seeing it through. Sometime before 1197, John Buchart of Wilberton set off on crusade, only to be turned back by 'William, king of Apulia, [who had] stopped the Mediterranean crossing'. This was presumably William II, king of Sicily (r. 1154–89), a descendent of the first Norman lord Tancred of Hauteville. John Buchart was given a papal indult excusing him from completing his

the king, Stephen, was certainly in no position to lead an army to the East as he had spent the last twelve years fighting a civil war to keep his throne. When Bernard of Clairvaux wrote to the English in 1146 to try and move them to take the Cross, he was aware of the obstacle that civil war posed, and asked them:

> For how long will your men continue to shed Christian blood; for how long will they continue to fight amongst themselves? You attack each other, you slay each other and by each other you are slain. What is this savage craving of yours? Put a stop to it now, for it is not fighting but foolery. Thus to risk both soul and body is not brave but shocking, is not strength but folly. But now, O mighty soldiers, O men of war, you have a cause for which you can fight without danger to your souls; a cause in which to conquer is glorious and for which to die is gain.[57]

His request was not overly successful. Although the worst of the fighting was over, there were still tensions; many of the elite were concerned with protecting their estates in England, Wales and Normandy should fighting break out again, despite the ecclesiastical sanctions against such attacks.[58]

The same considerations may have influenced men who held lands in Wales and the Welsh March, as they were often involved in conflict which might deter them from going overseas. The potential problems posed by the Welsh who were trying to regain lands lost to the Anglo-Normans was recognised by Richard I, who sought to make a peace with the 'petty-kings of the Welsh'; he also sought a peace with the Scots so that they would 'not cross their borders to do harm to England' while Richard was on crusade.[59] Moreover, it seems likely that many potential Welsh recruits saw the crusade as synonymous with Anglo-Norman military activity and aggression, and as such were reluctant to engage with it when it was proposed to them by Anglo-Norman representatives. Although the tour of 1188 may have attracted hundreds, if not thousands, of men, some were reluctant to support the tour, and few actually set out on the crusade. Suspicion of the archbishop's motives for coming to Wales, in particular in relation to his authority

---

vow: 'Schedule of Crusaders from Lincolnshire', *Reports of the Historical Manuscripts Commission, Various Collections I* (London, 1901), p. 235.

[57] *The Letters of St Bernard of Clairvaux*, trans. Bruno Scott James (Stroud, 1998), p. 462. The same letter was sent to other places in Europe, but the language still fits the English situation perfectly.

[58] King, *King Stephen*, p. 231; Marjorie Chibnall, *The Empress Matilda: Queen Consort, Queen Mother and Lady of the English* (Oxford, 1991), p. 147.

[59] *The Chronicle of Richard of Devizes*, p. 7.

over the Welsh church, and his alienation of potential supporters through various actions whilst on tour, cannot have helped.[60]

Men who had been exiled or fallen from favour used the crusade as a means of escape, allowing them to distance themselves from an angry king, perhaps in the hope that relations would improve on their return. Some, like Odo, bishop of Bayeux, former earl of Kent, were already exiled some years before the First Crusade was launched, in his case for rebelling against William Rufus in favour of Robert Curthose. Odo died on crusade, at Palermo, in 1097. Another failed rebellion in 1095 appears to have provided the catalyst for the crusading of several important men from England. In 1095, having refused to answer the king's summons to respond to the complaints of traders whose vessels had been seized off the Northumbrian coast, Robert de Mowbray, earl of Northumbria (d. 1115/1125), was attacked by the king and imprisoned. Some of those involved in the rebellion understandably earned the king's enmity, and took the Cross, eager to escape the ensuing 'witch-hunt ... in which a variety of aristocratic scores were paid off'.[61] Among them was Arnulf of Hesdin, a major beneficiary of the conquest of 1066, who held land in more than ten English counties; although he was a Fleming, his decision to join the crusade was directly influenced by involvement in a failed Anglo-Norman rebellion.[62] David Crouch suggests that Arnulf 'quit England in disgust at the tyrannical and barbaric proceedings he had witnessed' when accused of treason and forced into trial by combat, 'and joined the crusade'. Frank Barlow and the editors of the *Hyde Chronicle* suggest that his decision to join the crusade 'may have been an act of penance as a result of his involvement in the rebellion'.[63]

Ivo of Grandmesnil, lord of Leicester in England and Grandmesnil in Normandy, was another whose involvement in the 1095 rebellion made it convenient to go abroad. His heart was perhaps not in it, as he fled the First Crusade army by climbing down the walls of Antioch in the middle of the night. He may have aimed to atone for this shameful action by going on crusade again in 1101, though again he had been involved in a

---

[60] Hurlock, 'Power, Preaching and the Crusades in *Pura Wallia*', pp. 95–7; Hurlock, *Britain, Ireland and the Crusades* pp. 106–8; *IC*, pp. 15, 125–6; Thorpe, *Journey*, pp. 76–7, 185.

[61] David Crouch, *The Normans: The History of a Dynasty* (London, 2002), p. 148.

[62] OV, v, pp. 208–11; The reasons for his unrest are unclear, though it is possible that he was planning a military venture to Rome with English troops to make himself pope. David Bates, 'The Career and Character of Odo, Bishop of Bayeux (1049/50–97)', *Speculum* 50 (1975), 18. The bishops of Evreux and Sees also attended the council: Aird, *Robert Curthose*, p. 153. Riley-Smith, *The First Crusaders* p. 91.

[63] Crouch, *The Normans*, p. 149; *The Warenne (Hyde) Chronicle*, ed. and trans. Elisabeth M. C. van Houts and Rosalind C. Love (Oxford, 2013), p. 40, n. 75; Frank Barlow, *William Rufus* (Berkeley, 1983), p. 358.

failed attempt to see Robert Curthose on the English throne over Henry I. According to Orderic Vitalis (c. 1075–1142), Ivo 'would never recover the king's friendship that he had lost, so he decided to go on crusade'.[64] Philip the Grammarian of Montgomery, fourth son of Roger de Montgomery, earl of Gloucester, was also implicated in the rebellion of 1095. He joined Robert Curthose on crusade, and died at Antioch.[65] Fifty years later the same motive was still playing out, as Roger de Mowbray of Yorkshire took the Cross having lost lands in England and Normandy during the civil war under King Stephen.[66] According to the chronicler John of Hexham, Roger 'won renowned fame by conquering, in single combat, a pagan king'.[67]

Another group – the Anglo-Saxons – had lost their lands after the Norman conquest in 1066, and some of these now landless men may have joined the First Crusade as an alternative to a potentially uncertain and unprofitable life in England under Norman rule. There were already Anglo-Saxons in the service of the Byzantine emperor, Alexius Comnenus (r. 1081–1118), by the early 1080s, so the idea of military service in the East was already established as an option; thus the Anglo-Saxons who had been displaced since the Norman victory at Hastings in 1066 had an alternative presented to them in the form of the crusade. Anglo-Saxons appear in the sources relating to the First Crusade. Some of these may have been the men termed *angli* in the sources, who sought the protection of Robert Curthose at Lattakiah.[68] During the course of the First Crusade, there were 'English' fleets in the Mediterranean, one arguably populated by the emperor's mercenaries but the other probably made up of Anglo-Saxon crusaders who came over with the crusading army.[69] The highest ranking of these crusaders may have been Edgar the Ætheling, claimant to the English throne in 1066, who had fled to Scotland in 1068 and entered into rebellion against William I in 1069–70; it is more likely, however, that he joined the crusade

---

[64] OV, vi, p. 18.

[65] Hurlock, *Britain, Ireland and the Crusades*, p. 66.

[66] John of Hexham, 'Continuation of Simeon of Durham's *Historia Regum*', in Simeon of Durham, *Historical works*, ed. T Arnold (London, 1882–85), p. 319; for Roger of Mowbray's career in context, see Janet E. Burton, '*Fundator Noster*: Roger de Mowbray as founder and patron of monasteries', in *Religious and Laity in Western Europe, 1000–1400: Interaction, Negotiation and Power*, ed. Emilia M. Jamroziak and Janet E. Burton (Turnhout, 2006), pp. 23–39.

[67] *The Church Historians of England*, vol. 1: *The Chronicles of John and Richard of Hexham*, ed. J. Stevenson (London, 1856), p. 25.

[68] Tyerman, *England and the Crusades*, pp. 20–1.

[69] Shepard argues that there were mercenary troops under the Byzantine emperor sent as a first wave of the crusade. J. Shepard, 'The English and Byzantium: A Study of Their Role in the Byzantine Army', *Traditio* 29 (1973), 53–92; For Raymond of Aguilers, see *RHC*, iii, pp. 290–1. There is some debate over the composition of the English fleets: see Tyerman, *England and the Crusades*, pp. 19–21; John France, 'The First Crusade as a Naval Enterprise', *The Mariner's Mirror* 83 (1997), 397.

in 1102.[70] Orderic Vitalis thought that he took part in the first wave of the First Crusade, stating that when Edgar Ætheling was at the fall of Antioch 'he immediately took the city under his protection and, preserving his loyalty to Duke Robert transferred it to him after the victory over the pagans'.[71]

A considerable volume and range of information on crusades and crusading found its way into the written works produced in England in the twelfth century. Whilst this was not actively used as promotional material, the dissemination and recording of ideas can only have helped to spread the message of the crusades and keep it alive in the consciousness of those who had connections to these works and the communities that produced them. In the wake of the successes of the First Crusade, there was considerable interest in the events of the Holy Land, spread by returning crusaders and those who sent letters home.[72]

One of the most enduring, and yet most passive, ways in which the Normans influenced crusading from England in the long term was by creating an historical mythology largely based on the crusade of Robert Curthose. The decision to do this may have been promoted by interest in the Anglo-Norman's ancestral homeland, or an attempt to emphasise the martial abilities of the Norman *gens* by highlighting the achievements of the most prominent Norman to join the crusade. This mythology flourished in England, not Normandy where Curthose had ruled, and it clearly had an impact; after the First Crusade, the Norman aristocracy of Normandy played little part in the crusades, yet in England interest in crusading steadily grew alongside the interest in the First Crusade shown in written and visual works. William of Malmesbury (*c.* 1090–1142) devoted a large section of his work to the activities of the Normans on the First Crusade, and even stated that Robert Curthose had been offered the crown of Jerusalem.[73]

---

[70] N. Hooper, 'Edgar the Aetheling: Anglo-Saxon Prince, Rebel and Crusader', *Anglo-Saxon England* 14 (1985), 206–10; *The Anglo-Saxon Chronicles*, trans. and ed. Michael Swanton (London, 2001), pp. 201–3; Hurlock, *Britain, Ireland and the Crusades*, p. 67; William of Malmesbury, *Gesta Regum Anglorum*, ed. and trans. Mynors *et al.*, i, p. 467. Other crusaders (or possibly pilgrims) of Anglo-Saxon descent who joined the crusades but were not dispossessed include Godric of Finchale and Robert, son of Godwin of Winchester, who was martyred in Cairo in 1102 after his capture at the siege of Ramlah. Reginald of Durham, *Libellus de vita et miraculis S Godrici, hermitae de Finchale* (London, 1847), pp. 33–4, 53–8. For the argument that Godric was a pilgrim rather than a crusader, see William J. Purkis, *Crusading Spirituality in the Holy Land and Iberia, c. 1095–1187* (Woodbridge, 2008), p. 63.

[71] OV, v, p. 270.

[72] For examples of crusading letters from across Europe, see *Letters from the East: Crusaders, Pilgrims and Settlers in the 12th–13th Centuries*, trans. Malcolm Barber and Keith Bate (Aldershot, 2010).

[73] Rodney M. Thomson, *William of Malmesbury* (Woodbridge, 2003), esp. ch. 10, 'William as Historian of the Crusade', pp. 178–88; Aird, *Robert Curthose*, p. 186; *Gesta Regum Anglorum*, i, pp. 702–3. Roger of Wendover (d. 1236) repeated and embellished the story in the early thirteenth century: *Matthaei Parisiensis Monachi Sancti Albani, Historia Anglorum*, ed. F. Madden, 3 vols (London, 1866–69), i, pp. 149–50, 205.

Towards the end of the twelfth century, the events of the crusade were recorded in the works of Ralph of Coggeshall, Ralph of Diceto, William of Newburgh and Roger of Howden, influenced no doubt by the number of knights, nobles and other men who took part and, in Roger of Howden's case, by his own involvement. Twelfth-century writers often emphasised the role of Robert Curthose as crusade leader and, in the case of William of Newburgh, Robert was the only crusader identified by name.[74] It was clearly the activities of England's Norman connections, rather than the crusade as a whole, which caught their imagination. Although many of these works were produced by monastic or clerical writers, information on the crusades appeared in secular writing too and was clearly performed and discussed at the royal and other courts in England. The Anglo-Norman writer Walter Map, for example, included crusade-inspired tales in his *De nugis curialium* (*Courtier's Trifles*), written for the entertainment of the Anglo-Norman court.[75] Interest in the First Crusade and Curthose's role continued into the thirteenth century, when it is likely that wall paintings commissioned by Henry III depicted the heroic (though perhaps legendary) actions of the duke on the First Crusade.[76]

So, what impact did the Normans have on participation from England and Wales? And was it unique in any way? In terms of unique influences, it seems that the Norman influence in England and Wales was much the same as the influence of nobles and lords elsewhere in Europe; what was perhaps different was the impact of recent conquest on groups like the Anglo-Saxons, who were dispossessed, and the Welsh, who may have stayed at home in order to defend their lands and thus resisted attempts at recruitment. Overall, despite the reputation of the Normans as leaders of the crusades – particularly at the time of the First Crusade – their influence on potential participants from England and Wales was rather limited; in reality, those Normans who joined the crusade who had ties with England and Wales in the 1090s did so because those ties were threatened and escape overseas was expedient. There appears to have been little common interest between the Normans who travelled under Robert Curthose and those in England for only thirty years, suggesting that the idea of the Normans as a united race on crusade did not hold sway at all. Throughout the twelfth century, domestic warfare during Stephen's reign, and against the Welsh

---

[74] William of Newburgh, *The History of English Affairs*, ed. and trans. P. G. Walsh and M. J. Kennedy (Westminster, 1986), pp. 44–45.

[75] Walter Map, *De nugis curialium: Courtier's Trifles*, ed. and trans. M. R. James (Oxford, 1983), pp. 41–3.

[76] S. Lloyd, *English Society and the Crusade, 1216–1307* (Oxford, 1988), pp. 199–200.

and Scots stopped many potential crusaders from travelling from England and Wales. The arrival of the Normans in England in 1066 and their continued determination to fight one another and enemies on their borders meant that their presence was probably more of a hindrance when a help in terms of crusade recruitment. The lack of leadership meant there was no concerted effort to recruit fighters until 1188. Until this time, instead of positively promoting the earlier crusades, the crown actively inhibited crusade activity, denying individuals permission to travel, failing to engage in crusade promotion or overseeing domestically turbulent politics that made absence inadvisable. What the Normans did give to England and Wales was a legacy of participation and interest in the crusades that influenced participation in the thirteenth century, suggesting that the Norman influence on crusading was strongest once the Norman period in England and Wales had effectively come to an end. In the thirteenth century, family traditions were continued by many families with Norman roots, and the crusade of Richard I became a popular motif in floor tiles in abbeys across England and Wales, and was chosen by Henry III as the theme to decorate rooms in royal palaces.[77]

---

[77] Hurlock, *Britain, Ireland and the Crusades*, pp. 87, 121; Lloyd, *English Society* pp. 199–200; Roger Sherman Loomis, 'Illustrations of Medieval Romance on Tiles from Chertsey Abbey', *University of Illinois Studies in Language and Literature* 2 (1916), 20–27, 84–5.

5

The Secular Clergy of Normandy and the Crusades[1]

DAVID S. SPEAR

The goal of this chapter is to add to current crusading scholarship focusing on regional studies.[2] Work has appeared previously on the Normans and the crusades.[3] In fact, the story of the central role of the Normans and the crusades extends back at least a century to that great researcher and populariser Charles Homer Haskins, and continues right up to the present with the recent study of John France on precisely this topic.[4] However, far fewer studies have dealt with Normandy itself (as opposed to Anglo-Normans and Italo-Normans),[5] and no one, to my knowledge, has examined exclusively the role played by the Norman clergy. Thus one of the angles here is to further evaluate France's assertion that 'Normandy ceased to have any distinctive crusading role after the First Crusade'.[6] Such a discussion leads necessarily to the issue of Norman identity that I hope also to touch upon.

A few words of definition. I have used the inelegant term 'the clergy of Normandy' to avoid the ambiguity inherent in the phrase 'the Norman clergy', which could (and often does) mean 'the Anglo-Norman clergy',[7]

---

[1] In memory of William A. Chaney, d. 15 March. 2013. I thank Richard Allen and Richard Heiser for their substantive comments, and Jim Guth and Kathryn Hurlock for their editorial suggestions.
[2] Christopher Tyerman, *England and the Crusades 1095–1588* (Chicago, 1988); K. Hurlock, *Wales and the Crusades, 1095–1291* (Cardiff, 2011); Kathryn Hurlock, *Britain, Ireland and the Crusades 1000–1300* (Basingstoke, 2013).
[3] David C. Douglas, *The Norman Achievement, 1050–1100* (Berkeley, CA, 1969), and Douglas, *The Norman Fate, 1100–1154* (Berkeley, CA, 1976).
[4] Charles Homer Haskins, *The Normans in European History* (Boston, 1915), esp. pp. 127–31, 208–17; John France, 'The Normans and Crusading', in *The Normans and Their Adversaries at War: Essays in Memory of C. Warren Hollister*, ed. Richard P. Abels and Bernard S. Bachrach (Woodbridge, 2001), pp. 87–101.
[5] On the Normans see Charles W. David, *Robert Curthose, Duke of Normandy* (Cambridge, MA, 1920), chapter 4 and appendices C, D and E. On the Anglo-Normans see Tyerman, *England and the Crusades*. On the Normans in Sicily and South Italy, see G. A. Loud, *The Age of Robert Guiscard: Southern Italy and the Norman Conquest* (Harlow, 2000).
[6] France, 'The Normans and Crusading', p. 87.
[7] Tyerman, *England and the Crusades*, p. 15, makes this point from the English side of the Channel: 'Any narrow definition of the term "English", however, even in the sense of being "from England"

and, too, to indicate that the focus is on the secular – in this case cathedral – clergy, as opposed to the regular – monastic – clergy. In general, monks were discouraged from going on armed crusades, and examining what transpired at Norman monasteries, as the religious prayed about the Holy Land, would take this essay in a very different direction. Further, I intend to concentrate on the duchy of Normandy, which for ecclesiastical purposes corresponds very closely to the borders of the archdiocese of Rouen. Even so, it has proven difficult to avoid bleeding into neighboring regions such as England, the Perche or the Ile-de-France.

Norman clergy were present at the very inception of the First Crusade, for Bishops Odo of Bayeux, Gilbert of Evreux, and Serlo of Sées attended the Council of Clermont in 1095.[8] As regards the First Crusade (1096–99) itself, the main Norman protagonist is, of course, Duke Robert Curthose, who made many contributions to its success.[9] He seldom alienated his fellow crusaders; he fought at the Battle of Dorylaeum; he participated at the siege of Antioch; he helped to storm Jerusalem; and he won at the Battle of Ascalon. Along the way, he had amicable meetings with the pope and with the Byzantine emperor. His bravery was universally acknowledged. While he eschewed any formal political position in the Holy Land, it is clear that he had significant influence over development of the ecclesiastical make-up of the crusader kingdoms. Robert had close association with several clerics. At the start of the crusade, he was accompanied by his uncle, Odo, bishop of Bayeux, along with Gilbert, bishop of Evreux. His chaplain, Arnulf of Chocques, became the patriarch of Jerusalem and another of his possible chaplains, Robert of Rouen, became the bishop of Lydda.

Of Robert's clerical associates, Arnulf of Chocques in particular has been underappreciated.[10] He was not without flaws: he had a flamboyant personality that sometimes grated, and he kept mistresses. Some contemporary chroniclers – especially those from the south of France – were put off by Arnulf, and William of Tyre actively despised him. These negative aspects have often influenced modern assessments. Nevertheless, that Arnulf was well educated and an effective preacher was conceded even

---

distorts the nature of the cross-Channel Anglo-Norman aristocracy, especially at the highest levels.'

[8] OV, v, p. 18.

[9] David, *Robert Curthose*; Aird, *Robert Curthose*.

[10] On Arnulf see David, *Robert Curthose*, pp. 217–20; and Raymonde Foreville, 'Un chef de la Première Croisade: Arnoul Malecouronne', *Bulletin philologique et historique du comité des travaux historiques et scientifiques* (1953–54), 377–90. Arnulf was significant enough that he is mentioned by virtually all of the chroniclers of the First Crusade. These references are listed in Jonathan Riley-Smith, *The First Crusade and the Idea of Crusading* (London, 1993), p. 186, n. 168, and Alan V. Murray, *The Crusader Kingdom of Jerusalem: A Dynastic History, 1099–1125* (Oxford, 2000), pp. 182–3.

by his enemies. Moreover, he was battle tested, having marched with the crusaders throughout their arduous journey, at times encouraging the troops from quite near the battlefield with both prayers and relics. He had sub-legatine powers on the crusade itself, and had received the deathbed blessing of Adhemar of Le Puy, the primary papal legate on the expedition.

More to the point, Arnulf's eighteen years in Jerusalem, attached in one way or another to the church of the Holy Sepulchre, almost by definition made a large impact. He was patriarch-elect briefly in 1099, then patriarch proper from 1112 to 1118. During the intervening years, from 1100 until 1112, he was certainly the *force majeure* behind the scenes, as archdeacon and chancellor of the church of Jerusalem, at the same time serving King Baldwin as advisor and sometime chancery official. Thus, Arnulf remained well connected and involved in administrative matters for both church and state. At the church of the Holy Sepulchre, he established twenty Latin canons, which necessitated finding incomes for these clergy.[11] He eventually instituted the Augustinian rule for the clergy there. As noted by Bernard Hamilton, among his accomplishments as patriarch,

> he freed the Hospital of Saint John from the payment of tithe in his diocese; he had a devotion to the Blessed Virgin and gave benefactions to the community of Josaphat to enable them to rebuild their church which was the chief Marian shrine in the patriarchate; and ... made financial arrangements for [his canons'] support which were honoured throughout the years of the first kingdom.[12]

Like any good bishop, he worked at building up a relic collection: he discovered the long-lost True Cross and received a battle standard procured at great cost by Duke Robert Curthose for the church of the Holy Sepulchre. He had a strong sense of ritual and worship, leading processions and commissioning new bells for that church and, as we now know, establishing the Latin liturgy there. Liturgical books that had been in the possession of Bishops Odo of Bayeux and Gilbert of Evreux were handed over to Arnulf

---

[11] Eugène de Rozière, ed., *Cartulaire de l'église du Saint Sépulcre de Jérusalem* (Paris, 1849), nos. 25, 29. On the incomes see Bernard Hamilton, *The Latin Church in the Crusader States: The Secular Church* (London, 1980), pp. 150–1. On the thorny issue of how the Greek clergy were treated at the church of the Holy Sepulchre, see Jonathan Riley-Smith, 'The Latin Clergy and the Settlement in Palestine and Syria, 1098–1100', *Catholic Historical Review* 74 (1988), 539–57, esp. 551–4. For Arnulf as Baldwin's *scrinarius*, see AA, pp. 454–5, n. 64.

[12] Hamilton, *The Latin Church in the Crusader States*, p. 62, and cf. p. 94.

in Palermo in 1096 and he seems to have kept them in his custody during the crusade, and then brought them into use in Jerusalem.[13]

Arnulf's successes were due to his own talents, but what got him the job was his close association with Duke Robert of Normandy.[14] Although Arnulf was from the village of Chocques in Flanders, he had become by most measures a Norman cleric. Arnulf was no mere acquaintance of the duke; rather, he was Robert's chaplain and his notary before the crusade. They travelled together throughout the expedition to the Holy Land, and it was almost certainly Curthose's backing that secured Arnulf's nomination as patriarch. We know, too, that Arnulf taught at Caen, and was the long-time tutor of Curthose's sister, Cecilia, a nun at Holy Trinity.[15] Arnulf was the teacher of Ralph of Caen who went on to write the *Gesta Tancredi*, and who himself journeyed to the Holy Land. At Caen, Arnulf would likely have encountered William Bona Anima who was abbot of Saint Stephen (1070 to 1079).[16] Bona Anima was the son of Radbod, bishop of Sées, and kinsman of William, bishop of Evreux. He had previously been an archdeacon of Rouen, but had become a monk at Bec, then at Saint Stephen where he had been instructor of the novitiates. It is possible that Arnulf taught at the monastery's external school. His presence at Caen also allowed for ongoing contact with Odo of Bayeux (Bayeux being but seventeen miles from Caen). All of this demonstrates that Arnulf was a cleric of long-standing in the duchy, well connected, and familiar with the church–state relations there.

Arnulf would have found other things at Caen as well, especially a welcoming environment for sons of priests. William Bona Anima, Theobald of Étampes and Serlo, the canon of nearby Bayeux, were all sons of priests. Arnulf would also have seen the monastery of Saint Stephen put together a large endowment, much of it in Caen itself, perhaps providing a model

---

[13] Christina Dondi, *The Liturgy of the Canons Regular of the Holy Sepulchre of Jerusalem: A Study and a Catalogue of the Manuscript Sources* (Turnhout, 2004), pp. 47–57; *The Deeds of God through the Franks: A Translation of Guibert of Nogent's* Gesta Dei per Francos, trans. Robert Levine (Woodbridge, 1997), p. 136.

[14] Guibert of Nogent claimed that Duke Robert promised Arnulf a bishopric, which promise was fulfilled in spades at Jerusalem: *ibid.*, p. 135.

[15] For the educational milieu at Caen see David S. Spear, 'The School of Caen Revisited', *Haskins Society Journal* 4 (1992), 55–66 wherein for 'Arnulf of Rohes' read 'Arnulf of Chocques' (David, *Robert Curthose*, pp. 217–18 notes that 'Rohes' is an incorrect rendering of 'Chocques'). Raymonde Foreville, 'L'École de Caen au XIe siècle et les origines normandes de l'Université d'Oxford', *Études médiévales offertes à M. le Doyen Augustin Fliche* (1952), 81–100, alleges that Arnulf was a student as well as a teacher at Caen, but I have been unable to verify this assertion.

[16] Véronique Gazeau, *Normannia Monastica*, 2 vols. (Turnhout, 2007), i, p. 171; ii, pp. 41–3; David S. Spear, 'William Bona Anima, Abbot of St. Stephen's of Caen, 1070–79', *Haskins Society Journal* 1 (1989), pp. 51–60.

THE SECULAR CLERGY OF NORMANDY AND THE CRUSADES

for his later efforts for the church of the Holy Sepulchre in Jerusalem. From Bishop Odo he would have learned the realities of sustaining a church with many canons to provide for (Bayeux had thirty canons). More importantly for his experience in the Holy Land, Arnulf knew the importance of a *regnum* run by a duke or a king who could freely elect his own bishops and abbots, was willing to endow monasteries and cathedrals, and expected to work in tandem with his bishops. This was the perspective that Arnulf embodied in Jerusalem. It is not coincidental that he easily gravitated to King Baldwin's inner circle, and was able to work better with him than were any of the other patriarchs.[17]

Another Norman cleric in Curthose's entourage – probably another of his chaplains – was Robert of Rouen.[18] As the crusaders approached Jerusalem, they appointed Robert as the bishop of Lydda in June 1099, only the second Latin cleric to be given a bishopric in the Holy Land, and the first in Palestine. His choice was largely due to Curthose's influence. The shrine of Saint George at Lydda was to be the new cathedral and, as Ramla was quite close to Lydda, Robert was given both cities and the surrounding territory. The whole ensemble was conceived of as an ecclesiastical lordship because its military role was crucial to holding southern Palestine, and Robert's episcopal responsibilities included the defence of his diocese. He died *c.* 1110.

Norman clergy were clearly an important part of Robert's crusade entourage, but they may also have played an important role in his decision to take up the Cross. I agree with William Aird that 'Robert's reasons for vowing to make the journey to Jerusalem were more complex than those described by Orderic. It was not simply a case of the duke trying to escape from difficulties at home.' Aird calls attention to the probable influence of the example of his grandfather and namesake, Duke Robert I, who died on a pilgrimage to the Holy Land in 1035. He also suggests a role for several Norman bishops, especially William Bona Anima, archbishop of Rouen.[19] I would like to spin Aird's thread out a bit longer.

The figure of William Bona Anima is important, not only because of his connection to the milieu at Caen, but also because, as archbishop of Rouen

---

[17] John Gordon Rowe, 'Paschal II and the Relation between the Spiritual and Temporal Powers in the Kingdom of Jerusalem', *Speculum* 32 (1957), 470–501, esp. 497–500.

[18] Hamilton, *The Latin Church*, pp. 11–12, 58, 129, 137; Riley-Smith, *The First Crusade* pp. 79–80, and p. 186, n. 155 for references; and idem, 'The Latin Clergy', p. 548; Murray, *The Crusader Kingdom of Jerusalem*, pp. 64, 226–7; Hans Eberhard Mayer, 'The Origins of the Lordships of Ramla and Lydda in the Latin Kingdom of Jerusalem', *Speculum* 60 (1985), 537–52.

[19] Aird, *Robert Curthose*, pp. 157–8.

from 1079, he had continued contact with Robert Curthose (as well as with Arnulf of Chocques and possibly with Robert of Rouen).[20] Bona Anima was in close association with Curthose over several years, probably acting as an *ex officio* advisor.[21] Bona Anima had taken a pilgrimage to the Holy Land in 1057, and it would not be a stretch to imagine him speaking to Duke Robert about the experience.[22] Perhaps he was one of the 'certain men of religion' who encouraged Robert to take up the Cross.[23] Bona Anima was related to the Fleitel family.[24] It is not often remembered that Gerard Fleitel had accompanied Duke Robert I on his pilgrimage to Jerusalem.[25] Gerard survived the experience and retired to the monastery of Saint-Wandrille upon his return.[26] Thus, Bona Anima himself was upholding a family tradition of pilgrimage to the Holy Land. The Fleitels in turn were closely connected to the Gournay family.[27] William Bona Anima gave the veil to Basilia (wife of Hugh) Gournay, to her niece, Amfrida, and to Eva (wife of William) Crispin when the three women became nuns, living a life of seclusion near Bec.[28] It is interesting therefore that Hugh and Basilia's son, Hugh II (as well as his wife Edith) participated in the First Crusade.[29] It is once again possible that Bona Anima was the catalyst.

Another Norman crusader known to Bona Anima was Stephen of Aumale.[30] He and the Gournays (and others) had rebelled against Robert Curthose in the early 1090s.[31] One wonders if the crusade can be seen, at least in part, as the physical embodiment of reconciliation between Robert and his enemies. If so, it is something that Bona Anima may have helped to broker. He was present for the accord drawn up on behalf of Duke Robert

---

[20] Rouen MS. Y 44 (1193), no. 42 (Cartulary of the See of Rouen); Charles Homer Haskins, *Norman Institutions* (New York, 1925), p. 70, no. 31, where Arnulf appears as the chancellor of Duke Robert in a document also attested by Archbishop William.

[21] Curthose was at the dedication of Saint Stephen's abbey in 1077 when William Bona Anima was abbot there (David, *Robert Curthose*, p. 16). In August 1095 Duke Robert made a grant to Rouen cathedral which William attested (Rouen MS. Y 44 (1193), no. 42).

[22] OV, ii, p. 68. Gundulf, a cleric at Rouen cathedral and later bishop of Rochester, also went on this pilgrimage. Rodney Thomson, ed., *The Life of Gundulf Bishop of Rochester* (Toronto, 1977), p. 27.

[23] OV, v, p. 26.

[24] *Ibid.*, ii, p. 254.

[25] Elisabeth M. C. van Houts, ed. and trans., *The Gesta Normannorum Ducum of William of Jumièges, Orderic Vitalis, and Robert of Torigni*, 2 vols (Oxford, 1992–95), ii, p. 116, n. 1.

[26] OV, iii, p. 84; Marie Fauroux, ed., *Recueil des actes des ducs de Normandie de 911 à 1066* (Caen, 1961), nos. 30, 108.

[27] Daniel Gurney, *The Record of the House of Gournay* (London, 1848), pp. 54–5.

[28] *Ibid.*, pp. 52–3.

[29] David, *Robert Curthose*, pp. 222–3.

[30] *Ibid.*, p. 228.

[31] *Ibid.*, p. 58; Aird, *Robert Curthose*, p. 138.

between Stephen Aumale and the monastery of Saint Lucien of Beauvais on 14 July 1096,[32] and was on friendly terms with all the parties involved.

One final, admittedly remote, connection between William Bona Anima, Robert Curthose and the First Crusade is the cult of the protomartyr Saint Stephen. I have mentioned that William was the second abbot of Saint Stephen's monastery in Caen. His kinsman, Gerard Fleitel, had procured several relics of Saint Stephen when he was in Jerusalem in 1035, which he gave to the monastery of Saint Wandrille when he retired there.[33] Was it merely a coincidence that when Jerusalem was surrounded by the crusaders Robert Curthose ended up at Saint Stephen's Gate, doubtless encamping around the church or shrine of Saint Stephen, located about one-quarter mile north of the city walls?[34]

It is evident that William Bona Anima remained cognisant of the Holy Land, because in 1106 he sent a parishioner on a pilgrimage to Jerusalem as penance for having alienated some of Rouen cathedral's lands in the Vexin.[35] In addition, in that same year the crusader Bohemond visited Rouen where a member of his entourage gave to Archbishop William some hairs from the Virgin Mary, relics had been in the custody of the patriarch of Antioch.[36]

Which Norman clergy were actually *crucesignati* in 1096? If we set Robert of Rouen aside because so little is known of him, we are left with Arnulf of Chocques, Odo, bishop of Bayeux, and Gilbert, bishop of Evreux. Are there attributes that unite all three figures? Aside from Robert Curthose, someone who knew all three was William Bona Anima. Not much is known about Gilbert, but he had consecrated William as archbishop of Rouen.[37] Gilbert was called 'Gilbert, son of Osbern'. If he was related to William, son of Osbern – this is merely supposition – he would have been in the family of close supporters of William the Conqueror, and thus, like Odo, closely linked to the Conqueror. Even Arnulf was so connected, albeit loosely, as the long-time tutor of the Conqueror's daughter. A letter of Bishop Gilbert survives denouncing a royal *dapifer* for having unlawfully imprisoned one

---

[32] P. Piolin, ed., *Gallia Christiana* (Paris, 1874), xi, Instrumenta, cols. 19–20.

[33] Lucien Musset, *Les actes de Guillaume le Conquérant et de la Reine Mathilde pour les abbayes caennaises* (Caen, 1967), p. 17.

[34] AA, p. 404; OV, v, p. 156. In the twelfth century, Saint Stephen's gate was on the north side of the city. Through a name change over the centuries, today it is on the east side. Adrian J. Boas, *Jerusalem in the Time of the Crusades* (London, 2001), p. 53.

[35] Archives de la Seine-Maritime G 8740.

[36] Eadmer, *Historia Novorum in Anglia*, ed. Martin Rule (London, 1884), pp. 179–81; OV, v, p. 170.

[37] *Ibid.*, iii, p. 22.

of Gilbert's parishioners who had set out on a pilgrimage to Vézelay.[38] The incident shows that, at the very least, Gilbert was sympathetic to the rules governing pilgrimage. Both Gilbert and Odo had attended the Council of Clermont in 1095 and the Council of Rouen in 1096.[39] Odo's career, on the other hand, is well known.[40] Half-brother to the Conqueror, he was present at the Battle of Hastings. As bishop of Bayeux, he was a builder and patron on a grand scale and was accused of having designs on the papacy itself when he left on crusade. Aside from the material wealth he left, his legacy to Arnulf of Chocques, a mere chaplain who became a patriarch, may have been the motto, 'Live large'. Of course, Odo died in Palermo in 1097 but Gilbert returned to Normandy, as he was present at the dedication of Saint Evroul in 1099.[41]

Thus, the two clergymen who represented Normandy on the entirety of the First Crusade were Arnulf of Chocques and Robert of Rouen. Jonathan Riley-Smith's observation – 'that the ecclesiastics on the crusade were not the cream of the contemporary Church, being made up, by and large, of the magnates' house priests' – rings true.[42] Still, it is worth considering whom the cream might have been, and how they would have reacted to unpredictable and volatile circumstances in the Holy Land. If one thinks of bishops like Daimbert, the archbishop of Pisa, who came as a papal legate in the aftermath of the siege of Jerusalem, then I am not sure they were any more effective than the clergy who had marched their way there. Given the frontier conditions prevailing in the Levant, men with a different set of talents were required, namely, clerics who could work closely with their rulers. These were men of action more than of theology, men who knew through bitter experience the lay of the land; in short, clergy such as Arnulf of Chocques and Robert of Rouen. Those in the mould of Odo of Bayeux would have flourished more happily than those like, say, Anselm of Canterbury or, manifestly, Daimbert of Pisa.[43] Arnulf of Chocques may have

---

[38] Gilbert's letter is embedded in one of Hugh, archbishop of Lyon, to Ivo of Chartres (J.-P. Migne, ed., *Patrologia Latina* (Paris, 1834), clvii, p. 520). On this see Richard Allen, 'The Norman Episcopate, 989–1110', unpublished PhD thesis (University of Glasgow, 2009), pp. 235–6.

[39] OV, v, pp. 18–20 where it is stated explicitly that they attended Clermont and implied that they attended Rouen.

[40] David Bates, 'The Character and Career of Odo, Bishop of Bayeux', *Speculum* 50 (1975), 1–20.

[41] OV, v, p. 264.

[42] Riley-Smith, *The First Crusade*, p. 80.

[43] 'Dai[m]bert's loyalty to the principles of reform underlay his successes in Pisa as well as his uneven conflict with Baldwin I of Jerusalem and his ultimate failure in the hostile environment of the Holy Land': Michael Matzke, *The Crusades: An Encyclopedia*, ed. Alan V. Murray, 4 vols. (Santa Barbara, 2006), ii, p. 340.

been contumacious, but what counted was that he knew his way around a battlefield.

What happened when the First Crusade ended? Robert Curthose returned to Normandy, as did other warrior-pilgrims. A knight named Odard, who went to Jerusalem in 1098, perhaps not even as a part of the official crusade, came home and donated lands to the monastery of Jumièges in repayment for his safe return.[44] Another Norman knight, Adjutor, from the town of Vernon in the Vexin, returned from the crusade around 1115. In a battle outside Antioch, he had been saved through his prayers to Mary Magdalene. He stayed in the Holy Land another seventeen years until he was miraculously transported home from a Saracen prison. He entered the Percheron monastery of Tiron that had close connections to the duchy.[45] Miracles continued as Adjutor followed a hermitic life under the aegis of Bernard the founder of Tiron. Adjutor died on 30 April 1131. It was Hugh, archbishop of Rouen (1130–64), who wrote the *vita* of the former crusader. And Ralph of Caen, a former student of Arnulf's, went to the Holy Land, serving 'in the entourages of Bohemund I of Antioch (1107) and Tancred (1108)',[46] writing the *Gesta Tancredi* sometime between 1112 and 1118.[47]

Ralph of Domfront, a knight from Normandy's southern perimeter who took clerical orders, had become archbishop of Mamistra in Cilicia.[48] When the previous patriarch of Antioch died in 1135, Ralph vaulted up the ecclesiastical hierarchy by becoming the new patriarch. Although elected 'by the vote of the people',[49] Ralph's enthronement was resented by other bishops, thwarted by certain members of his cathedral chapter, opposed by the count of Antioch, and eventually investigated by the papacy. All this made for an embattled tenure. He seems to have had a clear conception of Antioch as a patriarchate, arguing that since Saint Peter visited there before

---

[44] Riley-Smith, *The First Crusade* p. 21; *Chartes de l'Abbaye de Jumièges*, ed. J. J. Vernier, 2 vols (Rouen, 1916), i, pp. 121–3. Riley-Smith, *The First Crusade* p. 121, notes that after their crusading experience Richard fitz Fulk and a certain Gilbert became monks at the Norman monasteries of Bec and Saint-Ouen of Rouen, respectively.

[45] David Knowles, *The Monastic Order in England*, 2nd edn (Cambridge, 1966), p. 202, observes that although Tiron was founded a decade after Citeaux, 'it attracted attention in Normandy and England sooner than Citeaux'. Adjutor's life can be found in 'Vita Sancti Adjutoris', *Patrologia Latina*, ed. J.-P. Migne (Paris, 1855), cxcii, cols. 1345–52. See also Claire Biquard, 'Saint Adjutor, sa vie et son culte (XII–XX siècle)', *Cahiers Léopold Delisle* 45, fasc. 3–4 (1996), 1–30; *Bibliotheca hagiographica latina antiquae et mediae aetatis* (Brussels, 1898), no. 81. p. 15.

[46] Peter Orth, 'Radulf of Caen', in *The Crusades: An Encyclopedia*, iv, p. 1001; *GT*, Bachrach, pp. 1–15.

[47] Hodgson, 'Reinventing Normans', pp. 117–32, at page 117 for the dates.

[48] William of Tyre, *A History of the Deeds Done beyond the Sea*, trans. E. A. Babcock and A. C. Krey, 2 vols (New York, 1943), has a long section on Ralph, esp. ii, pp. 113–23. See also Bernard Hamilton, 'Ralph of Domfront, Patriarch of Antioch (1135–40)', *Nottingham Medieval Studies* 28 (1984), 1–21.

[49] William of Tyre, *A History of the Deeds*, ii, p. 60.

coming to Rome, the patriarch was in no way subordinate to the papacy. He made two trips to Rome to defend himself from accusations that his election was uncanonical, and that he was guilty of simony and fornication.[50] He attended the Lateran Council of 1139, 'the first such office-holder from the Latin East to attend at any of the great Church assemblies of the twelfth century'.[51] He had some ecclesiastical tact, respecting Orthodox traditions when he established new sees, and in general followed the examples set by his predecessor.[52] He was removed from his position in 1140, and died in unfortunate circumstances around 1146. William of Tyre adds the human dimension:

> This same Lord Ralph, whom I saw in my youth, was a tall and handsome man, slightly cross-eyed, but not to such an extent that he was uncomely. Although but little learned, he was a very fluent speaker, graceful and agreeable in conversation. His generous disposition had won him much favor, not only with the knights but also with the common people. He was, however, very forgetful of his promises and agreements. Changeable and inconstant in his words, subtle and devious in all his ways, he was yet provident and discreet. In one respect alone he showed some lack of wisdom, in that he refused to receive adversaries whom he had justly roused against him, when they wished to return favor with him. He was called arrogant (and so indeed he was) and presumptuous beyond measure.[53]

He was a decisive figure, perhaps, and one capable of administrative competence, but without a hint of the spiritual.

The Second Crusade (1147–49), while led by King Louis VII of France and King Conrad III of Germany, again, had a strong Norman clerical flavour in the person of Arnulf, bishop of Lisieux.[54] Like Arnulf of Chocques, he was controversial, a good orator and a sub-legate on the crusade.[55]

---

[50] Bernard Hamilton, 'Ralph of Domfront', in *The Crusades: An Encyclopedia*, iv, p. 1003.

[51] Rudolf Hiestand, 'The Papacy and the Second Crusade', in *The Second Crusade: Scope and Consequences*, ed. J. Phillips and M. Hoch (Manchester, 2001), p. 34.

[52] Hamilton, *The Latin Church*, pp. 30–8, esp. 37.

[53] William of Tyre, *A History of the Deeds*, ii, p. 121. Hans Eberhard Mayer has tentatively proposed that Anschetinus, first a cantor at Bethlehem, and then *c*. 1108 its bishop, was a Norman. He bases his supposition on the name, which appears at least once in a Norman version as Ansquitillus: 'Angevins *versus* Normans: The New Men of King Fulk of Jerusalem', *American Philosophical Society* 133 (1989), 1–25, at p. 21. This is interesting but tenuous; even if a Norman, he may not have come from the duchy, but perhaps from south Italy.

[54] For the crusade in general see Jonathan Phillips, *The Second Crusade: Extending the Frontiers of Christendom* (New Haven, CT, 2007). On Arnulf of Lisieux see Frank Barlow, *The Letters of Arnulf of Lisieux* (London, 1939); Carolyn Poling Schriber, *The Dilemma of Arnulf of Lisieux: New Ideas versus Old Ideals* (Bloomington, IN, 1990).

[55] Hiestand, 'The Papacy and the Second Crusade', p. 38.

Indeed, he was one of the three main clerics serving the Frankish army.[56] Arnulf of Lisieux definitely had a position of responsibility on the crusade: he was in charge of leading the English and Norman contingent to the Rhine.[57] On the march to Antioch, Arnulf was given the unenviable task of trying to placate the Byzantine emperor in the aftermath of a scuffle between the Greeks and Western crusaders.[58] We know, too, that in the debates about whether or not to attack Constantinople, his view that the Byzantines should be left alone finally prevailed.[59] In addition, he attended the council of elites held on 24 June 1148 at Palmarea, near Acre, where it was decided to attack Damascus, a flawed decision that Arnulf had apparently opposed. Disappointed by the choice, he returned to the West. That Arnulf was among the circle of elites is confirmed by the fact that he loaned money to King Louis to continue the crusade, which payment was collected upon Arnulf's return.[60]

What animated Arnulf of Lisieux, especially before his departure on the crusade? Or, put another way, why of all the Norman bishops was it Arnulf who actually took up the Cross? For one thing, although Arnulf was by ancestry a Norman, he was pulled early and often into the French orbit. In the words of Frank Barlow: 'Certainly Arnulf, as a churchman, had many more ties with France than with England.'[61] Coming as he did originally from Sées, he was close to the French border and he had been a protégé of the bishop of Chartres.[62] He had studied at the University of Paris and throughout his life was drawn towards the monastic experience – not so much the Benedictine as the Augustinian and the Cistercian. Indeed, he had watched his brother establish Augustinian canons at Sées cathedral. He had hoped during a mid-life crisis to retire to the Cistercian abbey of Mortemer in Normandy and at the end of his life, he actually retired to Saint Victor in Paris. Probably of the greatest importance was his early acquaintance with Bernard of Clairvaux. Bernard had admired a treatise

---

[56] Phillips, *The Second Crusade*, p. 273. Guido of Saint Grisogono was the official legate to Louis' forces, but his overly mild personality allowed for a rivalry to occur between Bishops Arnulf of Lisieux and Geoffrey of Langres. See John of Salisbury (who despised Arnulf) on this rivalry. *Historia pontificalis*, trans. Marjorie Chibnall (Lonodn, 1956), pp. 52–9.

[57] Odo of Deuil, *De profectione Ludovici VII in Orientem*, ed. and trans. Virginia Gingerick Berry (New York, 1948), p. 22.

[58] *Ibid.*, pp. 74–6.

[59] *Ibid.*, p. 70, and n. 23.

[60] Schriber, *Arnulf of Lisieux*, p. 22.

[61] Barlow, *Letters of Arnulf*, p. li.

[62] Lindy Grant, 'Arnulf's Mentor: Geoffrey of Lèves, Bishop of Chartres', in *Writing Medieval Biography, 750–1250: Essays in Honour of Professor Frank Barlow*, ed. David Bates et al. (Woodbridge, 2006), pp. 173–84.

written by Arnulf in 1133, had supported Arnulf's election to Lisieux in 1141, and had joined Arnulf in opposing the episcopal election at Sées in 1144.[63]

Thus, when Arnulf heard Bernard preach the crusade at Vézelay at Easter 1146, he took up the Cross. There may have been other motives. He seems almost certainly to have been reacting to recent disappointments in both political and ecclesiastical arenas in Normandy. In the political world, serious discord with Count Geoffrey of Anjou had fractured his vision of the correct relationship between the *regnum* and *sacerdotium*, namely that the two orders should work in harmony. In the clerical realm, he had to watch as all his family's labours at Sées unravelled. His brother had established Augustinian canons at the cathedral, but now, with the election of Gerard, this plan was undone. As a consequence, Arnulf had recently asked to be allowed to resign his episcopacy and retire to a monastery, but Pope Eugenius denied his request. No doubt, Arnulf was in a receptive frame of mind to leave his diocese and to begin some sort of adventure, partially secular, partially spiritual. Carolyn Schriber may be correct, too, in noting that by going on the Second Crusade, Arnulf could move more closely into the orbit of the king of France: Arnulf was nothing if not ambitious. Late in life, Arnulf claimed that 'the holy father Pope Eugenius sent me against my will,'[64] but this seems to be belated self-justification. At a minimum, though, we may say that Arnulf's participation reflected several motives.[65]

Aside from Arnulf, very few identifiable Normans, clergy or no, went on the Second Crusade. We know that a contingent of Anglo-Normans went by sea, stopping to help King Alfonso of Portugal take Lisbon from the Saracens.[66] In the Levant, 'Drogo II of Mouchy-le-Châtel was the son of Drogo I, who had taken part in the First Crusade. The latter was also the stepfather of Hugh II of Gournay, another Second Crusader; and Hugh's natural father, Gerard, was on the First Crusade, too.'[67] We may add Roger of Clinton, bishop of Coventry, who was possibly born in Normandy in the Cotentin. He took up the Cross in 1147, arriving at Saint Simeon in March 1148, and dying at Antioch in June of that same year. Unfortunately, 'Bishop Roger's motives for becoming a crusader ... are entirely unknown'.[68]

Rotrou, bishop of Evreux (1139–65) and then archbishop of Rouen

---

[63] Barlow, *Letters of Arnulf*, pp. xvi–xviii.
[64] Schriber, *Arnulf of Lisieux*, p. 21.
[65] The material for this paragraph comes from Barlow, *Letters of Arnulf*, esp. pp. xi–xl, and Schriber, *Arnulf of Lisieux*, esp. pp. 1–24.
[66] *DEL*, pp. 55, n.2, 100–8.
[67] Phillips, *The Second Crusade*, p. 100.
[68] M. J. Franklin, 'Clinton, Roger of (d. 1148)', *Oxford Dictionary of National Biography*, Oxford University Press, Oct. 2009 [www.oxforddnb.com/view/article/95152, accessed 2 Nov. 2013]

(1165–83), was related to several crusaders. 'The rulers of the small northern French county of the Perche, the Rotrou family, contributed to all the significant crusading initiatives from 1096 until the beginning of the thirteenth century.'[69] Archbishop Rotrou was the son of Henry, earl of Warwick and Margaret, granddaughter of Rotrou, count of Mortagne (d. 1079), the founding father of the dynasty. Archbishop Rotrou was therefore the brother-in-law of Rotrou II who participated in the First Crusade, and was related more distantly to the dozen or so crusaders from that family. Through his father, Rotrou was a member of the Beaumont family, which also provided crusaders such as Waleran of Meulan, an important figure on the Second Crusade.[70] Rotrou served as caretaker-bishop for Arnulf of Lisieux when Arnulf was on the crusade, and it is in Rotrou's entourage that we first find the cleric Peter of Blois, a courtier of King Henry II.

Henry had taken up the Cross on 21 January 1188.[71] Peter of Blois may have influenced that decision.[72] Most scholars know Peter as a French-born cleric with an English career, which is true, but he was also a personal letter writer for two successive archbishops of Rouen – Rotrou and Walter of Coutances – and held prebends both at Rouen and Bayeux cathedrals. Peter had been at the papal court at Verona in 1187 when the stunning news arrived of the disastrous defeat of the crusaders at Hattin. Moved by what he heard, he immediately wrote to King Henry II, informing him of Hattin and the subsequent loss of Jerusalem. Peter also composed a vigorous defence of Reginald of Chatillon who was killed – martyred in Peter's view – in the aftermath of Hattin. In addition, he wrote a treatise on *The Speeding-up of the Crusade* and encouraged Baldwin, archbishop of Canterbury, to make a preaching tour of Wales to build support for the crusade, an expedition that Peter apparently joined.[73]

Another Norman cleric who may have had an influence on Henry II's

---

[69] Kathleen Thompson, 'Family Tradition and the Crusading Impulse: The Rotrou Counts of the Perche', *Medieval Prosopography* 19 (1998), 1–33, quotation at p. 1.

[70] David Crouch, *The Beaumont Twins: The Roots and Branches of Power in the Twelfth Century* (Cambridge, 1986), pp. 16, 64–8.

[71] See Mayer, 'Henry II of England and the Holy Land', 721–39 for Henry's numerous vows and his financial commitments.

[72] David S. Spear, *The Personnel of the Norman Cathedrals* (London, 2006), pp. 70, 251; John D. Cotts, *The Clerical Dilemma: Peter of Blois and Literate Culture in the Twelfth Century* (Washington, DC, 2009), pp. 218–30; R. W. Southern, *Scholastic Humanism and the Unification of Europe*, vol. 2: *The Heroic Age* (Oxford, 2001), pp. 196–204; R. W. Southern, 'Peter of Blois and the Third Crusade', in *Studies in Medieval History Presented to R. H. C. Davis*, ed. H. Mayr-Harting and R. I. Moore (London, 1985), pp. 207–18; Michael Markowski, 'Peter of Blois and the Conception of the Third Crusade', in *The Horns of Hattin*, ed. Benjamin Z. Kedar (Jerusalem, 1992), pp. 261–69.

[73] See Hurlock, *Wales and the Crusades*, pp. 58–91 for a current account; Cotts, *The Clerical Dilemma*, p. 37 for Peter's participation on the preaching tour.

decision to go on crusade was Wace, canon of Bayeux, who wrote his *Roman de Rou* in part to remind Henry, his patron, about the great deeds of his ancestors, including the crusading feats of Robert Curthose.[74] Whatever the Norman clerical backdrop for the decision of 21 January 1188, we know that the immediate impetus for both Henry II and Philip II of France to take up the Cross was the impassioned pleadings of the archbishop of Tyre.[75] Their joint armed pilgrimage in effect represented a peace treaty between the two kings, especially since they became *crucesignati* at the border between their two territories. Once the planning for the joint crusade began, yet another Norman cleric, Richard Barre, whose career as a *familiaris* of Henry II straddled the Channel (he was simultaneously a canon at Salisbury and archdeacon of Lisieux),[76] was put to work. He was dispatched to parlay with Barbarossa, the king of Hungary, and the Greek emperor to line up supplies and safe passage. The scheme, however, came to nothing, and the crusade itself ended with Henry II's death on 6 July 1189.

The Third Crusade (1189–92), like the First, hinged on secular leadership. Richard the Lionheart was at once king of England and duke of Normandy. Indeed, the Third Crusade could be called 'Richard's Crusade'[77] and several Norman clerics joined him. Peter of Blois himself went with the king as far as Sicily, and then in the retinue of Baldwin, archbishop of Canterbury, to Tyre. When Baldwin died on 20 November 1190, Peter turned back to England. On his return, Peter joined the entourage of Queen Eleanor of Aquitaine, who had just arrived in Sicily. Later Peter wrote letters on Eleanor's behalf, trying to free Richard from the captivity he suffered in Germany upon his return from the crusade.[78]

Walter of Coutances, although born in Cornwall, was of Norman extraction.[79] He held numerous ecclesiastical positions on both sides of the Channel, culminating in the bishopric of Lincoln (1183–84) and the archbishopric of Rouen (1185–1207). He was an important *curialis* of Henry II

---

[74] Spear, *The Personnel of the Norman Cathedrals*, p. 83; Jean Blacker, 'Wace (*b.* after 1100, *d.* 1174 × 83)', *Oxford Dictionary of National Biography*, Oxford University Press, 2004 [www.oxforddnb.com/view/article/28365, accessed 2 Nov, 2013]; N. L. Paul, *To Follow in Their Footsteps: The Crusades and Family Memory in the High Middle Ages* (Ithaca, NY, 2012), pp. 55–6, 180–4, 228–33.

[75] John Gillingham, *Richard I* (New Haven, CT, 1999), p. 88.

[76] Spear, *The Personnel of the Norman Cathedrals*, pp. 176–7.

[77] Gillingham, *Richard I*, 'The Third Crusade was very much [Richard's] crusade'. pp. 113–14.

[78] R. W. Southern, 'Blois, Peter of (1125 × 30–1212)', *Oxford Dictionary of National Biography*, Oxford University Press, 2004 [www.oxforddnb.com/view/article/22012, accessed 2 Nov. 2013]

[79] On Walter see Peter A. Poggioli, 'From Politician to Prelate: The Career of Walter of Coutances, Archbishop of Rouen, 1184–1207', unpublished PhD thesis (Johns Hopkins University, 1984); Ralph V. Turner, 'Coutances, Walter de (*d.* 1207)', *Oxford Dictionary of National Biography*, Oxford University Press, 2004 [www.oxforddnb.com/view/article/6467, accessed 2 Nov. 2013]; Gillingham, *Richard I*, pp. 104, 227–9.

and later of Richard the Lionheart. When Henry II became a *crucesignatus* in 1188, he received the Cross personally from Walter (and the archbishop of Tyre). After the death of Henry II, Archbishop Walter absolved Richard of bad conduct against his father, then consecrated him duke of Normandy.[80] In anticipation of the crusade, in February 1190 Walter held a council at Rouen, which adopted legislation to protect crusaders' property and family while abroad. After committing the ecclesiastical province of Normandy to his nephew, John of Coutances, the dean of Rouen, Walter left Normandy on crusade with Richard. He played an important role on the crusade, serving as treasurer and spiritual caretaker. At Messina Walter was sent by King Richard to make a peace settlement between the locals and the crusaders. While still at Messina, Richard began hearing about unrest in England, so he sent Walter back with Queen Eleanor. (Walter received papal release from his crusading vow.) As justiciar of England, he later found himself in charge of raising the enormous ransom for Richard's release from captivity in Germany. When Richard was freed, Walter himself stayed on as a hostage until the balance of the king's ransom was paid. Indeed, he paid part of Richard's ransom himself, but was never reimbursed.

Another Norman cleric on the Third Crusade was John, son of Luke, bishop of Evreux (1182–92). In Limassol, Cyprus, on the way to the Holy Land, Richard the Lionheart married Berengaria of Navarre. She was crowned there by Bishop John on 12 May 1191.[81] At Acre he, along with other bishops, rebuilt a chapel.[82] We know, too, that he bolstered the strength of the crusade, bringing with him 'good men who were his vassals'.[83] He died at Joppa on 1 June 1192. He had been a long-time cleric of Walter of Coutances, and seal-bearer for King Henry II.[84] He was probably related to the Rouen family of John Luke, and possibly to John, son of Luke, the *chevalier de Richard*, who also participated in the Third Crusade.[85] In addition, John of Alençon, archdeacon of Lisieux, was with King Richard at the launching of the crusade at Vézelay, for he was the king's vice-chancellor. Although he did not take part in the crusade itself, he travelled to the Holy Land in late May 1192 to apprise Richard of political machinations taking

---

[80] Gillingham, *Richard I*, pp. 103–4.
[81] Lionel Landon, *The Itinerary of King Richard I* (London, 1935), p. 49. For the political context of this wedding see Gillingham, *Richard I*, pp. 123–6, and idem, 'Richard I and Berengaria of Navarre', *Bulletin of the Institute of Historical Researc*. 53 (1980), 157–73.
[82] *Gallia Christiana* xi, col. 580.
[83] *Ambroise's Estoire de la Guerre Sainte: The History of the Holy War*, trans. Marianne Ailes (Woodbridge, 2002), p. 96.
[84] Spear, *The Personnel of the Norman Cathedrals*, p. 135; Poggioli, 'Walter of Coutances', pp. 23–5.
[85] J. Horace Round, 'Some English Crusaders of Richard I', *EHR* 18 (1903), 477.

place between Philip Augustus and John Lackland.[86] At about this time, William Burel, bishop of Avranches (1183–96), is associated with a trip to the Holy Land while his cathedral church possessed relics that had been brought back from the East.[87]

Some crusaders may have been related to cathedral clergy in Normandy. If so, we can presume the clergy would have been instructed to pray for the crusaders, and to aid them by sending money or reinforcements. This was certainly the theme of many letters sent to family from the East.[88] We know that Walter of Saint-Valery, archdeacon of Rouen, was the brother of Bernard of Saint-Valery who went on the Third Crusade, and was no doubt related to the Walter of Saint-Valery who went on the First Crusade. Perhaps Ivo of Vieuxpont, the archdeacon of Rouen was related to the crusader of the same name.[89]

Of Rouen canons on crusade, Drogo of Trubleville may have been the most interesting.[90] He was in the train of Walter of Coutances, first at Lincoln, then at Rouen. This may partially explain his participation in the Third Crusade: he was simply following his ecclesiastical lord. We may add into the mix the fact that Drogo was a grand patron of the Norman Cluniac establishment of Longueville and indeed was buried there near the altar of the priory. Cluny had an important role in the calling of the First Crusade, and perhaps that association still had spiritual purchase. If at first Drogo was in the service of his archbishop, he grew in his attachment and devotion to King Richard, for he offered to Rouen cathedral a reliquary with King Richard's name inscribed upon it, and perhaps even his portrait.[91]

There is good evidence that Ambroise, author of the verse chronicle of the Third Crusade, was from the Evrecin. His language was Norman; he displayed a general admiration for the Normans; and he had detailed

---

[86] Spear, *The Personnel of the Norman Cathedrals*, p. 179, citing Landon, *The Itinerary of King Richard I*, pp. 36–7, 64; *Itin. Peregr.*, p. 320.

[87] Richard Allen, 'Les reliques de la cathedrale d'Avranches' *Recueil d'études offert en homage à Emmanuel Poulle, Revue de l'Avranchin et du Pays de Granville* 87 (2010), 501–35, at pp. 515–16. I thank Richard Allen for calling this reference to my attention.

[88] *Letters from the East: Crusaders, Pilgrims and Settlers in the 12th–13th Centuries*, trans. Malcolm Barber and Keith Bate (Aldershot, 2010); for example, letters 3, 7, 12, 13.

[89] Cf. Tyerman, *England and the Crusades*, pp. 66, 69; Spear, *The Personnel of the Norman Cathedrals*, pp. 214–15.

[90] Spear, *The Personnel of the Norman Cathedrals*, pp. 237–8. He was also known as Drogo de Fréville. Two other cathedral clergy are worth mentioning by virtue of their names: William de Sancto Sepulchro was a possible canon at Avranches in 1188, and Ranulf Templarius was a possible canon at Bayeux at about the same time. *Ibid.*, pp. 28, 74.

[91] A. Deville, 'Sur la châsse de Saint-Sever', *Mémoires de la Société des Antiquaires de Normandie* 10 (1836), 340–68. See David S. Spear, 'Les chanoines de la cathedrale de Rouen pendant la periode ducale', *Annales de Normandie* 41 (1991), 152–3 for photos of the reliquary.

THE SECULAR CLERGY OF NORMANDY AND THE CRUSADES

knowledge of crusaders who came from that part of Normandy.[92] Moreover, his most recent editors observe that, 'Both the strong moral purpose which runs through the poem and the level of language employed suggest that Ambroise was a cleric, at least in minor orders, and a man of some education'.[93]

Then, too, there are subsidiary ways in which the Norman clergy interacted with the crusades. Nicholas of L'Aigle – another cross-Channel cleric who was both dean at Chichester and *scholasticus* and later dean at Avranches – was a canonist who discussed two controversies that related to events touching upon the Third Crusade.[94] In the first case, Nicholas decided that King Richard's crusading status protected his properties: even papal legates could not intrude into the affairs of the duchy of Normandy. In the second case, it was found that King Richard was justified as a crusader in attacking the bishop of Beauvais, who had arrested Richard while returning from crusade and had seized his lands.

In contrast to their involvement in earlier crusades, I find no examples of Norman clergy on the Fourth Crusade.[95] The explanation may be quite simple: because the kings of France and England were fighting at precisely this time over possession of the duchy of Normandy, bishops were preoccupied with immediate issues of war, survival and accommodation, and could not be distracted by an expedition to the East.[96]

There was some Norman involvement in the Albigensian Crusade (1209–29). William Burel, bishop of Avranches, was responsible for circulating a letter calling people to join the Albigensian Crusade.[97] Both Robert d'Ablèges, bishop of Bayeux (1206–31), and Jordan du Hommet, bishop of Lisieux (1202–18) were in the south of France in 1211,[98] and Robert Poulain, archbishop of Rouen (1208–21), was there in the spring of 1212.[99]

The Fifth Crusade (1217–21) also witnessed Norman clerical participation.[100] Herbert of Andely, canon of Rouen, was recognised by Innocent

---

[92] *The History of the Holy War*, p. 2; Round, 'Some English Crusaders', 475–81.
[93] *The History of the Holy War*, p. 2.
[94] Spear, *The Personnel of the Norman Cathedrals*, p. 14; James A. Brundage, 'The Crusade of Richard I: Two Canonical *Quaestiones*', *Speculum* 38 (1963), 443–52.
[95] Cf. Jean Longnon, *Les compagnons de Villehardouin: recherches sur les croisés de la Quatrième Croisade* (Paris, 1978).
[96] For a glimpse of the internal concerns see Jörg Peltzer, 'The Angevin Kings and Canon Law: Episcopal Elections and the Loss of Normandy', *ANS* 27 (2004), 169–84.
[97] Avranches, BM, MS. 149, fol. 78v. I thank Richard Allen for calling this reference to my attention.
[98] *The History of the Albigensian Crusade: Peter of les Vaux-de-Cernay's* Historia Albigensis, trans. W. A. and M. D. Silby (Woodbridge, 1998), p. 112.
[99] *Ibid.*, pp. 151, 157–8.
[100] James M. Powell, *Anatomy of a Crusade, 1213–1221* (Philadelphia, 1986), pp. 232, 241. We should note the role played by Gervase, abbot of Prémontré. He preached the Albigensian Crusade. Then in

III as one of the preachers of the crusade.[101] Robert, bishop of Bayeux, and Jordan, bishop of Lisieux, who had taken part in the Albigensian Crusade also went on the Fifth Crusade in 1217.[102] Upon his return, Robert founded a college at Caen dedicated to the Holy Sepulchre whose revenues were to support a prebend for his cathedral church.[103] Given the date of his arrival, in 1218, it is more likely that Jordan, for his part, joined the crusaders in Egypt rather than in the Levant. Jordan du Hommet's family was originally based in the Manche region of Normandy, but had become a duchy-wide power, with recent members serving as constable.[104] Jordan's interest in the crusades doubtless antedates his actual departure for the East, for in 1215 he founded the Norbertine monastery of Mondaye.[105] The Premonstratensians had clear associations with the Holy Land: the Norbertines had several abbeys in Palestine.[106] Moreover, Jordan's ancestor of the same name had taken part in the Third Crusade.[107] He died on crusade.[108]

Drogo II of Trubleville, the nephew of Drogo I, above, and a canon of Rouen cathedral, seem to have gone on the Barons' Crusade in 1237.[109] Hugh, bishop of Sées (1229–40), helped raise funds for the expedition, and may himself have started on the crusade in 1239.[110]

Eudes Rigaud, archbishop of Rouen (1248–75), was closely connected to the Tunisian Crusade (1270) of Louis IX. Eudes was not Norman by birth,

---

1216 he wrote to Popes Innocent III and Honorius III about the logistics of collecting taxes for the Fifth Crusade. He became bishop of Sées in 1220. See *Crusade and Christendom: Annotated Documents in Translation from Innocent III to the Fall of Acre, 1187–1291*, ed. Jessalynn Bird et al. (Philadelphia, 2013), pp. 133–41; and Pierre Desportes et al., *Fasti Ecclesiae Gallicanae*, vol. 9: *Diocèse de Sées* (Turnhout, 2005), pp. 77–80.

[101] Spear, *The Personnel of the Norman Cathedrals*, p. 244; A. Potthast, *Regesta Pontificum Romanorum* (Berlin, 1874), no. 5259, dated to late 1215 or early 1216.

[102] Matthew Paris, *Chronica Majora*, ed. Henry R. Luard (London, 1876), iii, p. 9.

[103] *Gallia Christiana*, xi, col. 367.

[104] Lewis C. Loyd, *The Origins of Some Anglo-Norman Families* (Leeds, 1951), p. 52; Maurice Powicke, *The Loss of Normandy, 1189–1204*, 2nd edn (Manchester, 1961), p. 343; Thomas Stapleton, *Magni Rotuli Scaccarii Normanniae*, 2 vols (1840–44), ii, p. clxxvii; Daniel Power, 'Henry, Duke of the Normans', in *Henry II: New Interpretations*, eds. Christopher Harper-Bill and Nicholas Vincent (Woodbridge, 2007), pp. 109–17.

[105] Marion Thébault, 'Le 'premier cartulaire' de l'Abbaye de Monday, *Annales de Normandie* 61 (2011), 25–47. Jordan was regarded as the founder by the cartulist and in the necrology, but other documents recognise the role of Ralph of Percy who was a relative of Jordan's through marriage.

[106] *The Catholic Encyclopedia* (New York, 1911), xii, pp. 388–9. The Norbertine houses included Saint Abacuc, Saint Samuel, an unnamed monastery at Bethlehem and one at Acre.

[107] Howden, *Chronica*, iii, pp. 62–3. I thank Richard Heiser for calling this connection to my attention.

[108] Spear, *The Personnel of the Norman Cathedrals*, p. 171; *Gallia Christiana* XI, cols. 781–2.

[109] Jörg Peltzer, 'Master Arnulf, Archdeacon of Rouen, Unlicensed Pluralism, and Idoneitas: Defining Eligibility in the Early Thirteenth Century', *Haskins Society Journal* 19 (2007), 58, n. 33. On the Barons' Crusade, see Michael Lower, *The Barons' Crusade: A Call to Arms and Its Consequences* (Philadelphia, 2005).

[110] *Ibid.*, pp. 123, 155; *Fasti Ecclesiae Gallicanae*, *Diocèse de Sées*, p. 81.

but rather from the Ile-de-France. He was educated at Paris, and became a Franciscan regent master at Paris. Eudes had been a friend of Louis IX even before becoming an archbishop and remained a close companion until Louis's death in 1270. In 1260, when word came of the Mongol threat in the Holy Land, Eudes had raised the issue of a new crusade with his suffragans. In 1264, he allowed the archbishop of Tyre to preach at Rouen cathedral on the need for a new crusade. On 25 March 1267, King Louis took the Cross for his second crusade; two months later Eudes became a *crucesignatus*. In 1268, he preached the crusade in Rouen, climaxed by a procession of the relics of Mary Magdalene. Finally, in 1270 Eudes left on crusade with the king from the royal port of Aigues-Mortes. Eudes was with Louis on his deathbed, perhaps administering the last rites, and was one of the executors of Louis' last will and testament. The crusade collapsed with Louis' demise,[111] but even after the fall of Acre in 1291, Normans continued to be interested in the Holy Land. Pierre Dubois, born in or near Coutances, wrote his famous treatise, *The Recovery of the Holy Land*, in 1306.[112]

After this review of Norman clerical participation in the crusades, we can assess the contention that 'Normandy ceased to have any distinctive crusading role after the First Crusade'. Clearly, this might be true for secular participation, but would be manifestly false from an ecclesiastical point of view. Norman clerics were there for the whole crusading experience, from Arnulf of Chocques' accompanying of Robert Curthose on the First Crusade, to Eudes Rigaud's presence at the deathbed of Louis IX on the Eighth. And they played many roles in the crusading experience, from serving as patriarch and bishop to being *curiales* to kings, from being canonists to preachers. The question is if the word 'distinctive' is valid or not.

At one level, it is hard to argue for Norman uniqueness since many clergy discussed above were cross-Channel clerics, with part of their career in Normandy and another part in England. Moreover, after England and Normandy were severed in 1204, the clergy of the duchy found themselves drawn more fully into the Gallican church. Distinctive or not, the Norman clergy invariably followed their secular leader, be it the duke of an independent duchy, the king of England or the king of France. In part, this pattern is the necessary corollary of Alan Murray's observation that after 1101, 'crusades were increasingly led by kings, who could mobilise financial

---

[111] Most of the information in this paragraph comes from Adam J. Davis, *The Holy Bureaucrat: Eudes Rigaud and Religious Reform in Thirteenth-Century Normandy* (Ithaca, NY, 2006), esp. pp. 13, 30, 157–8, 166–9. See also *The Register of Eudes of Rouen*, trans. Sydney M. Brown (1964), pp. xxxv–xxxvi.
[112] Pierre Dubois, *The Recovery of the Holy Land*, trans. Walther I. Brandt (New York, 1956), p. 3.

resources which were not available to most of their vassals'.[113] Again and again we have seen that the Norman clergy *crucesignati* were *familiares* of the duke-king. There were very few 'free-lancers' – only Ralph of Domfront comes to mind – especially after the First Crusade.

Of course, the judgement on Norman distinctiveness depends on what scholars will find in other regions, but for the Norman clergy, we can offer the following tentative foray. One critical aspect derives from their view of church–state relations. The assumption on the part of Norman clergy was that there would be close co-operation between the two, with the *regnum* leading the *sacerdotium*. This vision is often implicit, but is exhibited in most of the relationships we have seen, such as that between Arnulf of Chocques and Baldwin I of Jerusalem, the many Norman bishops and Richard I, and even Eudes Rigaud and Louis IX.

While the clergy were close to their duke-king, they were less close to the papacy. There were some exceptions, such as Arnulf of Chocques, Arnulf of Lisieux and later Eudes Rigaud. However, papal legates were not allowed in Normandy without the duke's permission, and this remained true up to 1204: we need only recall the case involving papal legates and Richard the Lionheart. Ralph of Domfront was happy to ignore the papacy, although later he was forced to recognise its authority over him. In contrast to their distance from papal influence, many clergy were closely tied to monasteries with prior connections to the crusades. Drogo of Trubleville favoured the Norman Cluniac foundation of Longueville, Arnulf of Lisieux was partial to the Cistercians and Victorines, and Jordan du Hommet founded the Norman Premonstratensian house at Mondaye. Both Arnulf of Chocques and Arnulf of Lisieux had a special fondness for the Augustinian rule.

One of the contemporary characteristics attributed to the Normans was eloquence,[114] so perhaps it is not surprising that several of the clergy – Arnulf of Chocques, Ralph of Domfront, Arnulf of Lisieux and Eudes Rigaud – were known as good speakers. Others were accomplished writers, known for their adroit style and learning, such as Peter of Blois, Wace, Ambroise and Ralph of Caen. Yet as many were called arrogant or contumacious. Arrogance could hardly be considered a uniquely Norman vice, but it is clear that the idea of celibate clergy was not highly regarded by the Norman clergy. Arnulf of Chocques, Ralph of Domfront and Odo of Bayeux were known to have had mistresses.

---

[113] A. V. Murray, 'National Identity, Language and Conflict in the Crusades to the Holy Land 1096–1192', in *The Crusades and the Near East: Cultural Histories*, ed. C. Kostick (Abingdon, 2010), p. 120.

[114] Marjorie Chibnall, *The Normans* (Oxford, 2006), p. 118, citing Geoffrey of Malaterra.

One unanticipated disposition is that there may have been a uniquely Norman acceptance of the Byzantines. On the surface, this would seem unlikely, as several Italo-Normans made a career of gnawing at the flanks of the Byzantine Empire. Yet Robert Curthose got on well enough with Emperor Alexius I, Arnulf of Chocques allowed the Greek canons to remain in the church of the Holy Sepulchre (even if he did take away their stipends), and Arnulf of Lisieux argued against attacking Constantinople. I would not see this as a pro-Greek stance, but neither did they seem anti-Greek.

One final angle on the issue of Norman uniqueness is to what extent does region matter within Normandy itself? Lower Normandy, for example, is weakly represented. Coutances has some representation in that Walter of Coutances' family roots were in Coutances, as were Roger of Clinton's. One Coutances bishop, Richard de Bohon (1151–78), made a donation to the Templars of lands and rents in his diocese.[115] However, no bishops of Coutances were known to have participated in the crusades. Avranches provided but one bishop. Perhaps the reason for this dearth is that it is a smaller geographical territory, with fewer people and fewer resources, or perhaps it is simply a gap in the historical record. Whatever the cause, the relative lack of crusaders from western Normandy is worth noting.

On the other hand, Rouen was a very active centre for interest in the crusades. Most of the archbishops – William Bona Anima, Hugh, Rotrou, Walter of Coutances, Robert Poulain and Eudes Rigaud – had some link to the crusades. William Bona Anima, in particular, seems to have been instrumental in helping to lay the foundations for the First Crusade. This observation, then, might counterbalance Nicholas Paul's argument that for King Henry II, the Angevin-Poitevin story of crusading ancestors was more powerful than the Norman story line (which was too diffuse).[116] Paul's evidence tends to be monastic, while we have focused on cathedrals. Still, Paul seems not to recall that Henry II's eldest son, King Henry the Younger (d. 1183), who had taken a crusading vow, while first buried at Le Mans, was then moved to Rouen. It was canons of Rouen Robert of Neubourg and Ivo of Vieuxpont who persuaded Henry II to honour his son's last wishes to be buried at Rouen and who had reclaimed the body. Robert was the nephew of Rotrou[117] and so was related to several crusaders, and Ivo was doubtless kin to the crusader who bore the same name. We may link this incident with the close connection between canon Drogo of Trubleville and Richard

---

[115] Michel Miguet, *Templiers et hospitaliers en Normandie* (Paris, 1995), p. 27.
[116] Paul, *To Follow in Their Footsteps*, pp. 221–50.
[117] Spear, *The Personnel of the Norman Cathedrals*, p. 202.

the Lionheart. Drogo had gone on crusade with Richard, and had given a reliquary to Rouen cathedral that bore Richard's name. Although we don't know how it transpired, Rouen cathedral obtained the heart of Richard the Lionheart.[118] These circumstances suggest, cumulatively, a conscious effort by its canons to reinforce the associations between Rouen, the ducal crown and the crusades.

On one level, the story of the Norman clergy and the crusades is merely a sustaining part of the European experience as a whole. But given the evidence presented here, without Norman clerical participation, the crusades would have looked very different indeed.

---

[118] *La Cathédrale de Rouen: seize siècles d'histoire*, ed. J.-P. Chaline *et al.* (Rouen, 1996), p. 126 for an illustration of the lead coffinette that once held Richard's heart.

6

Norman and Anglo-Norman Intervention in the Iberian Wars of Reconquest before and after the First Crusade

LUCAS VILLEGAS-ARISTIZÁBAL

The Normans were interested in various parts of Iberia from the eleventh to the twelfth centuries. In the eleventh century, the main arena of Norman participation was the valley of the Ebro, but by the mid-twelfth century, Anglo-Norman arrivals gravitated towards the Portuguese frontier. Norman and Anglo-Norman participants came from different social groups over time. For example, during the late eleventh and early twelfth centuries, the Norman contingents were largely from the higher nobility.[1] In the mid-twelfth century, when their interest moved from the east to the west of the peninsula, most were from the lower ranks of the nobility and other social levels.[2] This chapter will address how the Normans' motives and aims changed as a result of the First Crusade and the transformation in the ideas of holy war in Iberia in the twelfth century. More importantly it will show how the idea of crusade was central to Norman involvement especially after the conquest of Jerusalem in 1099. Finally, it will explore

---

[1] Lucas Villegas-Aristizábal, 'Roger of Tosny's Adventures in the County of Barcelona', *Nottingham Medieval Studies* 52 (2008), 4–16; Lucas Villegas-Aristizábal, 'Algunas notas sobre la participación de Rogelio de Tosny en la reconquista ibérica', *Estudios humanísticos* 3 (2004), 263–74; Milo Crispin, 'On the Origins of the Crispin Family', in *Normans in European History*, ed. Elisabeth van Houts (Manchester, 2000), pp. 84–5; Lynn Nelson, 'Rotrou of Perche and the Aragonese Reconquest', *Traditio* 26 (1970), 113–33; Kathleen Thompson, *Power and Border Lordship in Medieval France: The County of Perche* (Woodbridge, 2002), pp. 71–8; Lawrence J. McCrank, 'Norman Crusaders in the Catalan Reconquest', *JMH* 7 (1981), 67–82; Eloy Benito Ruano, 'El principado de Tarragona', in *Misel·lània Ramon d'Abadal* (Barcelona, 1994), pp. 107–19.

[2] Marcelin Defourneaux, *Les français en Espagne aux XIe et XIIe siècle* (Paris, 1949); Ramon Miravall, *Immigració britànica a Tortosa* (Barcelona, 1970); Matthew Bennett, 'Military Aspects of the Conquest of Lisbon, 1147', in *The Second Crusade, Scope and Consequence*, ed. Jonathan Phillips and Martin Hoch (Manchester, 2001), pp. 71–89; Lucas Villegas-Aristizábal, 'Revisión de las crónicas de Ralph de Diceto y la Gesta regis Ricardi sobre la participación de la flota angevina durante la tercera cruzada en Portugal', *Studia historica. Historia medieval* 27 (2009), 153–70; Lucas Villegas-Aristizábal, 'Anglo-Norman Involvement in the Conquest and Settlement of Tortosa, 1148–1180', *Crusades* 8 (2009), 63–129.

how the Norman collaboration with the Iberian rulers differed, making them a singular external group whose involvement transformed with the changing nature of the conflict.

The ideological effect of the events of the First Crusade to the Holy Land (1095-99) cannot be underestimated. The Normans in Italy, as well as in Normandy and England, were obviously attracted by the appeal of crusade from both a religious and a secular perspective. It is well known that important figures such as Robert, duke of Normandy, Bohemond of Taranto and Tancred were among the leaders of this expedition.[3] Moreover, in the case of the last two, they were able to acquire great material rewards from their involvement.[4] As has been demonstrated by a succession of historians, the religious as well as the material appeal of this expedition attracted the attention of any Norman prepared to leave their homeland for adventure or pilgrimage elsewhere.[5] In this way, it diverted their interest from other theatres of war, and notably Iberia, where the Normans had been active participants before 1095.

The First Crusade also helped to transform the Iberian struggle from a secular conflict between political entities of different religious and cultural tendencies, towards a long-term Christian military struggle with a clear theological justification.[6] In the eleventh century after the collapse of the Umayyad caliphate of Cordoba, the Christian kingdoms and counties of the peninsula had seen this as an opportunity for expansion and profit.[7] The Taifa kingdoms that were formed as a result of the power vacuum left in al-Andalus by the fall of the Umayyads were intrinsically unstable. They lacked legitimacy in the eyes of their multi-ethnic subjects and were constantly at odds with each other over territory. In this atmosphere, the Christian Iberian realms could expand through outright conquest, but in most cases they were more keen to extort payments for protection known as *parias*.[8] The most daring and successful conquests that were achieved during this period were those of Fernando I of Leon and his son Alfonso

---

[3] Norman Housley, *Contesting the Crusades* (Oxford, 2006), pp. 90-1; Thomas Asbridge, *The Creation of the Principality of Antioch* (Woodbridge, 2000).

[4] RCaen, pp. 603-716; Annliese Nef, *Conquérir et gouverner la Sicile islamique aux XIe et XIIe siècles* (Rome, 2011), pp. 56-7.

[5] Jonathan Riley-Smith, *The First Crusade and the Idea of Crusading* (London, 1993), pp. 91-119.

[6] Francisco García Fitz, 'La Reconquista: Un estado de la cuestión', *Clio & Crimen* 6 (2009), 142-215; Joseph F. O'Callaghan, *Reconquest and Crusade in Medieval Spain* (Philadelphia, 2003), pp. 1-22.

[7] Adam J. Kosto, 'Reconquest, Renaissance and the Histories of Iberia c. 1000-1200', in *European Transformations: The Long Twelfth Century*, ed. Thomas F. Noble and Jon Van Eugene (Notre Dame, IN, 2012), pp. 98-9.

[8] Manuel González Jiménez, 'Frontier and Settlement in Castile (1085-1350)', in *Medieval Frontier Societies*, ed. Robert Barlett and Angus Mackay (Oxford, 1989), pp. 52-3.

VI. In Alfonso's case, he conquered the symbolically important city of Toledo in 1085, which pushed the Christian–Islamic frontier south to the Tagus River and made the Leonese crown the largest by far of all the Christian realms of the peninsula.[9] These relationships based on the extortion of money, which appeared most often during this period, did, however, at times place the Christian realms at odds with each other.[10] The recognition of this kind of conflict involving Christians and Muslims fighting side by side in wars against Christians and Muslims alike, which was a particular feature of the Iberian experience in the high Middle Ages, has been used to question how appropriate it is to define these conflicts through the use of the term crusade.[11] The long-standing existence of the Christian–Muslim Iberian frontier (711–1492) encouraged the rulers of both faiths to have a more pragmatic relationship with each other, even in periods of heightened religious animosity, than other rulers who lived far from the borderlands.[12] In a frontier society there was always a degree of tolerance and at times co-operation; an important factor that would produce misunderstandings with Norman immigrants, not unlike that caused between the crusaders and their Frankish and Byzantine allies in the Latin East during the crusader expeditions of the twelfth and thirteenth centuries.[13]

Alongside this, from the eighth century, the Mozarab clerical chroniclers of the Cantabrian realms had gradually produced an ideological justification for the Christian expansion into the Muslim dominated territories of al-Andalus. They argued that the Leonese monarchy was the direct decedent of the Visigothic state that had been overthrown by the Islamic invasion in 711. Based on this assumption and on the Christian theological arguments for 'just war' that had been developing, they argued that it was Leon's duty to reconquer those territories.[14] From this, therefore, the concept of the *Reconquista* was forged, a concept that has been controversial in Iberian historiography in the last fifty years because of its nationalistic

---

[9] *Ibid.*, pp. 60–4.

[10] Richard Fletcher, *The Quest of El Cid* (London, 1989), pp. 112–13.

[11] Simon Barton, 'Traitors to the Faith? Christian Mercenaries in al-Andalus and the Maghreb, c. 1100–1300', in *Medieval Spain: Culture, Conflict and Coexistence*, ed. Angus MacKay, Roger Collins and Anthony Goodman (London, 2002), pp. 23–45.

[12] Robert I. Burns, 'The Significance of the Frontier in the Middle Ages', in *Medieval Frontier Societies*, ed. Bartlett and Mackay, pp. 316–30.

[13] Villegas-Aristizábal, 'Roger of Tosny's Adventures', 15–16; Benjamin Z. Kedar, 'Subjected Muslims of the Frankish Levant', in *Muslims under Latin Rule 1000–1300*, ed. James M. Powell (Princeton, NJ, 1990), pp. 143–74.

[14] Augustine of Hippo, *The City of God*, trans. Henry Bettenson (London, 1984), p. 32; Frederick H. Russell, 'Love and Hate in Medieval Warfare: The Contribution of St Augustine', *Nottingham Medieval Studies* 31 (1987), 108–24.

overtones. However, whether or not the Iberian kingdoms did have a grand idea of reuniting Iberia under a single ruler, the term *Reconquista* will be used here to define the conflict with Islam that, as Garcia Fitz has postulated, cannot be ignored as a defining feature of the Iberian Christian frontier societies that developed throughout the high Middle Ages.[15]

Also during the latter half of the tenth century, the Christian realms of the peninsula started to attract the newly formed monastic order of Cluny to their realms, as a way of re-establishing more direct links with the rest of western Europe.[16] Examples of this can be found in the close relations created by Sancho III of Navarre and his son and successor, Fernando I of Leon, with the Burgundian monastery. These two leaders started a policy of endowment of the Burgundian order from around the turn of the millennium. It has been suggested that this new order helped to transform the ideology behind the conflict with Islam. Furthermore, it has been proposed that the Cluniac reformers, in their self-proclaimed mission to purify the church from the unwanted hands of the local rulers as well as to reduce the constant state of fratricidal conflict that characterised the period, inspired the formation of the crusading theological argument.[17]

Whether this was so or not, it is certain that the Cluniac monastic order profited directly from the policies of the Iberian rulers with regards to the Muslims. For example, Fernando I of Leon accepted a feudal relation with Cluny in which he paid to the order large sums that he had extorted from the Taifa kingdoms. In this context the Cluniac order, if not directly preaching it, might have introduced the Norman nobility to the idea of holy wars in Iberia.[18] As the Normans in the early eleventh century started to undertake pilgrimages, they perhaps were able to hear about the potential for loot in Iberia as they travelled on their way to the famous shrine of

---

[15] García Fitz, 'La Reconquista', 205.

[16] Charles J. Bishko, 'Fernando I y los orígenes de la alianza castellano-leonesa con Cluny', *Cuadernos de Historia de España* 47 (1968), 31–51.

[17] Carl Erdmann, *The Origins of the Idea of Crusade*, trans. Marshall W. Baldwin (Princeton, NJ, 1977), pp. 288–9; Pierre Boissonade, 'Cluny, la papauté et la première grande croisade internationale contre les sarrasins d'Espagne: Barbastro (1064–1065)', *Revue des questions historiques* 60 (1932), 257–301; Vicente Cantarino, 'The Spanish Reconquest: A Cluniac Holy War against Islam?' in *Islam and the Medieval West*, ed. Khalil I. Semaan (Albany, NY, 1980), pp. 88–9; Étienne Delaruelle, 'The Crusading Idea in the Cluniac Literature of the Eleventh Century', in *Cluniac Monasticism in the Central Middle Ages*, ed. Noreen Hunt (London, 1971), pp. 209–10; O'Callaghan, *Reconquest and Crusade*, pp. 1–22.

[18] Jonathan Riley-Smith, *The Crusades, A Short History* (London, 2001), pp. 3–7; Marcus Bull, *Knightly Piety and the Lay Response to the First Crusade: The Limousin and Gascony, c. 970–c. 1130* (Oxford, 1993), pp. 21–3, 33–9, 258–81; Marcus Bull, 'Origins', in *The Oxford History of the Crusades*, ed. Jonathan Riley-Smith (Oxford, 1999), pp. 15–34; Herbert E. J. Cowdrey, *Pope Gregory VII 1073–1085* (Oxford, 1998), p. 468; Lucas Villegas-Aristizábal, 'Norman and Anglo-Norman Participation in the Iberian Reconquista, c. 1018–c.1248', PhD thesis (University of Nottingham, 2007), pp. 49–52.

Santiago de Compostela. Wace, for example, claimed that Walter Giffard, who supposedly took part in the siege of Barbastro, visited the famous shrine.[19] Also in the late eleventh century, during a rebellion in Galicia, the local bishop was accused of instigating a Norman invasion by William I of England. Whether this is true or not, the fact that the *Historia Compostelana* refers to such a plot does suggest that Normans might have been present in the area.[20] Since the Cluniac order acquired several monastic houses on the famous trail to the shrine from southern France all the way to Galicia, it was in a privileged position to inform and persuade pilgrims.[21]

An early example of this was the involvement of Roger of Tosny on behalf of Countess Ermesinda of Barcelona that was described by Ademar of Chabannes in his chronicle and in the northern French chronicle of *Saint Pierre le Vif de Sens*.[22] In this case, it is impossible to know what exactly motivated this high-ranking Norman to go especially to the county of Barcelona. However, it seems from the limited sources that his desire to abandon his homeland temporarily was the result of some dispute with his overlord: 'Roger ... returned to his father in Normandy, making peace with Duke Richard.'[23] It is possible to speculate that he might have gone on pilgrimage to Santiago and on his way there might have been informed of the local opportunities in the Catalan counties. However, it is also possible that he was coming back from Italy or the Holy Land by sea instead. The sources do not give us any itinerary for his journey. It is likely that he might have passed on his return home through Limoges or Angoulême where he might have met Ademar of Chabannes, who recorded his career in Iberia.[24] The adventures of this Norman certainly produced a precedent that later Norman contingents might have been acquainted with, as is evident in Orderic Vitalis' work.[25]

The conflicting interests of the Iberian realms, from the final decades of eleventh-century made popes, such as Alexander II and Gregory VII,

---

[19] Derek W. Lomax, 'The First English Pilgrims to Santiago de Compostela', in *Studies in Medieval History Presented to R. H. C. Davis*, ed. Henry Mayr-Harting and R. I. Moore (London, 1985), p. 166.

[20] *Historia compostelana*, ed. Emma Falque (Madrid, 1994), p. 299.

[21] Otto K. Werckmeister, 'Cluny III and the Pilgrimage to Santiago de Compostela', *Gesta* 27:1/2 (1988), 103–12; Theresa Martin, 'Recasting the Concept of the "Pilgrimage Church": The Case of San Isidro de Leon', *La Corónica* 32:2 (2008), 169.

[22] Adémari Chabannensis, *Chronicon*, ed. Pascale Bourgain (Turnhout, 1999), p. 174; Richard Landes, *Relics, Apocalypse and Deceits of History: Adémar of Chabannes* (Cambridge, MA, 1995), p. 124; *Chronique de Saint-Pierre-le-Vif de Sens*, ed. R. H. Bautier and M. Gilles (Paris, 1979), p. 112; Villegas-Aristizábal, 'Roger of Tosny's Adventures', 8.

[23] *Ibid.*, 8.

[24] *Ibid.*, 11–16.

[25] OV, ii, pp. 68–9; For more information on this particular participant see: Villegas-Aristizábal, 'Roger of Tosny's Adventures', 4–16.

encourage the Iberian rulers and some Frankish nobles to engage the Muslims in the peninsula. Examples of these efforts were the ephemeral conquest of Barbastro in 1064 and Gregory VII's planned expedition to Iberia by the northern French count, Ebulus II of Roucy.[26] These expeditions, it has been argued, were to a certain extent the result of the exasperation felt by the papacy with the less than aggressive policies of the Iberian rulers towards their Muslim neighbours. Bishko argued that the Barbastro expedition was called as a result of the outrage caused when an Aragonese attempt to take Cinca in 1063 failed when it was intercepted by the Castilian forces of El Cid at the Battle of Graus.[27] Furthermore, the expedition against Barbastro, according to the papal letter attributed to Pope Alexander II, granted remission of penance similar to those received by the crusaders from Urban II in 1095. Even if the letter was not referring to this specific venture, the expedition attracted the attention of multiple Norman knights of fortune, such as Robert Crispin and perhaps Walter Giffard. These Norman contingents, whose motivations are unclear, certainly seemed to have profited financially from the expedition but then continued their careers elsewhere.[28]

Following the success of the First Crusade in capturing Jerusalem and other Eastern cities and territories, popes such as Gelasius II and Calixtus II were prepared to grant the conflict in Iberia the same status.[29] Furthermore, the church throughout the twelfth century continued to encourage the Iberian rulers, with only limited success, to lay aside their local squabbles and fight the Muslims. Especially in the eyes of foreign participants, the papal endorsement, therefore, made the Iberian struggle and its associated military campaigns into true crusades. Here lies an important distinction, namely that although the church was increasingly eager to glorify and sanctify the Iberian war against Islam, the local rulers were only eager to accept this designation gradually and when it suited them. One can say that the pragmatism of the frontier society clashed with the idealism of the clergy. For the Iberian rulers, their Muslim neighbours had always been a well-known evil that could be used in certain circumstances. Examples of this were numerous from the fall of the caliphate of Cordoba

---

[26] Herbert E. Cowdrey, *The Cluniacs and the Gregorian Reform* (Oxford, 1970), p. 221; José María Lacarra, *Vida de Alfonso el batallador* (Saragossa, 1978), pp. 15-17; Malcolm Barber, *The Two Cities: Medieval Europe. 1050-1320* (London, 1993), p. 346.

[27] Bishko, 'Fernando I y los orígenes, 55.

[28] Amatus of Monte Cassino, 'The Capture of Barbastro', in *Christians and Moors in Spain*, ed. Colin Smith (Warminster, 1993), pp. 84-7; Thomas A. Archer, 'Giffard of Barbastre', *EHR* 18 (1903), 303-5.

[29] William Purkis, *Crusading Spirituality in the Holy Land and Iberia c. 1095-c. 1187* (Woodbridge, 2008), p. 133; Johannes Dominicus Mansi, *Sacrorum conciliorum nova et amplissima collectio* (Graz, 1961), xxi, col. 217; Bull, *Knightly Piety* p. 81.

to the beginning of the thirteenth century. This facet of the Iberian conflict with Islam continued, even after the official endorsement by the papacy of the Iberian conflict as a crusade at the beginning of the twelfth century. Kings such as Alfonso IX of Leon and Sancho VII are obvious examples of rulers who allied themselves to the Almohads, in order to confront the hegemonic tendencies of their Castilian neighbours.[30] In these two cases they did so even when the pope threatened to excommunicate them. In the case of Alfonso IX, a crusade was even proclaimed against his kingdom as a result of his duplicity and constant military alliance with the Muslims.[31] On the other hand, the new sanctification of the conflict against Islam made it possible for the rising power of the local monarchies to use the financial and organisational power of the church to expand their domains and gain spiritual rewards. Furthermore, the fact that all the Christian rulers shared a religious affiliation did not necessarily mean that they were always at peace with each other. Therefore, they had to be realistic in their relations with their Muslim neighbours, especially when they were at war with their co-religionists. Thus, truces with the Muslim rulers were common among all the Christian realms of the peninsula even when the church opposed them on ideological grounds. In a way this situation was not dissimilar to what was occurring in the Latin East as a result of the formation of the Latin states. There, the newly established local nobility had to accept a more pragmatic relationship with the Muslims which was perceived as scandalous by Western visitors.[32] So the dilemma of the local rulers slowed the religious transformation of the Iberian conflict in the locals' minds during the twelfth century, but it did not eradicate it completely from the minds of the participants. This, of course, was the age in which the image of Saint James the Moor-slayer started to captivate the Christian-Iberian collective imagination and the promulgation of indulgences for crusades was widely used to recruit troops.[33] Also, there were some monarchs and rulers – like Alfonso I of Aragon, Afonso Henriques of Portugal, Alfonso VII of Leon and Count Ramon Berenguer IV of Barcelona – who actively used crusading indulgences to raise armies against the Muslim-dominated

---

[30] Damian J. Smith, 'The Papacy, the Spanish Kingdoms and Las Navas de Tolosa', *Anuario de la historia de la Iglesia* 20 (2011), 176; Antonio Ubieto Arteta, 'La participación navarro-aragonesa en la primera cruzada', *Príncipe de Viana* 8 (1947), 357–84; Colin Smith, *Christians and Moors* (Westminster, 1989), ii, pp. 6–11; Francisco García Fitz, *Relaciones políticas y guerra: La experiencia castellano-leonesa frente al Islam Siglos XI–XIII* (Seville, 2002), p. 274.

[31] Miguel Dolan Gomez, 'The Battle of Las Navas de Tolosa: The Culture and Practice of Crusading in Medieval Iberia', PhD thesis (University of Tennessee, 2011), pp. 64–5.

[32] Elizabeth Hallam, ed., *Chronicles of the Crusades* (Godalming, 1997), pp. 138, 146–8.

[33] Colin Smith, ed., *Christians and Moors in Spain* (Warminster, 1993), pp. 80–3.

lands of al-Andalus in the first half of the twelfth century.³⁴ In the case of the Portuguese monarchs they might have even encouraged northern European involvement through the flourishing cult of local saints in the Low Countries as Jonathan Wilson has recently pointed out.³⁵

For the Norman crusaders as well as other groups from northern Europe, the Muslims were the enemy of Christ and their destruction was the way to salvation. For them, the ecclesiastical propaganda was literally true; they knew little about Islam and what they saw was already tainted by their prejudice. This is evident in the contemporary sources.³⁶ For example, Bernard of Clairvaux said in his letter to the Anglo-Norman nobility: 'How great a number of sinners have here confessed with tears and obtained pardon for their sins since the time when these holy precincts were cleansed of pagan filth by the swords of our fathers.'³⁷ On the other hand, even if they were aware of the early Norman incursions into the peninsula, those stories would have been perceived within the context of holy or just war or even as part of the flourishing romantic tradition of Roland.³⁸ Since the great majority of Normans had never seen or had to deal with the Muslims, any story, such as the one described in the epic poem or the contemporary chronicles, could be interpreted at face value. This more simplistic view was what made the Iberian struggle very attractive to multiple waves of Normans in the century after the fall of Jerusalem. Also, the Iberian realms, especially those facing the Atlantic, offered an obligatory stopover on the sea route to the Holy Land.³⁹ Therefore, their plight could not be easily ignored. The local Iberian clergy, as well as the papacy, had been eager to present the Iberian struggle both as a Christian duty of divine restitution of Christian lands lost to the pagans and as true crusades.⁴⁰ All in all, this

---

[34] Derek W. Lomax, *The Reconquest of Spain* (London, 1978), pp. 61–93; O'Callaghan, *Reconquest and Crusade*, pp. 35–49.

[35] Jonathan Wilson, 'Tactics of Attraction: Saints, Pilgrims and Warriors in the Portuguese Reconquest', Institute of Historical Research Seminars: Crusades and the Latin East (Senate House, London, November 4, 2013).

[36] OV, v, pp. 4, 15, 36; Penny J. Cole, '"O God the heathen have come into your inheritance" (Ps 78.1): The Theme of Religious Pollution in Crusader Documents 1095–1188', in *Crusaders and Muslims in Twelfth Century Syria*, ed. Maya Shatzmiller (Leiden, 1993), pp. 100–1.

[37] *The Letters of St Bernard of Clairvaux*, ed. Bruno Scott James (London, 1998), p. 461.

[38] Wolfgang Van Emden, *La chanson de Roland* (Valencia, 1995), pp. 10–12; Michel Zink, *Le moyen âge littérature française* (Nancy, 1990), pp. 41–3; Lucien Musset, *Les relations littéraires franco-scandinaves au moyen âge* (Liège, 1975), pp. 193–213; Matthew Gabriele, 'Asleep at the Wheel? Messianism, Apocalypticism and Charlemagne's Passivity in the Oxford *Chanson de Roland*', *Nottingham Medieval Studies* 47 (2003), 46–72.

[39] John H. Pryor, 'A View from a Masthead: The First Crusade from the Sea', *Crusades* 7 (2008), 106–15.

[40] Richard A. Fletcher, 'Reconquest and Crusade in Spain', *TRHS* 37 (1987), 42; Defourneaux, *Les français en Espagne au XIe et XIIe siècles*, pp. 156–7.

made the Iberian struggle a very attractive theatre of action for those crusaders who wanted to return home soon after having received their spiritual as well as their secular rewards for their actions. An early example of this can be seen in the participation of the veteran crusader Count Rotrou of Perche, a vassal of Henry I of England, and his lieutenant Robert Burdet from Cullei in the campaigns of Alfonso I of Aragon. Rotrou, for his part, had already been involved in the First Crusade to Palestine and seems to have been keen to atone for his perceived later sins in Iberia at the behest of his relative, the Aragonese monarch.[41] Perhaps his misfortune of losing his wife Matilda (an illegitimate daughter of Henry I of England) in the White Ship tragedy pushed him to take the Cross. On the other hand, Robert Burdet seems to have gone to Iberia in a quest for land. However, it is likely that some religious impulse influenced his involvement in the restoration of the see of Tarragona.[42] After all, Tarragona had been for many years a pet project of the papacy in its desire to restore the see into Christian hands. Furthermore, although the possession of the Christian principality on the frontier might have appeal for a Norman adventurer, the precarious position of the ruined city certainly would have discouraged anyone interested in an easy venture to get rich. Unlike his early eleventh-century Norman predecessor in the peninsula, Roger of Tosny, Robert perhaps drew on his religious zeal and was prepared to stay in Iberia until his death in order to secure his new, albeit impoverished and exposed, domain.[43] Ultimately his principality became an obstacle to the rising aspiration of Count Ramon Berenguer IV of Barcelona, but Robert's venture had managed indisputably to return a permanent Christian population to the ancient city, as is clear from the documentary sources that survive from his principality.[44]

By the mid-twelfth century, it seems the Anglo-Norman involvement started to have a more complex justification within the crusading movement. During the general crusading promulgation known collectively as the Second Crusade, a great number of Norman and Anglo-Norman crusaders arrived in the Iberian peninsula, where they were involved directly in locally inspired ventures against the Muslim dominated lands of al-Andalus. In the case of Lisbon (1147), one can easily appreciate in the

---

[41] Nelson, 'Rotrou of Perche', 121–3; Villegas-Aristizábal, 'Norman and Anglo-Norman Participation', pp. 125–7.

[42] McCrank, 'Norman Crusaders in the Catalan Reconquest', 67–82; Benito Ruano, 'El principado de Tarragona', pp. 107–19.

[43] Villegas-Aristizábal, 'Norman and Anglo-Norman Participation', pp. 129–45.

[44] Villegas-Aristizábal, 'Anglo-Norman Involvement', docs 4, 7–9, 11, 13, 20, 21, 23, 26, 28–31, 34, 35, 37, 39, 45, 49, 64, 68, 78, 83, 112.

speech attributed to the bishop of Porto the logic employed by the Norman scribe for their involvement in this undertaking.[45] He explains that the prelate proclaimed that their war against the Moors was just on the grounds that the Muslims had unjustly violated the lands and its Christian people, and therefore it was a Christian duty to impose divine retribution for such action. The cleric furthermore explains to those hesitant to get involved in Iberia: 'Be not seduced by the desire to press on with your journey which you have begun; for the praiseworthy thing is not to have been to Jerusalem, but to have lived a good life while on the way.'[46] Here, the author of the chronicle is clearly justifying the Lisbon venture as part of the general crusade proclaimed by Eugenius III, three years earlier, in the papal bull *Quantum Prædecessores*.[47] The obvious question of whether the Iberian crusade was a deviation from the original aim of Jerusalem in the participants' minds is clear in the speech. This is especially relevant since it is still not very clear whether Pope Eugenius III had originally sanctioned the Lisbon expedition as part of the Second Crusade.[48] Despite this ambiguity, it seems that only a small fraction of the expedition was hesitant to get involved in the Portuguese venture and in this case it seems their reasoning had more to do with their earlier failed attempt to conquer Lisbon (in *c.* 1142) than with any religious qualms about the legality of this particular undertaking. This earlier expedition, mentioned briefly in the *De expugnatione* and described in more detail in the Portuguese annal *Historia Gothorum*, was certainly not an official crusade sanctioned by the papacy. This, however, did not seem to have bothered its Anglo-Norman participants. The *Historia* does refer to them as men of war with a vow to go to Jerusalem, suggesting their vocation as crusaders.[49]

Crusading indulgences in the form of papal bulls and letters were widely circulated, and the Norman and Anglo-Norman nobility were probably quite aware of their existence and meaning. Bernard of Clairvaux had appealed to the Anglo-Norman nobility to put aside their squabbles and disputes in the anarchic realms of King Stephen and join the Second

---

[45] Charles W. David, 'The Authorship of the *Expugnatione Lyxbonensi*', *Speculum* 7 (1932), 50–7; Harold Livermore, 'The *Conquest of Lisbon* and Its Author', *PS* 6 (1990), 1–16.

[46] *DEL*, p. 79.

[47] Peter Rassow, 'Der Text der Kreuzzugsbulle Eugens III', *Neues Archiv* 45 (1924), 302–5; Eugene III, 'Quantum prædecessores', in *Chronicles of the Crusades*, ed. Hallam, pp. 121–2; Riley-Smith, *The Crusades*, p. 94.

[48] Jonathan Phillips, 'St Bernard of Clairvaux, The Low Countries and the Lisbon Letter of the Second Crusade', *Journal of Ecclesiastical History* 48:3 (1997), 485–97; Alan Forey, 'The Conquest of Lisbon and the Second Crusade', *Portuguese Studies* 20 (2004), 1–13.

[49] Lucas Villegas-Aristizábal, 'Revisiting the Anglo-Norman Crusaders' Failed Attempt to Conquer Lisbon *c.* 1142', *Portuguese Studies* 29 (2013), 7–20.

Crusade.[50] It was a call that indeed seems to have attracted unprecedented acceptance, as is testified by the great number of participants who took part in the conquests of Lisbon and Tortosa. Furthermore, as was proclaimed by Henry of Huntingdon in his discussion of the failure of the Second Crusade, the Anglo-Norman detachment that had helped to conquer Lisbon had been more worthy of God's grace 'thanks to their humility'.[51] Here the Anglo-Norman cleric was obviously glorifying his compatriots' success in relation to the French and German failures in the Latin East. However, the fact that the Anglo-Norman victory was in Iberia shows that this theatre was widely accepted as a legitimate area for action by the mid-twelfth century. Furthermore, this might have been accentuated by the visit of the English bishop of Lisbon, Gilbert of Hastings, to England to recruit settlers in the 1150s.[52]

The different approaches followed by the northern crusaders in relation to their Muslim captives certainly antagonised the local Christian forces, as was the case in Lisbon and in the ephemeral conquest of Silves during the Third Crusade.[53] During the final assault on the city of Silves, the Anglo-Normans, as part of the larger crusader contingent and influenced perhaps by a combination of religious fanaticism and avarice, refused to allow the inhabitants to depart with their valuables as the Portuguese monarch had negotiated.[54] A similar attitude existed in the Latin East between the crusaders and their Byzantine allies in the twelfth century.[55] However, unlike the antagonism that was aroused against the Christians in the Latin East, in Iberia the local rulers could accommodate more easily to the newcomers' pressures. It is likely that the common Latin liturgical practices and relative cultural similarities made the Iberian Christians less alien to the Normans than the Byzantines or the Eastern Christians. Nonetheless, tensions remained. This is evident in episodes like the siege of Lisbon in 1147 and the sack of Silves in 1189 where the Portuguese were forced to allow the crusaders to carry out their sackings. This state of affairs continued right through to the thirteenth century. For example, during the crusader

---

[50] BNF, Paris, Fond Latin, Ms. 14845, f. 257; *Letters of Saint Bernard of Clairvaux*, pp. 460–3.

[51] Henry of Huntingdon, *The History of the English People*, trans. Diana Greenway (Oxford, 2002), p. 86.

[52] *Opera omnia historian regum, eadem historia ad quintum et vicesium annum continuata per Jonem Hagulsstadensem*, ed. Thomas Arnold, 2 vols (London, 1885), ii, p. 324.

[53] Jaime Ferreiro Alemparte, *Arribadas de normandos y cruzados a las costas de la península ibérica* (Madrid, 1999), p. 80 n. 2.

[54] Villegas-Aristizábal, 'Norman and Anglo-Norman Participation', p. 191.

[55] Thomas Asbridge, *The Crusades* (London, 2010), pp. 48–50, 531–2.

campaign of Las Navas de Tolosa the foreign crusaders departed the expedition before the battle after similar tensions emerged over strategy.[56]

The church in the twelfth century, especially after the Second Crusade, was eager to change its role from a position of simply accepting the status quo to one in which it acted as a more direct promulgator of military ventures in the peninsula. An important development that occurred in Iberia, that helped both in the ecclesiastical endeavour to maintain a constant struggle against Islam and to equalise this conflict with that of the Latin East, was the introduction of the military monastic orders. The Templars and the Hospitallers started to receive castles and properties in the peninsula from at least the 1120s onwards, and by the end of the century were well established in this frontier with Islam.[57] Furthermore, this inspired the formation of new local military orders such as Balchite, Santiago, Calatrava and Alcantara. These clerical military orders, like those involved in the Latin East, were less careful to maintain the local truces with the Muslims, since they had a more ideologically driven religious zeal embedded within their existence than their secular counterparts. They were in theory directly under the jurisdiction of the papacy, which arguably freed them from the concerns of the lay lords.[58] This became more prominent in the second half of the twelfth century when the wars against Islam in the peninsula suffered from a hiatus not unlike that which occurred in the Latin East after the failure of the Second Crusade. The existence of the military orders in the peninsula further helped to create a sense, at least from the perspective of the Norman crusaders, that the Iberian wars against Islam were indeed part of the crusading movement. The Templars, for example, were instrumental in the conquest of Santarem by Alfonso Henriques of Portugal and in the sieges of Lisbon and Tortosa during the Second Crusade, as well as in the defence of Tomar in the Third Crusade, a similarity that could not be overlooked by observers such as Caffaro and Roger of Howden.[59] Moreover, some Anglo-Norman settlers, like Gilbert Anglici in Tortosa, bequeathed some

---

[56] Francisco García Fitz, *Las Navas de Tolosa* (Barcelona, 2012), p. 219–22; Gomez, 'The Battle of Las Navas de Tolosa', pp. 147–60.

[57] Malcolm Barber, *The New Knighthood* (Cambridge, 1994), pp. 1–63; Desmond Seward, *The Monks at War* (London, 1995), pp. 1–13; Helen Nicholson, *Templars, Hospitallers and Teutonic Knights* (Leicester, 1993), pp. 1–5, 15–21.

[58] Peter Linehan, *History and Historians of Medieval Spain* (Oxford, 1993), pp. 293–4.

[59] Martin Hall and Jonathan Phillips, eds, *Caffaro, Genoa and the Twelfth-Century Crusades* (Aldershot, 2013), pp. 133–4; Caffaro di Rustico, *De captione Almerie et Tortuose*, ed. Antonio Ubieto Arteta (Valencia, 1973), p. 32; 'A conquista de Santarém', *Fontes medievais da história de Portugal*, ed. Alfredo Pimenta (Lisbon, 1960), pp. 94–106; Roger of Howden, *Chronica*, ed. William Stubbs (London, 1870), iii, p. 44; *Gesta Regis Henrici Secundi*, ii, pp. 118–19; García Fitz, *Las Navas*, pp. 114–33; Villegas-Aristizábal, 'Revisión de las crónicas', 169.

of their properties to the Templars,[60] and, according to an early charter of the repopulation of Tortosa, the English contingents were acknowledged to have a cemetery in the vicinity of the Church of the Order of the Holy Sepulchre, furthering the connection between the two theatres of conflict.[61]

The papacy did not see the apparent lack of interest by the Iberian rulers in the war against Islam as something to be commended and encouraged them to halt their constant disputes and engage their common enemy.[62] To say there was no activity against the Muslims would be erroneous, however, since the monarchs as well as their subjects did launch a series of raids across the frontier from time to time. However, this did not result in any major lasting conquest of territory, only a few frontier fortifications being given to the military orders. In attempting to push for more concerted actions, church councils like that of Segovia in 1166 encouraged secular fervour for crusade among the laity in the kingdom of Castile, but with limited success.[63]

On the other hand, this period saw the greatest increase of diplomatic contacts between the Anglo-Norman domains and the Iberian realms as a result of Henry II's marriage alliance with Eleanor, duchess of Aquitaine. The creation of the so-called Angevin Empire by the new English monarch made Iberia no longer a distant land for crusaders and adventurers, but a potential arena within which to forge alliances against the enemies of the crown. In these diplomatic endeavours the *Reconquista* seems to have been used by the Iberian rulers as a way to increase their prestige in the eyes of their new potential ally.[64] It is known, for example, that Henry contemplated the idea of launching a crusade in Iberia during the early period of his reign only to be warned against this by the English pope, Adrian IV, who, on this occasion, feared to antagonise the Iberian rulers, an inevitable eventuality if Henry entered their territories without their approval.[65] Furthermore, Henry II actually secured an alliance with Alfonso VIII of Castile by marrying Eleanor, one of his daughters, to the Castilian.[66] He

---

[60] Villegas-Aristizábal, 'Anglo-Norman Involvement', doc. 157.
[61] *Ibid.*, doc. 31.
[62] Linehan, *History and Historians*, pp. 288–9; Gonzalo Martínez Diez, *Alfonso VIII* (Burgos, 1995), pp. 11–38, 63–78.
[63] Peter Linehan, 'The Synod of Segovia', *Bulletin of Medieval Canon Law* 10 (1980), 31–44.
[64] Richard Barber, *Henry Plantagenet* (Woodbridge, 2001), pp. 95–6, 134; Wilfred L. Warren, *Henry II* (London, 1973).
[65] Demetrio Mansilla, *La documentación pontificia hasta Inocencio III* (Rome, 1955), doc. 103; Lomax, *The Reconquest*, p. 107.
[66] Rose Walker, 'Leonor of England and Eleanor of Castile: Anglo-Iberian Marriage and Cultural Exchange in the Twelfth and Thirteenth Centuries', in *England and Iberia in the Middle Ages*, ed. María Bullón-Fernández (Basingstoke, 2007), pp. 67–88.

also attempted to follow similar arrangements with the kings of Navarre and Aragon in an attempt to secure his southern frontier and fight against his enemies, the king of France and the count of Toulouse.[67] Henry seems to have been genuinely interested in the affairs of the Christian frontier in Iberia; as Lomax pointed out, he even granted a sum to the Spanish military order of Santiago.[68] Even after the infamous assassination of Thomas Becket, Henry managed to get permission from the church to join the fight in Iberia as part of his penance for his role in the assassination.[69] However, as with all his other promises of crusade, Henry never left his domains. Henry's prestige in Iberia reached such a level that he was requested to arbitrate in a land dispute between the Castilian and Navarrese monarchs.[70] Even with all these direct diplomatic contacts there is little evidence for any direct military activity by Normans or Anglo-Normans in the Iberian frontier during this period. However, as explained above, the *Reconquista* saw only limited activity from the part of all secular rulers and the lack of any large naval crusading expedition heading to the eastern Mediterranean during this period further reduced the likelihood of any substantial external involvement in Iberia.

The fall of Jerusalem to Saladin in 1187 produced a reaction in the West that inadvertently seems to have changed temporarily, at least in Portugal, the lack of activity from the Iberian rulers. In Portugal, as is narrated in a variety of chronicles, the Anglo-Normans as well as other nationalities arrived in multiple waves on their voyage to the Holy Land.[71] We know that the first contingents to arrive in Portugal proceeded to attack the port city of Silves.[72] In this case, their arrival did not coincide with a period of Christian hostilities towards the Muslims on the part of the Portuguese, but the crusader action precipitated their reaction even with some hesita-

[67] Martínez Diez, *Alfonso VIII*, pp. 43–6.

[68] José Lopez Argurleta, ed. *Bullarium equestris ordinis sanct Sanct Jacobi de Spatha* (Madrid, 1715), p. 30; Derek W. Lomax, *La orden de Santiago* (Madrid, 1965), p. 116.

[69] Dorothy E. Whitelock and Christopher N. L. Brooke, eds, *Councils and Synods with Other Documents Relating to the English Church* (Oxford, 1981), i, pp. 940–56; Anne Duggan, 'Diplomacy, Status and Conscience: Henry II's Penance for Becket's Murder', in *Forschungen zur Reichs-, Papst-un Landesgeschichte*, ed. Karl Borchardt and Enno Bünz (Stuttgart, 1998), pp. 265–90.

[70] Fernando Luis Corral, 'Alfonso VIII of Castile's Judicial Process at the Court of Henry II of England', *Nottingham Medieval Studies* 50 (2006), 22–42; Martínez Diez, *Alfonso VIII*, pp. 89–90.

[71] Villegas-Aristizábal, 'Revisión de las crónicas', 157–70.

[72] Christopher W. David, ed., 'Narratio de itinere navali peregrinorum Hierosolyman tendentium et Silviam capientum A. D. 1189', *Proceedings of the American Philosophical Society* 81 (1939), 591–676; Guðbrandur Vigfússon and George W. Dasent, eds, 'Orkneyinga Saga', *Icelandic Sagas and Other Documents Relating to the Settlement and Descent of the Northmen on the British Isles* (London, 1894), i, pp. 159–79; Ralph of Diceto, *Opera Historica*, ed. William Stubbs (London, 1876), ii, pp. 65–6; *Gesta Regis Henrici Secundi*, iii, pp. 115–21; Howden, *Chronica*, iii, pp. 43–5.

tion. Earlier, in 1184, the Portuguese ruler had been forced to confront an Almohad invasion on his city of Santarem.[73] After this, the Almohads had maintained a series of truces with their Christian enemies as a result of internal disputes in their empire.[74] Also, as mentioned, the Iberian rulers were far from eager to engage the Muslims in the preceding decades as a result of their political disputes and the Portuguese had been no exemption, although they had committed a few raids across the frontier. The crusader victory against Silves might have resonated in the imagination of those involved and have acted as a precursor to the victories envisaged in the East. However, as was the case in the Second Crusade, many crusaders stayed behind to settle in the newly exposed Christian city. The conquest and settlement of Silves, after most of the population had been massacred, shows the idea that the *Reconquista* in itself was considered sufficient for many to gain their spiritual reward, as they were prepared to stay and not continue on their journey to the Holy Land. Also, as is described in the Chronicle of Roger of Howden, a second wave of crusaders from London arrived in Silves just as the Almohad caliph was preparing a counter-attack. Here the crusaders were encouraged to participate with the promises that they would be repaid for their sacrifice by the Portuguese monarch.[75] The fact that this second wave of crusaders was prepared to delay their journey in order to defend the newly conquered city with only the promise that they would be repaid in kind for their action, does suggest that they understood that their engagement there could be counted as part of their crusading endeavour.[76]

The Third Crusade in Portugal had another facet in the involvement of the Anglo-Normans. The Islamic reaction to the fall of Silves to Caliph Abu Yassuf Ya'qub al Mansur, was to try to recapture the defensive perimeter of the Portuguese city of Lisbon.[77] For King Sancho I of Portugal the arrival of another wave of crusaders, as the caliph was simultaneously besieging Torres Novas and Santarem, seems to have been a godsend. The clerical author of the *Gesta Regis* and Roger Howden seem to have been convinced of the legitimate action of the crusaders in helping the Portuguese monarch in the defence of the city. As further proof that by the end of the twelfth century the *Reconquista* had been accepted as an intrinsic part of the cru-

---

[73] Hugh Kennedy, *Muslim Spain and Portugal* (London, 1996), pp. 235–6.
[74] Maria João Violante Branco, *D. Sancho I o filho do fundador* (Lisbon, 2010), pp. 153–4.
[75] Howden, *Chronica*, iii, p. 43; Matthew Paris, *Chronica majora*, ed. H. R. Luard, ii, p. 366; *Gesta Regis Henrici Secondi*, ii, p. 117.
[76] Ralph of Diceto, *Opera Historica*, ii, pp. 89–90; David, 'Narratio de itinere navali', 591–676.
[77] Villegas-Aristizábal, 'Revisión de las crónicas', 162–4.

sading movement, the chronicle claimed that the crusaders decided to die in war in the name of Christ when helping the Portuguese.[78]

However, after the main wave of the Third Crusade ended, the Portuguese *Reconquista* came to a halt and by 1191 the Almohads had recovered Silves. In the following years, Alfonso VIII of Castile became the leading ruler in the struggle against the Moors in the peninsula; however, his activities led him to the greatest military defeat of that generation in the Battle of Alarcos in 1195. It was a defeat that was recorded with anguish in chronicles and annals far away from the peninsula.[79] After this defeat the Almohads were able to threaten Castile's strategically crucial city of Toledo. The fear of an imminent Moorish invasion of Iberia did not materialise, thanks in part to the caliph's own political problems in north Africa. However, after the defeat, the Christian world would not have been able to predict the caliph's subsequent difficulties and there were multiple calls for a general crusade against the Muslims in Iberia. Richard I of England and Phillip II contemplated taking the Cross together once more to aid the Iberian rulers.[80] However, none of this came to pass as the English and French rulers, although worried about the Almohads, were more distrustful of each other's intentions than of a Muslim invasion. More crusades led by kings both in the peninsula as well as from the rest of Europe were hampered by similar disputes among the laity. The remainder of the reign of Richard as well as the troubled reign of his successor John kept the Anglo-Norman nobility engaged in their own disputes as well as those with the French monarchs over their continental domains.[81] Even though there were plentiful alliances and diplomatic contacts between the English monarch and their Iberian counterparts, these had to do more with protecting Gascony than with any attempt to launch a crusade in Iberia. The only exception to this was the expedition by the German emperor Henry VI to the Holy Land in 1197. On this occasion he attempted to retake Silves without Portuguese involvement but failed.[82] There is no reference to any Normans having taken part in that expedition but, since the expeditionary fleet stopped at Dartmouth on their way to Iberia, there might well have been some.

Although the crusading movement reached a new level of organisational

---

[78] *Ibid.*, 159–65.

[79] Miguel Ángel Ladero Quesada, 'Amenaza almohade y guerras entre reinos', *Historia de España Menéndez Pidal*, ed. Miguel Ángel Ladero Quesada (Madrid, 1998), ix, pp. 505–8; Carlos Alvar, *Textos trovadorescos sobre España y Portugal* (Madrid, 1978), pp. 235–6.

[80] John Gillingham, *Richard the Lionheart* (London, 1978), p. 258; Lomax, *The Reconquest*, p. 120.

[81] Wilfred L. Warren, *King John* (London, 1997), pp. 51–99, 105–10, 174–205.

[82] Howden, *Chronica*, iv, p. 26; 'Annales Stadenses', MGH Scriptorum 16, ed. Georgius Heinricus Pretz (Leipzig, 1925), p. 353.

sophistication after the Third Crusade and particularly following the Fourth Lateran Council, the involvement of Normans in the Iberian struggle suffered a drastic and final decline in the thirteenth century.[83] The reasons for this are varied but have mostly to do with the way the crusaders' ventures took place in the peninsula. They occurred mostly in the interior and in the Mediterranean zones of Iberia, making them less connected to other expeditions to the Holy Land as they had been in the previous century. Obviously Mediterranean expeditions could have technically attracted northern crusaders but there is little evidence that they did.[84] Furthermore, as the Iberian kingdoms grew in confidence after the great victory of Las Navas de Tolosa, their desire for foreign aid declined in importance. On the other hand, the fragmentation of the Anglo-Norman domains as a result of King John's loss of most of his continental possessions produced a series of conflicts against the French crown that distracted the monarch as well as the nobility from crusader ventures into the peninsula. The troubled reign of King John, with his conflicts with the nobility and the church, did not produce a fertile ground for crusaders. Without the assurance that the church could protect their properties from other lords or the king in their absence, the nobility was less keen to get involved in these types of ventures. There were even later suggestions by Matthew Paris that King John had come to an alliance with the Almohad caliph as his other Iberian allies (Sancho VII of Navarre and Alfonso IX of Leon) had done.[85] Obviously if this alliance was ever really attempted, as it was later suggested by Arab sources, it was a political one against their common enemy Alfonso VIII who, in 1205, had attempted to take Gascony from John.[86] In the end, the crusader ventures of the Iberian monarchs, Fernando III of Castile-Leon and James I of Aragon, gave those monarchs, in the eyes of

---

[83] Christopher Tyerman, 'Were There Crusades in the Twelfth Century?' *EHR* 110 (1995), 553–77; Jean Richard, *The Crusades c. 1071–1291*, trans. Jean Birrell (Cambridge, 1999), pp. 319–61; Hans E. Mayer, *The Crusades*, trans. John Gillingham (Oxford, 1972),pp. 228–38, 260–88; Riley-Smith, *The Crusades*, pp. 152–61, 173–216.

[84] Richard of Cornwall's crusade could have potentially been involved in Iberia on its way to Jerusalem but it seems that in this case he took the Mediterranean route from Marseilles, bypassing the peninsula. The Rothelin, *Continuation to the History of William of Tyre*, trans. Janet Shirley (Aldershot, 1999), pp. 38–9.

[85] Matthew Paris, *Chronica majora*, ed. Luard, ii, pp. 559–64; Nevill Barbour, 'Embassy Sent by King John of England to Miramamolin, King of Morocco', *Al-Andalus* 25 (1960), 373–81; Nevill Barbour, 'Two Embassies to the Almohad Sultan Mohammad al-Nasir at Seville 1211', in *Actas del primer congreso de estudios árabes e islámicos* (Cordoba, 1962), pp. 189–213; Ibn Abi Zar, *Rawd el-Qirtas*, trans. Ambrosio Huici Miranda (Valencia, 1964), i, pp. 457–60.

[86] Pierre Chaplais, ed., *Diplomatic Documents Preserved in the Public Records Office* (London, 1964), i, doc. 56; Joseph F. O'Callaghan, 'Innocent III and the Kingdoms of Castile and Leon', in *Pope Innocent III and His World*, ed. John C. Moore (Aldershot, 1999), pp. 320–5.

their contemporaries, a level of prestige unparalleled by any other crusader monarch in their time.[87]

Although during these campaigns the English crusaders might not have played an important role, their perception that the Iberian struggle was fully part of the crusader movement was maintained, as is evident from contemporary sources such as Mathew Paris.[88] It is obvious that this image was maintained a long time after, as can be seen in the English and French involvement in the Siege of Algeciras (1348) and the conquest of Granada (1492).[89] The Iberian victories contrasted dramatically with the failures in the Latin East, giving the Christian observers a sense perhaps of the worthiness of the cause, as Henry of Huntingdon had expressed when comparing the two endeavours.[90] However, the reinvention of the Iberian *Reconquista* as part of the crusades would have been very different without the success of the First Crusade in creating a group of vulnerable Christian states in the East that required an almost constant flow of crusaders to survive. The location of the peninsula on the sea route to the Holy Land undoubtedly played a pivotal role in the Anglo-Norman involvement there after the First Crusade, especially since this group had been so adept in using the sea route for their other overseas ventures. On the other hand, the gradual equalisation of the Iberian conflict with that of the Holy Land gave many Normans and Anglo-Normans an extra incentive to get involved in the *Reconquista* on their way to Jerusalem or elsewhere.

In the final assessment, the Normans and their Anglo-Norman successors seem to have become a constant in the wars against Islam from the early eleventh century to the beginning of the thirteenth century. The only other group that appears to have such a constant involvement was the nobility of southern France. However, in this case geographic, linguistic and ethnic proximity offers an obvious explanation for their interest in the affairs of the peninsula. The Normans' involvement in Iberia, although long and more or less constant, did not produce an independent state apart from the short-lived principality of Tarragona. This perhaps ultimately explains why Norman involvement in Iberia has attracted far less scholarship

---

[87] Matthew Paris, *Chronica majora*, ed. Luard, v, pp. 231–2.
[88] *Ibid.*
[89] *Crónicas de los Reyes de Castilla*, ed. Cayetano Rosell (Madrid, 1875); i, pp. 360–1; Peter Russell, *The English Interventions in Spain and Portugal* (Oxford, 1955), pp. 7–8; Luciano Serrano, *Alfonso XI y Clemente VI durante el cerco de Algeciras* (Madrid 1915), pp. 3–21; Eloy Benito Ruano, 'Un cruzado inglés en la guerra de Granada', *Anuario de Estudios Medievales* 9 (1979), 585–93.
[90] Henry of Huntingdon, *Historia Anglorum*, p. 753.

in comparison to other 'Norman' zones such as southern Italy, the Latin East and the British Isles.

Part III

7

The Pilgrimage and Crusading Activities of the Anglo-Norman Earls of Chester

ANDREW ABRAM

This chapter explores the devotional and political dynamics behind the promotion of shrines, pilgrimage centres and crusading by the Norman and Anglo-Norman earls of Chester. Following the Norman invasion and settlement of England the earldom of Chester was established as a powerful centre of lordship along the northern march with Wales. Owing to its vital strategic function and the loyalty to the Crown of its successive earls, the earldom of Chester enjoyed semi-independent status which invested authority in the earl, hence, the royal writ did not apply there, and the king possessed no property in the county of Cheshire. As leading lords and noblemen in both Normandy and England, earls such as Hugh d'Avranches (c. 1071–1101) and his son Richard (1101–20) were particularly active in promoting cult centres of former Anglo-Saxon saints, while later figures vigorously led and prosecuted military expeditions to the East. Moreover, the special status of the earls of Chester made their part in the crusading movement more crucial for recruitment and participation than perhaps noble leadership was elsewhere in England. Cheshire was the only county in England with no Templar property of any kind, and its Hospitaller holdings were scarce.

For the purposes of this study, the Norman and Anglo-Norman earls of Chester span the period from Hugh I, who was invested with the title around 1071, and the death of Ranulf III in 1232. The activities of John the Scot, the last of the earls before the honour passed to the Crown, are not covered, although he took the Cross in 1236 yet died before he could fulfil his vow.[1] John would have taken part in the crusade of Richard of Cornwall and, had he fulfilled his vow, it is likely that the greatest impact on Cheshire would have been financial, as he was one of the richest crusade leaders as

---

[1] Matthew Paris, *Chronica Majora*, ed. Henry Richards Luard (London, 1872–83), iii, pp. 368–9.

a result of his properties in England and Scotland.² This chapter, however, necessarily considers the activities of both the earls and their leading vassals, such as the constables of Chester, as they illustrate a range of features synonymous with the bellicose, acquisitive and religious nature of the Normans and their adherents. One such individual was Hugh d'Avranches, hereditary *vicomte* of Avranches in western Normandy, holder of lands in the Hiémois, Avranches and Bessin regions of the duchy and established as earl of Chester around 1071. Hugh's vast and newly acquired lordship dominated the northern part of the border with Wales, and extended to estates not only in Cheshire, but in twenty other English counties.³

The monastic and religious patronage of the earls of Chester in their Norman homelands and newly acquired English possessions was unsurprisingly extensive, and represented a significant element of their role as hereditary *vicomtes* of Avranches and important members of the Anglo-Norman nobility on both sides of the English Channel. Like most other Anglo-Norman magnates, Earl Hugh d'Avranches was an active monastic benefactor. In Normandy, he founded the Abbaye Notre-Dame de Saint-Sever, his family's senior house, around 1085, and endowed important monasteries such as Bec-Hellouin and Saint-Evroul.⁴ The promotion of monasteries, established at important pilgrimage sites such as Saint-Sever, was a significant feature of the religious, political and cultural landscape of lower Normandy during the late eleventh century. During the rule of Duke Richard I (942–996), the body of Saint Sever, the sixth-century bishop of Avranches, was translated to the cathedral church of Rouen, then in the late eleventh century partially removed to a recreated abbey dedicated to him in the diocese of Coutances.⁵

A Norman *translatio* from Richard's time relates that, whilst travelling to Mont-Saint-Michel (founded in 708 by the bishop of Avranches), two clerks from Rouen Cathedral stopped at Saint Sever's tomb, which was revered by a priest and housed in a rude wooden chapel. At the bidding of the clerks, Richard I assented to the removal of the saint's remains to

---

[2] Alan MacQuarrie, *Scotland and the Crusades, c. 1095–1588* (Edinburgh, 1988), p. 40.

[3] William Farrer, *Honours and Knights' Fees*, 2 vols (London, 1924), i, pp. 5–6. For the views of Orderic Vitalis and Florence of Worcester, see OV, v, pp. 214, 298; Florence of Worcester, *Chronicon ex Chronicis*, ed. B. Thorpe, 2 vols (London, 1849), ii, p. 57.

[4] Geoffrey Barraclough ed., *Charters of the Anglo-Norman Earls of Chester* (Gloucester, 1988), pp. 1–2, 11, 20–1; *Cartulary or Register of the Abbey of St Werburgh, Chester*, ed. James Tait, 2 vols (Chetham Society, 1920–23), i, p. 298.

[5] Lucien Musset, 'Reserches sur les pèlerinages en Normandie jusqu' à la Premiere Croisade', *Annales de Normandie* 12 (1962), 130; Mathieu Arnoux, 'Before the *Gesta Normannorum* and Beyond Dudo: Some Evidence on Some Early Norman Historiography', *ANS* 10 (1987), 29–48 (37–8).

the capital of the duchy, where, according to the *translation*, Saint Sever became the most prized relic of the cathedral church. Such events must be located within the context of the settlement of the ducal succession and the beginning of the process of ecclesiastical reforms within Normandy during the late tenth century. Powerful links between Rouen, the Cotentin region and the diocese of Avranches in the west of the duchy were vital to this process. Integral to the modernisation of the Norman church was the restoration of bishoprics in 989, and the first re-established bishop of Avranches, Norgod (989–1022). In common with all Norman historical writing from the early eleventh century onwards, the *Revelatio* of the abbey of Mont-Saint-Michel followed the somewhat historically inaccurate Dudo of Saint-Quentin in crediting Richard I with rebuilding the church and enforcing strict Benedictine monasticism on the community.[6]

Following the Norman invasion and conquest of England, the foremost religious act of Hugh d'Avranches was his foundation of Chester Abbey in 1093. The conversion or refoundation of Chester was achieved by supplanting the previous minster church of secular canons dedicated to the Anglo-Saxon Saint Werburgh, with monks.[7] Hugh was assisted in this by his friend, the reforming Abbot Anselm of Bec (the future archbishop of Canterbury), in supervising the transformation of the minster into a Benedictine house and important pilgrimage site.[8] Although the earl's gesture can be interpreted as a highly significant act of piety, it also reflected the political, familial and cultural nature of the earldom of Chester on a grand scale, indicative of other recent Anglo-Norman refoundations such as Much Wenlock Priory and Shrewsbury Abbey by Roger de Montgomery.[9]

As studies of the relationship between the Anglo-Normans and pre-existing religious sites, such as Durham Cathedral, demonstrate, shrines dedicated to saints' cults and relics, and thus frequented by pilgrims, were widespread in post-Conquest England.[10] In numerous cases the Anglo-Norman monarchy, bishops, founders and benefactors recognised, adapted and venerated them, and regarded them as the focus of devotion,

---

[6] For the details of the eleventh-century fight between the canons of Avranches Cathedral and the monks of Mont-Saint-Michel over the relic of the skull of Saint Aubert, see *The Cartulary of the Abbey of Mont-Saint-Michel*, ed. K. S. B. Keats-Rohan (Donington, 2006), pp. 14–15, 63–76

[7] Barraclough, *Charters*, pp. 2–11.

[8] *Ibid.*, pp. xxiii–xxv.

[9] J. F. A. Mason, 'Roger de Montgomery and His Sons (1067–1102)', *TRHS* 13 (1963), 1–28; Marjorie Chibnall, *Anglo-Norman England 1066–1166* (Oxford, 1986), pp. 15–18.

[10] William Aird, *St Cuthbert and the Normans: The Church of Durham, 1071–1153* (Woodbridge, 1998); Andrew Abram, 'Saints, Cult-Centres and the Augustinian Canons in the Diocese of Coventry and Lichfield', in *The Regular Canons in the British Isles in the Middle Ages*, ed. Janet Burton and Karen Stöber (Turnhout, 2012), pp. 79–95.

continuity and reform. Furthermore, the promotion of shrines by communities of monks and regular canons conforms to a more general pattern, and can be identified at sites such as Burton-upon-Trent and Stone in Staffordshire. Research has emphasised that, in particular, late Anglo-Saxon minsters were usually superior churches that provided pastoral care and administration to wide *parochia* from the tenth to the early twelfth centuries.[11] Additionally, they were associated with areas focused on the royal *tun*, and therefore connected with royal administration.

The pre-Conquest kingdom of Mercia contained several minsters where the ruling dynasties promoted cult centres of various royal saints. The administrative centre was located at Tamworth and the spiritual heart of the kingdom at Lichfield, with its cathedral dedicated to Saint Chad, while the traditional burial place of the Mercian royal house was at Repton. Moreover, Mercia's heartlands of Cheshire, Staffordshire, Shropshire and Derbyshire contained a group of royal free chapels that long preserved their substantial ancient parishes. Many of these chapels were later converted to Benedictine and Augustinian communities, while their patron saints were promoted by the Norman and Anglo-Norman incomers. The tenth-century princess, Æthelflaed, promoted cult centres and minsters at her various *burhs*, such as Chester, Stafford and Runcorn, which had been established as military and political centres of power along the north-western frontier of the Mercian kingdom.[12] Hence, when she constructed fortifications at Tamworth and Stafford in 913, she encouraged the cult of Bertelin, a local saint, who was enshrined in the ancient royal minster at Stafford. The fortification at Runcorn controlled the strategically important Runcorn Gap, a narrowing of the Mersey estuary, and was probably sited on the small promontory on the south bank of the River Mersey. Since the early tenth century, Halton, in north-west Cheshire (encompassing the parish of Runcorn), had been a manor of some importance. The strategic value of the site was thus appreciated by the first Anglo-Norman constables of Chester, who located their *caput* at Halton, the centre of their Cheshire estates.[13]

The pre-existence of a minster church at Runcorn is related to the early history of the site. Domesday Book lists two priests under the manor of

---

[11] John Blair, 'A Saint for Every Minster? Local Cults in Anglo-Saxon England', in *Local Saints and Local Churches in the Early Medieval West*, ed. A. Thacker and R. Sharpe (Oxford, 2002), pp. 455–94; Sarah Foot, *Monastic Life in Anglo-Saxon England, c. 600–900* (Cambridge, 2006), pp. 5–7.

[12] Thacker, 'Kings, Saints and Monasteries', p. 19; *The Anglo-Saxon Chronicles*, trans. and ed. Swanton, pp. 97, 99; N. J. Higham, 'The Cheshire *Burhs* and the Mercian Frontier to 924', *Transactions of the Antiquarian Society of Lancashire and Cheshire* 85 (1988), 193–221; N. J. Higham, *The Origins of Cheshire* (Manchester, 1993), pp. 155, 158–9.

[13] *Domesday Book: A Complete Translation*, ed. A. Williams and G. H. Martin (London, 1992), p. 727.

PILGRIMAGE AND CRUSADING ACTIVITIES OF THE EARLS OF CHESTER

Halton, at least one of which belonged to Runcorn and its extensive parish.[14] In 1115, an Augustinian community dedicated to the Blessed Virgin Mary and Saint Bertelin replaced the former church. When the community transferred to Norton in 1134 the co-dedication to the Mercian saint was abandoned, although such practice seems not to have been unusual. By 1200, the ancient royal minster and later royal free chapel at Stafford, dedicated to Saint Bertelin, was rededicated to Saint Mary in the same way.[15] At Stafford, the remains of the Mercian saint had been enshrined in an ancient royal minster and his cult encouraged. This is indicative of the Anglo-Saxon religious and political dynamic evident in the north-west and north midlands of England during the early tenth century. In 901 at Much Wenlock, in the heartlands of Shropshire, King Æthelred and Queen Æthelflaed donated a gold chalice in honour of Saint Milburga, whose cult had survived Danish incursions. Similarly, about 907 Æthelflaed probably refounded a minster at Chester, incorporating the existing relics of Saint Werburgh, whose cult was associated with King Oswald, another saint promoted by the queen.[16]

Significantly, unlike other followers of Earl Hugh of Chester, Constable William seems not to have made any gifts to Chester Abbey as part of its refoundation as a Benedictine community in 1093. Previous donations to the canons of Chester came from his Wirral fee, rather than the lordship of Halton, and it is likely that he was planning to establish his own religious house nearer to the centre of his estates.[17] There seems to have been a precedent for this in Earl Hugh himself. Alan Thacker suggests that before Bishop Peter of Lichfield's decision to relocate the centre of his see in Chester around 1075, Hugh intentionally withheld any potential gifts from his Cheshire fee to Saint-Sever Abbey in Gascony in order to keep them for what would eventually form the endowment of his new Saint Werburgh's in Chester.[18]

A much later and perhaps unreliable tradition existed at Chester Abbey that William the Constable was closely associated with Saint Werburgh.

---

[14] *Ibid.*, p. 727.

[15] Adrian Oswald, *The Church of St Bertelin at Stafford Excavation Report* (Birmingham, 1953–4), pp. 9–10; J. H. Denton, *English Royal Free Chapels* (Manchester, 1970), pp. 93–5, 97–102, 162–70.

[16] A. J. M. Edwards, 'An Early Twelfth-Century Account of St Milburga of Much Wenlock', *Transactions of the Shropshire Archaeological and Historical Society* 57 (1980), 134–42; A. T. Thacker, 'Chester and Gloucester: Early Ecclesiastical Organisation in Two Mercian Burhs', *Northern History* 18 (1982), 201.

[17] *Cartulary. St Werburgh* iii, pp. 15–22; Barraclough, *Charters*, pp. 2–7.

[18] *Earldom of Chester and Its Charters: A Tribute to Geoffrey Barraclough*, ed. A. T. Thacker (Chester, 1991), p. 55.

According to a *Life* of the saint by the sixteenth-century monk Henry Bradshaw,[19] William's devotion to her was the result of a vow made probably in 1117 during an arduous crossing of the River Dee to assist Earl Richard, who, during a pilgrimage to Holywell, was attacked by Welshmen and besieged at Basingwerk. Upon the intervention of Saint Werburgh, William the Constable returned to Chester and made an offering at her shrine. How accurate the story is, we cannot know, especially as the hagiography's intention was to emphasise Werburgh and the city of Chester. Even so, before his death in about 1130, William the Constable granted his body for burial with the monks of the abbey.[29] The twelfth-century constables of Chester were directly responsible for the establishment of a number of religious communities associated with their lordship of Halton, being Runcorn (which relocated to Norton in 1134); Stanlaw and Warburton. The constables also encouraged their supporters not only to contribute to these, but to establish houses of their own.

In 1115 a community of regular canons venerating Saints Mary and Bertelin was founded at Runcorn by Constable William of Chester.[20] The establishment of Runcorn is notable in that it was among the pioneering group of Augustinian foundations in England and Wales. It was only the third in the north of England and the first to be established in the diocese of Coventry and Lichfield. Located adjacent to the site of an Anglo-Saxon *burh*, the regular community at Runcorn superseded an associated minster. Elsewhere in the diocese of Coventry and Lichfield the transformation of religious communities and sites for religious and political reasons became a feature of the region. Cult centres were utilised at Stone, Repton, and Trentham among others. William the Constable recognised that the initial proposal for his foundation at Runcorn came from Bishop Robert de Limesey.[21] This reformist and former chaplain to William I probably saw the canons as agents of reform within his see, with the expectation that they would provide pastoral service in the churches of which they held the advowson. Janet Burton stresses that, in the archdiocese of York, Thomas II introduced Augustinian canons to Hexham and Bridlington, whilst Thurstan, with the close co-operation of Pope Calixtus II, stimulated the

---

[19] Henry Bradshaw, *The Life of St Werburge of Chester*, ed. C. Horstmann (London, 1887), pp. 179–81. Basingwerk had been established as an Anglo-Saxon frontier stronghold at the northern end of Watts Dyke, while a later fortification was destroyed during King Stephen's reign. In 1131 Earl Ranulf II of Chester founded a Savignac abbey nearby.

[20] J. Tait, 'The Foundation Charter of Runcorn (Later Norton) Priory', *Chetham Society Miscellany* 100 (1939), 1–26; Andrew Abram, *Norton Priory: An Augustinian Community and Its Benefactors*, Trivium Publications, Occasional Papers, no. 2 (2007), pp. 5–6.

[21] Manchester, Chetham Library, MS Towneley C8. 8, fols. 65–6.

foundations of Nostell, Guisborough, Embsay, Drax and Worksop.[22] Like Runcorn, a number of these were pre-Conquest cult centres. At Guisborough, established between 1119 and 1124, the founder, Robert de Brus, was influenced 'by the councel and advice of Pope Calixtus II and Archbishop Thurstan', while William Paynel, who established Drax, shared a close rapport with the churchman, declaring that he placed canons there 'with the advice and council of Lord Thurstan, archbishop of York'.[23]

The role of Earl Richard of Chester in the establishment of Runcorn Priory is also worth emphasising. In 1113 or 1114, Walter de Gant founded Bridlington Priory with the assent of Henry I and the support of Archbishop Thomas of York, while Kirkham was established by Walter Espec with royal support.[24] Richard may have been promoting Augustinian canons at Calke around the time of the foundation of Runcorn.[25] Moreover, he apparently considered converting Chester Abbey from a Benedictine community, perhaps to an Augustinian cathedral chapter, similar to that created at Carlisle in 1133.[26] The earl's taste for the Augustinians is likely to have been fuelled by the interest of the royal family, as most of his upbringing and connections were at court. In a similar way, the royal justiciar Robert I of Brus, wishing to establish an Augustinian community at Guisborough, at the centre of his north Yorkshire fee, probably accompanied Henry I in Normandy in 1118–20, and sought the advice of both the king and Archbishop Thurstan of York.[27]

A similar conversion of a pre-Conquest site occurred at Trentham in Staffordshire, where in 1153, towards the end of his life, Ranulf of Chester established a priory of Augustinian canons at the site of a late Anglo-Saxon minster. Evidence for the existence of an earlier parish church hinges first on the Domesday Book, which records the presence of a priest. An episcopal confirmation dated 1121 × 1126 refers to the *parochia* of Trentham, while in 1139 Empress Matilda presented John, chaplain to Earl Ranulf,

---

[22] Janet Burton, *The Monastic Order in Yorkshire, 1069–1215* (Cambridge, 1999), pp. 76, 79, 92.
[23] *Ibid.*, pp. 77–8; *Early Yorkshire Charters*, ed. C. T. and E. M. Clay, 12 vols (Edinburgh and Cambridge, 1914–65), vi, p. 90.
[24] Burton, *Monastic Order in Yorkshire*, pp. 69–70; J. S. Purvis, 'The Foundation of Bridlington Priory', *Yorkshire Archaeological Journal* 12 (1929), 241–2; *Early Yorkshire Charters*, ii, pp. 427–8.
[25] Barraclough, *Charters*, pp. 59–60.
[26] Bradshaw, *St Werburge*, pp. 182–3; J. C. Dickinson, 'Origins of the Cathedral of at Carlisle', *Transactions of the Cumberland and Westmorland Antiquarian and Archaeological Society* 45 (1946 for 1945), 134–46; Henry Summerson, *Medieval Carlisle: The City and the Border from the Late Eleventh to the Mid Sixteenth Centuries*, 2 vols. (Kendal, 1993), i, pp. 30–2.
[27] Burton, *Monastic Order in Yorkshire*, p. 78.

to its church.[28] The suggestion that an earlier nunnery or religious house associated with the Mercian saints Werburgh and Wulfad existed at Trentham, perhaps before the minster, stems solely from Ranulf's charter to his Augustinian foundation, made in December 1153, which mentions 'the restoration of an abbey of canons in the church of Trentham'. Seemingly, it was upon this tradition that the sixteenth-century monk of Chester, Bradshaw, alleged that Saint Werburgh was foundress and abbess of a nunnery at Trentham.[29] Although documentation concerning this connection between Trentham and Chester remains sketchy, the Anglo-Norman earls of Chester maintained the religious and political link between the two locations. Saint Werburgh had lived at Trentham, yet her remains had been taken to Chester and venerated by the earls of Mercia. The promotion of pilgrimage to both sites was therefore fundamental to notions of continuity and power.

Such a feature was typical of the north-west of Coventry and Lichfield diocese, and is also evident at the Anglo-Norman refoundations of Chester, Runcorn and Warburton. The importance of the role of the earls of Chester in founding, converting and promoting cult centres in post-Conquest England by earls Hugh I, Richard and Ranulf II in particular is noticeable, as is the role of prominent lords such as the constables of Chester and a range of knightly vassals. Although some places associated with shrines and minster churches, such as Mobberley in Cheshire and Rocester in Staffordshire, were located within the heartlands of the earldom of Chester, it is clear that a number of highly significant pre-existing religious sites were retained and developed at border locations such as Chester and the Mersey estuary in order to emphasise and define the political, cultural and regional identity of the recently formed earldom of Chester and to mark the arrival of the Anglo-Norman elite.

As noted, a number of sites and their associated saints were developed and promoted as focal points for the religious, social and cultural expectations of founders and benefactors. Yet the preservation of such sites was also linked to memory, corporate identity and transition, from the earlier political regime of the Anglo-Saxon royal house to the new Anglo-Norman and later medieval structures of authority. Equally, the retention of cults in the region by powerful lords, guided by reformist bishops of Coventry and Lichfield, like Robert Limesey (1102–17) and Roger of Clinton (1129–48),

---

[28] Stafford, Staffordshire Record Office, D593/B/1/23/2/4; *English Episcopal Acta*, xiv, *Coventry and Lichfield 1072–1159*, ed. M. J. Franklin (Oxford, 1997), pp. 8, 39–41, 72–3.
[29] *Victoria History of the Counties of England: Staffordshire*, iii, ed. W. Page (London, 1970), p. 255 notes 1–2.

marked the transition from the 'old' church to the 'reformed' church. Such patterns are paralleled in Yorkshire, where, in the early twelfth century, Nostell, Hexham and Bridlington were established by ambitious Anglo-Norman lords with the assistance of the curialist archbishops Thomas II and Thurstan.[30]

Bishop Roger de Clinton's monastic activities in terms of religious foundations within his diocese and reform of Lichfield Cathedral are particularly noticeable, yet less is known of his crusade participation. Taking part in the Second Crusade, he died at Antioch on 16 April 1148.[31] In general, during the years of civil war between Stephen and Matilda many ecclesiastics and noblemen stayed in England to safeguard their interests. Roger, it seems, took no direct role in the dispute, and had already gone to Rome in 1143–44. He did, however, associate himself with Ranulf II of Chester and the Angevin party, something which might warrant little surprise given that Coventry and Lichfield diocese largely fell within the earldom of Chester, and that Roger was the nephew of Geoffrey de Clinton, the former chancellor of Henry I. Perhaps there is some truth that the bishop opted to take the Cross in order to expiate his earthly pursuits, which may have included the alienation of property within his see to certain knights, for which he had already been reprimanded by the papal legate. Somewhat sourly, the author of the *Gesta Stephani* remarked that he, among others, was 'eagerly devoted … to pursuits so irreligious'.[32]

As Kathryn Hurlock points out, crusade participation from the earldom of Chester materialised rather slowly, which fits a more general pattern with Anglo-Norman England.[33] It is impossible to vouch for any crusaders who responded to the First Crusade from the region. In Normandy, though, the pattern was different. Although Robert Curthose led a substantial number of crusaders from Normandy to Jerusalem in 1096, Hugh d'Avranches was not one of them, probably owing to political expediency in the north-west of England and his increasing ill health. Yet he was connected to, and may have influenced, the actions of some participants, either kinsmen or vassals of his in the Avranchin. Hugh's great-nephew William of Bayeux took part in the First Crusade, being mentioned by Orderic Vitalis at the capture of Nicaea.[34] The devotional, political and geographical connection

---

[30] Burton, *Monastic Order in Yorkshire* pp. 69–72.
[31] Christopher Tyerman, *England and the Crusades 1095–1588* (Chicago, 1988), p. 32; R. W. Eyton, *Antiquities of Shropshire*, 12 vols (London, 1854–60), vi, p. 319.
[32] *Gesta Stephani*, trans. K. Potter (Oxford, 1976), p. 104.
[33] Kathryn Hurlock, *Wales and the Crusades c. 1095–1291* (Cardiff, 2011), pp. 106–7.
[34] OV, v, p. 58.

between the *vicomtes* of the Avranchin and the ducal foundation of Mont-Saint-Michel must not be overlooked. By the time of the First Crusade the monastery was firmly located on the pilgrim route to Jerusalem, and the cult of its patron saint appealed to the religious and martial sensibilities of Norman knights.

William Aird illustrates in his biography of Robert Curthose that although the duke possessed 'conventional piety' he may have taken the Cross at the abbey, and he undertook a pilgrimage to Mont-Saint-Michel on his return from the Holy Land in 1100 (presumably with many crusading knights of his retinue).[35] The significance of the bond between Norman crusaders (some of whom were from the Avranchin) and the monks can be gleaned from grants to the abbey. Moreover, the surviving cartulary of Mont-Saint-Michel reveals both the activities of crusaders and their close bond with the community. In 1109, William son of Irsoi gave the tithes of Saint-Broladre, which he held of the archbishop of Dol, before travelling to Jerusalem. A few years later the abbey took the knight Baldwin Blondel into confraternity and gave him 'the costs of a pilgrimage to Jerusalem', while, in the 1140s, Richard son of Richolin donated land in Boucey and Sacey, near Avranches, 'who dying of infirmities acquired after his return' from the Holy City became a monk.[36] Similarly, a significant number of kinsmen and vassals of the earls of Chester in Normandy, such as Robert d'Avranches and Robert de Doucey, made gifts to Mont-Saint-Michel which were confirmed by Earls Hugh I and Ranulf I.[37]

Although Earl Ranulf II of Chester is not known to have taken the Cross, his half-brother William de Roumare undertook a pilgrimage to Santiago de Compostela, possibly with Waleran of Meulan in 1144.[38] Waleran attended the preaching of the Second Crusade in Easter 1146 and served as co-leader of the Anglo-Norman crusaders in Palestine. Though some Marcher lords, such as John II Lestrange of Knockin, went on the Third Crusade, involvement was again limited, yet some notable crusaders did leave Cheshire for the Holy Land. Principal among these was John, constable of Chester, who had supported the Templars and Hospitallers by granting property from his lordship at Halton, and left on crusade in March 1190.[39] Roger of Howden recorded that John died outside the walls

---

[35] William Aird, *Robert Curthose Duke of Normandy, c. 1050–1134* (Woodbridge, 2008), p. 157.
[36] *Cartulary of the Abbey of Mont-Saint-Michel*, pp. 101–2, 161–2, 168–9.
[37] Ibid., pp. 149–53.
[38] Barraclough, *Charters*, pp. 82–3.
[39] *Annales Cestrienses*, ed. R. C. Christie (Record Society of Lancashire and Cheshire, 1887), xiv, p. 41; Barraclough, *Charters*, p. 209.

of Tyre in 1190.[40] The nineteenth-century historian William Beamont has it that John's son and heir, Roger de Lacy, served at the siege of Acre in 1191, but there is no supporting evidence for this.[41] Another known crusader was Bertram of Verdun, who farmed the honour of Chester in 1187.[42] It is possible that one of these participants was responsible for the appearance of the brothers Robert the Saracen and Ralph the Saracen in the service of Earl Ranulf III between *c.* 1170 and 1208.[43]

As the example of John the Constable shows, Cheshire was included in national attempts at recruiting for the Third Crusade. In 1188, the archbishop of Canterbury reached Chester during his preaching tour of Wales and the Welsh March.[44] Gerald of Wales reports that Baldwin arrived in the city three days before Easter, thus allowing time to foster enthusiasm for the crusade, claiming that, as a result of being moved by the archbishop's sermon, 'many people took the Cross'.[45] Yet Gerald, characteristically exaggerating his own contribution to the success of the tour, remains quiet about the fact that the response from Cheshire was low key, probably because Earl Ranulf himself did not take the Cross. The reasons why he stayed at home are unclear, but it is likely that, having only gained his majority and been belted as earl in 1187, he wanted to consolidate his English estates rather than join the military venture led by Richard I.[46] Despite the claim in the *Annals of Dieulacres Abbey* that he embarked on the crusade with Richard I, and shared his imprisonment in the early 1190s, Ranulf remained in Europe.[47] Whatever his motives, he was not in Chester to meet the preaching tour, instead leaving his mother, the dowager countess, to act as hostess.[48]

If the Third Crusade and the crusading zeal of Richard I attracted the popular imagination in England, then it was the Fifth Crusade to

---

[40] *Gesta Regis Henrici Secundi* ii, p. 148; Howden, *Chronica*, iii, p. 88.

[41] William Beamont, *A History of the Castle of Halton and the Priory or Abbey of Norton* (Warrington, 1873), p. 20.

[42] Beatrice N. Siedschlag, 'English Participation in the Crusades, 1150–1220', unpublished PhD thesis (Bryn Mawr, 1939), p. 113.

[43] Barraclough, *Charters*, pp. 190–1, 225, 229–30, 249–50, 279, 366–8.

[44] *English Episcopal Acta*, ii, *Canterbury, 1162–1190*, ed. C. R. Cheney and B. E. A. Jones (Oxford, 1991), note on p. 221.

[45] Thorpe, *Journey*, p. 200.

[46] Geoffrey Barraclough argues that the use of a cross on a shield on Ranulf's second seal suggests he may have taken the Cross in 1188, though there is no evidence to support his theory. Barraclough, *Charters*, p. 229; George Ormerod, *The History of the County Palatine of Chester* 3 vols (London, 1819), i, p. 33.

[47] James W. Alexander, *Ranulf of Chester, Relic of the Conquest* (Athens, GA, 1983), p. 4. Geoffrey Barraclough has suggested that the young earl was compelled to vow he would undertake a crusade on Henry II's behalf. Barraclough, *Charters*, p. 229. See also Iain Soden, *Ranulf de Blondeville: The First English Hero* (Stroud, 2009), p. 21.

[48] *The Journey through Wales and the Description of Wales*, trans. Lewis Thorpe (Harmondsworth, 2004), p. 199.

Damietta (1217–21) that witnessed the widest spread of participants from the earldom of Chester. This was no doubt due to the leadership of Earl Ranulf III, who had taken the Cross with King John in March 1215.[49] Accompanied by the earls of Arundel, Derby and Winchester, Ranulf played a leading role in the campaign in Egypt, and although the aims of the crusade were not realised, the crusaders captured Damietta on 5 November 1219. The French translation of William of Tyre's *Historia*, the *L'Estoire de Eracles Empereur*, reported that the earl undertook the crusade with one hundred knights, a substantial retinue.[50] It is likely that many such men were his vassals and officials, such as his nephew and constable, John de Lacy.[51] Most of John's own followers came from his lordship of Pontefract, such as his steward, Robert of Kent, his porter, Roger, and his physician, Roger.[52] More sense of the wider composition of John's retinue comes from a charter drawn up at Damietta in 1218, to the priory of Pontefract, of which he was patron. The witness list includes members of his honour court, yet it remains uncertain whether all of its members accompanied him on crusade.[53]

Less known, however, is the extent of participation from John de Lacy's lordship as constable of Chester. His brother-in-law, Geoffrey de Dutton, took the Cross in 1215, and leased his lands in north-west Cheshire in order to fund the journey to the east.[54] Like other crusaders, Geoffrey's motives were doubtless complex, but following his return he adopted a seal depicting two hands holding a palm frond, the mark of a pilgrim to Jerusalem.[55] Geoffrey may have been accompanied by William *crucesignati*, one of his vassals.[56] The Dutton family acted as principal benefactors of the Augustinian priory of Norton, and it is possible that the portion of the Holy Cross reported to be venerated there in the thirteenth century was brought back by Geoffrey and presented to the community. The link with Jerusalem is

---

[49] Gervase of Canterbury, *The Historical Works of Gervase of Canterbury*, ed. William Stubbs, 2 vols (London, 1879), ii, p. 109.

[50] 'L'Estoire de Eracles Empereur', in *RHC*, ii, p. 342.

[51] For Ranulf, see, *Chronicon Petroburgense*, ed. Thomas Stapleton (London, 1849), p. 7; for John of Lacy, see, *Chronica Buriensis, 1212–1301: The Chronicle of Bury St Edmunds, 1212–1301*, ed. Antonia Gransden (London, 1964), p. 7; Roger of Wendover, *Rogeri de Wendover Liber qui dicitur Flores historiarum: The Flowers of History by Roger of Wendover*, ed. Henry Howlett, 3 vols (London, 1886–9), ii, p. 135; for Henry de Bohun see, Radulphi de Coggeshall, *Chronicon Anglicanum*, ed. Joseph Stevenson (London, 1875), p. 188.

[52] Siedschlag, 'English Participation', p. 97; *Chartulary of St John of Pontefract*, ed. Richard H. H. Holmes, 2 vols (Yorkshire Archaeological Society, 1902), i, pp. 36–37, no. 21.

[53] *Ibid.*, i, p. 37 no 21.

[54] Manchester, John Rylands University Library, Arley Charters, i. 94. p. 21.

[55] Ibid, i. 55; Chester, Cheshire Record Office, DLT, B3, fol. 142.

[56] Arley Charters, i. 66a.

actually a strong one as it is known that some Anglo-Norman crusaders ventured to the Holy City before embarking for home in 1220. The Norton relic (and its healing properties) is mentioned in the annals of Whalley Abbey.[57] The constables of Chester, themselves a crusading dynasty, acted as patrons of both houses, and it is unsurprising that Norton would have received such a gift. A small canopy resembling the roof of a shrine, as well as an extension to the east end of the priory in the early thirteenth century, possibly to house it, further suggest that the site was associated with pilgrimage and promoted pilgrimage activities.[58] Clearly the Norton relic was not the only item brought back from the Holy Land by returning crusaders. Various sites in Cheshire received portions of the Cross. Edward I gave a fragment which he had personally seized and worn in the Holy Land to Vale Royal Abbey upon its foundation.[59] Saint John's in Chester had a piece of the True Cross in its Holy Rood, known as the Crucifix of Chester, possibly donated by Earl Ranulf on his return from the Fifth Crusade.[60]

To conclude, to differing extents the Anglo-Norman earls of Chester and their leading vassals promoted former religious sites and pilgrimage centres within their lordship, such as the shrine of Saint Werburgh at Chester. This was particularly emphasised by the establishment of monastic houses at a number of these sites, which possessed not only a essential devotional dimension, but a sense of political and strategic continuity. Generally speaking, this was a common feature of Norman and Anglo-Norman piety as well as an act of consolidation over newly conquered regions. The earldom of Chester, however, although in some sense a successor of the Anglo-Saxon kingdom of Mercia was a key marcher lordship possessing a distinctive complexion. Thus, the promotion of pilgrimage sites represented a key aspect of its establishment in a frontier zone. The distinctiveness here is perhaps in that forging new, dynamic lordships, the earls of Chester promoted these sites to a significant extent. Although participation in crusading from the earldom was at times substantial, it was nevertheless intermittent.

At the time of the First Crusade, Hugh d'Avranches was too old and

---

[57] M. V. Taylor, 'Some Notes on Documents Relating to the Abbey and Other Religious Houses of Cheshire', *Journal of the Chester and North Wales Archaeological Society* 19 (2) (1912), 187.

[58] Abram, *Norton Priory*, p. 21.

[59] *The Ledger Book of Vale Royal Abbey*, ed. John Brownbill (Record Society of Lancashire and Cheshire, 1914), ix; Jeffrey Denton, 'From the Foundation of Vale Royal Abbey to the Statute of Carlisle: Edward I and Ecclesiastical Patronage', *TCE* 4 (1992), 123–38.

[60] A. T. Thacker, 'Later Medieval Chester 1230–1550: Religion, 1230–1550', in *A History of the County of Chester, Volume 5 part 1: The City of Chester: General History and Topography*, ed. C. P. Lewis and A. T. Thacker (Woodbridge, 2003), pp. 80–9.

probably occupied in England, yet it is possible to detect a pattern of participation from his Norman patrimony, both through direct association with Robert Curthose as well as through close links to Mont-Saint-Michel, that potent symbol of knightly piety, crusading zeal and Norman identity. The participation of Ranulf III and his vassals in the Fifth Crusade also placed the earldom of Chester at the forefront of the thirteenth-century Anglo-Norman response to recover Jerusalem on behalf of Latin Christendom. Although such undertakings correspond largely with wider Norman and Anglo-Norman patterns, the singularity of action might lie in the unique political, strategic and tenurial nature of Chester, as much as the pious outlook of its earls.

8

The Use and Abuse of Pilgrims in Norman Italy

PAUL OLDFIELD

The figure of the pilgrim was a ubiquitous and unifying presence in southern Italy during the eleventh and twelfth centuries, the region's so-called Norman period. While the territories of southern Italy and Sicily hosted a variety of different religious and ethnic communities – Greek Christians, Latin Christians, Muslims, Jews – and featured numerous socio-ethnic, religious and political boundaries, these same lands and boundaries were traversed by an ever-increasing influx of pilgrims which created comparable, shared exchanges all over the region. Some were drawn to any number of the region's renowned shrine centres, perhaps to Saint Nicholas' at Bari, Saint Benedict's at Montecassino, Saint Michael the Archangel's at Monte Gargano, Saint Matthew's at Salerno, or Saint Agatha's at Catania; others were passing through en route to the Holy Land, as devotional travel to Jerusalem increased in conjunction with the crusading movement.[1] At the centre of Mediterranean shipping routes, connecting movement between the sea's eastern and western coastlines, and linking Rome to Jerusalem, medieval southern Italy was a veritable hotspot for pilgrimage activity. It should be no surprise then that, in a variety of ways, the pilgrim drew the attentions of the ruling elites of southern Italy, which, from the mid-eleventh century onwards, were dominated by immigrant Norman lords. Indeed, descendants of one of these incoming Norman kin groups, the Hautevilles, established a royal dynasty when in 1130 Roger II drew together Sicily and the mainland into a unified monarchy. The elites of Norman Italy, and all manner of other groups in the region, regularly showed themselves keen to articulate a relationship with the pilgrim, and it would be one which brought a plethora of benefits. Pilgrims were useful, and, in what follows, I

---

[1] I would like to thank Emily Albu and Kathryn Hurlock for their valuable comments on an early draft of this essay. For more on pilgrim identities and patterns of movement see P. Oldfield, *Sanctity and Pilgrimage in Medieval Southern Italy, 1000–1200* (Cambridge, 2014).

propose to examine just some of the many ways that they were indeed used and at times abused.

The very origins of the Normans in Italy are founded on an inter-play between power and pilgrimage. It represents an unusual case in which the first protagonists of a military conquest were pilgrims; the nearest echo, though profoundly different in many ways, is of course the crusader conquest of the Holy Land during the First Crusade. Two of the earliest and most influential narratives of the Norman infiltration into southern Italy depict the Normans as unarmed pilgrims. Amatus of Montecassino, writing c. 1078–80, narrates how Norman pilgrims returning from the Holy Sepulchre saved the city of Salerno from a Muslim raid, while William of Apulia, writing c. 1096–99, offered an account of Norman pilgrims visiting the sanctuary of Saint Michael on Monte Gargano in c. 1010 who were subsequently recruited to aid a Lombard rebellion against Byzantine rule in Apulia.[2] Whatever the veracity in commencing the Norman story in the south in the context of devotional travel, and it should be noted that Norman pilgrimage to the Holy Sepulchre as well as devotion to Saint Michael are unmistakably evident in eleventh-century Normandy, its presence, brief but conspicuous in the opening sections of both works, powerfully sets a type of *origo* myth, a construct so alluring to the medieval mind.[3] The pilgrim back-story embedded a substratum into the Norman character which might have mollified any voices critical of the ensuing Norman rise to power in southern Italy. And there were many such voices in the eleventh century. As the Normans' rise in Italy threatened to destabilise the agenda of the reforming papacy, tensions inevitably arose between both parties, and the Normans consequently were the targets for invective and polemic. Pro-papal commentators like Bonizo of Sutri deemed as martyrs those who had fallen in the papal defeat by the Normans at the Battle of Civitate in 1053.[4] Similarly, the author of the *vita*

---

[2] Aimé du Mont-Cassin, *Ystoire de li Normant*, ed. M. Guéret-Laferté (Paris, 2011), Bk I.17–19 pp. 249–51 [for an English translation see Amatus of Montecassino, *The History of the Normans*, trans., Prescott N. Dunbar, revised with introduction and notes by Graham A. Loud (Woodbridge, 2004)]; GRW, Bk I pp. 98–100, lines 11–27.

[3] Most famously evidenced in the pilgrimage to Jerusalem of Duke Robert I in 1035 (*The Gesta Normannorum ducum*, ed. and trans. van Houts, ii, pp. 80–4) and the sanctuary at Mont-Saint-Michel (see the collected essays in *Culte et pèlerinages à Saint Michel en occident: les trois monts dédiés à l'archange*, ed. Pierre Bouet, Giorgio Otranto, and André Vauchez (Rome, 2003). For further evidence of Norman pilgrimage to Jerusalem see also C. Harper-Bill, 'The Piety of the Anglo-Norman Knightly Class', ANS 2 (1979), 63–77. For the medieval *origo* myth see S. Reynolds, 'Medieval *Origines Gentium* and the Community of the Realm', *History* 68 (1983), 375–90.

[4] *Bonizonis episcopi Sutrini Liber ad amicum*, ed. E. Dümmler, Monumenta Germaniae Historica, Libelli de lite 1 (Hanover, 1891), pp. 589, 620; English translation in *The Papal Reform of the Eleventh Century: Lives of Pope Leo IX and Pope Gregory VII*, trans. I. S. Robinson (Manchester, 2004), pp. 193, 260–1.

of Pope Leo IX spoke of 'the most evil nation of the Normans' and of their savagery and fury.[5] Once the Normans had allied with the reforming papacy in 1059, though thereafter relations were often tense, they found themselves in the imperial firing-line: Benzo of Alba labelled them 'robbers and tyrants' (*latronibus et tyrannis*) and the 'dung of the world' (*stercora mundi*), and also spoke of cleansing the 'stench of the Normans' (*fetore Normannorum*).[6] Several other accounts of the Norman arrival in southern Italy emphasise their background as exiles along with their mercenary motives, and thus outlawry, warfare, lucre and the Normans were well-known allies in the eleventh century.[7] Indeed, superficially, both Amatus' and William's versions can be reconciled with the other narrative traditions, for in both the Normans rapidly jettison their spiritual vocation to embark upon the path to power and wealth via violence and combat. But certainly Amatus' pilgrim origin story, portraying the Norman concern to protect Christendom against the encroachment of Islam, fits with the wider framework of his chronicle which seeks to balance Norman predation with Norman piety, and which presents the papal rapprochement of the 1050s and the conquest of Muslim Sicily as the point at which God's plan to employ the South Italian Normans in divine service becomes conclusively apparent.[8] That the Normans were pilgrims at the outset of a transformative process which temporarily led them into sin before returning them to a more righteous path suggests the power of divine prophecy, the ability to identify the preservation of faith and goodness amidst the lures of worldly power and lust.

On the other hand, William of Apulia's work, devised as an epic poem, was ostensibly intended to entertain courtly circles, and the pilgrim-warrior dialectic at the heart of the Norman story could only engage audience curiosity further as the Norman success unfolded. Moreover, if we follow

[5] *Ibid.*, pp. 141, 149–52.
[6] Among the many examples see Benzo of Alba, *Ad Heinricum IV Imperatorem Libri VII*, ed. H. Seyffert, MGH Scriptores Rerum Germanicarum 65 (Hanover, 1996), Bk II.2 p. 196, Bk II.16 p. 246, Bk III.1 p. 268, Bk III.15 [16] p. 316. For the wider background see H. E. J. Cowdrey, *The Age of Abbot Desiderius: Montecassino, the Papacy, and the Normans in the Eleventh and Early Twelfth Centuries* (Oxford, 1983), pp. 107–76. For more on papal-imperial invective see: J. A. Yunck, *The Lineage of Lady Meed: The Development of Mediaeval Venality-Satire* (Notre Dame, IN, 1963), pp. 47–83; and more generally J. Benzinger, *Invectiva in Romam: Romkritik im Mittelalter vom. 9. bis zum 12. Jahrhundert* (Lübeck, 1968).
[7] *Chronicon Monasterii Casinensis*, ed. H. Hoffman, MGH Scriptores 34 (Hanover, 1980), ii. 37, pp. 236–9; *Radulfus Glaber Opera*, ed. J. France, N. Bulst and P. Reynolds (Oxford, 1989), pp. 96–101; G. A. Loud, *The Age of Robert Guiscard: Southern Italy and the Norman Conquest* (Harlow, 2000), pp. 60–6.
[8] On this theme, see the introduction by G. A. Loud in Amatus of Montecassino, *The History of the Normans* and also K. B. Wolf, *Making History: The Normans and Their Historians in Eleventh-Century Italy* (Philadelphia, 1995), pp. 87–122. Similar divine undertones are discernible in the Norman histories of Dudo of Saint-Quentin and William of Jumièges, see Emily Albu, *The Normans in Their Histories: Propaganda, Myth and Subversion* (Woodbridge, 2001), pp. 7–46, 47–105.

the arguments of Emily Albu and Paul Brown, William's work may have been a critique, perhaps subconscious, of the Normans and one sympathetic to the Byzantines who are vanquished by the warriors from north of the Alps.[9] If so, then William's recording and usage of the pilgrim encounter on Monte Gargano might serve to warn how spiritual devotion could be corrupted by lust for secular power. It would thus fit with the sub-textual theme, expertly examined by Albu, of a corrupting *Normannitas* evidenced in several Norman chronicles of the Middle Ages, most vividly so in the work of Orderic Vitalis (composed c. 1114–41).[10] In short, two traditions emerged which assimilated Norman and pilgrim at the outset of the Norman infiltration into southern Italy, and which could conversely be used as an apology or critique. Evidence suggests that these traditions may have engaged with audiences well beyond the borders of southern Italy. The imagery of Norman pilgrims in southern Italy was disseminated to northern France and by the early twelfth century enshrined in legendary tones, for Orderic Vitalis, who did not appear to know Amatus' text directly, inserted into his work a version of the pilgrim origin-account which claimed that 100 Normans overcame 20,000 Muslims who had been enjoying a Salernitan beach-party.[11] Furthermore, manuscripts of William of Apulia's poem found their way to two monasteries in Normandy, Bec and Mont-Saint-Michel (the latter dated to the twelfth century), while sections of the work appear to have been incorporated into the mid-twelfth-century *Alexiad* of the Byzantine princess Anna Comnena, suggesting familiarity at Constantinople with Norman history in eleventh-century southern Italy, and by extension with the pilgrim origin narrative.[12]

It would also seem significant that from the 1130s – another key juncture in the history of Norman Italy – the subject of pilgrims and pilgrimage formed part of a wider strategy to justify and underpin the ideology of the new monarchy established in 1130 by Roger II (of Norman lineage). The struggles faced by Roger II to create and legitimate the monarchy are well known.[13] To

---

[9] Albu, *The Normans in Their Histories*, pp. 106–44; P. Brown, 'The *Gesta Roberti Wiscardi*: A "Byzantine" History?', *JMH* 37 (2011), 162–79.

[10] E. Albu, 'The Normans and Their Myth', *Haskins Society Journal* 11 (2003), 123–35, and also Albu, *The Normans in Their Histories*, especially pp. 180–213.

[11] OV, ii, pp. 56–7.

[12] G. Nortier, *Les bibliothèques médiévales des abbayes médiévales de Normandie: Fécamp, Le Bec, Le Mont Saint-Michel, Saint-Évroul, Lyre, Jumièges, Saint-Wandrille, Saint-Ouen* (Paris, 1971), p. 212; G. A. Loud, 'Anna Komnena and Her Sources for the Normans of Southern Italy', in *Church and Chronicle in the Middle Ages: Essays Presented to John Taylor*, ed. G. A. Loud and I. N. Wood (London, 1991), pp. 41–57.

[13] H. Houben, *Roger II of Sicily: A Ruler between East and West*, trans. G. A. Loud and D. Milburn (Cambridge, 1997), pp. 60–75; P. Oldfield, *City and Community in Norman Italy* (Cambridge, 2009), pp. 55–81.

many he was fearsomely authoritarian, a usurper of lands which rightfully belonged to others, and dubiously legitimised by an anti-pope – as Anacletus II would be deemed after his death in 1138 which hastened the end of nearly a decade of papal schism. A varied collection of classically minded twelfth- and thirteenth-century commentators labelled the Sicilian kings as tyrants, building on ancient traditions of despotic rule on the island. The Norman archdeacon, Arnulf of Seés, who was opposed to the Anacletian party during the schism, called Roger 'that tyrant whom the nurse of tyrants, Sicily, has sustained, the successor of Dionysius'.[14] Commentators from the German imperial court – the likes of Otto of Freising – and from the Byzantine Empire – such as John Kinnamos and Eustathios of Thessaloniki – wrote of the tyrannical Sicilian monarchy, and from their perspective understandably so given that both empires had direct political claims over southern Italy.[15] Yet, the 'tyrant Sicilian king' became such a uniform concept that it found its way not only into 'hostile' narratives and native Sicilian histories (the chronicle of the so-called 'Hugo Falcandus') but also into wider cultural streams.[16] To take just two examples, it appears in the late twelfth-century satirical work known as the *Speculum Stultorum* by the Englishman, Nigel Wireker, and in the early thirteenth-century chronicle by Jacques de Vitry, who denounced the Sicilian students at the University of Paris as tyrants.[17] Even worse for Roger II and his heirs, the presence of Greek Christian and Muslim communities in their realm drew suspicion, as did the monarchy's eclectic oriental imagery and limited direct participation in that most high-profile of Latin Christian ventures – the Crusades. Finally, the papacy never truly reconciled itself to the Sicilian kingdom's existence, and relations remained frosty until the Treaty of Benevento in 1156. The Saxon

---

[14] Arnulf of Seés, *In Girardum Engolismensium Invectiva*, MGH. Libelli de Lite iii (Hanover, 1897), p. 107. Dionysius I was known as the 'tyrant of Syracuse' who ruled from c. 432–367 BC. See also G. A. Loud, 'The Kingdom of Sicily and the Kingdom of England 1066–1266', *History* 88 (2003) pp. 549–50.

[15] *The Deeds of Frederick Barbarossa by Otto of Freising and His Continuator, Rahewin*, trans. C. C. Mierow (New York, 1953), pp. 165–6; *Deeds of John and Manuel Comnenus by John Cinnamus*, trans. C. M. Brand (New York, 1976), Bk II.4 p. 38, Bk II.12 p. 58, Bk III.5 p. 80, Bk IV.3 p. 110; *The Capture of Thessaloniki by Eustathios of Thessaloniki*, trans. J. R. Melville Jones (Canberra, 1988), pp. 59, 140, 153; and see the important article by H. Wieruszowski, 'Roger of Sicily, *Rex Tyrannus* in Twelfth-Century Political Thought', *Speculum* 38 (1963), 46–78.

[16] *La Historia o Liber de regno Sicilie e la Epistola ad Petrum Panormitane Ecclesie Thesaurium di Ugo Falcando*, ed. G. B. Siragusa, FSI 22 (Rome, 1897), pp. 6, 176 (English trans. in *The History of the Tyrants of Sicily by 'Hugo Falcandus', 1154–1169*, trans. G. A. Loud and T. Wiedemann (Manchester, 1998), pp. 58, 257).

[17] *The Book of Daun Burnel the Ass: Nigellus Wireker's Speculum stultorum*, trans. G. W. Regenos (Austin, TX, 1959), p. 121; *The Historia Occidentalis of Jacques de Vitry*, ed. J. F. Hinnesbuch (Fribourg, 1972), p. 92,

annals appeared then to encapsulate a prevailing twelfth-century western view in its condemnation of Roger II as a 'semi-pagan tyrant'.[18]

Within the kingdom of Sicily measures were taken to counter this damaging polemic. While the evidence for this is fragmented, from what survives it seems clear that one strategy was to portray the monarchy as the guardian of travellers and pilgrims, reflective of a deep-seated programme of royal peace and piety.[19] Of course, to an extent, royal peace-keeping represented standard measures of virtuous rulership evident across medieval Europe, and ones which had already been expounded coherently by Charlemagne in the late eighth century.[20] If after the collapse of Carolingian rule royal prerogatives over the upholding of peace decayed, the meritorious notion of public peace was revived by the church, in alliance with lay lords, through the Peace and Truce of God movements of the tenth and eleventh centuries. This process provided a foundation for lay rulers in the eleventh century to begin to reappropriate their peace-keeping privileges. Several scholars have shown how the Peace and Truce of God movements were reclaimed by lay rulers in order to bolster secular authority and lay claims over criminal justice.[21] William the Conqueror was an instrumental force at the Council of Lillebonne (1080) which – according to Orderic Vitalis – reaffirmed the 'Peace of God', 'for the good prosperity of God's church, and of the whole kingdom'; little wonder William was praised for his protection of the poor and travellers, and for the peace his authority facilitated.[22] In some regions, in Capetian France under the reign of Louis VI (1108–37), and in Germany from the Council of Mainz (1103) under the direction of Emperor Henry IV, the movement gradually metamorphosed into a 'royal peace' or an 'imperial peace' (*Reichsfreide*).

In the fraught political climate orbiting around the new kingdom of Sicily in the mid-twelfth century, small and subtle attempts to standardise Roger's kingship in correlation with similar notions of peacekeeping were

---

[18] *Die Reichschronik des Annalista Saxo*, ed. K. Naß, MGH SS 37 (Hanover, 2000), p. 608.

[19] For Roger's broader efforts to promote an ideal of Christian kingship in Sicily see Houben, *Roger II of Sicily*, pp. 113–35.

[20] See particularly Charlemagne's letter to King Offa of Mercia of 796: *Alcuin of York, c. AD 732 to 804*, trans. S. Allott (York, 1974), letter no. 40, pp. 51–3.

[21] H. E. J. Cowdrey, 'The Peace and the Truce of God in the Eleventh Century', *Past and Present* 46 (1970), 58–66; A. Grabois, 'De la trêve de Dieu à la paix du roi: etude sur les transformations du mouvement de la paix au XIIe siècle', in *Mélanges offerts à René Crozet*, vol. 1, ed. P. Gallais and Y.-J. Riou (Poitiers, 1966), pp. 585–96. I. S. Robinson, *Henry IV of Germany, 1056–1106* (Cambridge, 1999), pp. 319–20.

[22] OV, v, pp. 25–37 (quote at 25); see *The Gesta Guillelmi of William of Poitiers*, ed. and trans. R. H. C. Davis and M. Chibnall (Oxford,1998), p. 81; *The Anglo-Saxon Chronicle*, ed. and trans. M. Swanton (London, 2000), p. 220.

crucial and conveyed deeper significance. They were able to build upon earlier traditions of the Truce of God movement in southern Italy which had been proclaimed, with papal sanction, at the Councils of Melfi (1089) and Troia (1093, 1115, 1120).[23] Thus, in his chronicle, Roger's chief propagandist, the abbot Alexander of Telese, praised the king for establishing a general peace at a council held at Melfi in 1129; one which brought security and justice to the region and which, among its commands, proclaimed the protection of pilgrims who had previously been victims of robbery and murder.[24] The *Vita* of Saint William of Montevergine (d. 1142), which was composed in stages mostly after Roger's death (1154), makes comparable connections, for William had been mugged in Apulia in the 1120s while heading to Jerusalem as a pilgrim, and his hagiographer stated that this would not have occurred under the kingship of Roger II 'the exterminator of all evils and the best patron of peace and tranquillity'.[25] In the 1130s, Roger's subjugation of key territories within his realm, and the negotiation of truces, also harnessed the potent symbolic act of pilgrimage and drew upon the spiritually charged power of pilgrim-shrines. This was most apparent in relation to the key Apulian city of Bari. The urban community there had previously enjoyed wide autonomy under a regime led by a local ruler, Prince Grimoald Alfarinites, and offered some resistance to Roger's attempts to control the south Italian mainland.[26] At the same time, since 1087 the city had hosted the relics of Saint Nicholas, which were a source of great civic pride and prestige as the basilica of San Nicola soon developed into one of Christendom's premiere pilgrimage destinations. Consequently, part of Roger's strategy to subdue the city was framed in relation to the shrine and this saint. A royal charter of privileges, granted to the city in 1132, prioritised the autonomy and distinction of the shrine of Saint Nicholas, while an enamel plaque produced in the same decade depicted Saint Nicholas holding the crown on Roger II's head.[27] Later, once Pope Innocent II had formally acknowledged the formation of the kingdom of Sicily,

---

[23] Loud, *The Age of Robert Guiscard*, p. 227. For the 1120 council see *Les Chartes de Troia: Edition et étude critique des plus anciens documents conservés à l'archivio capitolare, 1 (1024–1266)*, ed. J.-M. Martin, Codice diplomatico pugliese 21 (Bari, 1976), no. 43.

[24] *Alexandri Telesini Abbatis Ystoria Rogerii Regis Sicilie Calabrie atque Apulie*, ed. L. De Nava, Fonti per la storia d'Italia 112 (Rome, 1991), pp. 3, 18–19.

[25] *Scrittura agiografica nel Mezzogiorno normanno: la Vita di San Guglielmo da Vercelli*, ed. F. Panarelli (Lecce, 2004), p. 10.

[26] Oldfield, *City and Community*, pp. 47–9.

[27] *Rogerii II Regis Diplomata Latina* (Codex Diplomaticus Regni Siciliae, Ser. I.ii (1)), ed. C.-R. Brühl (Cologne, 1987), pp. 54–6 no. 20; P. Belli d'Elia, M. S. Calò Mariani and L. Todisco, 'Architettura e arti figurative: dai bizantini agli svevi', in *Storia di Bari: Dalla conquista normanna al ducato sforzesco*, ed. F. Tateo (Bari, 1990), p. 301.

Roger performed a ritual entry into the papal enclave at Benevento where he visited, as a pilgrim would, an array of the city's renowned shrines, including Saint Bartholomew the Apostle's, and completed his tour in the monastery of Santa Sofia before the altar of Saint Mercurius (*ante altare Sancti Mercurii prostravit*).[28] It is perhaps equally significant that this ceremonial visit was recorded in the chronicle of Falco of Benevento, a work which for large sections is one of the most hostile of all to Roger II and his takeover of the mainland.

Such actions clearly assisted in rehabilitating Roger's reputation, a process increasingly apparent in the 1140s. It perhaps encouraged a figure no less than the eminent Cluniac abbot, Peter the Venerable, to write to Roger in 1139/40 praising the continual peace he had established in a traditionally discordant land, and likening the monarch to King Solomon (*velut alterius pacifici Salomonis*), who was renowned as a promoter of peace. Certainly, royal patronage for the Cluniac order and hopes for an alliance between France, Sicily and Germany against the Byzantines motivated Peter's communication, but it remains significant that so much of it, and a subsequent letter to Roger, was framed around the model of a peaceful realm.[29] This important facet of rulership, which was so visibly reflected in the security of pilgrims and other travellers, was still acknowledged towards the end of our period, in the reign of Roger's grandson King William II (1166–89). The Sicilian royal delegation at the Venice peace conference of 1177 presented William II as a king who invested great resources into defeating 'the enemies of the Cross', and who 'secured the road for those travelling to the Holy Sepulchre'.[30] Later, in 1178, William II made a very public spectacle of punishing the individuals responsible for an attack on the envoys of the Emperor Frederick Barbarossa as they passed through the kingdom. The guilty were hung at key junctions on the route-ways through southern Italy, thus showing that attacks on foreign visitors would be dealt with severely.[31] When passing comment on William's reign, the Campanian chronicler

---

[28] *Falcone di Benevento, Chronicon Beneventanum*, ed. E. D'Angelo (Florence, 1998), p. 224.

[29] *The Letters of Peter the Venerable*, ed. G. Constable. 2 vols. (Cambridge, MA, 1967) i, pp. 330–3, no. 131; M. Saurette, 'Peter the Venerable and Secular Friendship', in *Friendship in the Middle Ages and the Early Modern Age: Explorations of a Fundamental Ethical Discourse*, ed. A. Classen and M. Sandidge (Berlin and New York, 2010), pp. 301–4; Houben, *Roger II of Sicily*, pp. 94–5.

[30] *Romualdi Salernitani Chronicon*, ed. C. A. Garufi, Rerum Italicarum Scriptores 7 part 1 (Città di Castello, 1935), p. 290. See also: H. Houben, 'La politica estera di Guglielmo II tra vocazione mediterannea e destino europeo', in his *Mezzogiorno normanno-svevo: Monasteri e castelli, ebrei e musulmani* (Naples, 1996), pp. 150–1.

[31] *Romualdi Salernitani Chronicon*, p. 296.

Richard of S. Germano boasted that 'the traveller was not scared of the robber's trap, nor did the sailor fear injury from pirates by sea'.[32]

Articulating a concern for the pilgrim, and an affinity with pilgrimage, reflected a potent royal statement when considered alongside the geopolitical situation of southern Italy and Sicily in the twelfth century. This was the era of the great boom in devotional travel, exponentially intensified after the beginning of the crusading movement in 1095 which witnessed the emergence of the armed pilgrimage. Pilgrimage to Rome and, more so, to Jerusalem significantly increased in volume. Located in the central Mediterranean at the cross-roads of major travel route-ways, southern Italy and Sicily functioned as a crucial transit stage for much of this traffic; it was – as I have termed it elsewhere – a bridge to salvation, both logistically and metaphorically.[33] Once these territories were unified, a single dynasty effectively controlled a potential major checkpoint on the map of Christian pilgrimage. Furthermore, the unusual status of the kingdom of Jerusalem – founded by the crusaders in 1099 – needs to be factored in. As Smail demonstrated, this kingdom was regarded as the common responsibility of all Christians, it was a territory in which all had a stake and where no Christian could truly be an outsider.[34] Failures in crusading expeditions and setbacks in the Crusader states were blamed on the sinfulness of Christendom at large, and responses, evidenced in preaching and kingdom-wide taxes, show how the abstract duty of protecting a spiritual homeland was converted into tangible responses.[35] In the same understanding, from the moment of receiving their ritual blessing at the start of their journey, pilgrims performed an *imitatio Christi* and, particularly those bound for the Holy Land, were granted a type of extraterritorial immunity as they moved towards their final destination, conferred by the sacrifices they were undertaking on behalf of all Christendom.[36] This same ethos, the meritorious and universal duty to protect the pilgrim, was also from 1119 the initial *raison d'être* of the Templars in the Holy Land and contributed to the military monastic order's spectacular rise in the twelfth

---

[32] *Rycardi de Sancto Germano Notarii Chronica*, ed. C. A. Garufi, Rerum Italicarum Scriptores 8 part 2 (Bologna, 1937), p. 4.

[33] Oldfield, *Sanctity and Pilgrimage*, chapter 5.

[34] R. C. Smail, 'The International Status of the Latin Kingdom of Jerusalem', in *The Eastern Mediterranean Lands in the Period of the Crusades*, ed. P. M. Holt (Warminster, 1977), pp. 23–43.

[35] Cole, *The Preaching of the Crusades to the Holy Land*, pp. 37–61; E. Siberry, *Criticism of Crusading, 1095–1274* (Oxford, 1984), pp. 69–108.

[36] See generally W. J. Purkis, *Crusading Spirituality in the Holy Land and Iberia, c. 1095– c. 1187* (Woodbridge, 2008). For ritual blessings see: D. A. Rivard, '*Pro Iter Agentibus*: The Ritual Blessing of Pilgrims and Their Insignia in a Pontifical of Southern Italy', *JMH* 27 (2001), 365–98.

and thirteenth centuries. In short, perhaps more than in any other zone of Latin Christendom, by facilitating pilgrimage in their territories, Roger II and his heirs could advertise their Christian responsibility and commitment to a crusading movement which they were, for good reason, reluctant to participate in directly. Such reluctance seemingly stemmed from King Baldwin I of Jerusalem's humiliatingly abrupt divorce of Roger's mother Adelaide in 1117.[37] The Sicilian willingness, however, to offer indirect support was most visible when Roger II allegedly pledged all the facilities of his realm to aid the transit of the crusading force of King Louis VII in 1147.[38] The experience of the pilgrim in southern Italy and Sicily advertised an alternative public face of the kingdom, one which could be reflected back across Europe to counter the charges of Sicilian tyranny and illegitimacy, and which could demonstrate other ways of supporting crusading.

Indeed, Roger II and his heirs later in the twelfth century reigned during a period which saw the travel infrastructures within their kingdom improved and expanded, most notably with an increase in monastic houses and other hospices which sheltered pilgrims at key junctions and ports. If much of this originated not from direct royal initiative, it was certainly indirectly supported through royal patronage for certain monastic orders – Montecassino, Montevergine, Cava – and royal control of ports. Moreover, Roger II's commissioning of the so-called *Book of Roger*, a geographical survey of the world which was completed by the Muslim geographer al-Idrisi shortly after the king's death in 1154, showed the monarch's interest in the travel infrastructures, facilities and route-ways which connected the varied settlements within his kingdom.[39] A later commentator added that Roger was especially concerned to control movement into and across his kingdom by taking advantage of its landscape. Thus mountains formed natural barriers, and rivers which could only be crossed by bridges, valleys which were barred by walls, and coasts monitored by towers and naval forces, all provided natural checkpoints.[40]

---

[37] Adelaide had married King Baldwin I of Jerusalem in 1113, and then saw the marriage suddenly annulled in 1117 when the king opted to restore relations with his first wife who, it seems, had never formally been divorced. Other factors – the political instability within the kingdom of Sicily, eastern Mediterranean diplomacy and rivalries, the presence of a Sicilian Muslim community – equally played their part; for more see G. A. Loud, 'Norman Italy and the Holy Land', in *The Horns of Hattin*, ed. B. Kedar (London, 1992), pp. 49–62.

[38] *De profectione Ludovici VII in orientem: The journey of Louis VII to the East by Odo of Deuil*, ed. and trans. V. G. Berry (New York, 1948), p. 11.

[39] For an accessible French translation see: *Idrisi, La premiere géographie l'Occident*, revised translation by H. Bresc *et al.* (Paris, 1999).

[40] *Chronicon Ignoti Monachi Cisterciensis Sanctae Mariae de Ferraria*, ed. A. Gaudenzi (Naples, 1888), pp. 26–7.

If protecting pilgrims was a useful tool to revise hostile perceptions of the monarchy and indeed the region, it also came with risk. This was most notable in the early history of the kingdom of Jerusalem. Albert of Aachen's work is littered with Muslim attacks on Christian pilgrims which demoralised Christian morale and weakened the visage of royal power during the reign of Baldwin I (1100–18); hence the king's savage punishment of any perpetrators he could capture and the demand for a 'specialist' organisation like the Templars.[41] In Latin Christendom itself, no medieval monarchy could guarantee security throughout its realm, and the very public and special nature of pilgrimage to Jerusalem would always draw external observation. Unsurprisingly, pilgrims often suffered as part of the collateral damage arising out of localised conflicts. As early as 1016, the French chronicler Adhemar of Chabannes reported great disruption for pilgrims on what he called the *via Hierosolimae* in southern Italy, caused by warfare in Apulia between the Normans, Lombards and Byzantines.[42] In the 1050s, John abbot of Fécamp complained to Pope Leo IX that the disorder created by the Normans in southern Italy was so enraging the local communities that they were attacking any foreigners, including pilgrims.[43] The abbot's protest no doubt formed part of Leo IX's dossier to justify his ill-fated offensive against the Normans of southern Italy at the Battle of Civitate in 1053. Afterwards, in the fall-out that followed Roger II's death in 1154, the kingdom suffered a period of rebellion in 1155–56, and such was its effect on travel conditions there that William of Tyre, the leading chronicler of the Crusader states, reported news of the problems it caused for travellers.[44] Later in the twelfth century, the diplomat and poet Peter of Blois signalled the inherent vulnerability of pilgrims, and perhaps questioned their safety in the kingdom of Sicily, when he beseeched the archbishop of Palermo to aid northern Europeans (*cisalpini*) on their journeys to or from the Holy Land, where they stood in the footsteps of the Lord (*in qua steterunt pedes Domini*).[45] But it was the monarchy itself that was responsible for an episode that, in the eyes of some, harmed the dynasty's reputation. In 1185 King William II was preparing a huge naval expedition for an attack on the Byzantine Empire, and in the process, as recorded by the *Continuator*

---

[41] See, for example, the attack on 700 pilgrims between Jerusalem and the River Jordan in 1119, and, earlier, Baldwin I's order to execute or enslave members of a community of cave-dwellers south of the Dead Sea who had been attacking pilgrims, AA, pp. 880–1; Bk VII.39–40 pp. 542–7.

[42] *Ademari Historiarum Libri III*, ed. G. Pertz, MGH SS 4 (Hanover, 1841), p. 140.

[43] *Epistola Joannis I abbatis Fiscamnensis ad S. Leonem IX*, Patrologia Latina 143 (Paris, 1882), pp. 798–9.

[44] Guillaume de Tyr, *Chronique*, ed. R. B. C. Huygens, CCCM63 (Turnhout, 1986), p. 819.

[45] *Petri Blesensis, Opera Omnia*, Patrologia Latina 207 (Paris, 1855), no. 66 c. 196.

of the Chronicle of William of Tyre, the king 'retained the pilgrims from other lands who were passing through his territories'. Whether they were forced to join the naval force, or were simply held up by the preparations is not entirely clear. Either way, it was said that as a result, 'for two years he [William II] prevented the passage so that no one could cross to Outremer'. The *Continuator* went on to record the belief held in some circles that William II's actions paved the way for Saladin's victory over the Christians at Hattin (in 1187) which led to the fall of Jerusalem.[46] An unfair claim, no doubt, but in the context of the time perhaps one of the most injurious accusations possible. Protecting the pilgrim and enabling safe transit were praiseworthy; failing to do so could be damning.

The protection of pilgrims within the kingdom was not, of course, purely an exercise in public relations. The passage of pilgrims offered a variety of quite diverse opportunities. In 1085, for example, Count Roger I of Sicily encouraged certain priests *transmontanis partibus* to abandon their journey to the Holy Sepulchre and populate instead a new church foundation in Calabria.[47] In the 1160s the beleaguered Sicilian royal chancellor, Stephen de Perche, fearing for his safety in Palermo, benefited from the fortuitous arrival of some French knights heading for Jerusalem, and recruited them into his personal retinue.[48] Pilgrims could also be used in military campaigns. This occurred regularly in the special climate of the Crusader states; for example, crusader-pilgrims assisted in the siege of Jaffa in 1102, and Scandinavian, English and Flemish contingents were used in two offensives against the city of Sidon in 1106 and in 1110.[49] Later, the pivotal capture of Ascalon by the king of Jerusalem in 1153 was achieved with an army notably bolstered by recently arrived sailors and pilgrims. As William of Tyre tells us:

> Having heard [of their arrival], a council was held and men were sent from the army, who by royal authority forbid those sailors and pilgrims wishing to return [home] from doing so. They invited them all, with promises of money, to help in a siege and a work so acceptable to God, and they also brought small and large ships. Having done this rapidly, within a few days, following a good coastal wind, all the ships which had arrived in that [recent] passage, arrived before the city [of Ascalon] and a vast force of

---

[46] *La continuation de Guillaume de Tyr (1184–1197)*, ed. M. Morgan (Paris, 1982), chap. 72, p. 82.
[47] K. A. Kehr, *Die Urkunden der Normannisch-Sizilischen Könige – eine diplomatische Untersuchung* (Innsbruck, 1902), no. 2, pp. 410–11.
[48] *La Historia o Liber de regno Sicilie*, p. 129 (*History of the Tyrants*, p. 180).
[49] AA, pp. 658–9, 718–27, 804–9.

pilgrims – both knights and infantry – joined our expedition and every day increased the army.[50]

But, as we have seen, in the case of William II's preparation for the Sicilian attack on Byzantium, pilgrims could be conscripted into military service in European territories, and in 1194, when Henry VI of Germany invaded southern Italy, he supplemented his army with fellow-German pilgrims who were travelling along the same routes for the Holy Land.[51]

It is apparent, also, that legitimate financial profit was associated with the presence of pilgrims. Indeed, the pilgrim was heavily tied to the notion of money, and the carrying of a purse was a visible symbol of the pilgrim's status.[52] Impossible to quantify as it is, numerous local religious houses and hostelries benefited from payments made by pilgrims, and the Sicilian monarchy undoubtedly took a share of various tolls which pilgrims would have contributed to. We certainly should not underestimate the volume of pilgrims passing along the region's roads and through its ports. Evidence is fragmented, indirect and anecdotal, but points towards huge concentrations of pilgrim traffic in the region.[53] The Jewish traveller Benjamin of Tudela passed through southern Italy in c. 1170 and noted the city of Trani, 'where all the pilgrims gather to go to Jerusalem', and Messina, at which 'most of the pilgrims assemble to cross over to Jerusalem, as this is the best crossing'.[54] Muhammad al-Idrisi, in his *Book of Roger*, wrote that at Messina 'one finds congregated the greatest ships and that one encounters travellers and merchants from every sort of country, Christian and Muslim'.[55] The lucrative pilgrim–profit interrelationship could however lead to open abuse. In the 1160s at Messina, illegal financial exactions made on boats heading for the Holy Land sparked violent civil unrest. A certain Odo Quarrel of Chartres, an advisor in the household of the aforementioned Chancellor Stephen de Perche, was discovered extorting money at Messina from ships bound for Syria, and not allowing them to leave the

---

[50] *Guillaume de Tyre, Chronique*, p. 793.

[51] *Die Chronik Ottos von St. Blasien und die Marbacher Annalen*, ed. and trans. F.-J. Schmale (Darmstadt, 1998), p. 121.

[52] L. K. Little, *Religious Poverty and the Profit Economy in Medieval Europe* (New York, 1978), pp. 31–2.

[53] For more see Oldfield, *Sanctity and Pilgrimage*, chapter 5.

[54] *The Itinerary of Benjamin of Tudela*, trans. M. N. Adler (London, 1907), pp. 66, 137. For German crusaders arriving at Messina in the 1190s see *Arnoldi Chronica Slavorum*, ed. J. M. Lappenberg, MGH SS 21 (Hanover, 1868), p. 204.

[55] English translation in *Roger II and the Creation of the Kingdom of Sicily*, trans. G. A. Loud (Manchester, 2012), p. 361 (French trans. in *Idrisi*, p. 312). For a comparable description of Messina see *The Travels of Ibn Jubayr*, trans. R. J. C. Broadhurst (London, 1952), pp. 338–9.

harbour until payment had been made. Some of these, quite likely, were local Messinesi ships which had been accustomed to be free from such charges, and such additional payment might have threatened to raise the costs of transit for pilgrims, which in turn might have discouraged them from utilising the port city and its services. This sparked a series of volatile disturbances in the city which gave vent to other grievances which had been crystallising for some time, and ultimately led to the brutal murder of Odo Quarrel.[56]

Local customs show further financial benefits which were associated with the presence of pilgrims, for if they died under certain circumstances in these cities, local inhabitants could claim a share of their moveable goods. The inclusion of these clauses within these documents are testament to the significance of the subject. At Troia a set of privileges, granted by Pope Honorius II in 1127, established that if *viatores* and *peregrini* died in the city then a quarter of their possessions were to go to the papal court, with the remainder due to whoever else they chose; if they died without a will then all possessions could be claimed by the city's bishop, according to an earlier concession made by the Norman Duke Robert Guiscard (d. 1085) with the exception of the deceased's clothes which, following ancient custom, were due to whoever had given hospitality to the traveller or pilgrim.[57] In 1190, King Tancred of Sicily issued a set of privileges to Barletta, including a lengthy clause on the wills of deceased pilgrims: royal bailiffs could only take the king's share from pilgrims who died intestate, and procedures were established to ascertain, if doubt existed, whether the deceased was in fact a pilgrim.[58] A year later, the master of the Hospital of the Germans (*domus Alamannorum hospitalis*) which had been newly constructed in Brindisi, and was part of the new German order founded at Acre 1190 which would eventually evolve into the Teutonic Knights, acknowledged his subjection to the authority of Brindisi's archbishop.[59] In doing so, the German hospital could administer the Eucharist for, and hear confession from, pilgrims and was also permitted to bury pilgrims in its associated church and to receive three-quarters of the deceased's estate (it does not specify if this related only to those who died intestate).

Clearly, such situations bred abuse, as a document from Benevento in 1169 makes clear. A decree issued by the city's overlord, Pope Alexander

---

[56] *La Historia o Liber de regno Sicilie*, pp. 147–53 (*History of the Tyrants*, pp. 200–6).
[57] *Chartes de Troia*, no. 50.
[58] *Tancredi et Willelmi III Regum Diplomata*, ed. H. Zielinski (Cologne, 1982), no. 1, pp. 4–5.
[59] *Codice diplomatico brindisino*, vol. 1 *(492–1299)*, ed. G.-M. Monti (Trani, 1940), no. 26.

III, abolished a distasteful custom in the city of Benevento. It was outlined as follows:

> Now a certain practice, or rather an unlawful practice, is said to have come into existence in your city, which is acknowledged to be incompatible with human and divine laws, and the practice is bringing both those who practice it and those who set it up to risk divine punishment. Merchants and indeed travellers and pilgrims who have been received hospitably at someone's house in the city, if it should happen that they fall ill there, are not permitted to go home, or to make a will concerning their property, or to choose burial where they want, if they should die … As a result of this many people suspect that it happens on occasion that sometimes the sick are so badly looked after by their hosts that the death of the sick seems to have occurred through the greed of their landlords and helped along by their hands and their wish.[60]

Matters might well have been made worse by ambiguities in actually identifying genuine pilgrims, an issue already alluded to in the Barletta document. The addition of a new type of devotional traveller – the armed pilgrim – with the commencement of the crusading movement accentuated the confusion and contradictions, when individuals could seamlessly mutate between the secular and the spiritual, the warrior and the pilgrim. Such uncertainties must have been intensified too by a continuing backdrop of opposition to pilgrimage, mostly from monastic circles which espoused the importance of faith internalised over external expressions such as pilgrimage.[61] To choose one of countless examples of these scrambled identities, Albert of Aachen recorded the arrival of King Sigurd of Norway in the Holy Land in 1110, presenting the Scandinavian monarch's ardent desire to first visit the holy places in Jerusalem before participating in an offensive with King Baldwin I against the city of Sidon.[62] Christopher Tyerman has powerfully demonstrated the absence of defined crusading institutions prior to the late twelfth century, and famously *peregrinus* was one of many terms used for crusaders before the introduction of *crucesignatus* in

---

[60] *Le più antiche carte del capitolo della cattedrale di Benevento (668–1200)*, ed. A. Ciarelli et al. (Rome, 2002), no. 89. This translation was revised by comparison with one made by Ian Moxon to whom I am grateful. In 1039 a Spanish pilgrim heading for Rome was reported to have died at Benevento: P. Skinner, *Medieval Amalfi and Its Diaspora, 850–1250* (Oxford, 2013), p. 243.

[61] G. Constable, 'Opposition to Pilgrimage in the Middle Ages', in his *Religious Life and Thought (11th–12th Centuries)* (London, 1979), pp. 125–46.

[62] AA, pp. 804–9.

c. 1200.⁶³ Many contemporaries clearly struggled to disentangle the identity and status of participants in crusading expeditions. Furthermore, the identity of a pilgrim, and the immunity it afforded, could be subverted. This uncertainty, combined with an ability to provide information, one might even say 'intelligence', on distant lands, transferred a certain power to the pilgrim.⁶⁴ Already in the late eighth century Charlemagne had warned of merchants who joined bands of pilgrims and were thus evading the payment of tolls.⁶⁵ Later, when Bohemond II, Prince of Antioch, died in 1130, Roger II of Sicily, as a relative, had a claim to succeed to the principality. Instead, a party from Antioch offered the principality to Raymond of Poitiers who was forced to travel through southern Italy in 1135/36 to claim his prize. William of Tyre colourfully described how Raymond covertly escaped Roger's clutches:

> The lord Raymond, wisely hiding his plans, laid down all pride and, travelling as one from the common people, now on foot, now riding on a lowly beast of burden, he undertook his journey among the people ... Thus, dressed in a humble pilgrim's habit, and generally taking on the duties of servants, in appearance he deceived everyone and avoided the traps of his wise and most powerful enemy.⁶⁶

Raymond was thus more successful than Richard I of England who was famously taken captive in 1192 by his enemy Duke Leopold of Austria, despite, according to some accounts, being disguised as a low-ranking pilgrim returning from Jerusalem.⁶⁷ The use of pilgrimage to mask other activities was certainly a common theme in medieval sources: in the late eleventh century, the pro-Gregorian reformer, Bonizo of Sutri alleged that Guibert of Ravenna (the anti-pope Clement III, d. 1100) 'lingered in Rome, going about the city under the pretext of a pilgrimage', while secretly fomenting conspiracies.⁶⁸

Finally, the attraction, protection and cure of pilgrims at individual

---

⁶³ Tyerman, 'Were There Any Crusades in the Twelfth Century?', 553–77; M. Markowski, 'Crucesignatus: Its Origins and Early Usage', *JMH* 10 (1984), 157–65.

⁶⁴ It is perhaps interesting to note how frequently in *Chansons de Geste* and courtly romances the figure of the pilgrim played a role at a pivotal moment in the hero's quest, often providing crucial information on far-away territories, or allowing the hero to reflectively articulate the purposes of his mission. See for example: *Aiol: A Chanson de Geste*, trans. S. C. Malicote and A. R. Hartman (New York, 2014), 36–40, verses 1492–1723, pp. 38–42 and Gottfried von Strassburg, *Tristan*, trans. A. T. Hatto (Harmondsworth, 1975), pp. 75–7.

⁶⁵ *Alcuin of York*, letter no. 40 p. 52.

⁶⁶ Guillaume de Tyr, *Chronique*, pp. 657–8.

⁶⁷ *Radulphi de Coggeshall, Chronicon Anglicanum*, ed. J. Stevenson (London, 1875), pp. 52–8.

⁶⁸ *Bonizonis episcopi Sutrini*, p. 603; English trans. in Robinson, *Papal Reform*, p. 225.

shrines across southern Italy replicated at a local level many of the dynamics thus far considered. Here I can do no more than briefly draw attention to them.[69] Shrines competed with each other to demonstrate the superiority of their saint, and by extension of the local community. This could be measured by the presence of pilgrims who had travelled long distances, or who had turned away from other shrines. Pilgrims also, obviously, brought with them money for local services and donations to the shrine. Those heading for Jerusalem were deemed particularly prestigious and were pointedly noted at Trani, where the city's cult of Saint Nicholas the Pilgrim was established barely a decade or so after the famous arrival of the relics of Saint Nicholas from Myra to Bari in 1087.[70] Apulian urban, economic and ecclesiastical rivalries were at play here. Fuelled by similar motives was the production in *c.* 1100 of a polemical tract known as the *Adventus Sancti Nycolai in Beneventum*. Its underlying premise asserted that the patronage of Saint Nicholas had moved to Benevento from Bari because the latter city was so inhospitable to the visitor that the saint had urged pilgrims to head to the more salubrious climes of Benevento where his spiritual assistance could henceforth be found.[71] Indeed, the ultimate expression of the utility and value of the pilgrim can be reflected in the development of several cults around saints who had been heavily associated with pilgrimage during their lifetimes: Saint Nicholas the Pilgrim at Trani, Saint William of Montevergine and several Campanian saints fit such a pattern.

It is, I hope, apparent that pilgrimage was simultaneously fulfilling, complex, lucrative, sanitising, dangerous and manipulated. How an individual or community placed itself in relation to the pilgrim could be read as a critically important statement – be it as a protector, imitator or subverter. Indeed it must be remembered too that authentic expressions of piety and charity could co-exist in some of those individuals or groups who made gains from pilgrimage. At the same time, the figure of the pilgrim was far from passive or victimised; the potential for multiple identities (and motives) within any one pilgrim seriously redressed the balance, and could engender discomfiture in the surrounding community. Thus far we might apply these conclusions to many regions of Europe. However, as we have seen, in the complicated sociocultural landscape of Norman Italy, a landscape endowed with huge geopolitical importance in the eleventh and

---

[69] For more on local patterns of pilgrimage see Oldfield, *Sanctity and Pilgrimage*, chapters 2 and 6.
[70] P. Oldfield, 'St Nicholas the Pilgrim and the City of Trani between Greeks and Normans, *c.* 1090–c.1140', *ANS* 30 (2008), 168–81.
[71] G. Cangiano, 'L'*Adventus Sancti Nycolai in Beneventum*', *Atti della società storica del Sannio* 2 (1924), 131–62.

twelfth centuries, the multivalent figure of the pilgrim carried a special significance for both local communities and the region's elites (particularly its Norman rulers). This was due to three interlocking factors: the unusually high quantity of pilgrims in the region; the large proportion of those pilgrims who were heading for Jerusalem, an enterprise of interest to all Latin Christian Europe; and the enduring need for southern Italy's Norman elites to promote the legitimacy of their rule. In a land such as medieval southern Italy where travel and movement across its various borders was both frequent and significant, and where political rule was rarely uncontested and was often the subject of fierce polemic, the presence of the pilgrim was thus encoded with various meanings, and served equally numerous purposes, all of which offer us valuable perspectives on the complexities of Norman Italy.

Part IV

9

Antioch and the Normans

EMILY ALBU

In an assault engineered by Bohemond, a South Italian Norman and eldest son of Robert Guiscard, Antioch fell to the Latin forces of the First Crusade on 3 June 1098. Those first crusaders encountered this highly fortified city as the most formidable obstacle on their journey to Jerusalem. After a contentious struggle for control, Bohemond claimed lordship over the ancient city. He and his successors then held it as the heart of a territory now known as the Norman principality of Antioch, longest lived of the Latins' possessions in the Levant (1098–1268) and outlasting Latin Jerusalem for more than eighty years.

What made the Normans especially well prepared for crusading in the East? What distinctive skills or qualities of the Normans contributed to their success at Antioch? How did Antioch so often come to define the crusading experience for many participants and admirers of the crusading enterprise? These are the questions at the centre of this chapter.

When the Normans in Bohemond's troop first reached Antioch, after a long and harrying trek to Constantinople and across Asia Minor, they were astonished to confront such a vast and magnificent city, its two square miles enclosed within awe-inspiring fortifications, massive double walls built in the sixth century. The oldest surviving chronicle of the journey, the *Gesta Francorum* written by a member of Bohemond's fighting force, celebrates Antioch with a striking *status urbis*/description of the city, inserted in the manuscripts immediately following the account of the capture and defence of Antioch, before the armies headed south toward Jerusalem:

> This city, namely Antioch, is very lovely and distinguished. Within its walls are four enormous and really high mountains. On the highest one is the citadel, a remarkable edifice and very strong. Down below is the city, distinguished and well laid out, adorned with all sorts of sacred buildings, since it holds many churches, some 300, and sixty monasteries. Its patriarch oversees 153 bishops.

Two walls enclose the city. The larger of these is very high and remarkably broad, built of great stones, with 450 towers arranged on it. By all measures the city is beautiful. On the east it is enclosed by four big mountains; on the west, along the city walls, runs a river called Farfar. This is a city highly invested with royal authority, because seventy-five kings had founded it, the first of them being King Antiochus, from whom Antioch gets its name. This remarkable city the Franks besieged for eight months and a day.[1]

Nearly the middle half of the *Gesta Francorum* features events at Antioch as the site of the crusade's defining moments, from the crusaders' arrival there to their stunning victory, on 28 June 1098, in the great battle against the Muslim forces commanded by Karbuqa, emir of Mosul and the sultan's agent. The crucial importance of Antioch in the crusader imagination places it at centre stage in this first crusading chronicle.

For the writer of that descriptive passage, as for other Latins on crusade, Antioch was a city of legendary antiquity and splendour, a fortress made even grander by its intimate connections with royal and imperial powers. Founded by one of Alexander's generals, it enjoyed prominence under the Seleucids and then the Romans, whose fourth-century CE emperors sometimes made it their imperial residence. With the rise of Christianity, Antioch joined Alexandria, Constantinople and Jerusalem as one of the four patriarchal sees. Antioch's harbour tied it to Mediterranean shipping, and its place on the Roman road network made it an important stopping place on trade routes to the East. Earthquakes and plague weakened its position in the sixth century, however, as did a siege by Arabs in 529 and a pillaging by Persians in 540. When Byzantium and Persia fought for domination in the early seventh century, Antioch found itself at a flash-point in their struggle. Persians occupied the city (609/10–628) until Herakleios' miraculous victories captured it once again for Byzantium. But the rise of a new power in the East cut short the empire's jubilation. Antioch fell an early victim to the Arab conquests that swept south and west along the Mediterranean all the way to Spain. Yet in the Christian empire's rejuvenation under the Macedonian emperors, Byzantium took the city back in 969, holding it until an Armenian rebel, Philaretos Brachamios, seized control in 1078, aided by Norman mercenaries. Seljuks captured it from Philaretos

---

[1] Hill, *GF*, pp. 76–7. Translations from the Latin are my own except where otherwise noted. Some scholars have thought this a composite text by slightly later sources. See Jay Rubenstein, 'What Is the *Gesta Francorum*, and Who Was Peter Tudebode?' *Revue Mabillon* 16 (2005), 179–204. I have argued that it was largely a single-authored work, partly written en route: Emily Albu, *The Normans in Their Histories: Propaganda, Myth and Subversion* (Woodbridge, 2001), pp. 145–79.

in turn in December 1084, making Antioch a prized part of their Sultanate of Rum.

This history of conquest notwithstanding, Antioch's site and formidable walls made the city quite defensible whenever it could muster loyal forces sufficiently numerous to man the towers. As the crusaders began their siege on 21 October 1097 Antioch held a mixed population, reflecting its contentious recent past, with Turks, Armenians and Greeks living together in uneasy community. Perhaps it is not surprising, then, that it was probably an Armenian who let Bohemond climb into a tower he was guarding, giving up the city after an eight-month siege.[2] As we shall see, it comes as no surprise, either, that a Norman's initiative and machinations engineered the capture of a city associated with imperial power. Just as the South Italian Normans were especially well prepared for the crusading enterprise, so Bohemond was best positioned among them to take and hold Antioch.

The Italo-Norman Advantage

Compared with crusaders from more northern lands, Normans of southern Italy reached the East better suited to conditions of the Levant. Their greater ease in adapting to a familiar climate must have played a small part in this. But Normans of the south especially benefited from long contact with Byzantines and Arabs in Italy and Sicily. From fighting alongside eastern Christians and Muslims as well as against them, Normans thoroughly understood the art of negotiation and the strategies of siege warfare. Having adapted armour and fighting techniques learned from Byzantines and Arabs, southern Normans came equipped to engage those foes in physical combat and in a battle of wits.

William of Apulia's *Gesta Roberti Wiscardi* presents some of this preparation in striking detail.[3] Writing in southern Italy c. 1095–99, during the years of the First Crusade, William followed the Norman conquests in Italy and Sicily from the early years of that century, with the arrival of the first Norman mercenaries serving Byzantines and Lombards, to the death in 1085 of Bohemond's father, Robert Guiscard, whose ambitions and exploits

---

[2] For the suggestion that Firuz was a 'renegade Armenian' with his own reasons for betraying Antioch, see Steven Runciman, 'The First Crusade: Antioch to Ascalon', in *A History of the Crusades*, 3 vols. (Cambridge, 1951–4), i, p. 317. John France has explained the confusion in the sources concerning the traitor's ethnicity: John France, *Victory in the East: A Military History of the First Crusade* (Cambridge, 1994), pp. 257–8.

[3] This section draws on chapter 3, 'Normans in the South', in Albu, *The Normans in Their Histories*, pp. 106–44, and on my PhD dissertation, 'William of Apulia's *Gesta Roberti Wiscardi* and Anna Comnena's *Alexiad*: A Literary Comparison' (University of California, Berkeley, 1975).

the *Gesta* features.[4] The first three of the *Gesta*'s five books chronicle the Normans' struggles against their former employers as the Hauteville brothers – 'men without peer from the time of Caesar or Charlemagne' (5.405–6) – especially Guiscard and his youngest brother Roger, succeeded in carving out their own realms in southern Italy and Sicily. The final two books turn to Guiscard's venture against Byzantine lands in Dalmatia, concluding with the Norman leader's death and funeral in 1085.

Sieges played a dominant role in Norman aggression, and William has devoted considerable attention to the sieges of Trani, Salerno, Iuvenacus (Giovinazzo), Dyrrachium (Durazzo), Cephalonia and many other cities.[5] Some campaigns, like the one against wealthy Bari, William has related in detail, describing attacks and counter-attacks, the building of siege machinery drawn up to the wall on the land side, the blockading of the port by Guiscard's navy, and the overturning of Guiscard's tower and bridge by the men of Bari.[6] Only after an exhausting three-year siege did the city fall to Normans at last in 1071. Bohemond and many of his companions took part in some of these assaults, gaining experience they could draw upon during the crusade. Bohemond was besieging Amalfi when he caught his first sight of crusaders and joined their ranks.

Italo-Normans learned how to fight and arm themselves like the adversaries they faced in those conquests. Carvings over the north door of the church of San Nicola at Bari, for instance, illustrate the influence of Arab and Byzantine warriors. The church held the precious relics of Saint Nicholas, stolen in 1087 from their resting place in the Lycian city of Myra by traders from Bari who were sailing home from a mercantile expedition to Antioch.[7] Bari's church-door scene may depict the capture of Jerusalem during the First Crusade but most likely celebrates the 1098 siege of Antioch, engineered by Bohemond. The turbans, helmet, hauberk and weaponry of the Muslim defenders probably imitate equipage of Sicilian Muslims. As Gravett and Nicolle have noted, the four horsemen on the observer's left, with their mail hauberks and spears, look much like the Norman knights on the Bayeux Tapestry.[8] Three of those attacking from the right, however, carry swords or spears and wear lamellar armour characteristic of

---

[4] John France has dated their arrival in southern Italy to 1017: France, 'The Occasion of the Coming of the Normans to Southern Italy', *JMH* 17.3 (1991), 195–205.

[5] For Trani, *GRW*, pp. 184–5; Salerno, pp. 186–9; Iuvenacus, pp. 194–5; Dyrrachium, pp. 216–31; Cephalonia, pp. 248–9.

[6] *GRW*, pp. 158–63, 170–3.

[7] Latin, Greek and Russian sources tell this famous story. See Marjorie Chibnall's brief account of the sources and historical background: OV, iv, pp. 353–4.

[8] Christopher Gravett and David Nicolle, *The Normans* (Oxford, 2006), p. 58.

Byzantine warriors. Those three carved fighters may well demonstrate Byzantine influence on Italo-Normans, the likely models for those depictions.

Italo-Normans knew much more about eastern peoples than simply their weaponry and tactics. William of Apulia's *Gesta Roberti Wiscardi* demonstrates just how deep that familiarity might run. The mercantile interests of southern Italy provided some of William's connections to the wider world, as the port of opulent Amalfi enjoyed a lucrative trade with many lands, expressly including royal Antioch:

> Huc et Alexandri diversa feruntur ab urbe,
> Regis et Antiochi; gens haec freta plurima transit;
> His Arabes, Libi, Siculi noscuntur et Afri:
> Haec gens est totum notissima paene per orbem
> Et mercanda ferens et amans mercata referre.
>
> Various items are brought here from the cities of Alexander
> and King Antiochus; Amalfi's people cross many seas.
> Here they come to know Arabs, Libyans, Sicilians, and Africans.
> Its people are very well known throughout almost the entire world,
> as they move their merchandise and delight in bringing back their
> purchases.[9]

Military and diplomatic contacts, too, offered William an impressive awareness of foreign affairs, especially those that concerned the Byzantine Empire. Perhaps not surprisingly, he reported the stories of Normans who rebelled against Guiscard and then sought refuge in Byzantium: Jocelyn, lord of Molfetta, for instance, who returned to Italy with a Byzantine fleet and unwittingly played a role in the blinding of the emperor Romanos Diogenes;[10] and Guiscard's recalcitrant nephew Abelard, who fled to Alexios Komnenos.[11] William could identify the succession of catapans, the governors of Apulia and Calabria under Byzantine rule, and the generals who directed campaigns against the Normans in southern Italy: the catapan Tornikios and his legate in the first battle, Leo Pakianos;[12] general Michael Dokeianos who humiliated the mercenary Hardoin;[13] Michael Dokeianos' replacement, the son of Basil Bojoannes;[14] Emperor Michael V's ineffectual

---

[9] *GRW*, pp. 190–1.
[10] *Ibid.*, pp. 156–7, 162–3, 168–9.
[11] *Ibid.*, pp. 200–1.
[12] *Ibid.*, pp. 102–3.
[13] *Ibid.*, pp. 108–11.
[14] *Ibid.*, pp. 116–21.

appointee Synodianos, who was soon recalled by imperial order;[15] the notorious George Maniakes, whose handsome appearance was his only virtue;[16] and Stephen Pateranos, sent to Bari to assassinate Robert Guiscard.[17]

William also frequently interjected into his narrative remarks about the succession of Byzantine emperors. Constantine VIII and Basil II were reigning when the Normans first joined the Lombard Melus to raid Apulia;[18] it was Michael IV the Epileptic who ordered an assault on Sicily and later left the throne to his nephew Michael when the disease finally took his life.[19] William knew about the blinding of this imprudent Michael V, following his ill-advised refusal to share power with the empress Zoe, who then married Constantine IX Monomachos.[20] The death of Constantine X in 1067 has introduced a long description of the disastrous reigns of Romanos Diogenes and Michael VII, including details of Romanos' heroic but ill-fated campaign against the Seljuq Turks, his capture at Manzikert, and a legendary confrontation with the Sultan Alp Arslan.[21] In an allusion to the First Crusade, the *Gesta Roberti Wiscardi* claims that the folly of Michael VII, who blinded Romanos when Alp Arslan spared his life, would have left the East to the Turks even to the writer's present moment if God had not inspired the Normans to open up the roads to the Holy Sepulchre, closed by Seljuq Turks wreaking havoc on the Christians in Romania (Asia Minor).[22]

William of Apulia's history follows Michael's removal from the seat of power to a monastic retreat and the succession by the shrewd but cowardly Nikephoros III Botaneiates.[23] William seems to have known a great deal about the vigorous young general Alexios Komnenos, who defeated the pretenders Nikephoros Bryennios and Nikephoros Basilakes before rebelling and dethroning Botaneiates.[24] William's *Gesta* includes details of this rebellion with its three-day sack of Constantinople by Alexios' Turkish mercenaries. Intimating regret that Guiscard then attacked Byzantium under the pretense of attempting to avenge the scoundrel Michael VII, who had betrothed his son Constantine to Guiscard's daughter Helena, William

---

[15] *Ibid.*, pp. 120–1.
[16] *Ibid.*, pp. 122–3.
[17] *Ibid.*, pp. 162–3.
[18] *Ibid.*, pp. 102–3.
[19] *Ibid.*, pp. 108–9, 120–1.
[20] *Ibid.*, pp. 124–5.
[21] *Ibid.*, pp. 164–70.
[22] *Ibid.*, pp. 168–71, 164–5.
[23] *Ibid.*, pp. 204–5, 208–9.
[24] *Ibid.*, pp. 208–13.

protested that the new emperor, Alexios, was treating the girl with suitable honour.

William's knowledge of Byzantine affairs – along with his capacity to see, on occasion, the Greeks' point of view – demonstrates the affinity possible between Italo-Normans and Byzantines at the close of the eleventh century. Writing some four decades later, Anna Komnene somehow knew three episodes from William's *Gesta Roberti Wiscardi* and incorporated them into her *Alexiad*.[25] The worlds of South Italians and Byzantines intersected on many levels. On the Italian side, other chroniclers also showed an interest in Byzantine internal affairs. For example, the history by Amatus, a monk of Montecassino writing in the late 1070s, relates Roussel's rebellion against the empire and the emperor's appointment of Jocelyn to lead the fleet to Bari as well as some events within Constantinople, though his version does not always get the details quite right.[26] It is perhaps William of Apulia, though, whose narrative best displays the South Italian familiarity with Byzantium and nuanced attitudes toward the empire. However much his *Gesta* nods to his papal patron's rapprochement with Byzantium by displaying Byzantine sympathies and recognising Byzantine authority, his verse history also features the sense of Norman destiny strongly espoused by his protagonist, Robert Guiscard. The *Gesta Roberti Wiscardi* celebrates the House of Hauteville, Guiscard's family, and in a closely related vein suggests that Providence demands that the Normans succeed the Byzantines in power. Just as the feminine Greeks manifestly do not deserve to possess and enjoy fertile Apulia, so implicitly the Byzantine heartland, even Constantinople itself, might be the ultimate reward for Norman greatness.[27]

By the mid-eleventh century Normans had already penetrated deep into Byzantine Anatolia and its easternmost borderlands, where they were confronting and learning from forces that their compatriots would meet on crusade. When the Latins reached Antioch in 1097, therefore, Norman mercenaries already had more than half a century's experience with lands

---

[25] On these three episodes in both histories, see Marguerite Mathieu, Gesta Roberti Wiscardi, *La geste de Robert Guiscard* (Palermo, 1961) pp. 38–46.

[26] Amatus may have witnessed many of the events he recorded concerning Normans in Italy from 1016 to the death of Richard, the Norman count of Aversa and prince of Capua, in 1078. The Latin text of his *Historia Normannorum* no longer exists, replaced by a fourteenth-century Old French *Ystoire de li Normant*, more an adaptation than a precise translation: *Storia de' Normanni di Amato di Montecassino*, Fonti per la storia d'Italia, pubblicate dall'Istituto storico italiano per il Medio Evo. Scrittori. Secolo 11, no. 76, ed. Vincenzo de Bartholomaeis (Rome, 1935); Amatus of Montecassino, *The History of the Normans*, trans. Prescott N. Dunbar; revised with introduction and notes by Graham A. Loud (Woodbridge, 2004). In Dunbar's translation these passages are as follows: Roussel's rebellion, pp. 47–9; Jocelyn's appointment, p. 145; events in Constantinople, p. 67.

[27] *GRW*, pp. 110–11.

and peoples on Byzantium's volatile eastern frontier. Many of the 'Franks' that medieval sources place in the war zones of eleventh-century Byzantium were in fact Normans who made their way there from southern Italy. Those Normans certainly proved to be 'the most turbulent and intractable' of all the foreigners who entered Byzantine service.[28] Their leaders were men like Hervé, who worked for (and sometimes against) the Byzantine emperors Michael VI and Isaac Komnenos in the 1050s, confronting Turks, Arabs and Armenians in eastern Anatolia; Robert Crispin, who fought with Byzantine forces at Manzikert in 1071; Oursel and his successor Raimbaud, who allegedly commanded 8,000 Normans in the service of the Armenian rebel Philaratos in Syria during the 1070s. One of those Norman freebooters, Roussel of Bailleul, fought at Guiscard's side in southern Italy before leaving in 1069 to fight for the emperor Romanos IV Diogenes in the Balkans and then in Anatolia. After the debacle at Manzikert and his own attempt at rebellion against the emperor, Roussel tried to create his own domain in Byzantine Anatolia until Turks used trickery to capture him and send him back to Alexios Komnenos, whom he eventually served in turn.

The career of Hugh Bunel took a particularly fascinating trajectory, hurtling him from Normandy to southern Italy, then Sicily, and finally to the Levant. Hugh made a quick escape from Normandy after murdering the infamous countess Mabel of Bellême, seeking asylum first in southern Italy, then in Sicily, before abandoning Christendom altogether to hide out among the Turks. 'For twenty years', wrote Orderic Vitalis, 'he studied their customs and language.' When the crusaders reached the Holy Land, Hugh offered his service to the Normans in their ranks. 'Therefore', wrote Orderic, 'when he was received by the duke of Normandy he was able to do his countrymen great service, by explaining to them the habits of the pagans and their deceitful stratagems and the tricks that they practised against the faithful.'[29]

By understanding language and customs, expatriate Normans like Hugh brought invaluable resources to Normans on crusade. Some of them, like Hervé and Roussel, aimed to carve out a piece of the old Byzantine Empire for themselves to rule. Before Bohemond, none of these Normans held any of those territories for long. Where others had failed, however, Bohemond found auspicious circumstances that paired with his focused ambition and energies to bring him success at Antioch.

---

[28] Peter Charanis, 'The Byzantine Empire in the Eleventh Century', in *A History of the Crusades*, vol. 1, *The First Hundred Years*, ed. Marshall W. Baldwin (Madison, Milwaukee, and London, 1969), pp. 177–219, at p. 200.

[29] OV, v, pp. 157–9.

Bohemond's Advantage

Bohemond must have enjoyed contact with some of those expatriate Normans and benefited from their long experience in the East. Even if he had not, however, he brought the knowledge of eastern peoples that Italo-Normans had acquired over long familiarity. He was poised to seek the possessions that had eluded his Norman predecessors, and the crusade offered him that opportunity. Left without a landed inheritance when his father named his younger half-brother, Roger, as heir to the family's South Italian holdings, Bohemond set his sights on the eastern empire. Ten years after his father's death, Bohemond seemed far from that goal. He was working with his uncle, Count Roger of Sicily, besieging Amalfi when an army of pilgrims suddenly appeared, on their way to Jerusalem. The *Gesta Francorum* records Bohemond's reaction, as he interrogated these first crusaders. Satisfied that they answered only to God and had no leader on the ground, Bohemond saw his chance.

> Immediately, inspired by the Holy Spirit, Bohemond ordered the most precious cloak he had to be cut up and made into crosses. Then most of the soldiers who were at that siege rushed to join him with great eagerness, so that Count Roger remained almost alone, and he returned to Sicily grieving and mourning because he had lost his army.[30]

Bohemond does seem to have taken much of that army with him, provisioning the troops and transporting them across the Adriatic. He set out from Italy with clarity of purpose at odds with the expressed aims of the crusade, viewing this as his opportunity to wrest land from the failing Byzantines on their eastern frontier, as his father had done in the west. The sharp focus of his ambition gave him a distinct advantage over crusaders with mixed motivations. If his intent was not at once transparent to other Latins, Byzantines understood the threat. In describing Bohemond's earlier participation in his father's Byzantine campaigns, Anna Komnene wrote:

> Bohemond resembled his father in all respects, in daring, strength, aristocratic and indomitable spirit. In short Bohemond was the exact replica and living image of his father. He at once attacked Canina, Hiericho and Avlona like a streaking thunderbolt, with threats and irrepressible fury. He seized them, and fighting on took the surrounding areas bit by bit and destroyed them by fire. Bohemond was in fact like the acrid smoke which preceded

---

[30] Hill, *GF*, p. 7. See my discussion of this episode in Albu, *The Normans in Their Histories*, pp. 147–8.

the fire, the preliminary skirmish which comes before the great assault. Father and son you might liken to caterpillars and locusts, for what was left by Robert, his son fed on and devoured.[31]

Years later, when Bohemond reached Constantinople on the crusade, Anna's father Alexios received him graciously, Anna's *Alexiad* reports, but fully aware of his real objective.

> The truth is, [she wrote] that Bohemond was an habitual rogue, quick to react to fleeting circumstance; he far surpassed all the Latins who passed through Constantinople at that time in rascality and courage, but he was equally inferior in wealth and resources. He was a supreme mischief-maker. As for inconstancy, that follows automatically – a trait common to all Latins ... When he left his native land, he was a soured man, for he had no estates at all. Apparently he left to worship at the Holy Sepulchre, but in reality to win power for himself – or rather, if possible, to seize the Roman Empire itself, as his father had suggested. He was prepared to go to any length, as they say.[32]

If Bohemond could not extort all the empire from Alexios, he may have had designs at least on Antioch long before he ever saw the city. Among the crusaders, rumours circulated whispering of secret meetings between Bohemond and Alexios in Constantinople in 1097, with Bohemond promising loyalty to the emperor in exchange for extensive lands, 'fifteen-days-journey long and eight-days-journey wide', just beyond Antioch.[33] The offer may seem generous, even if the Latins would first have to conquer an area no longer under Byzantine control. Once regained, however, this territory would have been impossible to hold, and therefore virtually worthless, without possession of the city that protected it.

The *Gesta*'s author saw trouble brewing in this pact, as in the oaths that his lord and the other leaders openly swore to Alexios, taking the emperor's gifts in exchange for their pledges to restore to him any of his old lands they recaptured. The author of the *Gesta* feared that they were putting their private profit above the common cause of the crusaders. 'Maybe all along we were going to be tricked often by our leaders', he lamented. 'Knights so brave and so tough! Why did they do this?'

In any case, as we shall see, Bohemond soon found a loophole in the

---

[31] Anna Comnena, *The Alexiad of Anna Comnena*, trans. E. R. A. Sewter (Harmondsworth, 1969), p. 66.
[32] *Ibid.*, pp. 328–9.
[33] Hill, *GF*, p. 12.

treaties' conditions that he claimed invalidated the promises, allowing him to keep Antioch for himself. His nephew Tancred, meanwhile, slipped past the imperial city, altogether evading any oath of fealty. This hotheaded youth may have been behaving impulsively, in reckless defiance of all the crusading leaders, Bohemond included. Tancred's close co-operation with his uncle in later years, however, hints at the possibility that he was already acting with Bohemond's blessing when he moved swiftly to seize lands in Cilicia, on the route to Antioch. As Tancred sometimes colluded but often skirmished with Count Baldwin in Cilicia, their dueling claims to Tarsus fired the enmity festering among the crusaders and their leaders. The sources disagree on Tancred's loyalties and motivation, whether he was acting on his own or in concert with the crusading armies as he set out on foraging expeditions, formed alliances with Armenian Christians, and apparently conducted reconnaissance of the crucial Belen Pass through the mountains to Antioch. But if he was acting as his uncle's agent, Tancred's actions fit the pattern of someone already scheming to control Antioch and its environs.[34]

While Tancred was an early and aggressive claimant to towns on the route to Antioch, taking and holding Mamistra, for instance, a town that would prove important to the future Norman principality, Bohemond himself jockeyed with Raymond of Toulouse to occupy strategic positions. Thomas Asbridge has identified 'three key sites near the city which, it could be argued, were essential to the success of the siege of Antioch'.[35] We cannot now ascertain which crusading leader held two of these, the Iron Bridge across the River Orontes and the fourteen-kilometre road between Antioch and its Mediterranean port at Saint Simeon. It may be significant, though, that Bohemond and Raymond of Toulouse went together to retrieve supplies and essential personnel from the port during the siege.[36] The two rivals may have shared this hazardous duty because they represented the greatest strength of the crusading forces at that moment. Just possibly, however, each wanted to stake a reasonable claim to the port while keeping a close eye on the other's negotiations there. Raymond held the third critical site shortly after Antioch fell: the stronghold at Artah on the Roman road between Antioch and Aleppo, Ralph of Caen's 'shield of Antioch' against assaults from the east. In his chronicle honouring his lord Tancred, Ralph reported that Muslims surrendered the fortified town after

---

[34] See Thomas Asbridge, *The Creation of the Principality of Antioch 1098–1130*, (Woodbridge 2000) pp. 16–24.
[35] *Ibid.*, p. 24. For a detailed account and analysis of the sources for these occupations, see *ibid.*, pp. 24–34.
[36] Hill, *GF*, p. 39.

Karbuqa lost the Great Battle for Antioch, handing it over to Raymond because some of the count's men assured them that *their* lord's honour was worthy of trust.[37]

Although all the crusading leaders seem to have occupied sites around Antioch when assailing the city, Bohemond (along with Tancred) and Raymond were the chief competitors, with Bohemond especially holding the valley of Daphne and perhaps sites in Cilicia, where Tancred had been active, and Raymond establishing a power base south-east of Antioch. Those two men were the chief competitors for claiming and holding the city itself. Despite Raymond's apparently superior entitlement as a powerful nobleman of renowned integrity, with additional authority as defender of the emperor's rights, it was Bohemond who won and held the city.

Circumstances of the city's capture and the immediate aftermath played a role in this. Bohemond's extensive experience in siege warfare must have taught him the strategy of collusion, helping him win over the tower-guard Firuz. Bohemond had another strong advantage here, gained from growing up in southern Italy: he spoke Greek, a language he shared with the tower-guard at Antioch.[38] Anna Komnene snidely reported that, even decades later, Byzantines were mocking Bohemond's Italian accent by repeating his mispronounced Greek in a boast that came back to haunt him.[39] But Bohemond's Greek allowed him direct parley with Firuz, in secret and in a language foreign to other crusading leaders.

When those covert negotiations and bribery seemed about to win the traitor's towers, Bohemond tried his charm and rhetorical skill on the crusading leaders, asking them all to agree that they would surrender Antioch to anyone who could 'by some way or some contrivance … acquire the city or engineer its capture, either by himself or through others'.[40] The leaders rejected this proposal outright. 'To no one will this city be handed over', the *Gesta Francorum* reports them answering, 'but we will all share it equally. Just as we have had equal effort, so from that effort let us have equal privilege.' This adamant refusal sent Bohemond out of the meeting with his disarming smile turned to a scowl. As the Latins' desperation increased,

---

[37] RCaen, p. 672.

[38] Peter Frankopan, *The First Crusade: The Call from the East* (Cambridge, MA, 2012), p. 161. The only Greek in the Hill, *GF*, p. 46 comes from the mouth of Firuz, lamenting that too few Latins were scaling the wall to his tower: *Micro Francos echome* – 'We have few Franks': Albu, *The Normans in Their Histories*, pp. 158–9.

[39] *The Alexiad*, trans. Sewter, p. 149.

[40] Hill, *GF*, p. 44. On this episode, see Albu, *The Normans in Their Histories*, pp. 157–8.

though, even Raymond yielded at last to the Norman's assurance that Firuz was ready to betray his city.

Once Antioch fell to the crusaders, the hostilities between Bohemond and Raymond resumed, as each hastened to possess the most desirable quarters. As conditions in Antioch worsened and the Latins, caught in a stranglehold between Turks in the citadel above them and Karbuqa's vast army outside the walls, faced starvation and hallucinations, Raymond saw his chances improve with a Provençal-inspired miracle. When a Provençal peasant named Peter Bartholomew claimed visions of the Apostle Andrew revealing the burial place of the Holy Lance that had pierced Christ's side, Raymond joined the party charged with unearthing the precious relic. While others, Normans notable among their number, harboured suspicions about the authenticity of the Lance, even Bohemond used this discovery to roust the Latins out of their despair. After days of purification, the formerly bedraggled crusaders swept out of the city and routed Karbuqa's army in the Great Battle for Antioch. A gentle shower, divinely sent, refreshed the Latins and their horses as they rode into battle, confirming the Lord's approval, according to the Provençal chronicler, Raymond of Aguilers.[41]

With both Bohemond and Raymond holding claim to the city, though, it was unclear who would keep it after the battle. Bohemond snatched the highest towers and bullied the other leaders to surrender the ones they held, asserting that the leaders had ceded the city to him the moment his forces had climbed the city walls. Torn between their conflicting oaths to emperor and Norman, all at last bent to Bohemond's pressure, excepting only Raymond. Grave illness did not prevent the count from keeping Provençal forces at the Bridge Gate and at the palace of Yaghi Siyan, Antioch's former governor.

For his part, Bohemond relied on a technicality to release him from fealty to the emperor, who had failed to come to Antioch's relief as he had promised. Many among the crusaders knew that Alexios was marching with his army toward Antioch and turned back only when the defector, Count Stephen of Blois, intercepted him en route and persuaded him to retreat, since Antioch was surely lost and the crusaders annihilated. The *Gesta Francorum*, for instance, lays the blame squarely on the cowardly Stephen, whose feigned illness and shameful flight the *Gesta*'s Alexios mocks.[42] Ignoring the extenuating circumstances that worked to absolve

---

[41] Raymond of Aguilers, *Historia Francorum qui ceperunt Iherusalem*, trans. John Hugh Hill and Laurita Hill (Philadelphia, 1968), pp. 63–4.

[42] Hill, *GF*, p. 63.

the emperor, Bohemond held his ground. Norman propaganda, meanwhile, also succeeded in undermining confidence in the Lance's authenticity. The contemporary account of the *Gesta Francorum* delights in the discovery of the Holy Lance (9.28), but its author was about to transfer his own loyalty, leaving Bohemond's company for Raymond's. Writing about fifteen years later from the principality of Antioch, Ralph of Caen expressed the view more commonly held by Normans once the Lance had accomplished the task of rescuing morale and inspiring victory.[43] Though often willing to accept the miraculous, Ralph expressed scornful scepticism in the case of the Lance, wondering here why Saint Andrew would reveal a treasure to such an unworthy peasant.[44] Ralph's *Gesta Tancredi* has Bohemond exclaim in provocation, 'Who hid the lance, and why? *O rusticitas credula!*' When an ordeal by fire indicted Peter Bartholomew and led to his death, the Normans of the *Gesta Tancredi* exulted, vindicated by Peter's suffering.

Although Peter's death jeopardised Raymond's claim, the stalemate continued. At the appointed meeting on 1 November 1098, in Antioch's Church of Saint Peter, the leaders still could not agree on Antioch's lord or on plans for proceeding to Jerusalem. The assembly disbanded only with concessions that both Bohemond and Raymond would march to the holy city after some months of foraging and shoring up their new possessions in land. When the combined forces mustered again, Raymond and the other crusade leaders finally resigned themselves to surrendering their holdings around Antioch in order to concentrate maximum force against Jerusalem. At this moment Bohemond's ambition and clarity of vision served him especially well, letting him set out for the holy city with the others but soon turn back, reneging on his pledge to march to Jerusalem, the stated goal of the crusading mission, in order to safeguard Antioch. He argued that the crusaders could not risk losing the city. A Latin Jerusalem would need a Latin Antioch at its back for protection. This was a defensible position given the critical importance of guarding Antioch and preventing its recapture as the Latins pushed on to Jerusalem. Nonetheless, Bohemond's retreat to Antioch primarily served his own interests to rule over this powerfully fortified city, which he had good reason to fear might fall again to Muslims or, perhaps just as detestable a prospect for the Norman, to the hated Greeks. Bohemond would visit Jerusalem later, when it was safely in Latin hands.

---

[43] RCaen, pp. 599–716. *GT*, Bachrach.
[44] *GT*, Bachrach, pp. 118–20.

Bohemond's Disadvantage

If Bohemond's territorial ambitions to acquire imperial lands gave him an early advantage at Antioch, his enduring antagonism toward the Byzantine emperor brought a significant downside as well. Bohemond's enmity inflamed hostilities that long threatened the principality, forcing the Latins at Antioch to fend off Byzantine assaults instead of uniting with their Christian neighbours against common enemies. Only in 1137, when Raymond, prince of Antioch by virtue of his marriage to Constance, daughter of Bohemond II, finally agreed to terms with the emperor John Komnenos, did Antioch achieve some respite from Byzantine hostilities. Orderic Vitalis recalled the relief that followed this truce:

> The two princes [John Komnenos and Raymond] ratified a treaty of peace beneficial to pilgrims and all the believers in Christ living in Greece and Syria. So Raymond became the Emperor's vassal and received Antioch from him, and the Emperor promised to be his friend and provide help against Damascus and all the pagans. In this way the war, which had dragged on perniciously for almost forty years, and had been begun and carried on against Alexius by the Bohemonds and their successors, bringing captivity, death, and much suffering to countless thousands, was by God's will now brought to an end under the Emperor John and Prince Raymond the Poitevin, to the delight of many men on both sides.[45]

Still the old hostilities nurtured by Bohemond did not die. Raymond refused to surrender Antioch's citadel, and tensions resurfaced despite marriage alliances as elevated as the union of John's son, the emperor Manuel I, with Maria of Antioch, great-granddaughter of Bohemond I. At the death of Manuel in 1180, Bohemond III, the reigning prince of Antioch, abandoned his wife, Manuel's niece, surrendering any pretence of a Byzantine alliance.

A more immediate result of Bohemond I's anti-Byzantine fervour was his reckless campaign against the empire in 1107–8. Having returned to the West and gathered considerable resources to reinforce the Latin positions in the Levant, Bohemond instead led those forces against Byzantium with a siege of Dyrrachium, the city he had attacked at his father's side decades earlier. Guiscard had defeated the Byzantines there in 1081, but Alexios had soon regained the city, aided by a Venetian blockade. Bitter memories of that loss may still have haunted Bohemond. Then too, Dyrrachium sat at

---

[45] OV, vi, p. 509.

the start of the Via Egnatia, the old Roman road that could take the Norman prince across Bulgaria and Thrace to Constantinople, along the route the First Crusaders had travelled. This ill-conceived campaign instead led Bohemond to a devastating defeat. Compelled to make humiliating concessions to Alexios in the Treaty of Devol, Bohemond apparently agreed to surrender the independence of Antioch, to govern it on the emperor's behalf, and perhaps leave it to his newly acknowledged lord at his own death.[46] Humiliated, he returned to the West, never to return to Antioch, which he left to his nephew to protect. Fortunately for the Normans, Tancred had matured into a savvy ruler who learned how to assure the acceptance of a variety of ruled peoples. His death in 1112 left the principality to a Hauteville cousin until Bohemond's young son, Bohemond II, could come of age and claim his inheritance. With Bohemond II, the direct male line ended, but descendants of his daughter Constance carried Bohemond's name and memory all the way to the last prince of Antioch, Bohemond VII.[47]

Remembering Antioch

Antioch itself lingered long in the western imagination. It remained the heroic focus of epic cycles in Occitan (*Canso d'Antioca*) and Old French (*Chanson d'Antioche*).[48] In some respects, Antioch even more than Jerusalem came to define the crusading experience. The long siege, the subsequent privations of crusaders within the besieged city, the miraculous discovery of the Lance that led to an epic battle and astonishing victory – all these must have transformed the participants and inspired the generations who heard the tale.

During the period of the crusades, Antioch also served as a symbol of western imperial opportunities in eastern lands as its representation on the Peutinger map illustrates.[49] The map displays the inhabited world from Britain to Sri Lanka, as the Romans knew it. Yet our surviving map comes from southern Germany, drawn *c.* 1220 as a display piece asserting

---

[46] The treaty survives only in the *Alexiad*, p. 433. Asbridge, *Creation of the Principality of Antioch*, pp. 94–103.

[47] On the persistent Italo-Norman presence in the principality, see Alan V. Murray, 'How Norman Was the Principality of Antioch? Prolegomena to a Study of the Origins of the Nobility of a Crusader State', in *Family Trees and the Roots of Politics: The Prosopography of England and France from the Tenth to the Twelfth Century*, ed. K. S. B. Keats-Rohan (Woodbridge, 1997), pp. 349–59.

[48] *The* Canso d'Antioca, trans. Sweetenham; *The* Chanson d'Antioche: *An Old French Account of the First Crusade*, Crusade Texts in Translation 22, trans. Susan B. Edgington and Carol Sweetenham (Farnham, 2011).

[49] Emily Albu, *The Medieval Peutinger Map: Imperial Roman Revival in a German Empire* (Cambridge, 2014), pp. 95–105.

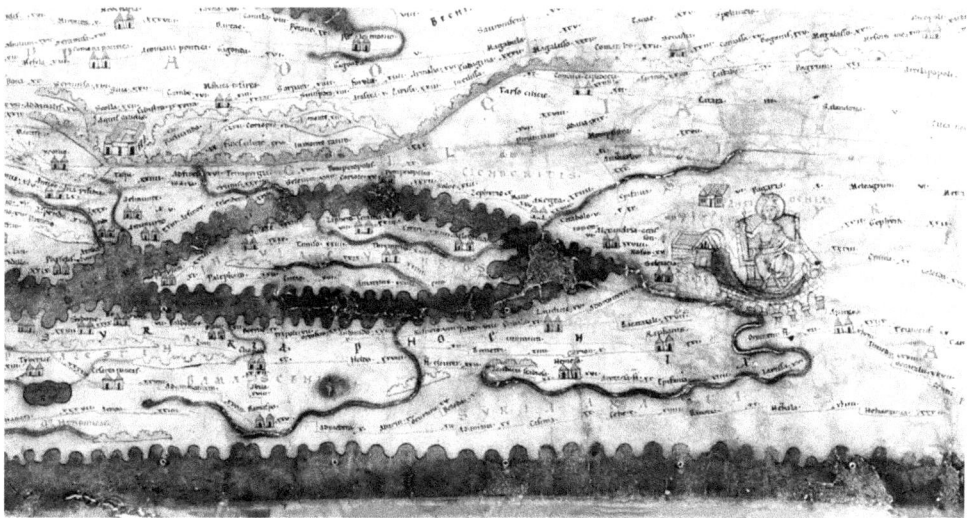

Antioch on the Peutinger map, near the Mediterranean shore, with Cyprus filling much of the eastern sea. ÖNB/Wien, Cod. 324

German (Holy Roman) imperial ambitions, emphasising sites of particular importance to its contemporary viewers, including notably the cities on the crusaders' routes to Antioch. Of the hundreds of vignettes on the map, Antioch's pictorial representation is the largest, larger and more detailed than the only other personified vignettes, at Rome and Constantinople. Antioch's image fills the eastern Mediterranean coastline and dominates the map's eastern stretches. Recent scholarship has identified it as a medieval addition onto an older mapping tradition.[50] Its insertion or magnification gives it particular significance on this medieval map with Roman imperial pretensions.

Antioch was a city that attracted variant interpretations. For Normans who first claimed the fortress in 1098 and who became its primary western settlers and defenders, Antioch formed the centre and bulwark of their own principality, protector of their eastern domain. For a thoughtful churchman like Orderic Vitalis, on the other hand, it became a symbol of the Normans' unholy violence and the attendant suffering. The prominence of Antioch on the Peutinger map suggests that, for the Hohenstaufen, it signified ancient power, royal and imperial, which western emperors could hope to acquire again. This was the Antioch of Bohemond's aspirations, the city that represented his imperial ambitions.

[50] Richard J. A. Talbert, *Rome's World: The Peutinger Map Reconsidered* (Cambridge, 2010), p. 124.

10

The Landscape of Pilgrimage and Miracles in Norman Narrative Sources

LEONIE V. HICKS

The chronicles we associate with the Normans are full of accounts of the miraculous, both good and bad. Some narrative sources, for example Orderic Vitalis's *Ecclesiastical History*, contain saints' lives and *miracula*. Sometimes the historian's encounter with the supernatural has elements of macabre humour as in the case of Wace's story of Duke Richard I's experience of a revenant, which led to his instituting a decree that dead bodies should be watched over and attended before burial. In reading these sources we also revisit familiar descriptions of the monastic landscapes and the trials and tribulations faced by the monks in establishing new communities, notably in the pages of William of Jumièges and Orderic. The crusade chronicles focus on what happened on the journey to Jerusalem and significant events such as the appearance of the ghostly army at Antioch, as well as descriptions of sacred geography. We can therefore consider how writers linked the experiences of the Normans who departed for the Holy Land with the readers of the chronicles. What many of the accounts of the miraculous have in common is their emphasis on place, movement and connections that link the familiar with the unfamiliar. This chapter examines a series of case studies from the narrative sources in order to consider what constitutes a landscape of pilgrimage or a setting for miracles and how those accounts relate to and reflect the wider themes of the chronicles.

The examples here are drawn from a variety of Norman sources that reflect different perspectives and experiences. William of Jumièges completed the *Gesta Normannorum Ducum* initially in the 1050s, returning to it in the late 1060s to write a short account, finished in 1070, of the Norman conquest of England. This work was then later interpolated by Orderic Vitalis, Robert of Torigni and a series of anonymous editors.[1] Orderic Vitalis

---

[1] *The* Gesta Normannorum Ducum *of William of Jumièges, Orderic Vitalis, and Robert of Torigni*, 2 vols, ed. and trans. Elisabeth M. C. van Houts (Oxford, 1992–95). For dating see, *ibid.*, i, pp. xxxii–xxxv.

in contrast started out writing a monastic chronicle detailing the history of his community at Saint-Évroult. His *Ecclesiastical History*, written between *c.* 1114 and *c.* 1141, rapidly expanded to encompass the activities of the Normans, particularly those such as the Giroie-Grandmesnil clan who had close connections with his monastery, further afield in Normandy, but also in England, southern Italy and the Holy Land.[2] The final chronicle considered here and which focuses more on Normandy is Wace's *Roman de Rou*. This work is an Anglo-Norman vernacular verse continuation of the *Gesta* tradition and was originally commissioned by Henry II. Wace, however, left it incomplete in the 1170s after Henry transferred the task to Benoît of Sainte-Maure.[3] This allows for a comparison across time in our consideration of the importance of pilgrimage and the miraculous in Norman historical writing. In looking at the Holy Land, the key sources here are the *Gesta Francorum*, Orderic Vitalis and Ralph of Caen's *Gesta Tancredi*. The anonymous *Gesta Francorum* is believed to have been written by a layman attached to the contingent led by Bohemond, son of Robert Guiscard, and was written shortly after the Battle of Ascalon in 1099. It is the earliest account of the expedition and provides the basis for many of the later narratives.[4] Orderic's account of the First Crusade in Book IX of the *Ecclesiastical History* substantially uses that of Baudri of Bourgeuil, who was archbishop of Dol. Ralph of Caen's *Gesta Tancredi*, as the name suggests, has as its main focus the deeds of Bohemond's nephew, Tancred. Ralph was a chaplain in Bohemond's retinue and his history was most likely completed before his patron, Arnulf of Chocques, later patriarch of Jerusalem, died in April 1118.[5] The focus in the crusade narratives is primarily on the relationship between the crusader army and the landscape, particularly how it helps and hinders their progress or demonstrates the qualities of the leaders. Similarities can therefore be drawn with Norman martial activity in England and southern Italy.

Within the historiography, there is a strong emphasis on the piety of the Normans in terms of both their foundation of monasteries and of their devotion to particular saints, and on the role of hagiography in the historical writing about the settlement of Rollo and his descendants.[6] This idea is

---

[2] The dates of various sections of the *Ecclesiastical History* are discussed in OV, i, pp. 45–8.
[3] Wace, *The Roman de Rou*, trans. G. Burgess with the text of A. J. Holden and notes by G. Burgess and E. van Houts (St Helier, 2002), with a discussion of the dating at pp. xiii–xv.
[4] Hill, *GF*, For dating and later use see pp. ix–xi.
[5] RCaen, pp. 587–716. Dating and Ralph's relationship with Arnulf are discussed at *GT*, Bachrach pp. 1–4.
[6] See for example C. Potts, *Monastic Revival and Regional Identity in Early Normandy* (Woodbridge, 1997); S. Herrick, *Imagining the Sacred Past: Hagiography and Power in Early Normandy* (Cambridge,

given added weight by accounts in the chronicles of papal endorsement of conquest: the granting of a papal banner to William the Conqueror in 1066 as recorded by William of Poitiers and Pope Nicholas II's investiture of Robert Guiscard with the title to the island of Sicily in 1059.[7] How this piety was expressed or experienced, both in terms of the purpose of historical writing and in relation to the landscape, is less well studied. Notable in this respect is the work of Carl Watkins who places the chroniclers' accounts of the miraculous in terms of the didactic purpose of their histories. This is, in part, achieved through their emphasis on the local, as illustrated in Orderic's *Ecclesiastical History*. The manuscript is marked with breathing points to aid reading aloud. Watkins points out that refectory readings would have reached a mixed audience as the community comprised a group of men ranging from child oblates to seasoned former warriors, meaning that the veracity of the account needed to depend not on 'shared ideologies' but instead on 'consonance with observed social, political and cultural realities'.[8] This, as he notes, is an important corrective to scholarship that privileges the role of narrative tropes, genre and the cohesiveness of the audience over shared experience and local concerns.[9] Amanda Jane Hingst also considers the place of the local in her study of Orderic's conception of the world, but the emphasis here is on ideology rather than connection with people.[10] Other examinations of landscape in the context of miracles and pilgrimage in narrative sources have focused on monastic foundation stories.[11]

Another point of concern when considering the relationship between landscape, miracles and pilgrimage is that of emotional engagement. If texts like those of Orderic and Wace were designed, at least in part, to be read

---

MA, 2007); F. Lifshitz, *The Norman Conquest of Pious Neustria: Historiographic Discourse and Saintly Relics 684–1090* (Toronto, 1995); *Culte et pèlerinages à Saint Michel en occident: les trois monts dédiés à l'archange*, ed. Pierre Bouet, Giorgio Otranto, and André Vauchez (Rome, 2003).

[7] William of Poitiers, *The Gesta Guillelmi of William of Poitiers*, ed. and trans. R. H. C. Davis and M. Chibnall (Oxford, 1998), pp. 104–7; *The Normans in Europe*, ed. E. van Houts (Manchester, 2000), no. 73, pp. 243–4.

[8] Carl Watkins, *History and the Supernatural in Medieval England* (Cambridge, 2007), p. 17. See also K. Quirk, 'Men, Women and Miracles in Normandy, 1050–1150' (pp. 53–71) and C. Watkins, 'Memories of the Marvellous in the Anglo-Norman Realm' (pp. 92–112), both in *Medieval Memories: Men, Women and the Past 700–1300*, ed. E. van Houts (Harlow, 2001).

[9] Watkins particularly critiques the work of Jean Blacker, Monica Otter and Gabrielle Speigel. See Watkins, *History and the Supernatural*, p. 16.

[10] Amanda Jane Hingst, *The Written World: Past and Place in the Work of Orderic Vitalis* (Notre Dame, IN, 2009). For comparison see J.-C. Schmitt, *Ghosts in the Middle Ages: The Living and the Dead in Medieval Society* (Chicago, 1998), pp. 93–122.

[11] Leonie V. Hicks, 'Monastic Authority, Landscape, and Place in the *Ecclesiastical History* of Orderic Vitalis', in *Authority and Gender in Medieval and Renaissance Chronicles*, ed. Juliana Dresvina and Nicholas Sparkes (Newcastle-upon-Tyne, 2012), pp. 102–20 and Carl Watkins, 'Landscape and Belief in Anglo-Norman England', ANS 35 (2013), pp. 305–19.

aloud either in the monastery or at court, then considering the response engendered on the part of the hearer is essential. This is particularly the case with the crusade narratives as many of those engaging with these texts would not have participated in the crusade itself. Thomas Bisson and, most notably, Vito Fumagalli, are key in understanding how landscapes and the natural world reflect states of mind.[12] For both these authors fear is the key emotion, but it is clear, as we shall see, that this is not the only response found in the chronicles, nor even the main one. Although descriptions of the landscape were grounded in local detail, they were primarily a means of making connections in a particular locale between time and space, between people, the past and the present.

Local Landscapes and Communities

Throughout the *Ecclesiastical History*, miracles and pilgrimage play an important role in Orderic's narrative of events in Normandy and elsewhere. Not only does he relate the foundations of the Merovingian community of Saint-Évroult and its refoundation in the mid-eleventh century, but he also wrote a monastic history of Crowland Abbey, included in Book IV, and incorporated material relating to the miracles of Saint Judoc in Book III. Beyond the hagiographical sections, Orderic included elements of the miraculous, in terms of both portents and pilgrimage, to examine the relationship between his monastery and its local community. Many of these incidents involve tenants of Saint-Évroult, clergy connected to the abbey or people within its confraternity. Two accounts in particular are of significance in terms of the link between events and the landscape within the context of pilgrimage and encounters with the miraculous: Geoffrey the Breton's journey through snow to bring bread to the monks and Ruald's escape from captivity in Domfront under Henry I.

Orderic includes Geoffrey's story in Book VI, which is devoted in the main to internal monastic history. This is an event which occurred during Orderic's own lifetime, in c. 1133, two years before the death of King Henry I, and in the chronicle it immediately follows on from the recovery of the relics of Saint Évroul from the community at Rebais. The episode is therefore designed to illustrate the power of the patron saint and to demonstrate the close link between the saint, his monastery and its people. The fact

---

[12] Vito Fumagalli, *Landscapes of Fear: Perceptions of Nature and the City in the Middle Ages*, trans. Shayne Mitchell (Cambridge, 1994); Thomas N. Bisson, 'Hallucinations of Power: Climates of Fright in the Early Twelfth Century', *Haskins Society Journal* 16 (2006), 1–11.

that Geoffrey was a Breton is significant as, within twelfth-century narrative sources, Bretons appear somewhat as a stereotype with fiery tempers and uncivilised habits. Elsewhere, in Book XII of the *Ecclesiastical History*, Orderic lays the blame for a riot in Rouen cathedral in 1119 at the door of Archbishop Geoffrey Brito's Breton temperament.[13] In the case of the more local Geoffrey, we know that he lived a life of 'brigandage and theft in his youth' (*rapinis et latronciniis studuit*), before he settled down, married and, following the influence of his wife's 'wise counsels, ceased to associate with his cruel and murderous followers and earned his living by the labour of his own hands' (*eiusque utilibus montitis adquieuit, et crudelibus letiferisque satelliciis renunciauit, et labore manuum quæ sibi necessaria erant procurauit*).[14] As part of this new life, Geoffrey was admitted into fraternity with the monks and took his duties towards them seriously visiting every saint's day with gifts. It was this dedication to the community that caused him to venture out on the feast of Holy Innocents after a blizzard.

Orderic goes to some lengths here to describe the weather and how it rendered the landscape unrecognisable, unfamiliar and threatening. The heavy snowfall, blocking houses and submerging birds, animals and people, was apparently the worst in living memory and we can expect that it was discussed by visitors to the monastery. Crucially, the snow made the landscape impossible to read and navigate as it 'covered up the roads' and 'levelled hills and valleys' (*viarum superficies obtexit, montes et ualles coequauit*), thus preventing many from attending church that day. As well as the snow, Geoffrey, his son and the horse carrying the provisions had to negotiate the River Risle. The account notes that there was no bridge. It is likely that the crossing-place was a ford, as Orderic notes that the water level was rising, making the river impassable. By setting the scene in this way, Orderic was then able to underline how strong faith and devotion to the saint enabled Geoffrey to negotiate the treacherous conditions. The route from home to monastery was one he must have known very well, but even so care was needed in order to stay on the road, maintain a sense of direction and, above all, cross the river. It was only through prayer that he was able to do so. His son, following with the horse, was least steadfast and only crossed with difficulty, getting very wet in the process. Nevertheless, the bread remained dry. On reaching the monastery, father and son were able to recount their adventures to the monks and others who had gathered there to celebrate the feast. In this episode the landscape is presented as

---
[13] OV, vi, pp. 209–95.
[14] OV, iii, pp. 342–5 with the quotation at pp. 342–3.

hostile and as a challenge to Geoffrey's faith. But by characterising it as such, Orderic makes it an active agent. It is precisely because the landscape was threatening that Geoffrey was able to demonstrate the full conversion of his life from one of crime to devoted service to the monastery and its saint. This point is underlined as the account of this journey is immediately followed by a description of the qualities and character of Abbot Warin who 'had a very real love and deep respect for this man [Geoffrey] because of his boundless devotion to God' (*et prefatum uirum pro magna deuocione qua erga Deum feruebat, uehementer diligebat, et ueneranter honorabat*).[15]

The landscape also serves to connect the people, monastery and saint in the case of Ruald, but this time with more earthly concerns. Ruald's story is told in Book VIII, which deals in the main with the disorders in Normandy under Robert Curthose. In this instance, events relate to Henry's capture of Domfront from Robert of Bellême and ensuing engagements with Robert Curthose. Among those captured during these troubles was Ruald, described as from 'the territory of Saint-Évroult' (*terra sancti Ebrulfi*).[16] Orderic states that he heard the tale from Ruald himself and he believed him because of his good character. In contrast to Geoffrey's journey, these events occurred in 1092, when Orderic, who had joined the monastery aged ten, was around seventeen. In this episode the landscape presented is not quite so menacing; indeed, it actually aided Ruald in his escape. Finding himself a prisoner, he called on Saint Evroul for aid. He was roused from sleep by someone taking him by the hand. This enabled him to have the faith and courage to attempt his escape. The bolt holding the door in place fell to the ground when he took hold of it. On stepping into the garden of the castle, he called on Saint Evroul again to lead him undetected past the knights in the courtyard. The castle at Domfront is situated on a rocky outcrop at the top of the town and to effect his escape, Ruald would have had to descend from the hill, a significant undertaking given his perilous position, without being recaptured. Handily placed bushes came to the rescue and he was able to evade his pursuer by hiding in them. Faith also helped him in that the men ploughing a nearby field denied having seen him, even though the knight offered them a bribe.

In the previous chapter of the *Ecclesiastical History*, Orderic listed various monks of Saint-Évroult who had gone on to become abbots in other major monasteries in Normandy, likening them to candles showing the

---

[15] OV, iii, pp. 344–5.
[16] OV, iv, pp. 256–61 with the quotation at pp. 258–9. For the background to the disorders in Normandy see Aird, *Robert Curthose*, pp. 99–152 and for discussion of Ruald's testimony, see Watkins, 'Memories of the Marvellous', pp. 96–7.

'way of salvation to those seeking to enter the house of the Lord by the path of righteousness' (*ingredi domum Domini per semitam iusticiæ aditum salutis ostenderent*).[17] He also comments that the monastic life was disturbed by the neglect and malice of secular rulers. It is surely no coincidence that Ruald's miraculously undetected escape then follows on from this passage. Orderic is drawing a direct contrast between the behaviour of the rulers and the faith shown by Ruald who, like the abbots, walked the path of righteousness. It is interesting also to stress, as Kathleen Thompson has noted, that the role of Henry causes some problems here for Orderic. In imprisoning a monastic tenant, he can hardly be the hero contrasted with the villainous Robert of Bellême or the incompetent Robert Curthose (as he so often appears to be in the *Ecclesiastical History*), but instead is seen as predatory and a threat to the monastery and its people.[18]

In both the cases discussed from Orderic's chronicle, there is also a strong contrast between inside and outside. Both Geoffrey and Ruald need to show a deep and steadfast faith in order to take the first steps towards spiritual safety (the monastery) or freedom (leaving the castle) and both attributed their success to the aid of the saints. The threat to Geoffrey came from a landscape rendered unfamiliar by the snow; in the case of Ruald, in needing to get to safety without being recaptured or worse. This contrast and visual plotting of the pilgrimages or miraculous journeys undertaken – to the monastery or to safety – allowed the readers or hearers of the chronicle to make those journeys in their own minds and ponder their significance, both for the monastery and for the relationship between God and humanity.

Rulers and the Miraculous

By considering chronicles written in the *Gesta Normannorum* tradition, it is possible to discuss the link between the dukes of Normandy and the miraculous. Two narratives in particular are useful here: the *Gesta Normannorum ducum* of William of Jumièges and Wace's *Roman de Rou*. In its initial form, the *Gesta Normannorum ducum* comprised books detailing the life of each duke up to and including William II (1035–87). For the early dukes, William relied heavily on the *History of the Normans* written by Dudo of Saint-Quentin, but he provides original information when it touches on the history of the monastery of Jumièges. Wace, by contrast, was writing in the second half of the twelfth century following a commission from Henry

---

[17] OV, iv, pp. 256–7.
[18] K. Thompson, 'Orderic Vitalis and Robert of Bellême', *JMH* 20 (1994), 133–41.

II to compose a history of his Norman ancestors in Anglo-Norman verse. His sources include Dudo, William of Jumièges and Orderic Vitalis, but like William he does provide original information. The examples discussed here relate to two dukes' encounters with the landscape of the strange and miraculous and shed light on the broad themes of these two histories.

In Book III, which records the deeds of William Longsword, William of Jumièges gives an account of the refoundation of his abbey following the settlement of the Vikings in the Seine valley by Charles the Simple. Duke William encountered two monks clearing the ground, described as 'a vast wilderness' (*vastam loci heremum*), on his return from a hunting trip.[19] The monks offered him a simple meal which he refused in preference for hunting an enormous wild boar. The boar attacked the duke, rendering him unconscious. On coming round. William realised that he had been somewhat unwise in refusing the monks' food. He returned to accept their hospitality, but also to refound the monastery:

> he sent them agents and had the site cleared of branches and brambles. Thus the church of Saint Peter, which for some time had been in decay, was skilfully roofed and repaired. And the duke rendered habitable the cloister and all the out-buildings.
>
> Immissis ergo actionariis, eum a ramnis et sentibus purgauit, Santicque Petri, quod aliquantisper deciderat, monasterium resarciens competenter texit. Claustrum vero et cuncta receptacula muniens a sui magnitudine breuiata habitabilia reddidit.[20]

The landscape here shows a strong contrast between wilderness and cultivation. This not only pertains to the site of the monastery itself, but to the fact that the land here is good for hunting. The attack on the duke by the boar is used by William to illustrate the importance of the restoration of the monastery and the need for the duke to engage with the monks. It was necessary that the community should be rebuilt, but also vital that it should be accomplished with the aid of the temporal powers. William after all sent additional men to help clear the site. William's conversion through his encounter with the wild boar in the wilderness allows Jumièges to flourish once again.

If William Longsword's encounter with the boar in the forests around Jumièges served as a means of introducing the importance of the

---

[19] *Gesta Normannorum Ducum*, i, pp. 84–5.
[20] *Ibid.*, pp. 86–7.

relationship between duke and church, then we see these themes continued in Wace's *Roman de Rou* albeit in a more secular and heroic context. Wace provides accounts of two particularly interesting episodes that fall into the category of the miraculous in a Christian context: Richard I's encounter with a revenant and his arbitration in a dispute between the devil and an angel about the fate of a monk's soul. Both of these stories have a very strong sense of place. These episodes also occur within a series of four anecdotes in which the miraculous and the fabulous are intermingled.[21] What is key here is that these happenings take place in the context of journeys, either those of the duke or someone else. Le Saux argues that, by doing this, Wace is placing the duke in the tradition of the Arthurian knight errant, which might well have been popular for a court audience.[22] They also place Richard squarely in the role of protector and governor of the church and as a properly courtly ruler. Richard was, after all, a man who 'loved clerics and learning, knights and knighthood' (*ama clers e clergie, / chivaliers e chevalerie*).[23]

Richard's encounter with the revenant occurs during one of his nocturnal journeys around the duchy.[24] Wace states that the duke travelled often at night, without fear. The veracity of this statement is not the key issue here. What is important to note is that Wace creates an image of a ruler who is able to control the lands under his authority and travel in safety. During his journey, Richard stopped at a church to pray, as was his custom, and found a body laid out on a bier prior to burial. The body began to move while he was praying and, on turning to leave the church once he had completed his devotions, he encountered the devil blocking his exit. Taking his sword, the duke cut the devil in half and left the church. His bravery was underlined by his returning to the church to collect his gloves.

The second episode involves Richard in his capacity as judge, but interestingly as judge of the clergy, in this case the sacristan of the monastery of Saint-Ouen in Rouen, who was tempted by the devil.[25] The monk, who was of good character, saw a beautiful woman and desired her greatly. They arranged to meet at night. It is at this point that important information about the landscape comes to the fore. Rather than the unfamiliarity of a snowy

---

[21] The other two stories involve hunting and encounters between knights and ladies on moorland: Wace, *Roman de Rou*, part 3, lines 511–610, pp. 118–21.
[22] See the brief discussion in F. Le Saux, *A Companion to Wace* (Cambridge, 2005), pp. 185–90, 281–2.
[23] Wace, *Roman de Rou*, part 3, lines 273–74, pp. 112–14.
[24] *Ibid.*, lines 275–336, pp. 114–15.
[25] *Ibid.*, lines 337–510, pp. 114–19.

Norman countryside or fear induced by captivity in a hostile environment, what Wace presents here is something initially very familiar. The sacristan was to meet the woman in her lodgings, which involved a short journey from Saint-Ouen outside the northern walls of the city across the River Robec. Crossing the Robec was apparently the only way the couple could meet. Although this was a very familiar journey, Wace describes the monk as fearful, no doubt because he was weighed down by the sin he was about to commit. While crossing the plank he fell into the river and drowned, whereupon the devil and an angel both tried to seize his soul. There follows a discourse on the nature of sin and intention and the devil and the angel agree to set the case before the duke in order to determine the fate of the monk's soul. Richard instructed them to set the monk back on the plank exactly where he fell off. If he stepped forward, the devil was to have his soul. After the monk was placed on the plank he came to his senses and ran home to the monastery. The truth of the matter was brought before the abbot when the duke visited the monastery the following morning and the hapless sacristan appeared before him in sopping wet clothes.

The landscape settings of these stories are key. Richard's encounter with the revenant takes place within a church and cemetery. The sacristan of Saint-Ouen meets his fate on a plank serving as a crossing place over the River Robec as it flows into the city of Rouen. Both encounters take place at night. If Orderic was drawing on the weather to highlight the familiar made unfamiliar, then Wace used temporality, the cover of darkness, a time when normal rules could be suspended and when people could well feel afraid. The sense of place here also serves to connect readers or hearers of the chronicle to the locations mentioned by Wace. Many of them might well have known the geography of Rouen sufficiently well that they could walk with the monk. That the story, regardless of veracity, passed into general knowledge is shown by the fact that the monk became the subject of a joke that then circulated in Normandy for a very long time: 'Lord monk, go quietly and mind how you cross the plank!' (*Sire muine, suëf alez, / al passer planche vus gardez!*).[26] The strangeness of churchyards at night would also have resonated with a court audience that knew its romantic and epic tales. These familiar, yet at the same time, unfamiliar topographies thus created a bridge between past and present, ancestor and descendant and chronicle and audience, demonstrating the character of Henry II's ancestor, Duke Richard.

---

[26] *Ibid.*, lines 509–10, pp. 118–19.

Crusade

Within the large body of historical work surrounding the crusade, the place of the landscape in reinforcing key themes or in understanding the purposes behind the chronicle has been neglected. Although the Normans were just one group within a larger movement and any sense of a separate Norman identity tended to be subsumed within the larger umbrella terms of 'Frank' or 'pilgrim',[27] there were occasions when the activities of individual Normans came to the fore and their topographical setting is key to our understanding. Ralph of Caen, for example, criticised (in verse) deserters, including the brothers Grandmesnil, from the army at Antioch with specific reference to their lineage: 'Alas and shame, it was Normandy who sent forth the brothers. Everywhere the Normans had victory and were the glory of the world ... Oh that shame should come from such a lineage!' (*At fratres, pudet, heu! pudet heu! Normannia misit / Illud ubisque genus, victoria, gloria mundi / ... horum patitur de stirpe pudorem*).[28] At other times the focus is on the ability of individual commanders like Tancred. Descriptions of the landscape here allow the various chroniclers to make significant points. They also serve to highlight the experience of the writers and the responses they might have been aiming for in their audiences. Two events in particular will be discussed here, which contrast nicely – Peter the Hermit's experience of command and Tancred's involvement in an engagement on the River Vardar – as well as the importance of biblical and liturgical markers.

The first episode involves the arrival of the army in Constantinople, initially led by Peter the Hermit.[29] In this account we see that experience of the landscape and its character was directly related to intention and action. Although Peter the Hermit's misadventure did not directly involve the Norman contingent, nor was it led by a Norman, it is necessary for understanding how the chroniclers chose to narrate Tancred and Bohemond's skirmish with the emperor's army on the banks of the Vardar. According to the anonymous author of the *Gesta Francorum*, Emperor Alexius initially welcomed Peter the Hermit's army and gave it provisions. Despite

---

[27] See in particular L. Ni Chlérigh, 'Gesta Normannorum? Normans in the Latin Chronicles of the First Crusade', in *Norman Expansion: Connections, Continuities and Contrasts*, ed. K. J. Stringer and A. Jotischky (Farnham, 2013), pp. 207–26 for a detailed comparison of the ethnic identifiers used to describe crusaders in a wide range of chronicles. John France emphasises the separateness of the contingents from Normandy and southern Italy: John France, 'The Normans and Crusading', in *The Normans and Their Adversaries at War: Essays in Memory of C. Warren Hollister*, ed. R. P. Abels and B. S. Bachrach (Woodbridge, 2001), p. 101.

[28] RCaen, pp. 662; *GT*, Bachrach, p. 101.

[29] Hill, *GF*, pp. 3–4.

this hospitality, the army pillaged the imperial city, stealing the lead from church roofs and burning the palaces. Alexius' response was to order this section of the crusade across the Hellespont, despite his earlier counsel that they should wait for the rest of the army in order to have sufficient numbers to defend themselves against the Turks. His actions can be read as deliberately exiling the army to territory that was dangerous, unsafe and unfamiliar, knowing that its chances of survival were slim. Peter's army continued to pillage and loot before fragmenting and choosing different leaders from among the men. The Germans were then besieged in the castle of Xenigordon and Walter 'the Penniless' was attacked by the Turks at Civetot. Some of the crusaders 'leapt into the sea, and others hid in the woods or mountains' (*alii precipitabant se in mare, alii latebant in siluis et montanis*), while others were killed, fled or were taken back to Constantinople by the emperor.[30] The author of the *Gesta Francorum* is very matter of fact in his account. The army behaved badly, was shipped across the Hellespont, continued to behave badly and was defeated. Crucially he notes that Peter the Hermit had returned to Constantinople prior to the engagements because 'he could not control such a mixed company of people who would not obey him or listen to what he said' (*eo quod nequibat refrenare illam diuersam gentem, quae nec illum nec uerba eius audire uolebat*).[31] Orderic, using Baudri, also includes this explanation, but, towards the end of this section goes further, stating that the French had been hasty and had 'scorned to wait for the help of Bohemond and other Christian armies and trusted too much in their own strength' and were therefore massacred on the Turkish frontiers (*Precipites itaque Galli auxilium Buamundi aliorumque fidelium expectare spreuerunt, sed in uirtute sua nimis fisi ad fines Turcorum appropriauernt*).[32]

It is clear from this episode that leadership was key. Bohemond and Tancred made their way east via Macedonia where they encountered the Greeks and fought a battle on the banks of the River Vardar.[33] The emperor would have been gravely concerned about the appearance of Robert Gusicard's son in his dominions, given Robert's previous attempts to invade and conquer parts of Byzantine territory.[34] It is hardly surprising, therefore,

---

[30] *Ibid.*, p. 5.

[31] *Ibid.*, p. 4.

[32] OV, v, pp. 40–1. See also the discussion of Peter's leadership in John France, *Victory in the East: A Military History of the First Crusade* (Cambridge, 1994), pp. 93, 95.

[33] *Ibid.*, pp. 103–4, 107.

[34] For Robert Guiscard's campaign in Byzantium see G. A. Loud, *The Age of Robert Guiscard: Southern Italy and the Norman Conquest* (Harlow, 2000), pp. 209–23 and in relation to the first crusade, France, *Victory in the East*, pp. 74–7.

that the crusaders encountered hostility. What is important, however, was the behaviour of Bohemond and especially Tancred. The author of the *Gesta Francorum* was an eye-witness to this event as he was travelling in the southern Italian contingent. Bohemond, as recorded by both the *Gesta* and Orderic (using Baudri), banned the army from pillaging the countryside, though later hostility from the local inhabitants meant they had to take provisions by force.[35] However, the intention and leadership could not be a greater contrast with that of Peter the Hermit. Leading by example was crucial in what follows as the army had to cross the Vardar, which was, according to Ralph of Caen, in full flood.

Rivers were significant obstacles to armies on the move as they delayed progress and also made the troops vulnerable to attack while they were waiting to cross. Estuarine rivers or those in flood also carried additional risks in that men and horses could be swept away. We see examples of this in accounts relating to the consolidation of William II's rule in Normandy at the battles of Val-ès-Dunes (River Orne) and Varaville (River Dives), as well as in his harrying of the north of England in 1069–70 (River Aire at Pontefract). Rivers also played a significant role in Robert Guiscard's attempts to conquer southern Italy.[36] All these examples serve to demonstrate the qualities of William and Robert as commanders. In this instance it is Tancred who is to the fore. The account in the *Gesta* is brief, recording that Bohemond crossed over while the count of Russignolo and his men remained on the other bank where they were attacked by the emperor's army.[37] Orderic (using Baudri) provides additional information that the Byzantines were 'reconnoitring and watching the roads' (*vias obsidentes explorabant*). On seeing this Tancred swam back across the river with his men to lend aid.

Ralph of Caen's account differs enormously.[38] Here it is Tancred who leads the initial section of the army across the river and is ambushed by the Turks, while Bohemond remained on the opposite bank. He only began to cross once it was evident that the Greeks were in retreat in the face of successful resistance from Tancred. However, a second troop of Greeks subsequently ambushed the lightly armed and wounded rear-guard. It is

---

[35] Hill, *GF*, p. 8; OV, v, pp. 44–5.
[36] For a discussion of the problems rivers posed to armies see L. V. Hicks, 'Coming and Going: The Use of Outdoor Space in Norman and Anglo-Norman Chronicles', *ANS* 32 (2010), 40–56; and 'Journeys and Landscapes of Conquest: Normans Travelling to and in Southern Italy and Sicily', in *Journeying Along Medieval Routes*, ed. A. Gascoigne, L. V. Hicks and M. O'Doherty (Turnhout: Brepols, forthcoming).
[37] Hill, *GF*, pp. 8–9.
[38] RCaen, pp. 607–9; *GT*, Bachrach, pp. 24–8.

at this point that Tancred crossed the river again to ensure safer passage for those still stuck on the opposite bank. In contrast to the remnants of Peter the Hermit's army, who had to use the cover provided by the landscape to escape from the Turks, here we see the Greeks fleeing 'over broken ground and into pathless areas' (*fugitur per abrupta, per avia*) in order to hide.[39] The culmination of this episode is fulsome praise for Tancred who is described as 'an offshoot of Normandy' (*tanta sobole Normanni*)'.[40] Of course, other leaders of the crusade were praised by chroniclers associated with their contingents, but what is significant here is that Ralph used the example of a military engagement fought on a river, something we see in other Norman, but non-crusade related, contexts, to underline the valour and courage of the individual.[41]

One of the other significant uses of the landscape in crusade narratives is in tying descriptions to liturgical or biblical markers. The battle on the banks of the Vardar took place on Ash Wednesday 1097. After that, the author of the *Gesta Francorum* tells us, the army camped at a town called Serres where it had sufficient victuals for Lent.[42] This would imply that the food was neither lavish nor plentiful, but of a suitable nature and quantity for the penitential season. As Bohemond continued on to Constantinople and his meeting with Alexius, Tancred remained with the main body of the army and continued to see to provisions. Rather than using limited money supplies to buy food, he led the army off the road to 'a certain valley full of all kinds of food and things which are good to eat' (*Denique intrauit in uallem quamdam plenam omnibus bonis quae corporalibus nutrimentis sunt congrua*) and it was here that the crusaders kept Easter.[43] If the author of the *Gesta* was indeed a pious layman, then key liturgical markers like these would have been integral to his personal experience of the crusade. The allusion to ideas of a promised land of milk and honey can hardly be accidental. Albu gives a more negative interpretation of this section, citing it as an example of Tancred's hot-headedness and lack of moderation in plundering the surrounding countryside;[44] however, neither the author of the *Gesta* nor Orderic is critical of Tancred's actions and they do not suggest he engaged in widespread plunder.

---

[39] RCaen, ch. 6, p. 609; *GT*, Bachrach, p. 27.

[40] RCaen, ch.7, p. 610; *GT*, Bachrach, p. 28.

[41] Emily Albu highlights the contrast between Ralph of Caen, who stresses Tancred's Norman background, and the author of the *Gesta Francorum* who 'neither emphasizes Normanness nor invokes Normandy'. See Emily Albu, *The Normans in Their Histories: Propaganda, Myth and Subversion* (Woodbridge, 2001), p. 166.

[42] Hill, *GF*, p. 10.

[43] *Ibid.*, p. 11. Orderic (using Baudri) also makes similar comments: OV, v, pp. 48–9.

[44] Albu, *The Normans in Their Histories*, p. 164.

In terms of biblical markers, both the *Gesta Francorum* and Ralph of Caen provide descriptions of biblical landscapes, mapping sacred geography onto the contemporary landscape. The description of the holy places in the *Gesta* is written in the same hand as the historical narrative in two twelfth-century manuscripts though there is no direct evidence, according to the text's modern editor, that the author wrote it. She does, however, suggest, based on style, that its inclusion indicates that the anonymous knight finished his pilgrimage after the siege of Jerusalem.[45] Various sites associated with the life of Christ, the Virgin Mary and episodes from the Old Testament are described and plotted in a way that enables the reader to locate them. Ralph of Caen also included a description of Jerusalem and the surrounding area prior to his account of the capture of the city. It seems, though, that he had one eye on the military side of things as he noted that the valley of Jehosophat would make a good camp.[46] Orderic does not include a detailed description of the holy places. Possibly this is down to his source material, but also, as a monk, he would be far more familiar with the sacred geography of Jerusalem in a conceptual sense through the repeated reading of scripture. What he does do, and crucially independently of Baudri, is refer to other sites of potential interest to his monastic audience. For example he discusses the biblical significance of Edessa, site of Thaddeus' mission and location of a relic in the form of the handkerchief on which Christ wiped his face on the way to Golgotha.[47] The brethren at Saint-Évroult may not have been as familiar with these details and so Orderic's inclusion of them would help tie in the progress of the crusaders with sacred history.

There are many other examples related to landscape in the crusade narratives, but those discussed above suffice to show how the progress of the crusade, broadly conceived as a military pilgrimage, through biblical and other landscapes, allowed the chroniclers to link the crusaders with other concerns. We see the emphasis placed on the Normans as good leaders. Ralph and Orderic especially echo details found in other aspects of Norman historical writing. The authors also link crusading back to local and biblical concerns, helping those who were reading or listening to their narratives to visualise and plot the course of the journey themselves.

---

[45] Hill, *GF*, p. 97, n. 1.
[46] RCaen, pp. 686–7; *GT*, Bachrach, p. 132.
[47] OV, v, pp. 120–1. The inclusion of this detail is probably based on Eusebius of Caesarea's *Historia Ecclesiastica* (p. 121, n. 3).

*

In considering the landscape of miracles, the miraculous and pilgrimage in Norman sources several key themes are evident. First, the chroniclers had a clear idea of what constituted an appropriate landscape setting for such encounters. Hagiography was not, after all, the main purpose behind these histories, even if monks like Orderic Vitalis included extended passages relating to the lives of saints and their miracles. Landscapes needed to be both familiar, in that people could visualise and relate to what they were reading or hearing, and also unfamiliar. An ordinary landscape that people might walk through every day was not suitable for demonstrating qualities of piety, faithfulness, devotion or authority. By using devices such as temporality, the weather and topography, these historians provided a suitable context in which these characteristics might be displayed. Geoffrey the Breton was not doing anything unusual in taking bread to the monks of Saint-Évroult, but what was different were his perseverance through the challenging weather conditions and his steadfast faith that God would guide him through. These landscapes were also liminal or marginal in some way: rivers, borders and the edge between cultivation and wilderness or city and suburb are key. They need to be liminal in order to allow for the potential for change and for creating a sense of distance between the everyday and the ordinary. We can imagine that it was a big step for Geoffrey to leave his house in the snow or for the crusaders to embark on their long journey to Jerusalem, but we can perhaps see this mostly clearly in the case of the sacristan of Saint-Ouen. Here the boundary between the right and wrong path, life and death, heaven and hell is most apparent. His biggest step was leaving the cloister and attempting to cross the plank. The crossing place on the Robec becomes a much larger metaphor in his actions: a spiritual boundary.

Bound up with a sense of what was considered an appropriate landscape in which to encounter the miraculous is where these ideas originated. Although in these instances the chroniclers do not necessarily quote the Vulgate directly, there are allusions to scripture evident in the text. When Orderic says the 'snow levelled the hills and valleys' (*montes et valles coequauit*), he surely echoes Isaiah 40:4 ('Every valley shall be exalted and every mountain made low'). The crusade narratives reference biblical and liturgical markers in the landscape more directly, as one would expect. This device also allows the readers or hearers of the chronicle to link the progress of the crusaders with their own reading of scripture and to map the journey mentally. This reflects the different experiences of the historians from eye-witnesses to cloistered monks. In all accounts there is an emphasis on deliverance, whether from hazardous conditions, human enemies or the devil. The question of orality is also an important one. Orderic, for example, explicitly states that Geoffrey and Ruald recounted their experiences to the monks of Saint-Évroult and Wace records the traditions that grew up around the sacristan's misadventures. Both the anonymous author of the *Gesta Francorum* and Ralph of Caen drew on their own experiences to record those of the crusaders.

In terms of the wider themes of the chronicles, we need to consider the significance of the Normans and Normandy in activities relating to pilgrimage and crusade. Neither activity was unique to the duchy and, indeed, the author of the *Gesta Francorum*, Orderic Vitalis and Ralph of Caen all refer to the other groups from different parts of Europe that made up the crusade army. What this brief survey does show is the variety of experiences and audiences for whom the chroniclers were writing. Orderic began his chronicle initially as a history of the monastery, but it expanded to include the activities of the Normans elsewhere, especially where they touched on the history of the monastic community. Wace, writing to praise the qualities of Henry II's forebears, stressed Richard's admirable qualities in terms of his rule and governance of the church. If pilgrimage, crusade and miracles were not necessarily unique to Normandy, their importance in the wider historical narrative when examined through the lens of the landscape adds significantly to our understanding of these important sources.

11

Normans and Competing Masculinities on Crusade

NATASHA HODGSON

In the late 1130s the Byzantine princess Anna Comnena wrote a history of the deeds of her father Emperor Alexius I, and described his encounter with the Italian Norman, Bohemond of Taranto, following the fateful siege of Dyrrachium (1107). Even in defeat, Anna was impressed by the masculine characteristics of this renowned war leader:

> Bohemond's appearance was, to put it briefly, unlike any other man of those days seen in the Roman world, whether Greek or barbarian. The sight of him inspired admiration, the mention of his name, terror … His stature was such that he towered almost a full cubit over the tallest men. He was slender of waist and flanks, with broad shoulders and chest, strong in the arms; in general he was neither taper of form, not heavily built and fleshy, but perfectly proportioned.

She went on to praise his stature, shaven skin and light-blue eyes 'which gave some hint of the man's spirit and dignity'. However, her appraisal of his masculine attributes was not without agenda, as she needed to cement in the minds of her audience just how significant a man her father Alexius had overcome:

> There was a certain charm about him, but it was somewhat dimmed by the alarm his person as a whole inspired; there was a hard, savage quality in his whole aspect, due, I suppose, to his great stature and his eyes; even his laugh sounded like a threat to others.[1]

Despite the debates over Anna Comnena's qualities as an historian, it is her image of Bohemond as a cunning, dangerous and overwhelmingly

---

[1] Anna Comnena, *Alexiade*, ed. and trans. Bernard Lieb, 3 vols, 2nd edn (Paris, 1967), iii, pp. 122–3; Anna Comnena, *The Alexiad of Anna Comnena*, trans. E. R. A. Sewter (Harmondsworth, 1969), p. 422.

masculine warrior which until recently informed most scholars' impressions of Bohemond's person and character; qualities which were also perceived to be quintessentially 'Norman'.[2] Although Bohemond was Italian by birth, his Norman heritage has been emphasised by a variety of subsequent historians.[3] His activities in the Mediterranean, on crusade and in the establishment of the principality of Antioch seemed to typify a Norman 'character' which formed a significant cornerstone of the arguments in favour of a unified rationale to Norman expansion in the eleventh and early twelfth centuries.[4] France and Murray, however, have done much to challenge established views about Norman identity in the specific context of the crusades: the former has considered problems with the application of Norman terminology in a crusading context, while the latter has explored ethnicity and identity during the settlement process.[5] Most recently, Ní Clerígh has undertaken a further comparison of the descriptive use of labels such as *Francigeni* and *Normanni* in first crusade histories, suggesting that in fact the Normans had minimal impact on the authors of crusade

[2] For example, Sir Steven Runciman asserted that 'genuine religious fervour was the strongest motive' for all of the leaders of the First Crusade except for Bohemond. He interpreted Bohemond's crusade as purely an excercise in personal ambition: Steven Runciman, *A History of the Crusades*, 3 vols (Cambridge, 1951–4), i, p. 113. For evaluations of Anna Comnena as an historian, see John France, 'Anna Comnena, *The Alexiad* and the First Crusade', *Reading Medieval Studies* 10 (1984), 20–38 and Peter Frankopan, 'Perception and Projection of Prejudice: Anna Comnena, the *Alexiad* and the First Crusade', in *Gendering the Crusades*, ed. Sarah Lambert and Susan B. Edgington (Cardiff, 2001), pp. 59–76. Frankopan has called for a re-evaluation of Alexius I, and by extension Bohemond, in the context of the First Crusade but still refers to the latter as a Norman. Peter Frankopan, *The First Crusade: the Call from the East* (London, 2012), especially pp. 185 and 186–206.

[3] For example Emily Albu, 'Probing the Passions of a Norman on Crusade: The *Gesta Francorum et aliorum Hierosolimitanorum*', *ANS* 27 (2005), 1–15; Kenneth Baxter Wolf, 'Crusade and Narrative: Bohemond and the *Gesta Francorum*', *JMH* 17 (1991), 207–16. France, however, has pointed out that relatively few contemporary authors of crusade narratives referred to Bohemond explicitly as a Norman: John France, 'The Normans and Crusading', in *The Normans and Their Adversaries at War: Essays in Memory of C. Warren Hollister*, ed. R. P. Abels and B. S. Bachrach (Woodbridge, 2001), p. 88. Albu, too, notes that the author of the *Gesta* only really describes Robert Curthose as Norman: Emily Albu, *The Normans in Their Histories: Propaganda, Myth and Subversion* (Woodbridge, 2001), pp. 153–4.

[4] See Charles Homer Haskins, *The Normans in European History* (Boston, 1915); David C. Douglas, *The Norman Achievement, 1050–1100* (Berkeley, CA, 1969); D. C. Douglas, *The Norman Fate, 1100–1154* (Berkeley, CA, 1976). John Le Patourel's *The Norman Empire* (Oxford, 1976), was less focused upon cultural issues but argued for the use of the term 'Empire' on the grounds of power stuctures. He did not consider what he saw as the colonisation of southern Italy, Sicily and Antioch as comprising a part of that empire (pp. 279–80). Such arguments have since been rigorously examined by historians, for example by R. H. C. Davis in *The Normans and Their Myth* (London, 1976), and most recently by David Bates in *The Normans and Empire* (Oxford, 2013).

[5] For example, see Alan V. Murray, 'How Norman Was the Principality of Antioch? Prolegomena to a Study of the Origins of the Nobility of a Crusader State', in *Family Trees and the Roots of Politics: The Prosopography of England and France from the Tenth to the Twelfth Century*, ed. K. S. B. Keats-Rohan (Woodbridge, 1997), pp. 349–59 and France, 'The Normans and Crusading', pp. 87–101.

narratives beyond a few significant sources.⁶ This chapter builds on the current debate by looking beyond explicit terminology and evaluating certain characteristics which were associated with Normans. It examines how far they were employed by the authors of crusade narratives to describe and explicate competing masculinities in the context of crusading activity. Taking issues such as identity, character and family into consideration, the Normans here provide a focal point for my wider attempts to establish parameters for understanding how crusaders fit into the contemporary spectrum of medieval maleness.

The eleventh and twelfth centuries were a crucial time for redefining gender identities in medieval Europe.⁷ Reforms instigated by the papacy and new monastic orders placed increasing pressure on clergy, both secular and religious, to conform to more restricted roles in terms of traditional 'manly' activities. At the same time, concerns about social interaction and religion led elite lay men to contemplate their own codes of behaviour and spiritual needs. The advent of crusading added yet another level of complex expectations to the medieval male experience. Most historians agree that the crusade was designed at least in part to offer knights an avenue for reform – famously Guibert of Nogent saw it as a new solution for knights who were concerned about their salvation but unable to embrace monastic life.⁸ However, bearing in mind that many of those who took the Cross were not knights, crusading evidently appealed to men across a range of social boundaries. As a result, crusade sources often expose a number of contemporary debates about masculine roles. Crusaders were not only contrasted with their enemies in terms of gender; contemporary narratives supplied opinions on what constituted a good Christian man and a good warrior: on sex, violence, hierarchies of power and social relationships.⁹ However, the experiences and actions of crusaders often fell short of this complex range of ideals.

When it came to the historical explanation of crusade expeditions in narrative, authors used even more nuanced ideas about male identity,

---

⁶ Lean Ní Clerígh, '*Gesta Normannorum*? Normans in the Latin Chronicles of the First Crusade', in *Norman Expansions: Connections, Continuities and Contrasts*, ed. Keith J. Stringer and Andrew Jotischky (Farnham, 2013), pp. 207–26.
⁷ See Jo Ann McNamara, 'The *Herrenfrage*: The Restructuring of the Gender System, 1050–1150', in *Medieval Masculinities: Regarding Men in the Middle Ages*, ed. Clare A. Lees, with Thelma Fenster and Jo Ann McNamara (Minneapolis, MN, 1994), pp. 3–29.
⁸ GN, p. 615.
⁹ Matthew Bennett, 'Virile Latins, Effeminate Greeks and Strong Women: Gender Definitions on Crusade?' in *Gendering the Crusades*, pp. 16–30 at pp. 16–18; Deborah Gerish, 'Gender Theory', in *Palgrave Advances in the Crusades*, ed. Helen Nicholson (Basingstoke, 2005), pp. 130–47.

gender and sexuality; drawing from the rhetorical mode of 'praise' and 'blame' for individuals or groups. A crusader force unified under the leadership of Christ was the ultimate ideal, but difference, inequality and disunity also played significant roles in describing events, especially military setbacks. Authors were therefore drawn to consider relationships between men: what have been described as competing masculinities, rather than simply establishing one type of masculinity in opposition to a feminine 'other'.[10] They also indicated degrees of social acceptability for crusaders' behaviour by employing concepts such as honour and shame. In order to highlight some of these debates, this chapter will take a focused look at Norman group identity and some select individual examples of crusaders traditionally identified as having 'Norman' characteristics, examining how these manifested in the context of crusader masculinities.

Norman Identity and Character

In some ways, the Normans are particularly well suited for a case study. Much groundwork has already been laid in terms of evaluating Norman identities on crusade. Loud has outlined some of the problems with accepting historical accounts of the *gens Normannorum* at face value, but recognises that certain sources played a formative role in defining and explaining the origins of a people who had made a substantial impact on several parts of Europe.[11] At a time when the secular aristocracy largely equated masculinity with prowess on the battlefield, the Normans were described by their advocates as the most warlike of races – *Normanni gentium fortissimo*, according to Henry of Huntingdon, while William of Poitiers talked in terms of *virtus normannica*.[12] In Orderic Vitalis' view they were cruel and warlike, their manliness stood in stark opposition to others, their 'bold roughness ... proved as deadly to their softer neighbours as the bitter wind to young flowers'.[13] They had, however, experienced a 'civilising' transition relatively recently in terms of their conversion to Christianity. Coupled with strong leadership these two elements were seen

---

[10] See Clare A. Lees, 'Introduction', in *Medieval Masculinities*, p. xx.

[11] G. A. Loud, 'The *Gens Normannorum*: Myth or Reality?' *ANS* 4 (1982), p.109 and G. A. Loud, 'Norman Italy and the Holy Land', in *The Horns of Hattin*, ed. B. Kedar (London, 1992), pp. 49–62. See also N. Webber, *The Evolution of Norman Identity, 911–1154* (Woodbridge, 2005) and H. M. Thomas, *The English and the Normans: Ethnic Hostility, Assimilation and Identity, 1066–c.1220* (Oxford, 2003)..

[12] Henry ascribed this term to William the Conqueror in his speech at Hastings. Henry of Huntingdon, *Historia Anglorum*, ed. Diana Greenaway (Oxford, 1996), pp. 388–9. *The Gesta Guillelmi of William of Poitiers*, ed. and trans. R. H. C. Davies and M. Chibnall (Oxford, 1998), p. 44.

[13] OV, v, pp. 24–7.

to provide the necessary checks for their tendencies towards unrestrained violence and in-fighting.[14] The Normans' reputation for military superiority was constructed through a series of eleventh-century histories and *chansons de geste*, developing the ideal of the *gens Normannorum*.[15] Their rapid territorial expansion was also a recognisable attribute, and Dudo of Saint-Quentin's use of Virgil's prince Aeneas as a model for Rollo, founder of the duchy of Normandy, leant classical support to the idea of Normans as heroic adventurers who settled overseas.[16] Dudo charted the gradual 'civilisation' of a succession of Norman princes; but, as Albu suggests, this was a thin veneer – the ravening wolf still lurked beneath.[17] Famously, Geoffrey Malaterra characterised the Normans as shrewd, duplicitous flatterers who loved luxury, hunting and the trappings of war. They were 'quick to avenge injury', adventurous, 'avid for profit and domination'. He asserted that they maintained 'a certain balance between avarice and largesse', but this was largely due to their princes' desire for 'a good reputation'. He praised their endurance but also emphasised their need for a strong hand in governance.[18] Such characteristics were inherently masculine. Women in positions of authority were usually viewed as having to transcend their gender in order to maintain such a role: thus they were often compared to men in descriptions of their activities: their dynastic origins might be important to establish their lineage, but distinguishing distinct qualities for

---

[14] OV, iii, p. 98; iv, p. 82; v, pp. 24, 300; vi, pp. 450–8, especially p. 457 'If the Norman people would live according to the law of God and be united under a good prince they would be invincible ... as their many victories in England and Apulia and Syria amply testify.'

[15] According to Loud, the *gens* combined common descent with cultural and physical traits. See Loud, 'The Gens Normannorum', pp. 110–11. See also Webber, *The Evolution of Norman Identity*; Davis, *The Normans and Their Myth*; Albu, *The Normans in Their Histories*, passim. Perhaps the most important eleventh-century authors in question are Dudo of Saint-Quentin, William of Jumièges and William of Poitiers, with Amatus of Montecassino, William of Apulia and Geoffrey Malaterra, emphasising Norman achievements in the Mediterranean. These sources were a great influence on later twelfth-century authors such as Wace and Orderic Vitalis. William of Poitiers himself was a knight turned chaplain, thus well acquainted with secular and ecclesiastical pressures: *Gesta Guilelmi*, pp. xv–xlvii.

[16] Albu demonstrates the strong links between Dudo's text and the *Aeneid*, with aspects of Aeneas' character being broken down 'in order to illustrate the progressive civilizing of the Norman dukes': Albu, *The Normans in Their Histories*, p. 15; see also pp. 7–46. This parallel was later employed directly by Ralph of Caen for the crusaders Arnulf and Tancred, whom he likened to Hector and Aeneas, see below p. 212.

[17] Albu, *The Normans in Their Histories*, pp. 13–26.

[18] Geoffrey Malaterra, *De rebus gestis Rogerii Calabriae et Siciliae Comitis et Roberti Guiscardi ducis fratris eius*, Rerum Italicarum Scriptores, 2nd edn, vol. 5, part 1, ed. Ernesto Pontieri (Bologna, 1925–28), pp. 8–9. Geoffrey Malaterra, *The Deeds of Count Roger of Calabria and Sicily and of His Brother Duke Robert Guiscard*, trans. Kenneth Wolf (Ann Arbor, MI, 2005), p. 56. See below n. 27 for parallels in Orderic Vitalis.

women within a *gens* is more difficult.[19] At times, however, the *gens* itself was portrayed as feminine, usually as a mother-figure.[20]

In literary accounts of their rise to power, the Christianisation of the Normans allowed authors to explore some of the inherent religious and social conflicts for an aristocratic society which prized success in warfare as the ultimate masculine ideal.[21] Christianity provided Norman leaders with a moral code and the means to restrict the behaviour of unruly followers, but they still needed to provide for their own defence. Dudo of Saint-Quentin's account of the murder of William Longsword, who was reportedly a devoted Christian, is interpreted by Albu as a cautionary tale.[22] William's faith made him too trusting, and believing in the better nature of his enemy he agreed to a meeting which turned out to be a duplicitous trap. On the other hand, Dudo approved of William's piety and emphasised that he became a martyr as a result.[23] Even at the height of their power, the Normans occupied a space on the cusp of socially acceptable ideals of lordship and nobility, especially in areas where they were newly established such as southern Italy.[24] Their reputation as mercenaries stemmed partly from the fact that they operated very openly as paid warriors in Italy, in Byzantium and in other areas of Europe. As Tyerman points out, this practice was probably widespread: even on crusade, Bohemond of Taranto is referred to as using paid troops several times.[25] This was one of the reasons why they were so keen to secure ecclesiastical approbation in written sources and papal recognition of their conquests. It might seem as if Baldric of Bourgeuil's version of Urban II's speech at Clermont was written explicitly with the Normans in mind as he described thieves anticipating pay for shedding Christian blood – sniffing out battles from afar and rushing to them like vultures.[26] By the time of the First Crusade, the Normans had a clearly es-

---

[19] See Susan M. Johns, *Noblewomen, Aristocracy and Power in the Twelfth Century Anglo-Norman Realm* (Manchester, 2003), pp. 13–30.

[20] See below p. 204 and Kirsten A. Fenton, *Gender, Nation and Conquest in the Works of William of Malmesbury* (Woodbridge, 2008), pp. 88–9.

[21] For a recent discussion, see Richard W. Kaeuper, *Holy Warriors* (Philadelphia, 2009).

[22] Albu, *The Normans in Their Histories*, p. 19.

[23] William was lured to his murder on the false pretext of arranging a truce by Arnulf I, Count of Flanders in 943. Dudo of Saint-Quentin, *De moribus et actis primorum Normanniæ ducum*, ed. Jules Lair (Caen, 1865), pp. 203–9.

[24] Ewan Johnson, 'The Process of Norman Exile into Italy' in *Exile in the Middle Ages*, ed. L. Napran and E. M. C. van Houts (Turnhout, 2004), pp. 29–38.

[25] For example, Hagenmeyer, *GF*, p. 156 and OV, vi, pp. 100–1. See Christopher Tyerman, 'Paid Crusaders. "Pro honoris vel pecuniae; stipendiarii contra paganos": Money and Incentives on Crusade', in idem. *The Practices of Crusading: Image and Action from the Eleventh to the Sixteenth Centuries* (Aldershot, 2013), pp. 1–40.

[26] BB, p. 9. Baldric's close association with powerful patrons linked to the Norman dynasty, such as Adela of Blois, are well known, as is his *Carmen* on the Norman Conquest. Biddlecombe has argued

tablished reputation for boldness, military tenacity and generosity when it suited them, but also for greed, cunning and in-fighting.[27] Their actions on crusade, from both pro-Norman and other commentators, attracted praise and controversy, demonstrating concerns about Normans backsliding into their old ways. In many respects the *fama* they had established provided a literary blueprint for warriors in the process of reform.[28]

Contemporary Masculinities

Given the aristocratic focus of most texts surviving from the time, the warrior, and the knight in particular, has held paramount position in the evaluation of secular ideals of masculinity. The rise of the Normans coincided with the highly significant period in the pre-chivalric *habitus* incorporating the transition of the *miles* from professional mounted warrior to the ideal of the knight. Not every powerful man was an active warrior, but prowess on the battlefield was an ideal towards which noble men aspired. Despite the tensions between secular and religious models of manhood, ecclesiastics too borrowed from military terminology to praise the men they wished to emulate. For example, asceticism was commonly linked to martial prowess.[29] It is difficult to establish whether these aspects of male identity were uniform across the rest of medieval society, largely because commentators were so focused on male hierarchies of power.[30] It has been argued that mainstream medieval masculinity could be distilled in its most basic form to three key activities: impregnating women, protecting dependants and serving as providers to one's family.[31] This model can be

---

that a later recension of Baldric's work was adapted to highlight the role of Breton and Norman Crusaders, perhaps at the behest of Alan, steward of the church of the archbishop at Dol: BB, pp. xxix–xxx.

[27] Geoffrey Malaterra, *De rebus gestis*, p. 8. Later, Orderic Vitalis also mentioned many of these as stock Norman features – their bellicose nature, greed and ambition to keep power, arrogance and adventurous need to seek new lands: OV, v, p. 24. He may have had access to the copy of Geoffrey Malaterra at Saint-Evroul, but Chibnall was not certain that he had used it. See Loud 'Gens Normannorum', pp. 106 and 206 n. 34.

[28] Hodgson, 'Reinventing Normans', pp. 117–32.

[29] See Janet L. Nelson, 'Monks, Secular Men and Masculinity c. 900', in *Masculinity in Medieval Europe*, ed. Dawn M. Hadley (Harlow, 1999), pp. 121–42; Jacqueline Murray 'Masculinising Religious Life: Sexual Prowess, the Battle for Chastity and Monastic Identity', in *Holiness and Masculinity in the Middle Ages*, ed. P. H. Cullum and Katherine J. Lewis (Cardiff, 2004), pp. 24–43. Katherine Allen Smith, 'Saints in Shining Armour: Martial Asceticism and Masculine Models of Sanctity, ca. 1050–1250', *Speculum*, 83 (2008), 572–602.

[30] See Ruth Mazzo Karras, *From Boys to Men: Formations of Masculinity in Late Medieval Europe* (Philadelphia, 2003), p. 2.

[31] Vern L. Bulloch, 'On Being a Man in the Middle Ages', in *Medieval Masculinities*, ed. Lees *et al.*, p. 34. See also David D. Gilmore, *Manhood in the Making: Cultural Concepts of Masculinity* (New Haven, CT, 1990).

projected with relative ease onto the men of the nobility and the Third Estate, but difficulties in relating it to the clergy, and indeed to crusaders, are self-evident.

Crusading was an innovation which directly reflected developing ideals of manhood but it is not sufficient to simply identify and typify the 'ideal crusader', whether by seeking a definition in canon law or by searching other records.[32] Historians have given detailed examination to the terminology surrounding crusade and the problems posed by the association of crusaders with pilgrims.[33] If there were ideal crusaders, they changed and developed alongside the idea of crusading itself, as participants were constantly measured against contemporaries as well as past exemplars. Like other men in medieval society, crusaders were constantly distinguished from one another other in terms of age, social status, career, dress, character, wealth, family relationships and – occasionally – *gens*. By comparing and contrasting the manly qualities of certain contingents on crusade, a greater insight is given into those individuals whose *gens* was seen to influence the masculine aspects of their character. Clerical masculinity is also a particularly significant issue for the crusades: both in terms of the role of clergy in the army and in the respect of the quasi-religious status held by crusaders as fighting pilgrims. Thus in the remainder of this brief study, four key figures have been chosen to represent issues relating to competing masculinities in the contexts of family, leadership and clerical masculinity: Bohemond of Taranto, Tancred, Robert of Normandy and Arnulf of Choques. First, however, the use of *gens Normannorum* as a measure of competing masculinities will be considered.

The *Gens Normannorum* and Masculinity

The authors of crusade narratives were usually keen to emphasise unity amongst crusaders. This could be demonstrated in a number of ways, one of which was to use 'catch-all' terminology such as Franks or Gauls. This method was employed even by pro-Norman authors such as Ralph of

---

[32] For an example, see Andrew Holt, 'Between Warrior and Priest: The Creation of a New Masculine Identity during the Crusades', in *Negotiating Clerical Identities: Priests, Monks and Masculinity in the Middle Ages*, ed. Jennifer D. Thibodeaux (Basingstoke, 2010), pp. 185–203.

[33] Tyerman has famously argued that the lack of specific terminology referring to crusaders in the twelfth century suggests that the idea of crusading was not clearly defined, and a recent research paper by Christoph Maier has challenged the existence of crusade itself as a distinct concept during the medieval period. See Christopher Tyerman, *The Invention of the Crusades* (London, 1998). Christoph Maier, 'What If There Were No Crusades in the Middle Ages?' Institute of Historical Research Crusades Seminar, 16 December 2013.

Caen, as France has established.³⁴ In addition, Ní Clerígh has argued that outside the 'immediate context of Norman-controlled heartlands' the use of *Normanni* and *Normannitas* was very limited in crusade histories. She suggests that the use of *Franci* in certain sources was not just an expression of unity, but simply reflected less regard for the Normans as a group in the minds of non-Norman commentators, especially when it was used in conjunction with other *gentes* such as *Longobardi* or *Allemani*.³⁵ The argument is a convincing one, but also indicates that we need to examine the context and circumstances more closely when *gens* was explicitly highlighted by authors. *Gentes* were often employed when commentators wanted to underline differences within the crusade armies. This was usually either to emphasise the wide appeal of the crusade message by listing a multitude of participants from far-flung geographical locations, to celebrate and commemorate participants or sometimes to explain military formations. The attention of the audience might be drawn to different contingents in order to describe traditional expertise or tactics among certain ethnic groups. They might be singled out for praise, or sometimes their failings were criticised – especially at times of hardship such as the desertions from the siege of Antioch in 1098, which I have discussed more detail elsewhere.³⁶ Of course, these judgements could simply reflect an author's agenda. For example Ralph of Caen, who supported Arnulf of Choques in his refutation of the Holy Lance and opposed Raymond of Saint-Gilles' claim to Antioch, was highly critical of the Provençals as a group, calling them unwarlike and greedy.³⁷

If we reduce our scope to those texts which are often identified with a pro-Norman perspective, we might expect all members of Norman contingents to present the most masculine qualities, but Normans who failed to live up to these high standards could expect severe criticism. Perhaps this is most amply illustrated by the Anglo-Norman priest Raol, in his *De Expugnatione Lxybonensi*. He placed an emphasis on the importance of unity throughout his text, but at times he deliberately highlighted the characteristics of certain *gentes*, Normans, English, Flemings and men of Cologne. These other groups did not share the exalted reputation of the Normans, but they were at least immune to some of their faults. When William Viel

---

³⁴ France, 'The Normans and Crusading', pp. 87–101. It is also significant that *gens* was differentiated from *natio* or *regnum* in medieval thought by virtue of the idea of shared stock, and by extension loyalties: Loud, '*Gens Normannorum*', pp. 109–10.
³⁵ Ní Clerígh, '*Gesta Normannorum?*' pp. 225–6.
³⁶ Hodgson, 'Reinventing Normans', pp. 129–32.
³⁷ RC, p. 651.

and his followers were threatening to leave the host rather than engage in the campaign against Lisbon, Raol attributed a rousing speech to Hervey of Glanvill in which he extolled the virtues of the Normans, but lamented their propensity for greed and envy. This, he asserted, made them more susceptible to discord than other groups on the crusade: the Flemings, the men of Cologne, even the barbaric Scots: 'what else can be said except that something abnormal appears in you, since we are all sons of one mother?'[38] He expressed concern about them bringing shame upon their *gens*, warning that:

> [You will become] objects of universal infamy and shame. Through fear of a glorious death you have withdrawn your support from your associates. The mere desire for booty yet to be acquired, you have bought at the cost of eternal dishonour. The race of your innocent colleagues will be held responsible for this your crime; and it is certainly a shame that Normandy, the mother of our race, must bear, and that undeservedly, in the eyes of so many peoples who are here represented the everlasting opprobrium of your outrageous action.[39]

Perhaps most astonishingly, Hervey broke down in tears and offered William Viel leadership of the contingent and all his possessions in order to achieve unity, attempting to kneel at his feet. While his actions might be seen as weak and far from masculine, his public show of humility obviously gained Raol's approval and had the desired effect. William Viel and his followers refused to accept Hervey's obeisance and agreed to remain with the army. It is strikingly similar to a scene carried out in Corfu over fifty years later when the Fourth Crusade army faced considerable dissent.[40] In some circumstances, a public demonstration of humility and an offer to transfer power placed a burden of honour on comrades to comply. In terms of affecting the reputation of one's *gens*, parallels can also be drawn with Ralph of Caen's lament at the desertion of Normans from the siege of Antioch in 1098. He highlighted William, Albert and Ivo of Grandmesnil, and Ralph of Fontanella as the key culprits.[41] He asserted that these were

---

[38] As Albu asserts, themes of treason and deception 'held particular resonance for Norman historians who sought the social origins of this pathology among their own people and identified stages of its development': Albu, *The Normans in Their Histories*, p. 5.

[39] *DEL*, pp. 100–11. The idea of Normandy as a mother was also used by Orderic Vitalis on the eve of the civil war, when she experienced sharp pains akin to childbrith and was reduced to tears because of her warring sons: OV, vi, p. 457.

[40] See Natasha Hodgson, 'Honour Shame and the Fourth Crusade', *JMH* 39 (2013), 220–39.

[41] The Grandmesnils were a well-known Norman family, but Murray identifies Ralph with La Fontanelle, in the Touraine region, an area held by the counts of Anjou from the counts of Blois. He was in

worthy and noble men 'inclined toward battle' who had received praise for their actions up until that point; but by their desertion they brought shame upon Normandy and upon their lineage.[42] Honour and shame were central features of aristocratic interaction, but the notion of shaming one's *gens* added yet another layer of social responsibility which could be extended to all members of a group linked by shared heritage.

Norman Leadership and Family Rivalry

Leadership raises its own issues for masculinity. Leading by example and personal bravery were important to inspire loyalty among followers, but the duties of a knight as fearless warrior of God were not the same as the expectations resting on the leader of an expedition. They were beholden not only to exercise strategic expertise but also to provide financial support, to exercise justice and to provide discipline. The leaders of the First Crusade were not kings, but the death or even injury of such powerful magnates was perceived to have severe consequences in terms of morale and the army's ability to wage war effectively.[43] Therefore bravery and prowess, key masculine qualities, needed to be tempered with prudence and foresight in a leader. Ralph of Caen gave a detailed appraisal of the characters and skills of the main First Crusaders, including their flaws. Raymond of Saint-Gilles was rich but not sufficient in largesse. Robert of Normandy was a miserable ruler of his own lands, but managed to restrain his profligate tendencies on

---

the contingent of Everard III of le Puiset: Murray *Crusader Kingdom*, pp. 222–3.

[42] 'Alas and shame, it was Normandy who sent forth the brothers. Everywhere the Normans had victory and were the glory of the world. This people were victorious over the English, the Sicilians, the Greeks, the Campanians and the Apulians. The people of Maine, Calabria, Africa and Japix serve them. Oh that shame should come from such a lineage!' RCaen, p. 662; *GT*, Bachrach, p. 101. These events were also mentioned by others: Guibert of Nogent omitted their family name for fear of bringing shame upon it, referring to them only as William of Normandy and his brother Alberic, but thereby highlighting their Norman origins: GN, p. 207. The *Gesta Francorum* identified them as William of Grandmesnil, Alberic his brother, Guy Troussel and Lambert the Poor (from Clermont, near Liège): Hagenmeyer, *GF*, p. 332. BB, p. 66 also mentioned these individuals, criticising their loss of courage and masculinity which engendered their eternal shame, *perpetuam suam ignominiam*. Orderic Vitalis changed this to *diuturnam ignominiam* perhaps, as Chibnall suggests, because he knew that other deserters, the Norman, Ivo of Grandmesnil and Miles of Bray (father of Guy Troussel), returned to the East and took part in the 1101 crusade: OV, v, pp. 98–9 and n. 3. Peter Tudebode explicitly added William of Bernella, William, brother of Richard, and Ivo of Grandmesnil to the *Gesta*'s version: Peter Tudebode, *Historia De Hierosolymitano Itinere*, ed. John Hugh and Laurita L. Hill (Paris, 1977), p. 97.

[43] For example, Guibert of Nogent blamed the desertion of some troops on an injury sustained by Duke Godfrey when he was out hunting and was attacked by a bear: GN, pp. 285–7. The impact of this may have been exaggerated, however. See Natasha Hodgson, 'Lions, Tigers, and Bears: Encounters with Wild Animals and Bestial Imagery in the Context of Crusading to the Latin East', *Viator* 44 (2013), 65–93.

crusade. Perhaps most telling was his assessment of Robert of Flanders, of whom we are told:

> [He] was praised above all the other leaders of the army for his skill with a sword and spear. But he shrank from taking a leadership role. As a result, he gained much more renown than the other leaders as a soldier, but much less as a leader, as he avoided the worries of command.[44]

Thus Ralph clearly distinguished between martial prowess and leadership abilities. The example of individual leadership in inspiring other men to take the Cross was also significant: Geoffrey Malaterra wrote of Bohemond's example,

> the war-oriented young men of the duke's and count's armies, attracted by the novelty of the thing as is customary for those of such a young age, hurried eagerly to Bohemond once they had seen his cross and been summoned by him to participate.[45]

Bohemond's actions and encouragement combined with the adventurous qualities attributed to *iuventes* to enable successful recruitment. Relationships between leaders could also be explained in terms of manliness and hierarchies of power. Family bonds were usually stressed in masculine terms, between Godfrey of Bouillon and his brothers for example, or Bohemond and Tancred. Kinship was seen to have the effect of adding strength to co-operative leadership, but could also incite competition.

It would be impossible to consider Norman masculinity on crusade without giving at least passing attention to Bohemond of Taranto, despite the complications inherent in distinguishing the Normans of Normandy from the southern Italians. From Anna Comnena's description to his controversial activities on crusade, Bohemond was unquestionably viewed as a man to be reckoned with. His legacy in crusade histories as *fortissimus Christi athleta* may be based predominantly on the influence of the *Gesta Francorum*, but as others have shown this was not always explicitly linked to his Normanness.[46] The *Gesta* did not refer to Bohemond as Norman at all, yet he did, however, exhibit recognisable traits which were traditionally associated with *Normannitas*: he was most often described as

---

[44] RCaen, p. 616, trans. *GT*, Bachrach, p. 38.
[45] Geoffrey of Malaterra, *De rebus gestis*, p. 102, trans. Wolf, p. 204. In Malaterra's view, Bohemond's motives in doing so were personal rather than religious – seeing a large number of leaderless men heading east he saw an opportunity to take control of an army.
[46] Hagenmeyer, *GF*, p. 247. See Ní Clerígh, '*Gesta Normannorum*', p. 214.

prudens, doctus and *sapiens*.⁴⁷ His use of flattery and trickery to gain the city of Antioch and the violation of his oath to emperor Alexius have also been characterised as typically Norman behaviour, especially when he was hedging his bets. The *Gesta* author highlighted the fact that Bohemond was not present when his troops started climbing the walls at Antioch, asking *Ubi est accerrimus Boamundus? Ubi est ille invictus?* suggesting concern or even disappointment at the lord's pragmatic decision not to put himself in the front line.⁴⁸ We are told that Bohemond, still addressed as *vir prudens*, had to be encouraged by a soldier – a *Longobardus* – to take part.⁴⁹ Essentially, limited knowledge about the authorship of the *Gesta* and changing attitudes towards Bohemond in the text create difficulties in presenting it as a pro-Norman text in any sense, but the author did colour the positive and negative features of this principal character with traditionally Norman attributes.

Perhaps more significant than *Normannitas* in the portrayal of Bohemond's masculine leadership was the sense of competing relationships with other male members of his family, echoing the Hauteville legacy.⁵⁰ His Norman father Robert Guiscard was often mentioned in connection with him – certainly Anna Comnena was keen to draw such comparisons in relation to Byzantine affairs – but in the context of the crusades it was his nephew Tancred who was to act in this capacity; he was a strong fighter and ally, but hungry for his own power. Ralph of Caen was keen to uphold Tancred's reputation in comparison to Bohemond, and was firm about establishing their shared Norman heritage, but he also spoke candidly about the rivalry which affected their relationship. When the two leaders met to hammer out the organisation of the crusade over a cup of wine, Ralph explained why Tancred agreed to be second-in-command:

> the first of these reasons was bound up in their love for one another ... the second was based on fear. If Tancred did not obey Bohemond, he might

---

⁴⁷ The Hagenmeyer edition includes more of these additional adjectives than Hill's, which is based on Vatican regiensis Lat 572. For Bohemond described as *prudens* see Hagenmeyer, GF, pp. 164, 178, 255, 267, 268 and 303. Tancred is the only other individual leader regularly referred to as *prudens*: Hagenmeyer, GF, pp. 197, 262 and 218. For *sapiens*, see *ibid.*, pp. 156, 198, 200, 241, 256, 268, 348, 371. The only other individuals to be described thus by the *Gesta* author are clerics: the bishop of Albara, Peter of Narbonne (*ibid.*, p. 393), and Arnulf of Choques (*ibid.*, p. 479). *Doctus* – learned or wise – is usually used only in conjunction with Bohemond: *ibid.*, pp. 165, 166, 226 and 270; except at p. 223 where Baldwin of Boulogne is described as *doctissimus* when he outplays Tancred at Tarsus.
⁴⁸ Hagenmeyer, GF, p. 303.
⁴⁹ *Ibid.*, p. 303. See Albu, *The Normans in Their Histories*, pp. 156–8.
⁵⁰ Anna Comnena saw him as the 'exact replica' of his father Robert Guiscard, sharing qualities of 'daring, strength, aristocratic and indomitable spirit': Anna Comnena, *Alexiad*, trans. Sewter, p. 66.

easily be accused of jealousy and seem to be worthy of being sent away from the expedition.[51]

Tancred later lamented the jealousy which had driven his uncle to force him into the oath to Alexius, even after pulling off his clever and thoroughly 'Norman' trick of crossing the Bosporus disguised as a foot soldier. Tancred, we are told, saw himself as 'captured by the weakness of another, the liberation of a relative'.[52] After the crusade, when Bohemond was taken captive and Tancred heard what had befallen his kinsman, Orderic Vitalis asserted that he had the grace to be upset 'but did not give way like a woman to vain tears and laments'. Nor did he go to Bohemond's immediate rescue, however. Instead he set about defending and even enlarging the principality of Antioch.[53]

Bohemond's relationships with women were presented in a rather more traditional fashion to highlight his manliness: the love-interest created by Orderic Vitalis was the Turkish princess Melaz, who was attracted not only to his masculine prowess but by his courteous, Christian behaviour.[54] Orderic portrayed Bohemond as a warrior devoted to God's cause, who turned down the proffered marriage to the princess in order to focus on martial affairs. Bohemond's actual marriage a couple of years later to Cecilia of France was a mark of the notoriety that his achievements on crusade received in the West, and cemented his heroic status. Part of Bohemond's enduring appeal as an historical character was at least in part a result of his reputation as a self-made, ambitious man. The *Gesta Francorum* explicitly outlined his personal qualities of leadership which inspired the other magnates to follow the Italo-Norman warlord in battle against the forces of Ridwan of Aleppo outside Antioch:

> You are brave and skilful in war, a great man of high repute, resolute and fortunate, and you know how to plan a battle and how to dispose your forces, so do you take command and let the responsibility rest with you.[55]

Other authors such as Guibert of Nogent and Robert of Reims, keen to capitalise on Bohemond's reputation for their own purposes, emphasised

---

[51] RCaen, p. 607, trans. *GT*, Bachrach, p. 24.
[52] RCaen, p. 615, trans. *GT*, Bachrach, p. 36.
[53] OV, v, pp. 354–5.
[54] See Natasha R. Hodgson, *Women Crusading and the Holy Land in Historical Narrative* (Woodbridge, 2007), pp. 69–70. See also Simon Yarrow, 'Prince Bohemond, Princess Melaz and the Gendering of Religious Difference in the *Ecclesiastical History* of Orderic Vitalis', in *Intersections of Gender, Religion and Ethnicity in the Middle Ages*, ed. Cordelia Beattie and Kirsten A. Fenton (Basingstoke, 2011), pp. 140–57.
[55] Hagenmeyer, *GF*, p. 171, trans. Hill, *GF*, p. 36.

what they saw as the Frankish elements of Bohemond's heritage instead of distinguishing him as Norman.⁵⁶ In addition, the Italian heritage of both Bohemond and Tancred introduces some problems for establishing a 'Norman' reading of their masculine qualities. However, the duke of Normandy, Robert Curthose, also presents a chequered image in First Crusade narratives, if for different reasons. The *Gesta Francorum* described the three together as *vir* Bohemond; *prudens* Tancred; and 'Robert the Norman' on more than one occasion.⁵⁷ It is unlikely that the author intended to damn by faint praise – perhaps being a Norman was deemed a suitable distinction in itself, but Robert maintained an unquestionably low profile in the *Gesta*.

Those early authors who drew from the *Gesta* usually followed suit: Robert's attack on the standard-bearer of a Turkish emir at the Battle of Ascalon was the heroic story most often retold.⁵⁸ Albert of Aachen highlighted Robert's lineage, prowess and wealth, calling him 'prince of Normandy, the son of the king of England, most warlike in military weapons and well endowed with property'.⁵⁹ However, these compliments came alongside an enormous list of the salient qualities of many crusaders as they settled in for the siege of Nicaea: Robert was not particularly distinguished elsewhere in the text. Later historians of the Anglo-Norman world made more overt attempts to attribute an heroic role to Robert. Orderic Vitalis highlighted his deeds of valour on crusade and Henry of Huntingdon had him chastising fleeing troops and performing feats of valour on the battlefield at Dorylaeum.⁶⁰ William of Malmesbury, like Henry, emphasised that Robert was offered the kingship of Jerusalem, although he refused the crown and 'brought a lasting stain upon his noble reputation'.⁶¹ Later poetic texts such as the *Roman de Rou* and the *Chanson d'Antioche*

---

⁵⁶ When recruiting crusaders, according to Robert of Reims, Bohemond encouraged his Italian troops by asserting 'After all, are we not French? Didn't our parents come from France and take this land for themselves by force of arms?' *The Historia Iherosolimitana of Robert the Monk*, ed. Damien Kempf and Marcus Bull (Woodbridge, 2013), p. 15; trans. in *Robert the Monk's History of the First Crusade: Historia Iherosolimitana*, trans. Carol E. Sweetenham (Aldershot, 2005), p. 92. Guibert of Nogent was more explicit about the connection. 'Since his family hailed from Normandy, which constitutes a part of France, he will most assuredly be considered to be Frankish on account of this, because he had now obtained by marriage the daughter of the King of the Franks': GN, p. 106. He later refers to this marriage as 'obscuring the base origins of his ancient ancestors': GN, p. 138.

⁵⁷ Hagenmeyer, *GF*, pp. 197, 202.

⁵⁸ *Ibid.*, pp. 494–5. Raymond of Aguilers did not mention this, however.

⁵⁹ AA, p. 97.

⁶⁰ OV, vi, p. 270; Henry of Huntingdon, *Historia Anglorum*, pp. 426–7. Immediately after he strikes a blow, *impiger* Tancred and *belliger* Bohemond join the fray.

⁶¹ Henry of Huntingdon, *Historia Anglorum*, p. 443; William of Malmesbury, *Gesta Regum Anglorum: The History of the English Kings*, ed. and trans. R. A. B. Mynors, Rodney M. Thomson and Michael Winterbottom (Oxford, 1998), i, pp. 702–3 Here William also relocates events at Ascalon to Antioch, suggesting that Robert killed Kerbogha in battle.

were also keen to capitalise on this heightened legacy. However, Aird has argued for a re-evaluation of Robert's contribution to the crusade, in both military and financial terms.[62] He underlined Robert's reputation for piety and devotion to the warrior-saint Michael, as well as a family tradition of pilgrimage.[63] Orderic, too, was keen to note that the duke was undertaking a pilgrimage and wished to atone for his sins.[64] Robert's main critic was Guibert of Nogent:

> It would hardly be right to remain silent about Robert, Count of Normandy, whose bodily indulgences, weakness of will, prodigality with money, gourmandising, indolence and lechery were expiated by the perseverance and heroism that he vigorously displayed in the army of the Lord ... He was bold in battle, although adeptness in foul trickery ... should not be praised unless provoked by unspeakable acts.[65]

However, even Guibert thought he should now be forgiven for these things because of his role on crusade and because he subsequently suffered in jail. Perhaps surprisingly, Ralph of Caen was also critical of Robert's masculinity despite his pro-Norman stance, seeing him as too soft to mete out justice and inclined towards tears. Like Guibert, though, Ralph interpreted Robert's crusade as counteracting his previous activities, providing him with an opportunity to redeem his leadership credentials.[66]

Clerical Masculinities and Conflict in a Norman Context

Both secular and religious clergy played important roles in crusading. They were essential to processes of recruitment, preaching and finance, for ministering to spiritual needs and regulating the behaviour of God's army. Certain key figures also had a pronounced role in military decisions and leadership of the army, especially papal legates such as Adhemar of le Puy on the First Crusade, who received special powers and authority to act on behalf of the pope.[67] A particularly significant aspect in the discussion of clerical masculinity on crusade was the role of clerical violence, something

---

[62] Aird, *Robert Curthose* pp. 189–90.
[63] *Ibid.*, pp. 159–60. Curthose's grandfather, Robert I, famously went on pilgrimage in 1034.
[64] OV, v, pp. 26–7.
[65] GN, pp. 132–3, trans Levine, p. 54.
[66] RCaen, p. 616.
[67] For a recent assessment of Adhemar's role in the context of medieval masculinities, see Matthew Mesley, 'Episcopal Authority and Gender in the Narratives of the First Crusade', *Religious Men and Masculine Identity in the Middle Ages*, ed. P. H. Cullum and Katherine J. Lewis (Woodbridge, 2013), pp. 94–111.

which we know that Raol the Anglo-Norman priest seems to have had no qualms about engaging in.[68] However, ecclesiastics were also expected to provide moral guidance and lead by example. Male clerics were particularly susceptible to criticism of their sexual reputations, as seen by the example of Adalbero of Metz in Albert of Aachen's *Historia* and the strict punishments meted out in the camp during the First Crusade.[69] Arnulf of Choques, chaplain to Robert of Normandy and controversial patriarch of Jerusalem, was reputedly the subject of scurrilous stories, according to Raymond of Aguilers and Guibert of Nogent, for his philandering on crusade.[70] His elevation to the patriarchy appears largely to have been through popularity but he was then discredited and replaced by the Pisan archbishop Daibert.[71] Perhaps as a result of Godfrey of Bouillon's fractious relationship with the latter, as well as his lack of dependence on the *Gesta* tradition, Albert of Aachen presented a positive image of Arnulf, who was seen to take on a fatherly role in sorting out disagreements among the army.[72] Ralph of Caen openly acknowledged a close relationship with Arnulf who had been his tutor and became his patron.[73] As a result, he emphasised Arnulf's role in a number of events, two of which have significance for this argument. The first occurred when Arnulf aroused the wrath of the Provençals by refusing to accept the veracity of the Holy Lance. Ralph told with some indignation how, after Peter Bartholomew's death, they treated Arnulf as if he were the fraud, sending a group of armed men to attack his dwelling. Forewarned, he sought the protection of his lord Robert of Normandy whom, we are told, 'he had served in a soldierly manner'. Arnulf's patron and the count of Flanders went to apprehend these bullies, but it was the approach of the Normans which struck fear into the heart of the Provençals, so they pretended to be looking for someone else.[74] This

---

[68] See Harold Livermore, 'The *Conquest of Lisbon* and its Author', *Portuguese Studies* 6 (1990), 1–16 and James A. Brundage, 'Crusades, Clerics and Violence: Reflections on a Canonical Theme', in *The Experience of Crusading*, 2 vols, ed. Norman Housely and Marcus Bull (Cambridge, 2003), i, pp. 147–56.

[69] For Adalbero see AA, pp. 208–11. Albert of Aachen asserted that a man and a woman were taken in adultery at Antioch, but Guibert of Nogent stipulated that the former was a cleric: AA, pp. 228–9; GN, p. 195.

[70] *Le Liber de Raymond d'Aguilers*, ed. John Hugh Hill and Laurita L. Hill (Paris, 1969), pp. 153–4; GN, pp. 290–3. Baudri of Bourgueil recounted a rousing speech by an anonymous cleric outside Jerusalem, and while some attribute this to Arnulf of Choques, Biddlecombe thinks it more likely to be Baldric's own composition: BB, p. li, n. 225. Albert of Aachen mentions that Arnulf gave a speech, but did not provide details of its content: AA, pp. 412–15.

[71] Ralph of Caen included a death scene for Adhemar in which he names Arnulf as his successor: RCaen, p. 674.

[72] AA, pp. 412–15.

[73] RCaen, p. 604.

[74] RCaen, pp. 682–3, trans. *GT*, Bachrach, pp. 126–7.

certainly shows the vulnerability of an outspoken cleric on crusade, and his need for lordly protection, and also how, in Ralph's view at least, the reputation of the Normans was well established among crusader contingents.

The second key event is the debate with Tancred which occurred after the capture of Jerusalem. At this point, the relationship between Arnulf and Tancred had soured – a difficult position for Ralph as an author. Arnulf and Tancred were cast as Hector and Aeneas, and Arnulf in particular seemed to demonstrate awareness of the Norman reputation. The cleric wielded Tancred's family relationships against him, highlighting Robert Guiscard's propensity for deception and trickery while pointing out that even this dubious character defended rather than destroyed the church. Arnulf was also portrayed as self-conscious of his own importance to the crusade 'with my encouragement, striving overcame sloth. It was I who urged on the young men and gave youth back to old men.'[75] He cited his own deeds of heroism in defence of his claim – at Dorylaeum, Antioch, Marra and Artah. Tancred, in turn, lamented his lack of eloquence as a martial man, but strove to uphold Guiscard's reputation and accused Arnulf ultimately of greed, fear and cowardice. In his view, a cleric could not hope to compete with Tancred's well-established reputation for bravery. The dispute was ultimately arbitrated and justice was dispensed by the crusade leaders, who ordered Tancred to give back 700 marks. Ralph's portrayal of the debate neatly encapsulates some of the chief conflicts between ecclesiastical and secular views on masculinity and authority, but also illustrates how personal conduct on crusade and the reputation of individual men were perceived to influence peers.

The study of masculinities in the context of the crusades is very complex, and requires a subtle and nuanced approach. Rather than trying to pin down one elusive 'ideal' of crusader masculinity which, after all, changed over time as Christian religious war developed, we need to move towards a model of scholarship which encompasses the wide range of masculine terminology employed in contemporary texts. Despite the desires of predominantly ecclesiastical authors to present the crusaders as a unified force working on behalf of God, they could not explicate their histories without at the very least commenting on the more obvious categories of male participants: kings, leaders, knights, sergeants, foot soldiers, secular and religious clergy, all of which invited contrast and comparison. For those authors who chose to comment on the 'maleness' of participants, masculinity was a descriptive tool which, used in conjunction with their factors

---

[75] RCaen, 700, trans. *GT*, Bachrach, p. 150.

such as age and social status, allowed them to communicate approval or disapproval of the actions of their subjects to audiences. The *gens* as an ideal added yet another layer of expectations and stereotypes on groups of men which were broadly associated with masculine characteristics. The appellation 'Norman' could be a simple statement of geographical origin but could also be a loaded term which incorporated a wealth of cultural meanings to the audience. Even without using the term 'Norman' explicitly, certain characteristics were likely to strike a chord for audiences familiar with contemporary perceptions about the *gens*. Ultimately, when authors felt it appropriate to highlight particular *gentes* to suit their own agendas, the Normans, perhaps precisely because of their pre-established *fama*, often became focal points for some of the more extreme instances of gendered praise and criticism in crusade narratives.

Select Bibliography

Primary Sources

Albert of Aachen, *Historia Ierosolimitana*, ed. and trans. Susan B. Edgington (Oxford, 2007)

Amatus of Montecassino, *The History of the Normans*, trans. Prescott N. Dunbar, revised with introduction and notes by Graham A. Loud (Woodbridge, 2004)

Ambroise, *The History of the Holy War: Ambroise's Estoire de la Guerre Sainte*, trans. Marianne Ailes and M. Barber (Woodbridge, 2002)

Anna Comnena, *Alexiade*, ed. and trans. Bernard Lieb, 3 vols, 2nd edn (Paris, 1967)

Anna Comnena, *The Alexiad of Anna Comnena*, trans. E. R. A. Sewter (Harmondsworth, 1969)

Anonymi Gesta Francorum, ed. Heinrich Hagenmeyer (Heidelberg, 1890)

Anonymous, *Gesta Francorum: The Deeds of the Franks and the Other Pilgrims to Jerusalem*, ed. and trans. R. Hill (Oxford, 1962)

Baldric of Bourgueil, *The Historia Ierosolimitana of Baldric of Bourgueil*, ed. Steven Biddlecombe (Woodbridge, 2013)

The Canso d'Antioca: An Occitan Epic Chronicle of the First Crusade, trans. Carol Sweetenham (Aldershot, 2003)

Cartulary of the Abbey of Mont-Saint-Michel, ed. K. S. B. Keats-Rohan (Donington, 2006)

The Chanson d'Antioche: An Old French Account of the First Crusade, trans. Susan B. Edgington and Carol Sweetenham (Farnham, 2011)

The Charters of the Anglo-Norman Earls of Cheshire, c. 1071–1237, ed. Geoffrey Barraclough (Chester, 1988)

The Chronicle of the Third Crusade: A Translation of the Itinerarium Peregrinorum et Gesta Regis Ricardi, trans. Helen J. Nicholson (Aldershot, 1997)

The Conquest of Lisbon: De Expugnatione Lyxbonensi, trans. Charles W. David, with Jonathan Phillips (New York, 2001)

La continuation de Guillaume de Tyr (1184–1197), ed. M. Morgan (Paris, 1982),

David, C. W. (ed.), 'Narratio de itinere navali peregrinorum Hierosolyman tendentium et Silviam capientum A. D. 1189', *Proceedings of the American Philosophical Society* 81 (1939), 591–676

Fulcher of Chartres, *Fulcheri Carnotensis Historia Hierosolymitana (1095–1127)*, ed. Heinrich Hagenmeyer (Heidelberg, 1913)

Fulcher of Chartres, *A History of the Expedition to Jerusalem 1095–1127*, trans. Frances Rita Ryan, ed. H. S. Fink (Knoxville, TN, 1969)

Geoffrey Malaterra, *De rebus gestis Rogerii Calabriae et Siciliae comitis et Roberti Guiscardi ducis fratris eius*, ed. E. Pontieri (Bologna, 1927–28)

Geoffrey Malaterra, *The Deeds of Count Roger of Calabria and Sicily and of His Brother Duke Robert Guiscard*, trans. Kenneth Wolf (Ann Arbor, MI, 2005)

Gerald of Wales, *The Journey through Wales and the Description of Wales*, trans. Lewis Thorpe (Harmondsworth, 2004)

Gerald of Wales, *Opera VI: Itinerarium Cambriae*, ed. James F. Dimock (London, 1868)

Gervase of Canterbury, *The Historical Works of Gervase of Canterbury*, ed. William Stubbs, 2 vols (London, 1879)

The Gesta Normannorum Ducum *of William of Jumièges, Orderic Vitalis, and Robert of Torigni*, 2 vols., trans. Elisabeth M. C. van Houts (Oxford, 1992–95)

Gesta regis Henrici Secundi Benedicti abbatis: The Chronicle of the Reigns of Henry II and Richard I. AD 1169–1192; known commonly under the name of Benedict of Peterborough, ed. William Stubbs, 2 vols (London, 1867)

Guibert de Nogent, *The Deeds of God through the Franks: A Translation of Guibert of Nogent's* Gesta Dei per Francos, trans. Robert Levine (Woodbridge, 1997)

Guibert de Nogent, *Dei Gesta per Francos et cinq autres textes*, ed. R. B. C. Huygens, CCCM 127A (Turnhout, 1996)

Guillaume de Tyr, *Chronique* ed. R. B. C. Huygens CCCM 63 (Turnhout, 1986)

Henry of Huntingdon, *Historia Anglorum*, ed. and trans. Diana Greenaway (Oxford, 1996)

The History of the Tyrants of Sicily by 'Hugo Falcandus', 1154–1169, trans. G. A. Loud and T. Wiedemann (Manchester, 1998)

Letters from the East: Crusaders, Pilgrims and Settlers in the 12th–13th Centuries, trans. Malcom Barber and Keith Bate (Aldershot, 2010)

Matthew Paris, *Chronica majora*, vol. 2, ed. Henry Richards Luard (London 1872–83)

Orderic Vitalis, *The Ecclesiastical History of Orderic Vitalis*, ed. and trans. Marjorie Chibnall, 6 vols. (Oxford, 1969–80)

Ralph of Caen, *Gesta Tancredi in expeditione Hierosolymitana auctore Radulfo Cadomensi*, in *RHC*, iii, pp. 587–716

Ralph of Caen, *The Gesta Tancredi of Ralph of Caen: A History of the Normans on the First Crusade*, trans. Bernard S. Bachrach and David S. Bachrach (Aldershot, 2005)

Ralph of Caen, *Radulphus Cadomensis, Tancredus*, ed. E. D'Angelo, CCCM 231 (Turnhout, 2011)

Raymond of Aguilers, *Le Liber de Raymond d'Aguilers*, ed. John Hugh Hill and Laurita L. Hill (Paris, 1969)
Raymond of Aguilers, *Raimundi de Aguilers canonici Podiensis historia Francorum qui ceperunt Iherusalem*, in *RHC*, iii, pp. 231–309
Regesta Regni Hierosolymitani (MCVII–MCCXCI), ed. R. Röhricht, 2 vols (Innsbruck, 1893–1904)
Robert the Monk, *The Historia Iherosolimitana of Robert the Monk*, ed. Damien Kempf and Marcus Bull (Woodbridge, 2013)
Robert the Monk, *Robert the Monk's History of the First Crusade: Historia Iherosolimitana*, trans. Carol Sweetenham (Aldershot, 2005)
Roger II and the Creation of the Kingdom of Sicily, trans. G. A. Loud (Manchester, 2012)
Roger of Howden, *Chronica*, ed. William Stubbs, 4 vols (London, 1868–71)
Roger of Wendover, *Flores Historiarum*, ed. H. G. Hewlett, 3 vols (London, 1886–89)
Rothelin, *Continuation to the History of William of Tyre*, trans. Janet Shirley (Aldershot 1999)
William of Apulia, *La geste de Robert Guiscard*, ed. and trans. Marguerite Mathieu (Palermo, 1961)
William of Malmesbury, *Gesta Regum Anglorum*, ed. and trans. R. A. B. Mynors, R. M. Thompson and M. Winterbottom (Oxford, 1998)
William of Poitiers, *The* Gesta Guillelmi *of William of Poitiers*, ed. and trans. R. H. C. Davies and Marjorie Chibnall (Oxford, 1998)

Secondary Works

Abels, Richard, '"Cowardice" and Duty in Anglo-Saxon England', *Journal of Medieval Military History* 4 (2006), 29–49
Abram, Andrew, 'Saints, Cult-Centres and the Augustinian Canons in the Diocese of Coventry and Lichfield', in *The Regular Canons in the British Isles in the Middle Ages*, ed. Janet Burton and Karen Stöber (Turnhout, 2012), pp. 79–95
Aird, William, *Robert Curthose, Duke of Normandy: c. 1050–1134* (Woodbridge, 2008)
Aird, William, *St Cuthbert and the Normans: The Church of Durham, 1071–1153* (Woodbridge, 1998)
Albu, E., *The Normans in Their Histories: Propaganda, Myth and Subversion* (Woodbridge, 2001)
Albu, E., 'The Normans and Their Myths', *Haskins Society Journal* 11 (2003), 123–35
Albu, E., 'Probing the Passions of a Norman on Crusade: the Gesta Francorum et aliorum Hierosolimitanorum', *ANS* 27 (2005), 1–15
Alemparte, Jaime Ferreiro, *Arribadas de normandos y cruzados a las costas de la península ibérica* (Madrid, 1999)
Alexander, James W., *Ranulf of Chester, Relic of the Conquest* (Athens, GA, 1983)

SELECT BIBLIOGRAPHY

Asbridge, T., *The Creation of the Principality of Antioch 1098–1130* (Woodbridge, 2000)

Barton, S., 'Patrons, Pilgrims and the Cult of Saints in the Medieval Kingdom of León', in *Pilgrimage Explored*, ed. J. Stopford (York, 1999), pp. 57–77

Bates, David R., 'The Character and Career of Odo, Bishop of Bayeux (1049/50–1097)', *Speculum* 50 (1975), 1–20

Bennett, M., 'Military Masculinity in England and Northern France c. 1050–c. 1225', *Masculinity in Medieval Europe*, ed. Dawn M. Hadley (Harlow, 1999), pp. 71–88

Birk, J., ' The Betrayal of Antioch: Narratives of Conversion and Conquest during the First Crusade', *Journal of Medieval and Early Modern Studies* 41 (2011), 463–85

Blair, John, 'A Saint for Every Minster? Local Cults in Anglo-Saxon England', in *Local Saints and Local Churches in the Early Medieval West*, ed. A. Thacker and R. Sharpe (Oxford, 2002), pp. 455–94

Bliese, J. R., 'The Courage of the Normans: A Comparative Study of Battle Rhetoric', *Nottingham Medieval Studies* 35 (1991), 1–26

Brundage, James A., 'Crusades, Clerics and Violence: Reflections on a Canonical Theme', in *The Experience of Crusading*, 2 vols, ed. Norman Housely and Marcus Bull (Cambridge, 2003), i, pp. 147–156

Brundage, James A., 'An Errant Crusader: Stephen of Blois', *Traditio* 16 (1960), 380–95

Bull, M., 'The Roots of Lay Enthusiasm for the First Crusade', *History* 78 (1993), 353–72

Charanis, Peter, 'The Byzantine Empire in the Eleventh Century', in *A History of the Crusades*, vol. 1, *The First Hundred Years*, ed. Marshall W. Baldwin (Madison, Milwaukee, and London, 1969), pp. 177–219

Chevedden, Paul, '"A Crusade from the First": The Norman Conquest of Islamic Sicily, 1060–1091', *Al Masaq* 22 (2010), 191–225

Cheynet, Jean-Claude, 'The Duchy of Antioch during the Second Period of Byzantine Rule', in *East and West in the Medieval Eastern Mediterranean*, vol. 1: *Antioch from the Byzantine Reconquest until the End of the Crusader Principality*, ed. Krijnie Ciggaar and Michael Metcalf (Leuven, 2006), pp. 1–16

Constable, G., 'Opposition to Pilgrimage in the Middle Ages', in his *Religious Life and Thought (11th–12th Centuries)* (London, 1979), pp. 125–46

Contamine, Philippe, 'Towards a History of Courage', in his *War in the Middle Ages*, trans. Michael Jones (Oxford, 1984), pp. 250–9

David, Charles W., *Robert Curthose, Duke of Normandy* (Cambridge, MA, 1920)

Drell, J., 'Cultural Syncretism and Ethnic Identity. The Norman Conquest of Southern Italy and Sicily', *JMH* 25 (1999), 187–202

Edgington, Susan, 'Pagan Peverel: An Anglo-Norman Crusader', in *Crusade and Settlement: Papers Read at the First Conference of the Society for the Study of the Crusades and the Latin East and presented to R. C. Smail*, ed. Peter Edbury (Cardiff, 1985), pp. 90–3

Fletcher, Richard A., 'Reconquest and Crusade in Spain', *TRHS* 37 (1987), 31–47

SELECT BIBLIOGRAPHY

Foreville, Raymonde, 'Un chef de la Première Croisade: Arnoul Malecouronne', *Bulletin philologique et historique du comité des travaux historiques et scientifiques* (1953–54), 377–90

Forey, Alan, 'The Conquest of Lisbon and the Second Crusade', *Portuguese Studies* 20 (2004), 1–13

France, John, 'The Fall of Antioch during the First Crusade', in *Dei Gesta per Francos: Etudes sur les croisades dédiés à Jean Richard/Crusade Studies in Honour of Jean Richard*, ed. Michel Balard, Benjamin K. Zedar and Jonathan Riley-Smith (Aldershot, 2001), pp. 13–20

France, John, 'The Normans and Crusading', in *The Normans and Their Adversaries at War: Essays in Memory of C. Warren Hollister*, ed. R. P. Abels and B. S. Bachrach (Woodbridge, 2001), pp. 87–102

France, John, 'The Occasion of the Coming of the Normans to Southern Italy', *JMH* 17 (1991), 195–205

France, John, *Victory in the East: A Military History of the First Crusade* (Cambridge, 1994)

Grabois, A., 'Anglo-Norman England and the Holy Land', *ANS* 7 (1985), 132–44

Hagger, Mark, ' Kinship and Identity in Eleventh-Century Normandy: The Case of Hugh de Grandmesnil, *c*. 1040–1098', *JMH* 32 (2006), 212–30

Hamilton, Bernard, 'Ralph of Domfront, Patriarch of Antioch (1135–40)', *Nottingham Mediaeval Studies* 28 (1984), 1–21

Herrick, S. Kahn, *Imagining the Sacred Past: Hagiography and Power in Early Normandy* (Cambridge, MA, 2007)

Higham, N. J., 'The Cheshire *Burhs* and the Mercian Frontier to 924', *Transactions of the Antiquarian Society of Lancashire and Cheshire* 85 (1988), 193–221

Hodgson, Natasha, 'Honour, Shame and the Fourth Crusade', *JMH* 39 (2013), 220–39

Hodgson, N., 'Reinventing Normans as Crusaders? Ralph of Caen's *Gesta Tancredi*', *ANS* 30 (2008), 117–32

Houben, Hubert, *Roger II of Sicily: A Ruler between East and West*, trans. G. A. Loud and D. Milburn (Cambridge, 1997)

Hurlock, Kathryn, *Wales and the Crusades, 1095–1291* (Cardiff, 2011)

Hurlock, Kathryn, *Britain, Ireland and the Crusades, c. 1000–c.1300* (Basingstoke, 2013)

Isaac, Steven, 'Cowardice and Fear Management: The 1173–74 Conflict as a Case Study', *Journal of Medieval Military History* 4 (2006), 50–64

Jamison, Evelyn M., 'Some Notes on the *Anonymi Gesta Francorum*, with Special Reference to the Norman Contingent from South Italy and Sicily in the First Crusade', in *Studies in French Language and Medieval Literature presented to Professor Mildred K. Pope* (Manchester, 1939), pp. 183–208

Jiménez, Manuel González, 'Frontier and Settlement in Castile (1085–1350)', in *Medieval Frontier Societies*, ed. Robert Barlett and Angus Mackay (Oxford, 1989), pp. 49–74

Johnson, Ewan, 'The Process of Norman Exile into Italy', in *Exile in the Middle Ages*, ed. L. Napran and E. M. C. van Hout (Turnhout, 2004), pp. 29–38

Karras, Ruth Mazo, *From Boys to Men: Formations of Masculinity in Late Medieval Europe* (Philadelphia, 2003)

Koytcheva, Elena., 'Civitates et Castra on Via Militaris and Via Egnatia: Early Crusaders View' [sic], *Revue des études sud-est européennes* 44 (2006), 139–44

Koytcheva, Elena, 'Travelling of the First Crusaders across the Byzantine Balkans', Ηπειρωτικα Χρονικα 36 (2002), 17–24

Lapina, Elizabeth, 'La représentation de la bataille d'Antioche (1098) sur les peintures murales de Poncé-sur-le-Loir', *Cahiers de civilisation médiévale* 52 (2009), 137–58

Lloyd, Simon D., 'William Longespee II: The Making of an English Crusading Hero', *Nottingham Medieval Studies* 35 (1991), 41–69; 36 (1992), 79–125

Loud, G. A., 'The *Gens Normannorum*: Myth or Reality?' *ANS* 4 (1981), 104–16

Loud, G. A., *The Age of Robert Guiscard: Southern Italy and the Norman Conquest* (Harlow, 2000)

Loud, G. A., 'Anna Komnena and Her Sources for the Normans of Southern Italy', in *Church and Chronicle in the Middle Ages: Essays Presented to John Taylor*, ed. G. A. Loud and I. N. Wood (London, 1991), pp. 41–57

Loud, G. A., 'Norman Italy and the Holy Land', in *The Horns of Hattin*, ed. B. Z. Kedar (London, 1992), pp. 49–62

Lyon, J. R., 'Fathers and Sons: Preparing Noble Youths to be Lords in Twelfth-Century Germany', *JMH* 34 (2008), 291–310

Mayer, Hans Eberhard, 'Henry II of England and the Holy Land', *EHR* 97 (1982), 721–39

Mayer, Hans Eberhard, 'Angevins *versus* Normans: The New Men of King Fulk of Jerusalem', *American Philosophical Society* 133 (1989), 1–25

McCrank, Lawrence J., 'Norman Crusaders in the Catalan Reconquest', *JMH* 7 (1981), 67–82

McQueen, William B., 'Relations between the Normans and Byzantium 1071–1112', *Byzantion* 56 (1986), 427–74

Morillo, Stephen, 'Expecting Cowardice: Medieval Battle Tactics Reconsidered', *JMH* 4 (2006), 65–73

Murray, Alan V., 'How Norman Was the Principality of Antioch? Prolegomena to a Study of the Origins of the Nobility of a Crusader State', in *Family Trees and the Roots of Politics: The Prosopography of England and France from the Tenth to the Twelfth Century*, ed. K. S. B. Keats-Rohan (Woodbridge, 1997), pp. 349–59

Murray, Alan V., 'Norman Settlement in the Latin Kingdom of Jerusalem, 1099–1131', *Archivio Normanno-Svevo* 1 (2009), 61–85

Nelson, Lynn, 'Rotrou of Perche and the Aragonese Reconquest', *Traditio* 26 (1970), 13–33

Ní Chléirigh, L., '*Gesta Normannorum*? Normans in the Latin Chronicles of the

First Crusade', in *Norman Expansion: Connections, Continuities and Contrasts*, ed. K. J. Stringer and A. Jotischky (London, 2013), pp. 207–26
Oldfield, Paul, *City and Community in Norman Italy* (Cambridge, 2009)
Oldfield, Paul, *Sanctity and Pilgrimage in Medieval Southern Italy, 1000–1200* (Cambridge, 2014)
Paul, N. L., *To Follow in Their Footsteps: The Crusades and Family Memory in the High Middle Ages* (Ithaca, NY, 2012)
Pryor, John, 'Modelling Bohemond's March to Thessalonike', in *Logistics of Warfare in the Age of the Crusades*, ed. John H. Pryor (Aldershot, 2006), pp. 1–24
Quesada, Miguel Ángel Ladero, 'Amenaza almohade y guerras entre reinos', in *Historia de España Menéndez Pidal*, vol. 9, ed. Miguel Ángel Ladero Quesada (Madrid, 1998), pp. 505–8
Riley-Smith, Jonathan, 'Family Traditions and Participation in the Second Crusade', in *The Second Crusade and the Cistercians* ed. Michael Gervers (New York, 1992), pp. 101–8
Riley-Smith, Jonathan, *The First Crusade and the Idea of Crusading* (London, 1993)
Riley-Smith, Jonathan, 'The Latin Clergy and the Settlement in Palestine and Syria, 1098–1100', *Catholic Historical Review* 74 (1988), 539–57
Round, J. Horace, 'Some English Crusaders of Richard I', *EHR* 18 (1903), 475–81
Shepard, Jonathan, 'Cross-Purposes: Alexios Comnenus and the First Crusade', in *The First Crusade: Origins and Impact*, ed. Jonathan Phillips (Manchester, 1997), pp. 107–29
Shepard, Jonathan, 'The English and Byzantium: A Study of Their Role in the Byzantine Army', *Traditio* 29 (1973), 53–92
Shepard, Jonathan, 'The Uses of the Franks in Eleventh-Century Byzantium', *ANS* 15 (1992), 275–305
Skinner, Patricia, *Medieval Amalfi and Its Diaspora 800–1250* (Oxford, 2013)
Slitt, Rebecca L., 'Justifying Cross-Cultural Friendship: Bohemond, Firuz, and the Fall of Antioch', *Viator* 38 (2007), 339–49
Smith, Damian J., 'The Papacy, the Spanish Kingdoms and Las Navas de Tolosa', *Anuario de la historia de la Iglesia* 20 (2011), 157–78
Smith, Jr, R. Upsher, '*Nobilissimus* and Warleader: The Opportunity and the Necessity behind Robert Guiscard's Balkan Expeditions', *Byzantion* 70 (2000), 507–26
Spear, David S., *The Personnel of the Norman Cathedrals* (London, 2006)
Spear, David S., 'William Bona Anima, Abbot of St Stephen's of Caen, 1070–79', *Haskins Society Journal* 1 (1989), 51–60
Stanton, Charles D., *Norman Naval Operations in the Mediterranean* (Woodbridge, 2011)
Thompson, Kathleen, 'Family Tradition and the Crusading Impulse: The Rotrou Counts of the Perche', *Medieval Prosopography* 19 (1998), 1–33
Tyerman, C., *England and the Crusades 1095–1588* (London, 1988)
Van Herwaarden, J., 'Pilgrimages and Social Prestige: Some Reflections on a

Theme', in *Wallfahrt und Alltag in Mittelalter und früher Neuzeit*, ed. G. Jaritz and B. Schuh (Vienna, 1992), pp. 27–79

Villegas-Aristizábal, Lucas, 'Anglo-Norman Involvement in the Conquest and Settlement of Tortosa, 1148–1180', *Crusades* 8 (2009), 63–129

Villegas-Aristizábal, Lucas, 'Revisiting the Anglo-Norman Crusaders' Failed Attempt to Conquer Lisbon c. 1142', *Portuguese Studies* 29 (2013), 7–20

Villegas-Aristizábal, Lucas, 'Roger of Tosny's Adventures in the County of Barcelona', *Nottingham Medieval Studies* 52 (2008), 4–16

Walsh, C., 'The Role of the Normans in the Development of the Cult of St Katherine', in *St Katherine of Alexandria: Texts and Contexts in Western Medieval Europe*, ed. J. Jenkins and K. J. Lewis (Turnhout, 2003), pp. 19–35

Webber, N., *The Evolution of Norman Identity, 911–1154* (Woodbridge, 2005)

Whalen, Brett, 'God's Will or Not? Bohemond's Campaign against the Byzantine Empire (1105–1108)', in *Crusades – Medieval Worlds in Conflict*, ed. Thomas F. Madden, James L. Naus and Vincent Ryan (Farnham, 2010), pp. 111–25

Wieruszowski, H., 'The Norman Kingdom of Sicily and the Crusades', in *A History of the Crusades*, vol. 2, *The Later Crusades: 1189–1311*, ed. R. L. Wolff and H. W. Hazard (Madison, WI, 1969), pp. 2–43

Wieruszowski, H., 'Roger of Sicily, *Rex Tyrannus* in Twelfth-Century Political Thought', *Speculum* 38 (1963), 46–78

Wolf, Kenneth Baxter, 'Crusade and Narrative: Bohemond and the *Gesta Francorum*', *JMH* 17 (1991), 207–16

Yewdale, R. B., *Bohemond I, Prince of Antioch* (Princeton, NJ, 1924)

Unpublished PhD Theses

Allen, Richard, 'The Norman Episcopate, 989–1110' (University of Glasgow, 2009)

Gomez, Miguel Dolan, 'The Battle of Las Navas de Tolosa: The Culture and Practice of Crusading in Medieval Iberia' (University of Tennessee, 2011)

Packard, Barbara, 'Remembering the First Crusade: Latin Narrative Histories 1099–c.1300' (Royal Holloway, University of London, 2011)

Siedschlag, Beatrice N., 'English Participation in the Crusades, 1150–1220' (Bryn Mawr, 1939)

Villegas-Aristizábal, L., 'Norman and Anglo-Norman Participation in the Iberian *Reconquista* c. 1018–c. 1248' (University of Nottingham, 2007)

Index

Abbaye Notre-Dame de Saint-Sever 126
Abbot Suger of Saint-Denis 14, 28
Abelard, nephew of Robert Guiscard 163
Abu yassuf Ya'qub al Mansure, caliph 117
Acre 95, 152
Acre, fall of (1291), 99
Acre, siege of (1104), 62, 135
Adela, daughter of William the
 Conqueror 16, 26
Adelaide, wife of Roger I 57, 59
Adhemar of Chabannes 107
Adhemar of le Puy, papal legate 36, 39, 83,
 210
Adjutor, Norman crusader 89
Adrian IV, pope 115
Æthelflaed, ruler of the Mercians 128, 129
Æthelred, king of the Mercians 129
Afonso Henriques of Portugal 109
Alarcos, battle of (1195), 118
Alberada, reputed mother of
 Bohemond 37
Albert of Grandmesnil 204
Albigensian crusade, Norman involvement
 in 97–8
Alcantara, order of 114
Aleppo 40, 169, 208
Alexander II, pope 107, 108
Alexander III, pope 152–3
Alexander, abbot of Telese 145
Alexandretta, castle of 17
Alexandria 160
Alexios I Comnenos, emperor of
 Byzantium 14, 17–18, 38, 39–40, 76, 101,
 164, 166, 168, 195, 208
Alferius, son of Ursus 55

Alfonso I Henriques, king of Portugal 91,
 114
Alfonso I of Aragon 109, 111
Alfonso IX of Leon 109, 119
Alfonso VI of Leon 104–05
Alfonso VII of Leon 109
Alfonso VIII of Castile 115, 118, 119
Algericas, siege of (1348), 120
Alice Peverel 71
Almohads 109
Alp Arslan, sultan 164
Altruda, wife of John 54
Amalfi 59, 163, 167
Amalfi, siege of (1096), 35, 55–6, 162
Ambroise 96–7, 100
Amfrida Gournay 86
Anacletus, pope 143
Anatolia, Normans in 165
Andrew, Apostle, visions of 171
Angevin empire 115
Anglo-Saxon crusaders 76, 78
Anglo-Saxon minsters 128
Anglo-Saxon saints 125
Anglo-Saxons 132
Anna Comnena 142, 165
Anselm of Bec, archbishop of
 Canterbury 73, 88, 127
Antioch 15, 22, 92, 159, 160, 163, 165, 168
Antioch, battle for 171
Antioch, capture of (1084), 160–1
Antioch, competing claims for 171–2
Antioch, conditions in 171
Antioch, fall of 159, 170–1
Antioch, Greek-speaking population of 32
Antioch, in epic cycles 174

INDEX

Antioch, Persian occupation of 160
Antioch, population of 161
Antioch, principality of 159
Antioch, recapture aim of Alexios I 39–40
Antioch, siege of (1097–98), 13, 14, 15, 16, 23–4, 25, 31, 42, 43, 77, 82, 89, 203, 204
Antioch, significance of 160
Antioch, symbolic meaning 174–5
Antioch, walls of 161
Apulia 14, 33, 165
Arabic interpreter 36
Arnulf bishop of Lisieux 90–2, 100–1
Arnulf of Choques, patriarch of Jerusalem 82–6, 87, 88, 89, 99, 100–1, 178, 202, 203, 211, 212,
Arnulf of Hesdin 75
Arnulf of Sees, archdeacon 143
Artah 160, 212
Arthur of Brittany 62
Arthurian Romance 62
Arundel, earl of 136
Ascalon, Battle of (1099), 33, 82, 178, 209
Ascalon, capture of (1153), 150
Aubre of Grandmesnil 13, 14, 18
Audience, for crusade narratives 179–80
Augustinian canons 128, 130, 131
Avranches 101

Bagrat, brother of Kogh Vasil 41
Balchite, order of 114
Baldwin Blondel 134
Baldwin I, king of Jerusalem 57, 83, 100, 148, 149, 153
Baldwin of Boulogne 34, 40–1, 42–3
Baldwin of Edessa 45, 46
Baldwin of Forde, archbishop of Canterbury 69–70, 74, 93, 94, 135
Baldwin, count of Cilicia 169
Barbarossa, king of Hungary 94
Barbastro, siege of (1064), 107, 108
Bari 58, 59, 145, 162, 164, 165,
Bari, painting in the church of San Nichola 162
Bari, shrine of Saint Nicholas 155, 162
Barletta 58, 59, 152
Barnwell Priory, relics of 67

Barons' Crusade (1240), Norman involvement in 98
Basil II, emperor of Byzantium 164
Basilia Gournay 86
Basingwerk, abbey of 120
Beauchamp family 72
Bec 84, 126, 142
Benedictines 128, 129, 131
Benevento 155
Benevento, city of, and pilgrims 153
Benevento, shrines of 146
Benevento, Treaty of, (1156), 143
Benjamin of Tudela 59, 151
Berengaria of Navarre, coronation of 95
Bernard de Saint-Valery 71, 96
Bernard of Clairvaux 74, 91–2, 110, 112
Bernard of Valence, patriarch of Antioch 47
Bertram of Verdun 135
Boccaccio 62
Bohemond II, prince of Antioch (d.1130), 154, 174
Bohemond III, prince of Antioch 173
Bohemond of Taranto 1105 embassy to Pope Paschal II 47
Bohemond of Taranto 5, 7, 14, 16, 20, 21, 24, 25, 28, 31–32, 33, 34, 41, 42, 43, 53, 66, 89, 104, 159, 161, 166, 167–74, 178, 187, 190, 195, 202, 206–07
Bohemond of Taranto, and Byzantine emperor 37–40, 41, 168–9, 71, 207
Bohemond of Taranto, and Byzantine relations 173
Bohemond of Taranto, and interested in Balkan conquest 37
Bohemond of Taranto, behaviour of 188–9
Bohemond of Taranto, Byzantine view of 167–8
Bohemond of Taranto, crusade journey of 35–6, 37
Bohemond of Taranto, crusade of 1107–8, 47
Bohemond of Taranto, crusade preparations 55–6.
Bohemond of Taranto, crusading contingent of 33, 36, 188

INDEX

Bohemond of Taranto, Frankish qualities 209
Bohemond of Taranto, fulfils crusading vow 45
Bohemond of Taranto, his knights enter service of Godfrey of Bouillon or Baldwin I of Jerusalem 45
Bohemond of Taranto, Prince of Antioch, recruitment tour of France (1106), 16, 173
Bohemond of Taranto, reaches Constantinople 35
Bohemond of Taranto, seeks title of *domestikos* 38–9
Bohemond of Taranto, using mercenaries 200
Bohemond VII 174
Bohemond, and relations with women 208
Bohemond, contingent massacred by Turks 40–1
Bohemond, description of 195–6
Bohemond, does not continue to Jerusalem 45
Bohemond, established principality of Antioch 34
Bohemond, speaks Greek 38, 169
Bohemond, takes Antioch 41
Bohemond, visits Rouen 87
Bohun family 72
Bonizo of Sutri, reformer 154
Boucey 134
Bridlington Priory 130, 131, 133
Brindisi 58, 59, 152
Brittany, crusaders from 33
Burton-upon-Trent 128

Cadmus, Battle of (1148), 68
Caen 84
Calabria, crusaders from 33
Calatrava, order of 114
Calixtus II, pope 130, 131
Calke 131
Campania, crusaders from 33
Carlisle 131
Cava, monastery of 148
Cecilia, sister of Robert Curthose 84

Cephalonia, siege of (1085), 162
Charlemagne, warning about pilgrims 154
Cheshire, crusaders from 133
Chester Abbey 127, 129, 131, 132
Chester 70, 128, 130, 132
Chester, constables of 126, 137
Chester, earldom of 125
Chester, earls of 126, 132
Cicilia, plans of 40
Cilicia, conquest of 46
Civitate, battle of (1053), 4, 140, 149
Clerical violence 210
Clerkenwell 69
Clermont, Council of (1095), 15, 35, 72, 82, 87–8, 200
Clifford family 72
Cluniac Order 96, 100, 106, 107, 146
Conrad III, king of Germany 90
Constance, daughter of Bohemond II 173, 174
Constantine IX, Monomachos, emperor of Byzantium 164
Constantine VIII, emperor of Byzantium 164
Constantine X, emperor of Byzantium 164
Constantinople 18, 91, 101, 142, 159, 165, 187
Constantinople, crusader attack on 187–8
Cordoba, caliphate of 104, 108
Courage 18–27, 29, 33
Coutances 101
Cowardice 19, 21–22, 27, 29
Crusade leadership 66–7, 94
Crusade recruitment 113
Crusade, appeal of 197
Crusade, historiography 4, 5–6, 7, 52–3
Crusade, status given to *Reconquista* 108–109
Crusaders, desertion by 28–9
Crusaders, from England 33, 62, 67, 150
Crusaders, from Flanders 150
Crusaders, from Scandinavia 150
Crusaders, from southern Italy 53, 53 n. 4,
Crusaders, from Wales 74–5, 79
Crusades, and church endowments 56
Crusades, criticism of 62
Crusades, economic impact on southern Italy 57–60

225

INDEX

Crusades, impact of Norman Italian *Regno* 54, 56, 60–1, 62–3
Crusades, impact on Norman Italy 54
Crusades, impact on those left behind 51–2,
Crusades, in written works in England 77
Crusades, used as a form of escape 75
Crusading lyrics 71
Crusading traditions 66
Crusading, family tradition and 71, 86, 92–3
Crusading, mythology of 77–8
Cult centres, promotion of 126

Daibert, archbishop of Pisa 46–7, 47 n. 57, 88, 211
Dalmatia 162
Damascus 40, 91
Damietta 135–6
Daphne, valley of 170
Dartmouth 118
Dee, river 130
Derby, earl of 136
Devol, Treaty of (1108), 174
Dionysius 143
Dol, archbishop of 134
Domfront 180, 182
Dorylaeum, Battle of (1097), 20, 82, 209, 212
Drax Priory 131
Drogo I 92
Drogo II of Trubleville, canon of Rouen 92, 96, 98, 100, 101–2
Durham cathedral 127
Dyrrachium siege of (1107), 162, 195, 273

Ebro valley 103
Ebulus II of Roucy 108
Edessa 43, 45, 191
Edgar the Ætheling 7–77
Edith Gournay 86
Edith, sister of William de Warenne 67
El Cid 108
Eleanor of Aquitaine 60, 61, 94, 95, 115
Eleanor, daughter of Henry II of England 115
Embsay Priory 131

Epiros 37
Ermesinda, countess of Barcelona 107
Eudes Rigaud, archbishop of Rouen 98–9, 100, 101
Eugenius III, pope 92, 112
Eustace of Fly 70
Eva Crispin 86

Fernando I of Leon 104, 106
Fernando III of Castile-Leon 119
Firuz (or Pirrus), betrays Antioch to the crusaders 31–2, 36, 41–42, 169, 170
Food and provisions 190
Fourth Lateran Council (1215), 119
Franks, reference to Normans as 32
Frederick II, emperor 52, 146
French, regional differences 44–5

Gascony 119
Gelasius II, pope 108
Gender, ideals of 197–8, 199, 201–02
Gender, identities of 19
Genoese trade 59
Geoffrey de Clinton 133
Geoffrey de Dutton 136
Geoffrey the Breton 180–2, 183, 193
George Maniakes 164
Gerald of Wales 70, 135
Gerard de Furnival 71
Gerard de Furnival, son of Gerald 71
Gerard Fleitel 87
Gerard Gournay 92
Gerard, bishop of Sées 92
Gerard, bishop of York 73
Germans, hospital of, and pilgrims 152
Gilbert Anglici 114
Gilbert of Hastings, bishop of Lisbon 113
Gilbert, bishop of Evreux 82, 83, 87, 88
Giroie-Grandmesnil family 178
Godfrey of Bouillon 34, 206, 211
Golgotha 191
Gournay family 86
Granada, conquest of (1492), 120
Grandmesnil brothers 187
Graus, Battle of 108
Gregory II, pope 107, 108
Grimoald Alfarinites 145

226

INDEX

Guibert of Nogent 22, 25
Guilbert of Ravenna/Clement III, anti-pope 154
Guisborough Priory 131
Guy Trousseau 13, 14–15, 28
Guy, half-brother of Bohemond of Taranto 17–18, 23, 27

Halton 128–29, 130, 134
Hardoin 163
Hastings, battle of (1066), 76, 88
Hattin, battle of (1187), 61, 93
Hauteville, family of 165
Hautevilles 139, 162
Helena, daughter of Roger Guiscard 164
Helenopolis 38
Henry I, king of England 67, 73, 76, 111, 131, 133, 180, 183
Henry II, king of England 61, 70, 93, 94–5, 101, 115, 116
Henry II, king of England, crusading vow 68, 94
Henry II, king of England, raises money for the crusade 68
Henry III, king of England 66, 72
Henry IV, emperor of Germany 144
Henry the Young King of England 101
Henry VI, emperor of Germany 118
Henry VI, emperor of Germany 151
Henry, earl of Warwick 92
Heraclius, patriarch of Jerusalem 69
Herakleios 160
Herbert of Andely, canon of Rouen, preaches Cross 97
Hereford 70
Hervé, Norman mercenary 166
Hervey de Glanville 68, 204
Hexham Priory (Yorks), 130, 133
Hohenstafuens 175
Holy Cross, portion of at Norton 136–7
Holy Cross, portion of at Saint John's Chester 137,
Holy Cross, portions of at Vale Royal Abbey 137,
Holy Lance 134, 171, 172, 140, 203, 211
Holy Sepulchre 83, 85, 100, 140, 150
Holy Sepulchre, church of the (Tortosa), 115

Holy war, ideas in Iberia 103–04, 105–06
Holy war, ideas of 19
Holywell 130
Honorius II, pope 152
Honorius III, pope 72
Hospitallers 114, 125, 134
Hugh Bunel 166
Hugh I d'Avranches, earl of Chester 125, 126, 127, 132, 133, 134. 137–8
Hugh II Gournay 86, 93
Hugh the Great, Count of Vermandois 15
Hugh, archbishop of Rouen 89
Hugh, bishop of Sées 98
Hugh, earl of Chester 129

Iberia, clergy of 110
Indulgences 112
Innocent II, pope 145
Innocent III, pope 97
Intermarriage 43
Investiture contest 34
Ireland, crusaders from 73
Isaac Komnenos, emperor of Byzantium 166
Italo-Normans, Byzantine influence on 163
Italo-Normans, relationship with Byzantines 165
Italy, crusaders from 32
Iuvenacus, siege of 162
Ivo of Grandmesnil 14, 18, 75–6, 204
Ivo of Vieuxpont, archdeacon of Rouen 96, 101

Jaffa, siege of (1102), 150
James I of Aragon 119
Jerusalem 7, 27, 45, 46, 57, 59, 67, 83, 85, 112, 120, 136–37, 138, 147, 153, 154, 160, 172
Jerusalem, as destination of First Crusade 18, 19, 24, 25, 26, 29, 45, 85, 88, 133, 136, 159, 167, 172, 174, 192
Jerusalem, capture of (1099) 5, 26, 33–4, 82, 88, 103, 108, 110, 162, 191, 212
Jerusalem, fall of (1187), 61, 93, 116, 150
Jerusalem, pilgrimage to 6, 55, 86–7, 134, 136, 139, 145, 149, 150, 151, 155, 156
Joanna, dowager queen of Sicily 61–2
Jocelyn, lord of Molfetta 163

INDEX

John Buchart of Wilburton 73 n. 56
John de Lacy, constable of Chester 70, 71, 134–5, 136
John from Avellino 54
John II Lestrange of Knockin 134
John Komnenos, emperor of Byzantium 173
John Luke 95
John of Alençon, archdeacon of Lisieux 95
John of Coutances, dean of Rouen 95
John of Oxeia, patriarch of Antioch 46, 47
John the Scot, earl of Chester 125–6
John, abbot of Fecamp 149
John, bishop of Exreux 94
John, chaplain to Ranulf, earl of Chester 131
John, king of England 66, 95, 118, 119, 136
Jordan du Hommet, bishop of Liseux 97, 98, 100
Jordan, bishop of Lisieux 98
Jumieges, refoundation of 184

Kerbogha/Karbuqa, emir of Mosul 13, 17, 28, 43, 160
Kirkham Priory 131
Knights, expectations places upon 19–20

Lambert the Poor 13, 15
Landscape 177–93,
Landscape, and biblical markers 190–1
Language 32, 36, 38, 41, 43–5, 158, 166, 170
Laodikeia, besieged by Bohemond 46, 47
Las Navas de Tolosa, battle of (1212) 114, 119
Lateran council, (1139), 90
Lattakiah 76
Le Man 101
Leo IX, pope 141, 149
Leo Palianos, legate 163
Leominster 70
Leopold, duke of Austria 154
Lichfield 128
Lillebonne, Council of (1080), 144
Limassol 94
Lincoln, bishopric of 94
Lisbon, capture of (1147), 92, 111, 113, 114, 117, 204

Lisbon, siege of (1147), 68, 92, 111, 112, 113, 114, 204
Longueville 96, 100
Louis IX, king of France 98, 99, 100
Louis VI, king of France 144
Louis VII, king of France 148
Louis VII, king of France 61, 67, 90, 91, 92
Ludlow 70
Lydda 85

Ma'arrat al-Numan 37
Mabel Courte Louve 14
Mabel of Bellême, countess of Shrewsbury 166
Macedonian emperor 160
Mainz, Council of (1103), 144
Mantzikert, battle of (1071), 38, 164, 166
Manuel I, emperor of Byzantium 173
Maria of Antioch 173
Marra 212
Mary Magdalene, relics of 99
Matilda of Perche 111
Matilda, Empress 131, 133
Melaz, princess 208
Melfi, Council of (1089), 144
Melfi, Council of (1129), 145
Mercia, kingdom of 128, 137
Mersey, river 128, 132
Messina 52, 58, 59, 60, 61, 62, 95
Messina, city of, as a pilgrim gathering place 151
Messina, impact of crusade and pilgrimage on 60–1
Michael Dokeianos 163
Michael IV the Epileptic, assaults Sicily 164
Michael V, emperor of Byzantium 164
Michael VI, emperor of Byzantium 166
Michael VII, emperor of Byzantium 164
Military orders 114
Milo, lord of Monlthéry 14
Miracles, and the dukes of Normandy 183–6, 191
Miracles, in crusade accounts 177
Miracles, in Orderic Vitalis 180
Mobberley (Cheshire), 132

INDEX

Mondaye, Norbertine monastery of 98, 100
Mongols 99
Monopoli 59
Monte Gargano 7, 142
Montecassino, monastery of 148
Montevergine, monastery of 148
Mont-Saint-Michel 7, 126, 127, 138, 142
Mont-Saint-Michel, as a pilgrim centre 134
Mont-Saint-Michel, links to Norman crusaders 134
Much Wenlock Priory 127, 129
Muslims, in Sicily 143
Muslims, trade with 57, 61

Navarre 115
Nicaea, capture of (1097), 20, 38, 133, 209
Nicholas of L'Aigle, dean of Chichester and Avranches 97
Nikephoros Basilakes 164
Nikephoros Bryennios 164
Nikephoros III Botaneiates, emperor of Byzantium 164
Norgod, bishop of Avranches 127
Norman and English, co-operation 68
Norman clergy, crusaders from among 87–8
Norman clergy, influence on Robert Curthose 85–6
Norman clergy, pro-Greek 101
Norman historiography 1–2, 4–5, 65–6
Norman identity 1, 2–3, 20, 29, 33, 65–6, 142, 196, 198–201, 203
Norman identity, on crusade 198–9
Norman language 44–5
Norman mercenaries 17, 161, 165–6, 200
Norman pilgrims, imagery of 142
Norman world 3–4
Normandy, loss of (1204), 99
Normandy, warfare in 97
Normans of southern Italy, descriptions of 141
Normans, and alliance with papacy 141
Normans, as pilgrims to Italy 140, 141
Normans, description of in crusade narratives 196–7
Normans, from southern Italy 13, 16

Normans, in Byzantium 166, 167
Normans, in the East 166, 167
Normans, leadership of 205–06
Normans, linguistic skills of 36–7
Normans, of southern Italy 161
Normans, origin myth 140
Normans, piety of 178–79
Normans, unity of 203–04
Norton, Augustinian priory of 129, 136
Nostell Priory (Yorks), 131, 133

Odard, donates lands to Jumièges 89
Odo Quarrel of Chartres 151–52
Odo, bishop of Bayeux 75, 82, 83, 85, 87–8
Oswald, king and saint 129
Oswestry 70
Oursel 166

Pagan Peverel 67, 71
Palermo 58, 61, 71, 150
Palmarea 91
Paris, university of 132
Paschal II, pope 26, 47
Peace and Truce of God 144, 145
Persia 160
Peter Bartholomew 171, 172, 211
Peter of Blois 70–1, 93, 94, 100
Peter the Hermit 15, 16, 187, 188, 190
Peter the Venerable 146
Peter, bishop of Lichfield 129
Peutinger map 174–5
Philarats, rebel 166
Philaretos Brachamios, Armenian rebel 160
Philip Augustus II, king of France of France, considers joining *Reconquista* 118
Philip Augustus II, king of France 94, 96
Philip I, king of France 15
Philip the Grammarian 76
Philomelium 17
Pierre Dubois 99, 101
Pilgrim protection, as a way to build reputation 148–9
Pilgrimage, family tradition of 210
Pilgrimage, historiography of 6–7
Pilgrimage, landscape of 177

INDEX

Pilgrims, accommodation for 148
Pilgrims, and financial profit 151, 152
Pilgrims, as fighters 150, 151
Pilgrims, as victims of local conflict 149
Pilgrims, concern for 146–7
Pilgrims, identity of 153–4
Pilgrims, in southern Italy 139
Pilgrims, Muslim attacks on 149
Pilgrims, protection of 150
Pilgrims, travelling by sea 59
Pisa 59
Poetry 51–3
Pontefract 136, 189
Porto, bishop of 112
Portugal 116
Preaching for the crusade 135
Preaching tour of Wales 93
Preaching, at Chester 135
Preaching, crusade recruitment and 69–71, 72

Quantum Prædecessores 112

Radbod, bishop of Sées 84
Raimaud 166
Ralph of Domfront 89–90, 100
Ralph of Fontanella 14, 204
Ralph the Saracen 135
Ramla 85
Ramon Berenguer VII, count of Barcelona 109, 111
Ranulf I, earl of Chester 134
Ranulf II, earl of Chester 132, 133, 134
Ranulf III, earl of Chester 125, 135, 136, 138
Ranulf, earl of Chester 131
Raol, priest 203–4, 210
Raymond of Poitiers 154
Raymond of Saint-Gilles, count of Toulouse 33–4, 36, 37, 43–4, 45, 203, 204
Raymond, count of Toulouse 169, 170, 171, 172
Raymond, prince of Antioch 173
Reconquista in Portugal stalls 118
Reconquista, 73, 104, 105–06
Reginald de Saint-Valery 71
Reginald of Chatillon 93

Relic 7, 8, 67, 83, 87, 96, 99, 107, 127, 129, 137, 145, 155, 162, 171, 180, 191
Religious diversity of Sicily and southern Italy 139
Repton 128, 130
Richard Barre 93
Richard de Bohon, bishop of Coutances 101
Richard I, consecrated duke of Normandy 94
Richard I, duke of Normandy 126–7
Richard I, duke of Normandy, encounters a revenant 185, 186
Richard I, king of England, captivity of 94, 95
Richard I, king of England, marries Berengaria of Navarre 95
Richard I, king of England, influence on later crusaders 72
Richard I, king of England 58, 60, 69, 74, 96, 100, 101–2, 135
Richard I, king of England, and decorative art 79
Richard I, king of England, captivity of 154
Richard I, king of England, considers joining *Reconquista* 118
Richard I, king of England, crusading army prevented from buying provisions 61
Richard I, king of England, heart of, at Rouen 101–2
Richard I, king of England, leads third crusade 94
Richard of S. Germano 147
Richard of the Principate, kinsman of Tancred 37
Richard son of Richolin 134
Richard, earl of Chester 125, 130, 131, 132
Richard, earl of Cornwall 125
Ridwan of Aleppo 208
Rinaldo d'Aquino, poet 52
Rivers, as obstacles 189
Robert Burdet 111
Robert Crispin 108
Robert Curthose, crusading contingent of 33, 67
Robert Curthose, duke of Normandy 5, 7, 20, 21, 22, 27, 66, 72, 75, 76, 77, 82, 84,

230

INDEX

85–87, 94, 99, 101, 104, 134, 138, 182, 183, 202, 205, 209–10, 211–12,
Robert Curthose, leadership of crusade 133
Robert Curthose, lineage of 209
Robert Curthose, mythology surrounding 77
Robert Curthose, offered the rule of Jerusalem 33–4, 77
Robert d'Ablèges, bishop of Bayeux 97
Robert d'Avranches 134
Robert de Brus 131
Robert de Ducey 134
Robert de Limesey, bishop of Chester 130
Robert de Mowbray, earl of Northumbria 75
Robert Guiscard 14, 152, 159, 161–2, 164, 165, 166, 167, 173, 178, 188, 197, 212
Robert Guiscard, investiture of 179
Robert Guiscard, leads invasion of Albania 37
Robert I of Brus 131
Robert of Bellême 182, 183
Robert of Flanders 206
Robert of Kent 136
Robert of Limsey, bishop of Chester/Coventry and Lichfield 132
Robert of Neubourg, canon of Rouen 101
Robert of Rouen, bishop of Lydda 82, 85, 87, 88
Robert Poulain, archbishop of Rouen 97, 101
Robert the Monk 20
Robert the Saracen 135
Robert, bishop of Bayeux 98
Robet Crispin 166
Rocester 132
Roger Borsa 35, 37, 55
Roger de Clinton, bishop of Chester/Coventry and Lichfield 68, 92, 101, 132–3
Roger de Lacy 135
Roger de Montgomery, earl of Gloucester 76, 127
Roger de Mowbray 76
Roger I, count of Sicily 35, 56–7, 150, 162
Roger I, marriage of 59
Roger I, relations with Muslims 57

Roger II, count of Sicily 56, 57, 61, 139, 142–3, 145, 148, 154, 167
Roger II, count of Sicily, reputation of 146
Roger II, death of 149
Roger II, interest in travel 148
Roger II, relations with Muslims 57
Roger of Tosny 107, 111
Roger, physician of Robert of Kent 136
Roger, porter of Robert of Kent 136
Rollo, founder of the duchy of Normandy 178, 199
Romanos Diogenes, emperor of Byzantium 163, 164, 166
Rome 19, 89, 133, 139, 154, 175
Rome, pilgrimage to 147
Ropes 13, 14, 15
Rotrou II 93
Rotrou of Perche 111
Rotrou, bishop of Evreux and archbishop of Rouen 92–3, 101
Rouen cathedral 99, 126
Rouen cathedral, riot in (1119), 181
Rouen 94–5
Rouen, as a centre of crusading interest 101–2
Rouen, council in, 88, 94–5
Rousel of Bailleul, rebellion of 165, 166
Ruald, escapes from captivity 180, 182, 183, 193
Runcorn Gap 128
Runcorn Priory 130, 131, 132
Runcorn 128–9, 130

Sacey 134
Saher de Archelle 68
Saint Agatha's shrine, Catania 139
Saint Bartholomer the Apostle, shrine of 146
Saint Benedicts' shrine, Montecassino 139
Saint Bertelin, Augustinian community of 128
Saint Bertlelin, cult of 128
Saint Chad 128
Saint Evroul 1099
Saint John's, Chester 137
Saint Leonard, monastery of 55
Saint Lucien of Beauvais, monastery of 86

INDEX

Saint Matthews' shrine, Salerno 139
Saint Mercurius, altar of 146
Saint Michael the Archangels' shrine, Monte Gargano 139, 140
Saint Michael 7, 210
Saint Milburga 129
Saint Nicholas, relics of 145
Saint Nicholas' shrine, Bari 139
Saint Sever, bishop of Avranches 126–7
Saint Simeon 92
Saint Stephen, monastery of 84
Saint Stephen, protomartyr 86–7
Saint Wandrille, monastery of 87
Saint Werburgh 127, 129–30, 132, 137
Saint William of Montevergine 145, 155
Saint Wulfad 132
Saint-Broladre 134
Saint-Evroul 126, 182
Saint-Évroult, monastery of 178, 180, 182, 191, 193
Saint-Ouen, monastery of 185–6
Saint-Sever, abbey (Gascony), 129
Saladin Tithe (1188), 69
Saladin 116
Salerno, saved from a Muslim raid 140
Salerno, siege of 162
San Nichola at Bari, church carving at 162
San Nicola, basilica of 145
Sancho I, king of Portugal 117
Sancho III, king of Navarre 106
Sancho VII, king of Navarre 109, 119
Santa Sofia 146
Santarem, siege of 114, 117
Santiago de Compostela 107, 134
Santiago, order of 114
Schism, papal 143
Scotland 126
Scots 69
Second Crusade, diverted to Lisbon 111–2
Second Crusade, preaching of 134
Sées, cathedral of 91, 92
Segovia, council of (1166), 115
Serlo, bishop of Sées 82
Serlo, canon of Bayeux 84
Shame 15, 17, 25, 27, 29, 75, 171, 187, 198, 204, 205

Ships and shipping 13, 35, 37, 51, 57, 58, 59, 61, 68, 69, 75, 76, 118, 151–2, 160
Shrewsbury Abbey 127
Shrewsbury 70
Sichelgaita, mother of Roger Borsa 37
Sicilian monarchy, as tyrants 143–4
Sicily, as a transit site for travellers 147
Sicily, crusaders from 32, 33
Sicily, crusading armies of Richard I and Philip II in 61
Sicily, languages spoken in 36
Sidon, city of 150, 153
Sieges, and Normans 162
Siesyll, abbot of Strata Florida 70
Sigurd, king of Norway 153
Silves, conquest of (1189), 113, 116, 117, 118
Silves, recovered by Almohads (1191), 118
Simon of Dover 68
Solomon of Salerno 59–60
Southern Italy, as a transit site for travellers 147
Southern Italy, its role in the crusades 53–4
Southern Italy, Norman conquest of 36
St Simeon's port 13–14
Stafford 128, 129
Stanlaw 130
Stephen of Aumale 86–7
Stephen of Perche, chancellor 150, 151–2
Stephen Pateranos 164
Stephen, king of England 27–8, 74, 112, 133
Stephen-Henry, count of Blois, Chartres and Meaux 15 n. 13, 16–18, 19, 22–4, 25–7, 29
Stephen-Henry, letter to his wife Adele 23
Stephen-Henry, motives for desertion 27
Stephen-Henry, returns to the Holy Land (1102), 27–8
Stone (Staffordshire), 128, 130
Students, from Sicily 132
Stuteville family 72
Synodianos 164

Taifa kingdoms 104, 106
Tamworth 128
Tancred 16, 24, 33, 40, 41, 61, 89, 104, 169, 170, 174, 187, 190, 202, 207–08, 209, 212

232

INDEX

Tancred, attempt to found the lordship of Galilee 34
Tancred, behaviour of 188–90
Tancred, king of Sicily 152
Tancred, swears allegiance to Godfrey of Bouillon 45
Tancred, takes Mamistra 169
Tarragona 111, 120
Tarsus, competing claims to 169
Tatikios, imperial general 42
Templars 101, 114, 115, 125, 134, 147, 149
Terror 17
Teutonic Knights 152
Theobald of Étampes 84
Thierry of Flanders 71
Thomas Becket, archbishop of Canterbury 116
Thomas II, archbishop of York 130, 131, 133
Thouars, lord of 73
Thurstan, archbishop of York 130, 131, 133
Tiron, monastery of 89
Toledo 118
Toledo, conquest of (1085), 105
Tomar, defence of 114
Tornikios, catapan 163
Torres Novas, siege of 117
Tortosa 69, 114, 115
Tortosa, siege of (1148), 113, 114
Tourraine 14
Trani 58, 59
Trani, city of, as a pilgrim gathering place 151
Trani, shrine of Saint Nicholas the Pilgrim 155
Trani, siege of (1080), 162
Trentham 130, 131, 132
Troia 152
Troia, Councils of (1093, 1115, 1120), 144
Tunisian Crusade of Louis IX (1270), 98
Turk, converts to Christianity 41
Turks 14
Tyre 94, 135

Umayyads 104
Urban II, pope 18, 34, 35–6, 72, 108, 200

Val-ès-Dunes, battle of 189

Varaville, battle of 189
Venice peace conference (1177), 146
Verdun family 72
Vernon 89
Vézalay 87, 92, 95
Virgin Mary, relics of 87

Wace, canon of Bayeux 94, 100, 178
Waleran de Beaumont, count of Meulan and earl of Worcester 67, 93
Waleran of Meulan, leads second crusade contingent 134
Walter 'the Penniless', 188
Walter de Gant 131
Walter Espec 131
Walter Giffard 107, 108
Walter of Coutances, archbishop of Rouen 93, 94–95, 96, 101
Walter of Coutances, archbishop of Rouen, as hostage for Richard I 95
Walter of Saint-Valery, archdeacon of Rouen 96
Warburton Priory 130, 132
Weather 181, 192
Welsh, preaching in 70
Whalley Abbey 137
Whitchurch 70
William Bona Anima, abbot of Saint Stephen, archbishop of Rouen 84, 85–7, 101
William Burel, bishop of Avranches 95, 97
William de Percy 67
William de Roumere, pilgrimage of 134
William de Warenne 67
William Ferrers, earl of Derby 71
William FitzAlan 70
William I, king of England 14, 16, 27, 87, 88, 107, 130, 144, 189
William I, king of England, granted a papal banner 179
William II, king of Sicily 61
William II, king of Sicily, donates supplies to Henry II of England 61
William II, king of Sicily, plans attack on Byzantine Empire 149, 151
William II, king of Sicily, prevents crossing to Holy Land 150

INDEX

William II, king of Sicily, secures travel for pilgrims 146–47
William Longespée, earl of Salisbury 71
William Longsword, duke of Normandy 184
William Longsword, murder of 200
William of Apulia 163
William of Bayeux 133
William of Grandmesnil 13, 14, 15 n. 13, 18, 29, 204
William of Warenne, earl of Surrey, joins crusade 67
William Paynel 131
William Rufus, king of England 72, 73, 75
William Rufus, king of England, inhibits crusading 72,
William son of Irsoi 134
William the Carpenter, viscount of Melun 15, 16, 18, 22, 23–5, 26, 28–9
William Viel 203–4
William Vitalis 68
William, bishop of Evreux 84
William, constable of Chester 129–130
Winchester, earl of 136
Worksop Priory 131

Xenigordon, castle of 188

www.ingramcontent.com/pod-product-compliance
Lightning Source LLC
Chambersburg PA
CBHW070342240426
43665CB00046B/2429